Praise for *Do It Wrong Quickly*

"What's the one thing companies care about? Conversion. Getting potential customers to convert into real, actual, customers. But how do you do that in a world of Facebook, Google, YouTube, blogs, and Flickr? Mike Moran shows you how—by trying lots of little things, studying the results, learning quickly from your failures, and doing it all over again. He gives you a framework for getting over your fears of talking with your customers without a committee to protect your behind. Great book."

—Robert Scoble
Video blogger of the Scoble Show and Co-author
of the top-selling corporate blogging book, *Naked Conversations*

"If you are in an enterprise that has trouble executing fast enough, then act now and read *Do It Wrong Quickly*. It is extremely common for businesses to identify major areas for improvement or benefit but get mired down in distractions or red tape. Businesses that don't learn to execute at the speed of business today are just going to be left behind—the same way cars sped past the horse and buggy. Anything worth doing is worth doing wrong."

—Bryan Eisenberg
Author of the #1 Wall Street Journal bestseller *Waiting for Your Cat to Bark?*

"Mike Moran is a true Web 2.0 marketing guru. This book is an ideal read for anybody who wants to gain a better understanding of what it takes to be successful and survive in today's new digital marketing landscape. Mike's book is a must-read!"

—Brian Fitzgerald
Director of Digital Media Marketing for the National Football League

"*Do It Wrong Quickly* captures the essence of data-driven approach to Internet marketing success. Accept that you won't always know the right thing to do, but instead of spending months convincing yourself, just try something and let your customers tell you how wrong it is. Then, fix it and try something else. Mike Moran's book offers practical examples and terrific tips to transform your marketing to the new way—all while keeping you both interested and amused. If you read only one book on Internet marketing this year, read this one!"

—Imran Khan
Chief Marketing Officer for E-LOAN

"Real insights that are easy and even fun to read. Mike has a wonderful way of seeing the new world for what it really is. *Do It Wrong Quickly* is a must-read."

—Gideon Sasson
Executive Vice President and Chief Information Officer for Charles Schwab

"Marketers who ignore the Web or think it's just a fad are missing out on reaping the benefits of harnessing one of the most powerful forces for connecting with customers ever. But online marketing isn't just an extension of traditional marketing: the rules are different. In *Do It Wrong Quickly*, Mike Moran describes the best practices of online marketing in a clear, compelling voice. This book should be a must-read for anyone serious about becoming a successful marketer in cyberspace."

—Chris Sherman
Executive Editor of SearchEngineLand.com and Author
of *Google Power* and *The Invisible Web*

"If you are one of the many who read Mike Moran's excellent book *Search Engine Marketing, Inc.,* you are already aware that Mike not only knows his stuff, but also makes his points logical and understandable. His new book will likely receive attention from a variety of business executives, marketing people, and observers of the online business.

Moran excels when describing his personal experiences and seeing the patterns that are changing the way we conduct business. The book is a well-researched look at how the Web has redefined marketing and how the Web will continue to be a reflection of culture. This is truly one of the best business books I have read!"

—Morten Kamper
Director of the Danish eBusiness Association

"Mike Moran has mastered a rare combination of marketing insight, technology instinct and consumer intuition that is critical to the future of smart marketing. He takes you on a comprehensive and entertaining tour through a rapidly-changing marketing landscape, making you feel comfortable about jumping off the bus to explore it on your own. For executives looking for a tour guide to this new terrain, Mike is your man."

—Steve Gehlen
Founder of the Internet Strategy Forum

"Why do some companies' marketing efforts stumble while others dominate in this new age of marketing on the internet? With *Do It Wrong Quickly*, Mike Moran offers clear and insightful guidance for budding "Millennium Marketers" on how to leverage both the old and the new of Web 2.0. Combining "conversations and personalization" with the measurability of direct marketing, Moran gives readers both strategic and practical tools for engaging internet savvy customers today and in the future."

—Lee Odden
CEO of TopRank Online Marketing and
Publisher of MarketingBlog.com

"The Web is wonderful at producing massive amounts of data that gets increasingly complex to interpret efficiently with each passing day, and let's not forget taking action. Yet, it is also an environment where technology enables experimentation and testing while controlling for risk. Mike's new book lays out why we all need a radical transformation in our approach to marketing on the Web, and he does not leave us guessing about how to accomplish that. You'll find specific ideas about how to score for your companies and your customers by doing it wrong quickly."

—Avinash Kaushik
Author of *Web Analytics: An Hour a Day* and the *Occam's Razor* blog

"Mike is a genius whose title should be IBM Distinguished Engineer *and* Marketer. This book captures the essence of how to build a winning Web site and conduct successful Web marketing in the 21st century. I highly recommend it for marketers of all kinds, both online and offline."

—Michael Yang
Founder, President, and CEO of Become.com

"*Do it Wrong Quickly* is the book I have been waiting for to give those super-perfectionist clients who won't pull the trigger on new things. In today's hyper-paced digital world, we don't have the luxury for everything to be completely tested and dialed in before we can act. This book is the roadmap for jump-starting projects and then making the course corrections to get perfection. Thank you, Mike, for making my job easier!"

—Bill Hunt
CEO of Global Strategies International and Co-author
of *Search Engine Marketing, Inc.*

"Damn! Just when I thought I had some great ideas for a book, I read Moran's manuscript and he beat me to them! So, take my advice and read Mike's book carefully. Then reread it. Because the onion that Mike's peeling back here reveals the essential realities we have to grasp to do marketing even half right in the wired world. It's faster, it's participatory, it's less predicable and it's certainly less controlled. That's why you can't deliberate too long. You just have to do it and damn the consequences."

—Gord Hotchkiss
President and CEO of Enquiro

"This book leads the way for new marketers, going beyond generalities, clichés, and quick fixes to offer the wisdom and insight needed to make the most of this new landscape. Not surprising really, because Mike has been a visionary in the search industry for over two decades. The real life examples and Mike's quick wit really bring the whats, whys and hows of this new era of marketing to life."

—Jane Paolucci
Vice President of World Wide Marketing at Coremetrics

Do It Wrong Quickly

Do It Wrong Quickly

How The Web Changes the Old Marketing Rules

Mike Moran

IBM Press

Pearson plc

Upper Saddle River, NJ • Boston • Indianapolis • San Francisco

New York • Toronto • Montreal • London • Munich • Paris • Madrid

Cape Town • Sydney • Tokyo • Singapore • Mexico City

ibmpressbooks.com

IBM Press Program Managers: Tara Woodman, Ellice Uffer
Cover design: IBM Corporation
Associate Publisher: Greg Wiegand
Marketing Manager: Kourtnaye Sturgeon
Publicist: Heather Fox
Acquisitions Editor: Bernard Goodwin
Managing Editor: Gina Kanouse
Designer: Alan Clements
Project Editor: Jovana San Nicolas-Shirley
Copy Editor: Language Logistics, LLC
Indexer: Erika Millen
Compositor: Nonie Ratcliff
Proofreader: Water Crest Publishing
Manufacturing Buyer: Dan Uhrig

Published by Pearson plc
Publishing as IBM Press

IBM Press offers excellent discounts on this book when ordered in quantity for bulk purchases or special sales, which may include electronic versions and/or custom covers and content particular to your business, training goals, marketing focus, and branding interests. For more information, please contact:

U.S. Corporate and Government Sales
1-800-382-3419
corpsales@pearsontechgroup.com

For sales outside the U.S., please contact:

International Sales
international@pearsoned.com

Library of Congress Cataloging-in-Publication Data

Moran, Mike, 1958-

Do it wrong quickly : how the web changes the old marketing rules / Mike Moran.

p. cm.

Includes index.

ISBN 0-13-225596-0 (pbk. : alk. paper) 1. Internet marketing. 2. Customer relations. 3. Internet advertising. I. Title.

HF5415.1265.M6646 2007

658.8'72—dc22

2007025648

Pearson Education, Inc.
Rights and Contracts Department
501 Boylston Street, Suite 900
Boston, MA 02116
Fax (617) 671-3447

ISBN-13: 978-0-13-225596-7
ISBN-10: 0-13-225596-0

Text printed in the United States on recycled paper at R.R. Donnelley in Crawfordsville, Indiana.
Third printing May 2008

To my wife Linda, and my children, David, Madeline, Marcella, and Dwight,
with great appreciation for their support for me.

Contents

Foreword xv
Preface xvii
Acknowledgments xxiii
About the Author xxvii

PART 1: THAT NEWFANGLED MARKETING 1

Chapter 1 ▪ They're Doing Wonderful Things with Computers 3
   The New Marketing Communication 6
   The New Marketing Segmentation 11
   The New Direct Marketing 15
   Summary 19

Chapter 2 ▪ New Wine in Old Bottles 21
   The "Three Rs" of Online Marketing 25
      You Must Be Relevant 26
      You Must Be Real 29
      You Must Be Responsive 32
   The New Marketing Is Not So New 35
      Advertising 35
      Direct Marketing 41
      Publicity 45
   Summary 53

Chapter 3 ▪ Marketing Is a Conversation 55
   Starting the Conversation 57
      When Your Customer Starts the Conversation 58
      When Marketers Start the Conversation 63
      How *Not* to Start a Conversation 70

xi

Learning to Listen 74
  Listening in Daily Life 77
  Listening in a Crisis 84
  Listening in a War 85
Getting Introduced to Others 90
  Introductions by Your Customers 90
  Introductions by Your Employees 96
  Introductions by Your Partners 98
Summary 101

PART 2: THAT NEWFANGLED *DIRECT* MARKETING 103

Chapter 4 ▪ Going Over to the Dark Side 105
  Find Your Purpose 109
    Your Web Site's Purpose 109
    Your Customer's Purpose 113
    A Common Purpose 121
  Measure Your Customer Activity 125
    Count Your Conversions 127
    The Conversion Process 131
    Count Your Impressions and Selections 135
  Measure Your Customer Relationships 142
  Summary 147

Chapter 5 ▪ The New Customer Relations 149
  The Look and Feel 153
    The Design 156
    The Navigation 164
    The Interactivity 169
  The Sights and Sounds 175
    The Words 176
    The Sounds 182
    The Pictures 184
  The Touch 186
    Deciding Which Customers to Target 188
    Getting to Know Your Customers 190
    Designing Your Experience for Each Customer 197
  Summary 208

Chapter 6 ▪ Customers Vote with Their Mice 211

    Where Do You Start? 215

    How Do You Know How Wrong It Is? 224

        How to Value Conversions 227

        How to Value Customers 232

        Test, Test, and Test Again 235

    How Do You Speed Up? 240

        Speed Up Your Targeting 241

        Speed Up Your Messaging 244

        Speed Up Your Feedback 247

    Summary 252

PART 3: THAT NEWFANGLED *YOU* 253

Chapter 7 ▪ This Doesn't Work for Me 255

    The Reasons Why Not 257

        "That's not my job." 259

        "I don't have permission." 259

        "No one will listen to me." 260

        "I don't have time." 261

        "I'm no numbers person." 261

        "I've never been fast at decisions—it's too much pressure." 262

        "We tried that already." 264

        "I can't stand being wrong." 265

        "It feels too overwhelming." 266

    Fear 266

    Change 270

    Summary 273

Chapter 8 ▪ This Won't Work Where I Work 275

    Leading People to Change 279

        Rally Your Allies 280

        Pick Your Target 284

        Declare Success 286

    Specialist Disease 287

        Put the Business First 289

        Speak Their Language 292

        Bring the Specialists Together 298

Personality Parade 307
    The Inattentive 309
    The Indecisive 311
    The Inept 312
Summary 313

Chapter 9 ■ This Stuff Changes Too Fast 315
How Do You Cope with Change? 317
What's Changing? 321
    More Participation 322
    More Context 325
    More Integration 328
How Do You Keep Up? 331
Summary 333

Glossary 335

Index 365

Foreword

"It's not just O.K. to fail...it's imperative to fail."

> —Seth Godin, bestselling author, entrepreneur, and agent of change

"Iterate, don't pontificate."

> —Rishad Tobaccowala, Chief Executive Officer, Denuo

When Mike Moran asked me to write the forward for this book, I jumped at the chance, despite the fact that I'm already hopelessly overloaded with books, magazines, Internet articles, blogs, e-mails, and research reports all demanding my frazzled attention. I simply had to say "Yes" because I knew that Mike was on to something big.

Do It Wrong Quickly, in my modest opinion, is a mandate for our times. Certainly it is a call to action for those of us who labor in the world of marketing, which we all know is being permeated, transformed, and upended by the liberating force of the Internet.

I will never forget the first time I heard the phrase "do it wrong quickly." I was speaking at and attending yet another Web conference, and Mike was on stage with a panel discussing Internet marketing strategies. I don't mean to suggest that I know it all, but it's not my usual practice at these events to take notes. After all, my entire business (eMarketer) is centered on aggregating and analyzing the constantly changing trends and stats related to every aspect of online marketing and advertising. Rarely at such confabs do I become "enlightened" with new data or concepts. But when Mike stood up and said emphatically to the attendees, "Do it wrong quickly!" I put down my Venti Starbucks and began scribbling furiously with a borrowed pen. Those four words, along with a Google-retrieved, grainy photo of Mike's face, are now a staple in my presentations around the globe.

In the digital age, where the costs of production and distribution are often negligible when compared with traditional means, and there are typically 1,001 options in front of you, marketers can't afford NOT to make mistakes. Our most precious resource today is not capital or production, but time. For any newfangled Web 2.0 trend, strategy, or tactic dangling itself in front of you, there are two choices in this binary world. You can either spend endless hours in heated meetings debating its likely benefits and risks for your business—or you can just go do it. The latter, as you'll see, represents the acid test.

Let me push this point even further, risking the possibility of implicating the very market research industry in which we operate. As a marketer, you can look at industry statistics and projections all day long, every business day. But if you don't try new things for yourself—such as blogs, podcasting, social networks, viral marketing, search marketing, wikis, virtual worlds, and so on—you won't ever know for sure if any of these (or any combination of them) will work for your business.

You should read this book for two reasons. First, you will want to fully absorb the "do it wrong quickly" concept into your personal philosophy as well as your daily business process. Second, you should read the book cover-to-cover (as I did) in order to learn how best to "do it wrong quickly." Mike is a veritable fount of knowledge when it comes to digital strategy and tactics. He can save you a lot of time and headaches. Read this book with a pen in hand so you can take notes for both yourself and for the benefit of others on your team. This book has already become mandatory reading for my managers, and I suspect it will be for yours, too.

Quite simply, you can't go *wrong* reading this book.

—Geoffrey Ramsey

About Geoffrey Ramsey

As CEO and co-founder of New York-based eMarketer, Mr. Ramsey is on the cutting edge of new research statistics, trends, and best practices covering every aspect of marketing in the digital age. He is frequently quoted by *The Wall Street Journal*, *Forbes*, CNN, *BusinessWeek*, *Business 2.0*, and *Advertising Age*. A highly regarded speaker, Mr. Ramsey keynotes at major industry and corporate events around the globe.

Preface

If you're getting to the age where you feel like everything is changing so fast that the world is passing you by, I want to reassure you: It's not just a feeling. (Uh, that wasn't terribly reassuring, was it?) Or if you're still young and vibrant (no one ever seems to be described as old and vibrant), you may be looking at the pace of change and saying, "But I didn't learn *that* in school." I can reassure you also: It's only going to get worse. (This reassurance stuff is not one of my core competencies, is it?)

Most of you know that marketing is changing—that's why you reached for this book. For some of you, that's exciting. For others, it's scary. Regardless of how you feel about the changes in marketing, they're here, and the pace of change is not slowing—it's accelerating. But whether change gets your blood pumping or leaves you in a pool of sweat, marketing is undergoing a revolution more profound than any of us are likely to see the rest of our lives. (Even you young and vibrant ones.) And we are just at the beginning of that revolution.

You see, for a long time, marketers were in control. For hundreds of years, marketers controlled the message, yes, but they also controlled the media. Now, they control neither, and customers still control their money. Control of marketing is shifting from marketers to customers.

Before we go any further, I want to talk about a word I use a lot in this book: *customers*. You might call them shoppers. Or clients. Or patients. Or something else entirely. In this book, I call them customers.

I won't spend a lot of time distinguishing customers from prospects, or leads, or target market segments, or any other term that tries to slice and dice people-who-already-bought-from-you from people-that-you-want-to-buy-from-you-but-haven't-yet. Maybe I should have, but I didn't.

I didn't split those hairs because most of the time it doesn't matter—you need to think the same way about existing customers (who you want to keep) as you do for prospects (who you want to buy for the first time). If you believe that you can do less for existing customers than you do for new ones, I think you're wrong—you need to work equally hard. Thinking about customers mostly the same way is smart, if only because it requires less thinking.

So because I like to think less (no, don't put the book down because I said that), you'll see me refer to this entire diverse group as "customers" a great deal of the time. There are great books written that help you treat new customers differently from old customers differently from people who bought once about eight years ago but don't return your calls anymore—but this isn't one of them. Instead, this book will talk to you about how to personalize what you do to give every customer what they really want, but with the same goal for all—*to give them what they really want.*

This also isn't one of those "sky is falling" books or one of those "put on your rosy glasses and look at the new stuff" books, either. This is because the Internet isn't good or bad for marketing any more than television was good or bad for marketing. The Internet's good if you know what to do with it. It's bad if you don't. After you read this book, the Internet will be good for *you* and for *your* marketing.

As an aside, I really struggled with names like "the Internet." Sometimes, such as in the subtitle of this book, it just sounded catchier to say "the Web" even though "the Internet" is bigger than the Web and encompasses e-mail and cell phones and other "online marketing" (or "interactive marketing"). I finally decided to use all of these words in the book because you're smart enough to apply the concepts where they make sense. And if you are reading this book a couple of years after I wrote it, then undoubtedly there will be more words to describe this stuff. So don't sweat the terminology because this book is not about terminology.

So what *is* this book about?

I was hoping you'd ask. This book could have been really short if everyone understood just two things: Marketing is now a conversation, and feedback from your customers helps you adjust what you do every day. That's it. But you're unlikely to plunk down any cash for a book that short, so I fleshed it out a little…just a few hundred pages more.

Perhaps you're asking yourself, "How can I *read this book* wrong quickly?" Good question.

Feel free to skip around. Look at the table of contents. Look at the one-page descriptions at the beginning of each part of the book. If you've been doing interactive marketing for a while and you know what your biggest problem is, dive into the section that covers it or use the index to dive in. I've tried to make it a good read if you go through it sequentially, but if you know the basics, there's no need for you to waste time reading them again.

I tried to make it an easy read, so I didn't fill it with footnotes every time I quote a statistic. For those who want to know where each stat comes from, you can head to my Web site (www.mikemoran.com/resources) to get all my research and lots more.

If you're *really* in a hurry (I like you already), you can look for the icon shown in the margin of this page—that icon appears everywhere I have a special tip to do something wrong quickly. You can start doing those things right away.

You might be asking yourself, "What's with that icon?" (And what about the picture on the cover of the book, for that matter?) To understand what I am getting at by advising you to do it wrong quickly, think about the two pictures below. Ask yourself, "Which target shows better results?"

Most people would say it's the one on the right. One arrow was shot, and one bullseye was hit—100% success.

But there's one problem. Suppose the game is being played based on the most points scored? The archer with three arrows on the board has a better chance to win than the archer with one. And that's the point. In business, you don't get any awards for the highest percentage of customers you win—you get awards for making the most money. So if you can take three shots in the same amount of time your competitor takes one, well, too bad for your competitor.

That's what "do it wrong quickly" is about—the new rules of Internet marketing. I'll summarize the book here, but you can also read the introductions to each part of the book or read the summaries at the end of each chapter to decide what to look at first, so you can read this book wrong quickly.

Part 1 explains how marketing is shifting from monologue to conversation. The Web is not just a new medium—it's an *active* medium rather than a *passive* one. Yes, the Web brings new advertising models, but the changes in direct marketing and in publicity are at least as profound for marketers. Customers don't just *hear* your message. They comment. They argue. They applaud (sometimes). And the rest of your customers hear what these vocal customers say. Marketers no longer have control over the marketing message—all participants in the conversation control their own voices.

Marketers must do more than *listen* to customers, however. Part 2 describes how you must *observe* your customers. Your customers vote with their mice. They click on your message to learn more. They sign up. They buy. If you're not watching what they do, you're missing an immense amount of free feedback. What customers *do* is just as important as what they *say*. You need to pay attention and change your marketing approach in response. And then watch them again, in a never-ending cycle that leads to continuous improvement.

So, those are the big ideas, really. Marketing is now a conversation. Customers give you feedback in word and deed. And you must become flexible enough to change direction every day based on that feedback. You need to do it wrong quickly and then fix it—just as quickly. Every blessed day. Try something and then see what happens, then try something new—all the time.

I know that when I urge you to do it *wrong* quickly, some folks bristle. They *so* want to do it right. And I do, too. But the way to eventually do it right is to admit that what you are trying right now is probably wrong. That's why you're *trying* it, see? Everything is an experiment—you need to find out what works. So we can't pore over the details for months and reach consensus before we try something. We need to accept the fact that our first try will stink on ice, and then we'll start making it better—so that it stinks a little bit less each day.

Am I the first one to say these things? Nah. But I set out to explain them in a different way than you may have seen before. I wanted to talk to the people that I meet every day who are struggling with the big changes the Internet is inflicting on our comfortable marketing practices.

When I meet these smart, hardworking folks, and I explain these big ideas, they almost always agree that the world is changing and changing fast. They agree that these ideas are imperative for marketers to understand, that all marketers must adapt, and that marketers must adapt now—with one glaring exception. None of them think that *they* personally need to adapt now. When I ask them what *they* are going to do about these changes, I get back a list of the *Reasons Why Not*. The reasons why it's too soon in their industry. Or why it won't work at their company. Or how they are doing a couple of things, but they're "not ready" for any more. Or (my personal favorite), "You don't know my boss."

And that's why I wrote Part 3 of this book. Because even though it's true that I really *don't* know your boss, I can help you work through whatever is blocking you from embracing the changes you need to make. (And if you don't feel comfortable embracing the changes, perhaps you can at least offer them a firm handshake.) You'll also learn how to help colleagues at your company make changes within themselves and in your organizational culture.

In addition, Part 3 helps you to think about the industry changes still ahead of us in marketing, with a pointer to my Web site (www.mikemoran.com/resources) to help you keep learning long after you close this book. There's also a glossary in the back to help you make sense of all the new jargon that Internet marketing has spawned—throughout the book, you'll see key terms in *italics* that are defined in the glossary. Between the glossary and my Web site, you should have enough resources to get started with the real work of adapting your marketing approach.

So that's what this book is about.

I wrote the book for marketers, but not only for marketers. Because Web marketing involves your whole company, every employee can be a marketer. So you need to know how to reach out to all those other folks who work with you so that *they* understand Web marketing and so that they know what they should do in their own jobs. This book has been written so that even non-marketers can understand the marketing stuff. (And you don't need to be a geek to understand the techie stuff.)

So if you're a veteran brand marketer, this book helps you adapt to the new way to market online—you'll learn to get feedback and adapt. If you have a background in *direct* marketing, you already understand how to adapt based on feedback, but this book shows you how to collect the feedback on the Internet and what to do with it. And if you're not a marketer at all, read this book to find out how everyone working in any business needs to be part of interactive marketing.

Gee, that takes in a whole lot of readers, doesn't? For anyone with a neck, this book's for you. (How's that for targeted marketing?)

Acknowledgments

If you've never written a book, it's hard to explain how many people help you create something that ends up with your name on the front cover. I got a lot of help from folks when I wrote my first book, in the process learning a lot about how to write a book. So you'd think I wouldn't need so much help this time around, right?

Wrong. I think I needed more.

I think books are like children. I have four of my own (children, that is), and each one is different. No matter how much you think you know about children, each one that comes along teaches you something else. One of the things each child teaches you is how much you don't know.

Each time I write a book, I find out how much I don't know. I think, in part, it's because a good book always explains more than the author knows. I mean, you think you know the subject when you start out, or you wouldn't propose to write a book on it. You think you're an expert. But as you write the book, you find out that you aren't as great an authority as you first thought. You aren't explaining it as simply as you thought. The book is longer than you thought it would be, and you're *still* leaving important stuff out.

So I wrote this book wrong quickly. You'll undoubtedly find that some of what I wrote could have been improved even now, but it's much better than it would have been because of all the folks who helped me improve it. I'll try to list them all, but I'm sure I'll do that wrong also and leave someone out.

I'd like to thank my management team at IBM Software Group, including Amit Somani, Feri Clayton, Tim Donofrio, and Carl Kessler for putting up with and occasionally encouraging the uncontrollable blogging habit that helped me work out these ideas. I'd also like to thank my fellow OmniFind Product Managers Sean Johnson and Jake Levirne, for listening to me incessantly whine about how swamped I am and how I am never going to finish this book and for covering for me as I tested the book's messages in speaking engagements that took me away from my day job.

Thanks to the folks who worked with me for eight years at ibm.com and helped me to experiment on a great Web site every day. A lot of what I did wrong, I did there, and other folks cleaned it up. Thanks to Jeff Schaffer and Bill Hunt, who helped me work out many of the big ideas in this book. Thanks also to David Bradley, Jeanine Cotter, John Rosato, and Lee Dierdorff, who gave me the room to try things, fail, and then try something else.

Thanks also to the folks at ibm.com who took the time to review early versions of my manuscript and tell me what I got wrong (and even helped me fix it). Keith Instone helped me improve the sections on information architecture and on the future—he was also the first to tell me that I needed to provide more examples of exactly how people can do it wrong quickly. Lots of reviewers told me they appreciated the humor in the book, but Charles Chesnut was willing to tell me which jokes weren't funny so I could prune them away—and he also told me when being snarky was becoming annoying to my readers. (My readers thank you.) Kevin Chiu provided insights into the design process and helped me do my Web site wrong quickly. Matt Ganis provided feedback on the section on agile development. Alex Holt tirelessly reviewed the book for technical inaccuracies and just plain bad writing, just as he did with my first book.

By picking the title I did, I knew I was leaving myself open to some snide reviewer saying that I had done this book wrong quickly, so the more folks that reviewed it to help me fix it, the better I felt. Thanks to everyone who looked it over and provided feedback to me, but I'd especially like to thank Edward O'Hara of JupiterMedia, who encouraged me when I needed it and who told me when I was confusing the heck out of anyone not from America. Piers Dickinson of BP, Margaret Jones from Kodak, and blogger Marshall Sponder also provided very helpful feedback.

I owe a debt of gratitude to Matt Ganis of IBM, Simon Matthews of Ion Global, Jane Paolucci of CoreMetrics, and my wife Linda for helping me locate just the right people to interview.

I am especially grateful to those people who talked to me for hours on end to provide real-world grounding for the "do it wrong quickly" approach. I decided early on that I would rather have deeper stories from a few people than many surface anecdotes, but that style required a lot of cooperation from some very busy people. Thanks so much to Scott Ambler of IBM, psychotherapist Nancy Fish, Al Hurlebaus of CompUSA, blogger Mike Kaltschnee, independent consultant Avinash Kaushik, Rob Key of Converseon, Imran Khan of e-Loan, Floyd Marinescu of infoq.com, Michael Petillo of W.L. Gore, Joel Reimer of ScottsMiracle-Gro, blogger Ryan Saghir, Curt Sasaki of Sun Microsystems, Devashish Saxena of Texas Instruments, Matt Schaub of

ReallyGreatRate.com, David Seifert of Bass Pro Shops, Steve Swasey of Netflix, and independent consultant Andreas Weigend.

The team at Pearson has always been very helpful, including Heather Fox, Kourtnaye Sturgeon, and especially my editor Bernard Goodwin. Producing a book isn't easy, and I appreciate their support.

Thanks also to best-selling authors Bryan and Jeffrey Eisenberg for their generosity in helping me get attention for my book. I liked writing it, but I'd really like people to read it, so I appreciated the advice of experts.

The biggest thank you, as always, goes to my family. Thank you David, Madeline, Marcella, and Dwight, for being so understanding about how much time Daddy stole to write this book. And thanks for providing several great quotes inside it!

I don't know how I would accomplish anything, much less write a book, without my wife Linda. You can imagine that it's not easy to manage a household of four kids when dear old dad is hunkered down over his keyboard at seemingly every waking moment.

But Linda was far more instrumental in producing this book than merely providing me room to write it. An accomplished writer and technologist in her own right, she went over every syllable in this book just as she did with the first one. Every time she circled something and scrawled, "Huh?" in the margin, she saved each one of you from the same fate. Every sentence marked "awk" prevented you from furrowing your brow in puzzlement.

Linda brought even more to this book. Her experience as a Web site owner, a blogger, and as a message board moderator, led her to say (numerous times), "That's not true, Mike." In addition to correcting my technical errors, she also alerted me to resources that you should know about, along with several real-world examples that illustrate the points I make. You have no idea how much better this book is now than when I wrote it.

Linda told me that she had less work to do when editing this book than with the first, which shows that she is not just a great editor but a gifted teacher. Whatever I know about writing, I learned from Linda.

About the Author

Mike Moran has worked on the Web since its earliest days, in both marketing and technical roles, including eight years at ibm.com, IBM's customer-facing Web site.

Mike has served as a product manager for several IBM products, currently performing in that role for IBM's OmniFind search engine, but has experience marketing IBM's full product line from its Web site. Mike led the adoption of search marketing at ibm.com back in 2001 and pioneered product search facilities that dramatically raised conversion rates. Mike's success led him to co-author the best-selling book, *Search Engine Marketing, Inc.*, in 2005 and to write a regular column on search marketing for *Revenue* magazine. He's a member of the Search Engine Marketing Council of the Direct Marketing Association and a charter member of the DMA's Interactive Marketing Advisory Board. Mike is a frequent conference speaker on Internet marketing and holds an Advanced Certificate in Market Management Practice from the Royal UK Charter Institute of Marketing.

Mike also has a broad technical background, with over 20 years experience in search technology working at IBM Research, Lotus, and other IBM software units. He led the product team that developed the first commercial linguistic search engine in 1989 and has been granted four patents in search and retrieval technology. He led the integration of ibm.com's site search technologies as well as projects in Content Management, Personalization, and Web Metrics. Mike was named an IBM Distinguished Engineer in 2005.

Mike can be reached through his Web site (www.mikemoran.com), which is also the home of his *Biznology* newsletter and blog.

PART **I**

That Newfangled Marketing

Chapter 1 ▪ They're Doing Wonderful Things with Computers   3

Chapter 2 ▪ New Wine in Old Bottles   21

Chapter 3 ▪ Marketing Is a Conversation   55

So exactly what is this newfangled marketing that the Internet has foisted upon us? Just what *is* all the fuss about? Marketing has always adapted to new technology.

This one's different.

The Internet (and the Web in particular) has produced a power shift in the relationship between marketers and customers. In the past, marketers could blanket the world with their message, and customers could take it or leave it. Now customers can tell you just what they think of your product or service—and they expect you to pay attention and do something about it.

For marketers to adapt to this brave new marketing world, we need to understand how interactive marketing is different from what we grew up with. And we need to learn what to do about it.

Chapter 1, "They're Doing Wonderful Things with Computers," introduces the changes the Internet has brought about. Our customers have far more control over which marketing messages they receive, and customers sometimes choose their own market segments. Increasingly, direct marketing practices are proving to bring success in new media.

Chapter 2, "New Wine in Old Bottles," explains the new approach the Internet is demanding for our tried-and-true marketing tactics. Much of what veteran marketers know is still true, but you need to learn a few new tricks to cope with blogs and search engines and other interactive techniques.

Chapter 3, "Marketing Is a Conversation," gives you the insight and tools needed to change the way you communicate from a monologue to a dialogue. You learn how it's less important to control the message than it is to listen to your customer and respond. It's not easy, but your customers expect nothing less from you.

By the end of Part 1, you'll understand how your marketing needs to change, not because the old ways don't work anymore, but because the new ways are beginning to work better. You'll understand the new techniques that interactive marketing has to offer, and you'll know the approach to take to begin engaging with your customers rather than delivering a message.

Let's get started!

I

They're Doing Wonderful Things with Computers

"Why, a child of five would understand this. Quick, someone fetch a child of five."

—Groucho Marx

Chapter Contents

- The New Marketing Communication   6
- The New Marketing Segmentation   11
- The New Direct Marketing   15
- Summary   19

My aunt, bless her heart, thought a *cursor* should have his dirty mouth washed out with soap. Any discussion about technology left her as confused as a sheepherder inside a Circuit City. So it was a challenge for her when I became a computer programmer—she felt compelled to ask me about my job, and I dutifully attempted to explain it. Those conversations always ended the same way, when Aunt Minnie quickly turned to the person next to her, exclaiming, "They're doing wonderful things with computers!"

Well, yes they are. But I can forgive you for thinking that the changes brought about by technological advances are not always so all-fired wonderful. As much as change provides new opportunities, it also poses new challenges. And nowhere are the challenges more obvious today than in the field of marketing.

But we're getting ahead of ourselves. (I have never understood how we could actually get ahead of ourselves, but cut me some slack here.) Let's start at the beginning.

In the beginning, there were no marketers. We had *entrepreneurs*, although they didn't call themselves entrepreneurs back then. I'm not sure they called themselves anything, but they were the smart guys (yes, back then they were guys) who thunk up the new stuff that people wanted. And they came up with some very cool stuff. And that was good.

Unfortunately, most entrepreneurs weren't very good at selling their stuff. They needed *salesmen*. Salesmen weren't so good at coming up with new products, but they sure knew how to sell them. Not only could an eloquent salesman persuade people to buy a vacuum cleaner after he spread the dirt on their carpets, but some seemed to be able to talk the dirt into jumping into the vacuum without turning it on.

Yes, salesmen could talk. They could look at a person, talk to him for a minute, and size him up on the spot. A good salesman could connect with people and figure out what they really wanted. And once he did, he'd use that to sell what was on the truck. Whatever the entrepreneur brought to market, the salesman could sell.

But then technology changed everything. Newspapers and magazines—and later radio and TV—created a new way to communicate. And while some used mass media to inform and entertain people, other people realized we had stumbled onto the greatest way to sell things ever invented. They discovered that media can drive demand for products. Those people were the first *marketers*.

Marketers discovered that *advertising* can deliver the *message* for your *brand* to your *target market*. (Just look at all those new italicized words that we marketers came up with just to explain what we do.) In fact, mass communication is what begat the need to have brand names at all.

Let's face it. Your customers don't need a name for what your salesperson is pressing into their palms. But without a brand name in your newspaper ad, your customers won't know what to ask for at the store—or have any way to connect the ad with what they now want to buy. The invention of advertising *requires* that products have brand names.

Now when all this branding stuff began, no one knew what they were doing—that's true at the start of just about anything. Whenever the world changes, there are no recipes for success, at least at first. In fact, when we consider how advertising evolved with the advent of newspapers, we can almost hear Ben Franklin's Aunt Minnie turning away from the young printer exclaiming, "They're doing wonderful things with printing presses!"

And so they were. They were experimenting like crazy because printing presses caused the invention of marketing—a big change. Any new world order forces experimentation, and the bigger the change, the more massive the scale of the experimentation. Gradually, over a long period of time, "best practices" were discovered by expert marketers and marketing consultants. (If you don't believe that best practices are discovered by consultants, just ask them.)

It's worth noting, however, that the best practices were *discovered*—everyone was forced to experiment precisely *because* no one knew what they were doing. Only as the world stabilized were successful experiments distilled into best practices so that people could be taught to follow them by rote. (I'm not really sure what *rote* means, but I tend to repeat that word a lot without thinking.)

The best practices of marketing evolved over just such a long period of time so that today we can scarcely think of a world without marketing (although some of our customers dare to dream). Marketers need to remember that marketing is all made up. It isn't chemistry, where laws of nature are discovered. Yes, market researchers do discover things about our customers, but the point is that marketing changes whenever people change—which is often.

Marketing is a set of ideas that people invented because they seemed to get other people to buy more of the stuff being hawked. The minute those things stop working, marketers will make something else up and call *that* marketing. Whatever works becomes the new best practice. Does that make marketing frivolous or unimportant? Certainly not. But it does make marketing as malleable as the customers it attempts to persuade.

Now then, this is all well and good, and this story about how marketing evolved is a necessary background for you to think about marketing in today's world. It has the one slight disadvantage of not being true. I mean, at least I don't know if it is true. I didn't research it, and I intended it to be an oversimplified history of marketing. But the story served my purpose as a way to get you to think about where marketing has been and where it is going.

And you'll likely remember it better than if I had painstakingly related the full history of marketing, replete with facts and dates and famous marketing thinkers and heroes. Why? That's just the way our minds work. We're all suckers for a good story, which marketers know better than anyone.

But my main purpose isn't to get you to remember the story. I want you to *do* something. I want you to change your thinking, change what you're doing, and get out there and become Millennium Marketers. Don't remain stuck in the old ways—start adapting to the huge changes that are right now remaking our profession. So I want you to remember what I said, but I also want you to take action.

That's what marketing is *really* all about, isn't it? That's why I told you a story, and that's why I am challenging you to change. Hey, I even branded you "Millennium Marketers," which might not go down in history like the "Pepsi Generation," but at least gives you a handle on what you are striving for. If you want to be in that select group of Millennium Marketers, then you've come to the right place.

And, come to think of it, if you don't have the slightest interest in all this new-fangled marketing on the Internet, you've come to the right place too. That's because, although I hate to have to break it to you, you don't get any choice. The world is changing, and the old ways are not working the way they once did. When you're born into a time of change, you don't get to coast along.

This is one of those times.

The Internet (and the World Wide Web in particular) is a new world order of amazing magnitude—probably the biggest change any of us will see in our marketing lifetimes. And that means that no one really knows what they are doing right now. The things that consultants call "best practices" today might seem laughable a couple of years from now. Right now, the successful marketers are experimenting like crazy and producing new best practices every day. Some of them will define what your children learn when *they* study marketing. So even if we're sure that we understand the basics of marketing, the change wrought by the Web forces us to go back and reconnect with the basics. (And maybe forces us to figure out the future tense of the word *wrought*.)

And so with no further ado (because I have already provided the perfect amount of ado), what is *really* changing about marketing? Let's start with the changes the Web is forcing on marketing communications.

The New Marketing Communication

Traditional mass media is a critical piece of many marketing communications plans today, and that's not going to change anytime soon. Coca Cola needs TV ads and billboards, and your company might too. The problem is that mass media's effectiveness in conveying your marketing message is fading.

The rise of the Web has ushered in huge changes in usage of mass media. Internet usage is beginning to overtake TV viewing in some countries, especially among younger market segments. Newspaper circulation has seen a steady, continuous drop over the last 40 years. What explains these dramatic shifts? Simply, people have only so much time in the day. Every time you see a stat that says Internet usage is up, understand that something else must be down.

Or that *multitasking* is up. More and more, people seem to be consuming multiple media sources simultaneously, such as watching TV while using the Web. When they do so, the effectiveness of the TV commercial is lessened because you don't have the full attention of the viewer the way you once did.

What's more, advertising-supported media is steadily losing ground to commercial-free sources. Of the time customers spend consuming media, the fraction spent with media directly supported by advertising has steadily dropped in recent years—it is expected to fall below half in the next decade. Consumers already spend more of their own money on media than advertisers spend for ads on ad-supported media—and that trend will only accelerate. Premium cable channels steal audiences from commercial-supported channels, iPods and satellite radio cannibalize free radio, and subscription information services lure readers from ad-supported media.

Smart marketers are adjusting their marketing mixes. Microsoft says that it's shifting half a billion dollars from offline to interactive marketing by 2010. And just listen to Al Hurlebaus, Senior Director of e-commerce for U.S. computer retailer CompUSA:

We're not going to completely abandon broadcast—we're still going to put out a circular every week. {But some} customers only want specific notifications, such as {content about} "Apple" or "notebook." An element {of the marketing mix} will continue to be broadcast and a portion will be personalized.

Even the remaining time spent on ad-supported media is less effective than in years past because your customers are increasingly ignoring or blocking the commercial messages. Tivo and similar machines allow viewers to "fast forward" through TV commercials. Households without Tivos use remote controls to channel surf when the commercials come on. The Web's so-called "banner blindness" (people completely ignoring banner ads) should give us a clue as to how much impact billboards and print ads *really* have.

And what else should we expect? Most people are exposed to thousands of marketing messages per day—one every few seconds during their waking day. When people ignore or block these intrusive messages, that behavior seems like a sign of their mental health.

"So what?" you might ask. (Well, you probably are not so rude to ask it like *that*, but you might be wondering it anyway.) Well, it adds up to fewer opportunities for traditional marketers to reach their markets, compounded by each opportunity getting less attention. Old media has not completely lost its effectiveness by any stretch, but it is less effective than it once was.

It might seem safe to continue to rely on TV and other traditional media, but Joel Reimer, Director of Interactive Marketing at lawn care company Scotts Miracle-Gro, says that "you need to try everything except TV." He further jokes, "The ship is sinking; it's on its way down—how long are you going to wait?"

Certainly, in many countries (and in many industries), TV, radio, and print advertising are still king. But in Japan, in much of Western Europe, and in the United States, the tide is turning toward the Internet. In consumer electronics, books, music, movies, and other information-rich products, marketing is moving online. Now is the time for marketers to adapt to the new ways, while there's still time.

OK, everyone who didn't know these things raise your hands. Hmmm, no hands up, huh? Yeah, I think most marketers understand that things are changing and I promise not to bore you with a whole book about how TV is dying and the Web is the new thing. Because even though the Web is the new thing, TV isn't actually dying, any more than radio died when TV came on the scene. But old media is becoming less important than it once was as the Internet becomes more important.

Now, in the face of such changes in the past, marketers always knew what to do. When radio made newspapers less important, we bought ads on the radio. When TV pushed radio farther back in the line, we flocked to TV ads. So, now the Web is the next big thing. We'll just buy ads there, right?

Wrong.

Well, it's partially wrong at least. (But it sounded so much punchier to merely say "Wrong," didn't it?) *Of course* we will buy ads on the Web. If there's a place to plaster our message, we will do it. We buy video ads in elevators, at gas pumps, and even above men's urinals. Oh yeah, we'll buy ads on the Web all right.

Beyond ads, the Internet has spawned a dizzying array of strange new ways to reach your markets. If you think that a "podcast" is a horror movie from the '80s, or a "Web feed" means buying pizza for your HTML coders, you'll want to study Chapter 2, "New Wine in Old Bottles." Once you do, you're sure to use all these new geeky toys along with Web ads.

But something more fundamental is going on. The rise of the Web is not merely a shift of media, the way print shifted to radio to TV. The Web is creating a shift of *control*. Your customers have more control than ever over which messages to see, which to ignore, and which to outright block.

Telephone solicitation has been curbed in the U.S. by the "Do Not Call Registry." Some companies responded by cranking up the spam e-mail, but they don't get it. Pop-up windows and other intrusive ads are not the answer either. If you feel the need to offer a "Skip this Ad" button, then you aren't doing it right.

Unless you engage your customers in *deciding* to view your ads, and you can convince them to *stick with* your ads, they won't see them. And they won't get your message.

Time was that your marketing program was limited by your budget—you could reach anyone if you had enough cash. Today, entire market segments are tuning out TV and other traditional media. Advertising money is easier to come by than your customers' time. Customers *choose* where to focus their attention. How do you become their choice?

Author Seth Godin has framed this dilemma as the "interruption model" versus the "permission model," and he's right. Advertising has traditionally been about interrupting people, blaring your message when they wanted to be doing something else. ("I was sitting in my living room, minding my own business watching the ballgame, when all of a sudden they're telling me about erectile dysfunction.")

The Web can change that model. Instead of showing a zillion car commercials in the hopes that customers remember your brand when they actually want to buy a car, what would it be worth to be able to talk to customers at that moment of readiness? To know exactly when your customers *want* to hear everything about your car?

Another way of describing this shift is "push" (interruption by the marketer) versus "pull" (permission from the customer). Godin describes deeper permissions where customers subscribe to regular messages from you or even have standing replenishment orders (for supplies, for example). Essentially, they are pulling your push.

So the real challenge of the Web is not the mastery of a new way of interrupting people. It's a lot harder than that. How do you get people to actually *want* to listen to you? Why should anyone choose to hear what you have to say?

Well, they might listen if your message is relevant to their needs and if you sound like an authentic and reliable source of information. And they might listen if they thought you were listening to them, too.

Yeah, I know. We all drone on about how we listen to our customers and how we "appreciate your feedback," and blah, blah, blah. Customers can talk to salespeople or the complaint department. That's the way it's always been, right? Unfortunately, on the Web, customers can talk back to us. Yeah, us. The marketers. Directly.

Uh oh.

By now, you probably realize that you need to use podcasts, blogs, and other new media to send out your message, but you might not realize that your customers will use them to talk back to you. Not only will customers comment on *your* blogs, but they will talk about you on their *own* blogs with other customers. And you might not like what they say. You might even need to respond.

So we *really* have to listen to customers now. Marketing communication is shifting to marketing conversation. You might say MarCom becomes MarCon. (OK, OK, you probably have better judgment than to say that.) The point is that you no longer deliver a message—you start a conversation.

Some pundits are going to the other extreme—saying that customers are now grabbing control. (And they say it with the same tone of voice as "The barbarians are storming the gates!") What's really happening is that instead of marketers conducting an old-fashioned monologue, marketers and customers are now *sharing* control of a real conversation.

MARKETS ARE CONVERSATIONS

Back in the mid-90s, I worked with Chris Locke, later one of the authors of the seminal book, *The Cluetrain Manifesto*. All Chris could talk about back then was how the Internet enabled *communities* to form around almost any subject—communities that would become more powerful than the hackneyed marketing messages that pervaded our public discourse. I could see his logic, but I wasn't smart enough to see what we should be doing about it at the time.

Later, Chris and his co-authors made "Markets are conversations" the first point of their 95-point manifesto. So why are we still talking about it now? Because it is finally happening.

The Cluetrain folks were visionaries. Back then, this conversational market phenomenon affected only a few industries. Today, average people are participating in communities in many markets. Soon, rating a product or commenting on a blog will be as common as e-mail, and many more methods of customer participation will arise too.

Chris was absolutely right, of course. He warned you this was coming years ago. Luckily, you still have a chance to do something about it before the vision is totally realized.

And it's not always a *private* conversation. Everything you say is just the starting point of where it will go in the new public discourse made possible by the Web. Sometimes the conversations are public; sometimes they are private. That used to delineate the difference between sales and marketing, but no more. The stark lines between sales and marketing disappear on the Web.

If you want a preview about how this new marketing conversation might evolve, check out one of the "rat-a-base" sites such as DontDateHimGirl.com, where you can see names and even pictures of men that women are warning other women about. In a world where alleged bad behavior in something as private as dating is plastered all over the Internet, you shouldn't have any expectations that your marketing message will go uncommented upon. Our customers are changing. They expect to comment on what companies say and do, and the Web lets them do it.

And you must be willing to adjust what you are doing at every moment. You need to be willing to change your message if it's not working. You must take responsibility for errors your company makes and ensure they are corrected. Your response to one customer might be seen by *all* your customers. So you must listen with new ears and take action if you want to appear responsive.

In the old days, public relations people handled these public discussions. Large companies needed to worry about negative publicity, but small companies were never interesting enough to be noticed by the media. With the Web, no company is so small that it can fly under the radar.

Your customers (or your competitors) can use the Web to give you whatever good or bad publicity they desire. So if your restaurant was cited for health violations or your products are assembled by child labor in a third-world country, you'll have to defend that. If someone took offense at one of your ads, you'll have to respond. Even if you are a very small company, someone will blog about the issue in front of your other customers, and you will be on the spot. Everything you say and do is public.

So if you prefer to *control* the marketing message, you might be in for some disappointment. No one can control a conversation—you can control what *you* say but not what your customers say. And honestly, when you have a dozen bloggers in your company, it's hard to impose traditional message control on even *your* part of the conversation. Can you strive to be relevant? Yes. Authentic? Definitely. Responsive? Absolutely. But can you exert control? Probably not.

Your marketing message is just the beginning of a conversation, which we'll discuss in depth in Chapter 3, "Marketing Is a Conversation."

The New Marketing Segmentation

If the changes in marketing communication didn't scare you enough, let's talk about the fundamental changes in market segmentation.

Market segmentation is the fancy marketer's term for dividing up the pool of potential customers based on shared characteristics. So a consumer marketer might segment markets based on demographics (such as age or gender) while a business-to-business (B2B) marketer might use firmographics (such as company size or industry).

With old-fashioned marketing, the best creative folks come up with a great message for the mass market (something clever, like "Coke is it!"), test it against focus groups, and push it out there—over and over again. It's on TV, on the radio, on billboards, on just about anything in front of a consumer's face. To decide exactly where to place those ads, we segment our markets based on their characteristics. Need to reach folks in the publishing industry? Buy an ad in *Publisher's Weekly*. Want authors, also? Put the same ad in *Writer's Digest*, too. For some companies, deciding where to place their ads is all they ever do with market segmentation.

Other businesses are more sophisticated—they might target *different* messages to different segments. Perhaps a B2B company might target by industry, using print ads emphasizing different concepts and examples in magazines for different industries. Some companies act like the politician with a different stump speech for each constituent group.

But the old-fashioned ways don't work on the Web because everything you say is now in public. If you publish conflicting messages in different magazines, your customers will "Google" their way to *every* message you've sent. If you sell "freedom fries" in your U.S. restaurants and "French fries" over the border in Canada, expect someone to call you on that. Hearing you talk out of both sides of your mouth won't do wonders for your credibility.

But that's not the biggest change. There *is* a way on the Web that you can differentiate messages to market segments (as long as they don't conflict). You allow the customers to segment themselves.

Segment *themselves*? Doesn't the marketer decide the market segments? The customers don't even know what segments we put them in. How can they segment themselves? Well, they can. The Internet allows customers to *self-segment* in ways never before possible.

One way of self-segmenting uses *search*. Every time people enter a few words into Google, they tell you what they are interested in. Subtle differences in wording identify different target segments. For example, a searcher who is looking for "lodging" is vastly different than one who searches for "hotel"—"lodging" searchers want a "bed and breakfast" or some other hotel alternative, which is why they search for a less-common word. These searchers are self-segmenting—they are dividing themselves into your target market segments.

Subscriptions provide similar self-segmentation possibilities. E-mail newsletters allow prospective customers to raise their hands and tell you they are interested in a certain subject. But some people are reluctant to give out their e-mail addresses because they don't know what else you'll send them. *Web feeds* (such as RSS) are a new way to subscribe to information with no loss of privacy—anyone using a blog reader (such as Bloglines) is already using Web feeds to subscribe to their favorite bloggers. We'll dive deeper into more of these new marketing methods in Chapter 2.

Self-segmentation goes beyond these marketing tactics, however. Because the Web is an interactive medium, anything your customers do has the potential to place them into a market segment. If you can get a customer to your Web site, every click reveals information you can use for segmentation. Every product viewed demonstrates interest. Rather than revealing the customer's demographics or firmographics for traditional market segmentation, however, you are instead learning what they are interested in. Customers self-segment based on their needs.

Traditional segmentation often ignores differentiation based on needs because it is hard to know when someone needs something, but the Web makes it much easier to do. And it is very powerful. If you know that the customer is in the market for your product now, you have a much better chance of selling it.

Clothing retailer Jo-Ann Fabrics set up their navigation to target different messages and products for people in various areas of their Web site. For example, if someone enters the sewing area, they assume she is a seamstress—interested in different products than knitters are, for example.

Web geeks even design software to respond to your customer's every click, called *personalization software*. If you've ever visited amazon.com, you've seen personalization in action. Anytime you look at a product or (even more telling) purchase a product, Amazon remembers what you did and designs your experience to suggest related products in the future. That's personalization. It's also self-segmentation based on needs—each Amazon customer creates a unique experience based on where they go and what they do on amazon.com.

But Web segmentation methods go farther than that. In classical marketing, the purpose of segmentation is to differentiate your entire offering—the communication about your product *and* your actual product. We've talked about differentiating the marketing communication, but how can the Web help differentiate the product itself?

At first, you might not see how the Web can differentiate your product. After all, you make what you make, and the Web can only sell it. This is true, but only up to a point. The Web excels in making vastly complex choices simpler, so your Web site can offer hundreds or thousands of variations on your product that can be customized in ways that would be expensive or impossible any other way.

Think about how Dell sells laptop computers—they let customers "build" their own computers on their Web site. By providing an easy way of selecting how much memory or disk space is desired, Dell simplifies a very complex task and provides exactly what the customer requested. Talk about self-segmentation! Dell can reach customers that want a three-to-five pound laptop built for games for under $1000—and show them exactly what they are looking for at the moment they want it. The Web is a great way to mask the complexity of a customized manufacturing process.

But you don't need to have Dell's customized manufacturing process to provide a similar experience to your customer. Retail Web sites can provide similar choices to customers without manufacturing anything. Look at Exhibit 1-1 to see how strikingly similar the experience can be. Circuit City allows customers to narrow down their choice of laptop using almost any characteristic (price, memory size, disk space, processor, brand, and many more) by listing all the choices and letting customers click what they want.

The Web allows a nearly endless number of variations to be chosen, which is the equivalent of custom manufacturing. So even though manufacturers and retailers might take different approaches, the customer's ability to get exactly what is desired doesn't change one iota. (For some reason, iotas never come in pairs.) A customer experience that formerly demanded a massive investment in custom manufacturing now needs not much more than a Web server. In Chapter 5, "The New Customer Relations," we'll see how you might provide this experience for your customer.

So what's the big change here? Market segmentation is becoming market personalization. You don't target markets anymore; you target individuals personally, using technology to do it. And you can't separate sales from marketing anymore—that clear dividing line is gone. You need to be ready to speak to customers as individually as possible from start to finish and to offer them the exact product they want, not just what's "on the truck."

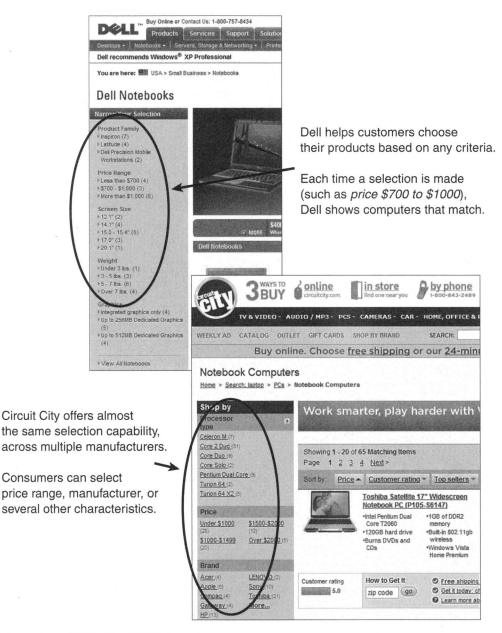

Dell helps customers choose
their products based on any criteria.

Each time a selection is made
(such as *price $700 to $1000*),
Dell shows computers that match.

Circuit City offers almost
the same selection capability,
across multiple manufacturers.

Consumers can select
price range, manufacturer, or
several other characteristics.

(Dell screen image ©2007 Dell Inc. All Rights Reserved)

Exhibit 1-1 Self-segmentation experiences from manufacturers and retailers

The New Direct Marketing

Direct marketing. All marketers know what it is, but many of them treat direct marketing as a backwater inhabited by hucksters. Well, direct marketers are getting the last laugh because the rise of the Web means that we're *all* direct marketers now...or at least we all need to be. We need to emulate direct marketers. Emulate their experimentation and their attention to details. But most of all, we need to emulate a direct marketer's obsession with measurement. No longer is it enough to be creative. To succeed in marketing, you need to measure your success.

Scary, huh?

For some of you, measuring success is a daunting prospect. It's true that the many successful marketers know how to analyze market segments based on market research and build a mean spreadsheet. But too many brand marketers have entered this field as a refuge from numbers. (After all, English majors deserve to make a living, too.) Maybe you are one of them.

Some slick marketers might even shirk accountability. (Not you or me, of course.) If you're a fast enough talker, no one can tell whether what you are doing really works or not. Let's not sugarcoat it—most brand marketing has no measurable correlation to sales. But that won't last, according to Imran Khan, Chief Marketing Officer at Internet lender E-LOAN, who says that "accountability will become more and more important."

In our everyday marketing world, we know that your commercial ran on TV last night, but how do we know whether it was effective? Did sales go up today? If they did, do we know whether the commercial was the reason? The impact of most marketing spending can't be measured very easily.

Geoff Ramsey of eMarketer likes to tell a story about the accountability of marketing spending. When the CEO asks the heads of manufacturing or sales or R&D what will happen if their budgets are cut 10 percent, they each can give a crisp answer with quantifiable business impact. But when that CEO asks the Chief Marketing Officer the same question, the answer comes back, "Well, our brand awareness will sure take a hit." So then the CEO says, "I see. Let's cut marketing *20* percent."

Such is the fate of all marketers that cannot measure their success in the real currency of the corporation—sales. "Traditional marketers tend to shy away from measurements," says Devashish Saxena, Manager of Worldwide Internet Marketing at Texas Instruments, "or they measure things that don't mean anything, like ad recall." At the end of the day (or even at lunch time), brand awareness doesn't mean anything if your product doesn't sell. It's not enough for marketers to talk a good game and then let the sales department be accountable for the company's revenue.

We do have a model for merging marketing and sales—*direct* marketing. With direct marketing, everything is measurable, and marketing no longer exists in a vacuum without sales. Direct marketing lives and dies by metrics—*response* metrics.

Think about how direct marketers work. Let's consider a new credit card application in a direct mail offer. (Ever see one of those in your mailbox?) That mailing piece has been painstakingly crafted to evoke a response. Every word on the envelope is designed to get it opened. Every word in the letter has been tested to persuade. And some guy made the Direct Marketers Hall of Fame when he came up with the idea for the handwritten Post-It note that says, "Before you throw this offer away, just read this." That gambit increased response rates by 0.7 percent, so it is worth millions.

Direct marketers never design their mail and then send out millions of copies indiscriminately. They carefully select the recipients—that's their market segmentation. They buy mailing lists of prospective customers that match their target markets, and they send out a few thousand pieces to see what the response rate is. They then pare down the lists they use to just the ones that get the highest response rates.

Measurement isn't an afterthought in direct marketing. Duane Schultz, Vice President of Internet Marketing for Xerox, likes to say, "The old model was Build, then Measure, while the new model is Measure, then Improve."

Direct mail marketers know this "new" model well because it's *always* been the direct mail model. Every aspect of a mailing piece is tested. They send different variations of the piece to their test mailing recipients to see whether different words on the envelope, a different offer, or even a different color for the Post-It note raises response. Direct marketers throw a party when they can get a 0.1 percent rise in response rates.

Catalog marketers are no different than direct mail marketers in their need to test everything possible to raise response rates. Catalogs are even personalized with different products or prices to different target market segments. Anything is fair game if it can raise response rates.

This is all very well and good but what's it got to do with the Web? What's the big deal about direct marketing, anyway? Well, the Web is the biggest direct marketing opportunity the world has ever seen.

Direct marketers pore over their response rates, but they don't have much information about what *caused* the response rates. They don't know how many envelopes were thrown away without being opened, for example. If they did, they would work feverishly on the envelope to get it opened more frequently. They'd change the words on the front. They'd change the size of the words, the typeface, and the color of the printing. They might even change the size and color of the envelope itself. If they knew what was lowering response rates, they'd attack that problem.

But they can't always do that because they just don't know how many people open that envelope. Michael Petillo, e-business Leader at W.L. Gore & Associates, notes, "In marketing, you always want to say you've created value today, but you didn't have the tools to show it."

On the other hand, the Web allows you to measure *everything*—every tiny step in the process. You know whether they saw your paid search ad on Google and whether they clicked it. You know whether they abandoned your Web site on the first page or they bailed out during checkout. You can know your response rate for every blessed step in the process, and you can experiment and tweak your marketing with far greater impact on the Web than in any traditional direct marketing campaign.

Both direct mailers and catalog marketers follow the same process of experimenting and testing the results before executing the campaign by sending out a million pieces of mail or a million catalogs. But the Web changes this aspect of direct marketing, too. With the Web, the most granular part of marketing is not the campaign. In fact, you can be as granular as you can afford. You can change something three times every hour if you want and see whether response rates go up each time.

Maybe this seems like small potatoes to you. (Strangely, nothing ever seems like *big* potatoes.) Maybe raising response rates by fractional percentages sounds like small-time thinking. Guess again.

The Web allows an accelerated pace of experimentation that is turning the world on its ear. The accumulation of changes that can be made at Web pace raise your effectiveness at blinding speed. If you change the copy on your product's Web page, you might know whether the change was a good idea in a couple of hours. If it's a dumb idea, you change it back or change it to something else. By relentlessly experimenting time after time, you gradually fine-tune your marketing to have the highest possible response rates. Web sites often improve their response rates ten-fold with this attention to detail.

But this requires a huge change in the way we think. We are accustomed to spending months in meetings reaching consensus on every detail of "the plan" and reviewing everything with executives for approval. And then we execute the plan and declare victory.

We often don't measure whether it worked. We frequently don't find out what is wrong with what we did. And we rarely spend months tweaking and polishing it to make it better than what we launched in the first place. Our basic approach is to spend almost any amount of time and money to get it right the first time. We do it right, slowly.

The reason that we do things slowly is very rational. In the old marketing world, it is dangerous to make a mistake. You make big decisions, such as the wording of the new slogan for the next calendar year. You spend money up front to make TV commercials and design print ads. You commit to commercial time and ad space months in advance. Then you debut your campaign...and hold your breath.

If your campaign is lousy, if it was a dumb idea, if it is embarrassing, if people make fun of it, if people ignore it, if no one likes it, if it is criticized in the industry, if the government investigates the claim, if there was an error in wording—you get the idea—then it is a *big* problem because it can't be easily fixed and because you will live with that problem for days or weeks or longer while it continues to embarrass you. And even if you can get it off the air and out of print, you have nothing to replace it with. You have no Plan B. If it is wrong, it will be a disaster!

You'll get fired!

So because you are rational, you take steps to mitigate all of these very real risks. You check everything with other people, ranging from PR people to lawyers to scientists. You ask anyone you can think of to help, to make sure *nothing is wrong*. You do focus groups with customers to make sure they like it. You ask your friends. You triple-check everything. You get "buy-in" from your boss, and you fix every problem that you uncover in this process, which makes the process very slow and very expensive. And the fact that it is expensive gives you even one *more* reason to be careful that you aren't about to waste a ton of money.

So make no mistakes. At all costs, this must be done right.

Except that we really *don't* do it right. At least, not as right as it could be. We gather all the smart people in a room and argue about the plan, and we convince each other it is right, but that doesn't make it so. All of us have to admit that every campaign we've ever done could have been better. Some of them, despite all of our time and effort, turned out to be downright lousy.

It's hard to admit, but many times we start off doing it wrong. It is the rare marketing campaign that would not be improved by testing it and making changes. And by taking so long to finally agree on what to do, we are losing a lot of the impact. Unfortunately, most of us are doing it wrong, slowly.

Sometimes, no matter how carefully we plan, something goes wrong. In late 2006, Chrysler's marketers came up with a great idea: On *Time* magazine's Web site, during the week that *Time* names their Person of the Year, Chrysler planned an eye-catching ad that began, "You might not be the Person of the Year…," which went on to address you as an important customer anyway.

There was only one problem—*Time* as it turned out, did name "You" as Person of the Year. The magazine had jumped on the whole Web 2.0 trend and highlighted that *everyone* is a participant. Chrysler wasn't prepared for that and could not have been.

But the Web lets us break free. Web sites are infinitely malleable, so you can change them whenever you want. Chrysler could remove that ad or change it into a joke—whatever works—while they could never have recovered from a similar misfortune in the print version of the magazine. On the Internet, you aren't committed to running that failing ad for a year—or even a day. If it's not working in the morning, change it after lunch. Alter the offer or the words or the picture—even start from scratch if you have to. Above all, you must experiment and see what happens.

Just like direct marketers, we can test *everything*. We can see what our customers do. We can see if they respond. Whatever they respond to, we do more of it and cut out the stuff they don't respond to.

And just like direct marketers, we can test in small groups. We can show the test Web pages to a small group of customers and show the regular ones to everyone else. If the test goes well, then we can show the new ones to everyone.

Remember, the Web is the biggest direct marketing opportunity to ever come along. You can try anything. You can measure its impact. You can fix it and measure it again. The more things you try, the more you will eventually get right. The faster you experiment, the faster you'll get everything right—or at least get close enough or closer than you were.

These are big changes in direct marketing. Part 2, "That Newfangled *Direct* Marketing," is all about them. Don't try to get it perfect the first time. Do it wrong quickly.

Summary

They *are* doing wonderful things with computers. But don't be like my dear old Aunt Minnie, sitting on the sidelines talking about what *they* are doing.

You need to get into the game. It's time to become a Millennium Marketer. Web analytics expert Avinash Kaushik, author of *Web Analytics: An Hour a Day*, tells marketers, "If you don't get the Web, you won't have a long future."

Extreme? Yes. But the fact is that the Web is no longer a great *potential* marketing tool. It *is* a great marketing tool—the potential is beginning to be realized, perhaps by your own competitors. As we've seen, the Web brings big changes to marketing as we know it:

- **MarCom is becoming MarCon**—Marketers who interrupt their customers to spew monologues are out. Marketing as conversation is in. What makes you someone your customers want to talk to? What makes you someone that your customers will say nice things about?

- **Marketing segmentation is becoming marketing personalization**—Web marketing makes it far easier to base market segments on needs rather than simple demographics and firmographics, and the Web lets customers segment themselves. Moreover, the Web allows segmentation to differentiate both the message and the product in ways not practical before. Do your customers feel like they get a personal message and a personalized product?

- **We're all direct marketers now**—The Web is one big direct marketing machine, and everyone is invited to the party. We can try anything, measure everything, and do it all over again 20 minutes from now based on what we learned. And we will change our culture from trying to be perfect from the outset to doing it wrong quickly.

Enough marketing philosophy! Let's dive right into what the Web has to offer. What are all those new Web marketing tactics with those funny names? Blogs and podcasts and wikis! Oh my! Check out Chapter 2 to find out what all this geeky stuff can do for your marketing.

2

New Wine in Old Bottles

"The very first law in advertising is to avoid the concrete promise and cultivate the delightfully vague."

—Bill Cosby

Chapter Contents

- The "Three Rs" of Online Marketing   25
- The New Marketing Is Not So New   35
- Summary   53

It's completely new. It's earth-shatteringly different. Nothing will ever be the same again. Business as usual is over.

Sounds a little scary, huh?

Well, that's how big changes seem to most of us. In spite of all the talk about embracing change (just give it a big hug), most of us like things the way they are. It's safer and more familiar and requires a lot less thought.

So if you think of Internet marketing as this breathtakingly new thing that changes *everything* and will send you into years of the unknown, you just might dampen your undies in fear.

But it doesn't have to be that way. Although there are many changes that the Web brings to marketing, you can be confident that many things stay the same. Much of what you know as an experienced marketer is still true. Many of the tactics in this new Web world are different, but in many ways they are new wine in old bottles. You can think of blogs as just a new form of publicity. Viral marketing is word-of-mouth on steroids. But before we leap into the analogies of the old world and the new, let's take a trip down Memory Lane (it's never Memory Avenue or Memory Road, for some reason) and see how the Web got us here.

You might be hearing a lot about *Web 2.0* and wondering what everyone is talking about. Less important than the name Web 2.0 is what the trend really means, what its business impact is, and what you should do about it. Long after people stop talking about Web 2.0, its impact will remain.

Right now, Web 2.0 is the flavor of the month, but expect a popular backlash as people attack Web 2.0 because it's nothing more than hype—or because something better has come along. Already people are talking about "Web 3.0." (They skipped right past Web 2.1 and 2.2.)

To understand what folks mean by the term Web 2.0, we need to understand what has come before. Calling it Web 2.0 makes it sound as if we need to know about only *one* thing that happened earlier, but we should dig deeper to get a better understanding.

Before there was a Web, we had the Internet. The Internet was about connecting computers together, and its biggest impact has been e-mail—once computers were connected, we could send e-mail between them to communicate with each other. Marketers did not discover the Internet right away (perhaps because Al Gore was not a marketer), but the invention of e-mail eventually allowed marketers to adapt direct mail practices to take advantage of the new technology.

Around 1994, we first started hearing about the World Wide Web. The Web was built on the Internet but was a breakthrough all its own because it connected information, not just computers. The HTML language, along with the Web browser, made it easy to display information on any computer and easy for each piece of information to link to any other piece of information. For marketers, the Web allowed marketing communications, such as brochures, to be available on demand from a Web site.

In the past, prospective customers had to contact you (by phone, for example) to request a brochure, and some did. But many more people will visit your Web site than contact you by phone. Why? Because they can be anonymous. They can find out what they want without giving up their identity and landing in your Rolodex (which would allow you to interrupt them more). Even in a physical store, people subject themselves to sales pitches just by showing up. Most people don't like sales pitches because they feel pressured. Your Web site is a pressure-free way to sell, so it's no wonder more people use it to research the early part of their purchases and that people tend to do a lot more research than they used to. For marketers, the Web is better than a brochure precisely because more people will look at the information.

Then came another leap forward when programmers invented *dynamic* Web pages. Instead of typing the HTML code into a file, a software program could generate HTML on the fly. Why do marketers care about such geeky stuff? Because dynamic pages can show different information to different people based on their identities and actions. The simplest uses of dynamic pages include shopping carts—each person who uses one has a different product in the cart. Dynamic pages turned brochure-ware Web sites into e-commerce sites.

At this point, the Web was suddenly discovered by business, including marketers. It became clear that the Web allowed any business to have a store—an online location where people could learn about what you sell and buy it (or learn about it and buy it offline). And interactive marketing was born.

Banner ads, e-mail marketing, search marketing—many new tactics arose to take advantage of this new medium. But the Web—what the gurus now quaintly call "Web 1.0"—still catered to *consumers*, in the marketing sense of the word. Web users consumed information (such as brochures and other product information), and they consumed products (that they bought either online or offline), but that's about all they did. Marketers were happy because marketers are always happy to reach consumers.

But before long, those consumers started turning into *participants*. They started rating merchants on eBay and reviewing books on Amazon. On message boards, they began complaining about poor service. This was new territory for marketers. No longer did Web users passively consume information and products. The Web had begun to change.

It didn't change all at once, although the name Web 2.0 makes it sound like a software release. Gradually, folks started writing blogs to share their opinions and to ask others to comment. They created wikis, such as Wikipedia, where Web users change the content of the site itself. They started sending messages of their own that competed with the messages of the marketers.

Before long, someone christened these participatory techniques "Web 2.0." But it's not the name that is important—some call this phenomenon *consumer-generated content*,

JUST WHAT *IS* SOCIAL MEDIA MARKETING?

Any emerging concept is hard to pin down—social media is no exception. Lots of people are talking about it, but they don't all agree on which Web techniques *are* social media and which are not. If you laid all the experts end-to-end, they'd all point in different directions.

But that won't stop me. You can think of social media marketing as any way to get attention for your message using people connected to the Internet. Here's a quick way to categorize different types of social media:

- **Content-based**—Some social sites are built around individual messages. YouTube and FlickR, for example, host videos and photos designed to be shared with others. Other content-based social media sites don't host the content—they link to it. Digg, del.icio.us, StumbleUpon, and other sites allow readers to bookmark certain content items to highlight them for others. (We'll talk more about those sites in Chapter 3, "Marketing Is a Conversation.")

- **Personality-based**—Social networking sites allow each member to create a profile description, which can then be linked to the profiles of friends or colleagues, forming a network. MySpace has gotten a lot of attention, but FaceBook and LinkedIn might be make more sense for marketers targeting adult market segments. (We'll tackle social networks later in this chapter.)

- **Interest-based**—Topic-oriented sites (such as Yahoo! Groups and Google Groups) form communities around specific subjects on message boards and similar sites, which we'll discuss later in this chapter. Increasingly, specialized search sites allow category searches, such as Technorati's search for blogs on a specific topic.

- **Fantasy-based**—Some folks believe that the emerging virtual worlds, such as Second Life, are also social media. (You can learn more about them in Chapter 9, "This Stuff Changes Too Fast.")

Now that you see the different types of social media, don't get too hung up on exact definitions. My list isn't any more insightful than anyone else's, and by the time you read this, an entirely new strain of social media may be emerging.

What *is* important, however, is paying attention so that when a new kind of social media appears, you'll recognize it and consider whether it could work for your marketing campaign. Rob Key, President of the consulting firm Converseon, suggests taking an approach drawn from cultural anthropology, "First become part of the community, understand its language, and give something altruistically to the tribe before expecting ROI." That will work for whatever comes along.

social computing, or *social media*. What *is* important is how these new techniques allow consumers to participate in the marketing conversation. Web 1.0 was for consumers, while Web 2.0 is for participants—those who create and add to information, not just read what others say.

Marketing in some industries, such as consumer electronics and high-tech, is already profoundly affected by what Web 2.0 customers expect. But even if marketing in your industry isn't affected yet, keep in mind the words of author William Gibson: "The future is here. It's just not widely distributed yet."

So settle in, and let's take a look at the ways that interactive marketing requires a different way of engaging these new Web 2.0 participants. Online marketing demands a change in both message and tone to something more personal than ever before.

How you approach online marketing is just as important as the tactics themselves. That's where we will start in this chapter. We'll get around to talking about what these new marketing tactics are, but first let's think about how interactive marketing changes the way you talk to your customers, using the "Three Rs" of online marketing. Later, we'll take a look at how these new marketing tactics fit into a more traditional view of marketing, using our offline marketing experience to conquer this brave new marketing world.

The "Three Rs" of Online Marketing

Classic marketing books expound upon the Four P's of marketing: Product, Price, Place, and Promotion. Well, when the Place you are marketing is the Internet, Product and Price continue to be critical to your marketing efforts, but so is Promotion. What's different is the way you *do* promotion.

Old-style promotion depends on filling every crevice with your marketing message—one-way communication, broadcasting the same message, over and over. You make the same claims and use the same attention-getting hype. That's the way we've always done it.

Old-style marketing is fading, however. It's fading because people pay less attention to traditional media as they begin to pay more attention to interactive media. But that's not the biggest reason it's fading. (After all, many people still don't even have Internet access.)

No, it's fading in large measure because people are sick of the hype. People are tired of being bombarded with marketing messages that they don't believe and aren't interested in. A Ball State University study says that Americans spend 70 percent of their waking time with media, much of that multitasking with multiple forms of media simultaneously and that media is *filled* with marketing messages—filled to the point of overload.

And when people are overloaded, they respond in predictable psychological ways. They pay less attention to each input (even disregarding inputs completely), and they filter (or completely block) reception. So it should come as no surprise that your customers are ignoring and blocking your marketing messages—they're overwhelmed.

You probably know that the younger your customer, the less credibility the traditional hard sell has. Customers are becoming more suspicious of marketing or advertising of any kind. So what *are* they looking for?

Promotion has always depended on getting attention and always will. The old way was to relentlessly pound your overblown messages over and over again. But Web 2.0 customers require a new approach to get their attention. You can summarize the new way as the "Three Rs." You must be *relevant*. You must be *real*. And you must be *responsive*.

You Must Be *Relevant*

"We're going to the store." Americans of a certain age remember our moms and dads making this announcement on Saturday morning. My, how times have changed! With the Web, the store can come to us.

But there's a less obvious change that's also occurred. If you grew up in a small town, you might really have gone to *the* store—maybe you had just that one Wal-Mart that satisfied most of your needs. But even if you lived in the largest city, you probably had a specific store you visited for each item you had to buy. You bought your tools at Sears, your cookware at Macy's, and "you know what" at Toys "R" Us. Often the most important factor in selecting a store was *proximity*. The Web has changed that forever.

You no longer have to visit a "store near you"—on the Web, all the stores are equally close. So what causes customers to choose one store over another? Frequently, it's *relevance*. If your Web site is the most relevant site for the task at hand, you might get the business. If not, it might not matter what your brand is. Proximity is being replaced by relevance.

You might agree that this insight is uncanny (it cannot be canned), but how do Web shoppers find relevant Web sites? And the answer is *Google*. Google and other search engines are designed to decide relevance. Each searcher's query is seeking the most relevant search results—the Web sites that best match the task being performed at that moment. Customers buying shoes want the best shoe store. Shoppers looking for computers want to see the widest selection with the best prices and the easiest purchasing experience. Those sites are the most relevant to the task at hand.

Google and other search engines provide that relevance. Today's typical Web shopper behavior is not to head to a favorite online store—shoppers go instead to their favorite search engine and let fly. The most relevant sites, as judged by the search engine, are where they go next. Sure, sometimes shoppers go directly to eBay or

Amazon, but there are far fewer brand-loyal shoppers on the Web than in the old world of physical proximity.

The use of search engines has fueled this shift in shopper attitudes. Web shoppers search mainly for detailed product information and price comparisons, not information about the retailer or the manufacturer. In fact, over 90 percent of all searchers never use brand names in searches that lead to purchases. Some might still argue that brand loyalty is not dead, but when loyalty is finally put to rest, its gravestone might say, "I told you I was sick."

If customers have any loyalty, it might be to their search engines ("I always use Google") because it saves them time. So the best test of relevance is whether your site helps customers do what they want to do at the moment they want to do it. Is it easy to find your site with a search? Easy for customers to find what they want on your site? Do you provide all the information needed? We'll tackle these questions starting in Chapter 4, "Going Over to the Dark Side."

Relevance continues to be important after the customer visits your store. At any moment the customer might decide that your store is no longer relevant enough—a few clicks of the mouse can bring up another one. Economists like to talk about "switching costs" (the drawbacks of changing the businesses you choose to patronize). Those living in small towns served only by Wal-Mart had very high switching costs. They might have been forced to pay more to shop elsewhere and also suffer from less selection—perhaps having to drive further as well. But on the Web, switching costs are extremely low.

Think about it. Few shoppers leave their half-full carts in the aisles of physical stores, but some Web sites find as many as half of their shopping carts are abandoned. The reason is low switching costs. It takes just a few minutes for a shopper to find a desired item at a rival Web site, while driving to another physical store takes considerably longer (and is not worth the time).

In such a world, brand loyalty is a thing of the past for many customers, although not for the majority of customers—yet. Brands continue to be strong in many areas; even Internet denizens respect brands such as Google and Amazon. And strong brands built offline have power that will last for years to come. But, as with old media habits, brand loyalty is becoming less strong than it once was, especially in countries with high Internet usage and especially with younger customers.

Brand loyalty is gradually being replaced by relevance. Obviously, your offering must be promising, and you must deliver on your promises. Your prices must be competitive. You must reliably provide your product or service. If your claims are hollow, then it's impossible for you to seem relevant for very long.

Relevance is at the top of your customers' list. They want what they want when they want it. They increasingly expect you not to waste their time. You can't keep finding more and more ways to interrupt people with irrelevant offers for products they don't want to buy now. If your customers don't want to receive your message, you can bombard them until the cows come home and get no response. (And the cows don't want to hear your message, either.)

So how do you make your interactive marketing the most relevant choice for your customers? You must adopt search marketing and Web site personalization approaches—a relevant ad is a winning ad. Instead of blanketing everyone with your 30-second TV spot, relevance-based marketing isolates the people most interested in what you are selling today.

But relevance is more than being there with the right ad at the right time. Relevance requires clarity. If no one understands you, how can you be relevant to them? You must dump the jargon and the marketing-speak. Being real requires real words. Let's talk about that next.

A "GETTING REAL" CASE STUDY

What do you do when you have customers counting on your service and you fail? Many of us marketers would do nothing—that kind of communication is for the tech support department. And of course the sales reps need to be briefed on what to say, because they might be dealing with some angry customers.

Few marketers would decide to post a blog entry entitled "Anatomy of a (an ongoing) Disaster"—but that is exactly what DreamHost did when they had a series of snafus that produced service outages for their customers.

DreamHost operates the computer servers that run other companies' Web sites, so when DreamHost fails, their customers' Web sites fail. Having a Web site down can be a disaster for many businesses, but how many marketers would use that word to describe their own service to their customers? DreamHost did.

DreamHost went into exhaustive detail on what went wrong, which was actually a series of errors, many by their own hand, but a few were out of their immediate control (by their suppliers).

And what was their customers' response? Some DreamHost customers switched to competitors, but most stayed. The comments posted to that blog entry were overwhelmingly positive:

- "I'm not going anywhere and this blog post is a big reason why."
- "Posts like this are the reason I love dreamhost and continue to pimp you guys out to all my friends."

You Must Be *Real*

Old-style promotion depends on hype. We know that it doesn't matter whether we *want* to hype our products or not. We *have* to. All of our competitors are breathlessly hyping their products, so we had better, too. That's what we tell ourselves.

After all, customers don't really believe those overheated ads, right? Everyone knows that customers discount the truth of everything they hear. So it stands to reason that with all of our competitors puffing up their claims, even if we tell the truth, our customers will *still* discount what we say, won't they? Then we'll look even worse than we really are. That's just the way it is, isn't it?

Then we tell ourselves that if all the other kids are doing it, we'd better continue to shade the truth, spin the message, exaggerate—you get the idea—or else we'll be

- "...try not to beat yourselves up too much over this period of bad luck..."
- "I have to say that without this post, I'd be outta here."
- "It's rare to find a company who is willing to own up to their mistakes and be honest with customers."
- "...I am rooting for you."
- "Without this post I would seriously consider moving."

Did every customer respond that way? No. There were a few flaming comments that took DreamHost to task. DreamHost left them in there along with all the positive comments for everyone to read.

And then a funny thing happened. Other bloggers linked to the DreamHost blog to show a great example of a company being honest under fire. For all we know, DreamHost actually attracted more customers than it lost.

Now will marketing like this make DreamHost a success? Not by itself. DreamHost must actually fix these problems, or their customers will flee no matter how honest they are about them. But this kind of authenticity might have forged stronger relationships. It would have been easier to keep a lid on information, to placate customers privately, or to make excuses—and customers are smart enough to know that.

Getting real is not just about avoiding ethical lapses, but about using truthfulness as a differentiator to build trust in your customer relationships.

hurt. That's the way old-style marketing promotion works. Our marketing better put the "hype" in *hyperbole* (or we fear they'll get someone else to do it "right").

Online marketing is turning this cozy little world upside down.

All this old-time hype makes customers more and more cynical—they automatically assume that companies are lying to them. They know their kids are being sold certain foods in the cafeteria because the schools get better deals for them. They know manufacturers are not "telling all" about the way laborers are treated in third-world factories. They know that food producers keep secrets about animal treatment. Customers have come to expect that everything they hear from you puts you in the best light, so they believe less and less of it. The entire anti-consumer movement demonizes companies as bad citizens of the world.

What does a marketer do in the face of this kind of cynicism? Well, it's not an easy answer, unfortunately. The only antidote to cynicism is honesty—honesty in large amounts over a long period of time.

This presents a problem for many companies. Abraham Lincoln once said that "what kills a skunk is the publicity it gives itself." If your company has not exactly been the poster child for ethical behavior, then suddenly "coming clean" is an unappetizing prospect. But those Web 2.0 customers will force you to do it sooner or later.

In the past, only big companies had to worry about a media exposé because no one cared about the bad behavior of small companies. But now every company can be held up on the Web and be made accountable. It costs nothing for one of your customers (or competitors) to write a blog entry or otherwise cause a ruckus. You might as well take a hard look at yourself and decide where your ethics need an overhaul. Then you can air your own dirty laundry with an apology and a commitment to fixing the problem. That's what "getting real" means in marketing today.

And don't assume that getting real is about only the big, Enron-style, horrible behavior. Being authentic is not just about preventing enormous lapses of ethics. Despite what the anti-consumerists say, the great majority of business people are not evil, and they have high moral standards. We just need to raise the bar.

We need to realize our customers want authenticity in every interaction, big and small. They want us to tell the truth even when we could get away with covering it up because that is what *really* builds trust. That's what long-term relationships are built on.

As you think about getting real, you no doubt appreciate that the logic is impeccable (it cannot be pecked), but you might be wondering how to *do* it. How can a *company* be real? Most companies large enough to have a slew of marketers are nothing more than a pile of stock certificates. Companies aren't real—people are. So the way to be real is to let the people out.

You have a whole company full of employee marketers itching to do your work for you. Some of them might want to write blogs. Some might just comment on blogs written by others. Others might haunt customer support message boards and explain how your product really works and how to make it work better. Today, these helpful, authentic people are probably hidden behind your corporate policies—only public relations people speak to the press, all external communication must be approved by legal, and all information is considered confidential until declassified by management, and on and on. Let your people go. Let them go out and be your best marketers.

When you do, you'll find out that your new marketers don't stay "on message." They don't stick to the "talking points." They speak in their own voices and say what they think they should in each situation. They sound like real people because they are real people. And customers eat it up.

Is this a risk? Yes. Your employees could do something dumb. They might say the wrong thing. They might embarrass you. They might even get you sued. If you are working in a highly-regulated industry, such as pharmaceuticals, you must consider the laws in each country in which you operate. But for most businesses, the risks are not terribly high.

If you go ahead and take the risk to allow your customers to see your company as a set of real human beings, your customers will cut you more slack. People are like that—we forgive many errors of people that we know, but we get royally ticked off at a faceless monolith.

Think about it. You hate to be told bad news in an e-mail or a letter—it's impersonal. ("Why didn't my sales rep call to tell me?") You ignore the fact that there's a real person in that car in front of you, even though you can see him, because you don't *know* him. (That's where road rage comes from.) You are nastier to someone on the phone than you would be in person and more frustrated yet with a voice response system. ("Your call is very important to us, but not so important that we hired enough people to answer it.")

Think how your customers respond to the faceless, nameless, personality-less voice from your marketing machine. In contrast, think of how customers respond when you let your product folks talk to them directly, apologize for what got screwed up, and promise that a fix is coming. You might just keep those customers, whereas you can lose them when your official tech support person minimizes the problem or quotes your company warranty policy.

After all, customers have policies too—they don't repurchase once they've been screwed. Then they tell everyone they know and lots of people they don't know—through the Web. Let your company show off its real people, and your customers will reward you instead.

Of course, you can simply move the old marketing hype over to the Internet and continue business as usual. But that's not the best approach. Online, your customers will call you on every little white lie, on every "best case" scenario. And you'll look bad in front of everyone. Better to let your competitors take that approach while you get real.

GETTING REAL ON FEATURES AND BENEFITS

Floyd Marinescu, creator of successful software community sites infoq.com and theserverside.com, disputes the traditional marketing dictum to "sell the benefits, not the features." Floyd says that he finds his software developer customers respond to the exact opposite approach—selling the features, not the benefits.

Floyd says that programmers perceive traditional marketing copy as spam: "When you sell the benefits, everyone's product sounds the same." He used copy soliciting registrants for a technical conference as an example:

- Increase your skill
- Network with others
- Learn what you need for your job

Floyd's point is that any conference can claim these benefits. He'd regularly rewrite this kind of copy to emphasize specific features—the speakers, the subjects, the precise technical information the customers were looking for: "No benefits. Just facts. Just features."

The marketers told Floyd that his copy was boring, but he says, "The feature-oriented ones did better—20 percent better click-through rates." If you're looking for a way to turn around your conversion rates, give fact-based marketing copy a try.

So shut off the hype machine. Your customers want facts. They want you to be authentic. They want to be able to trust you. Setting that authentic tone and providing the information your customers really want to know—that's the quickest way to "get real."

If you've always prided yourself on having that "just right" turn of phrase, don't worry. Being authentic means that you need to avoid the bombastic, overblown hype of typical marketing copy, but it doesn't force you to market sushi as "cold, dead fish." You can put your best foot forward in clear language.

Once you start talking to your customers like real people, an amazing thing will happen—they'll talk back. Then you'll need to know how to be responsive.

You Must Be *Responsive*

The Internet ends the one-way monologues of offline marketing. Online, you don't deliver a message—you start a conversation, or your customer starts a conversation with you. Either way, you need to be responsive, or the conversation ends. If your customers don't like some of your company's practices, for example, you must respond.

Even small companies can't hide from bad publicity any more because your customers will write about your bad behavior, even if the mainstream media does not. Your customers might complain in public about your product or your customer service, so you must be prepared to adroitly respond.

Blogger Ryan Saghir, the author of the popular Orbitcast blog covering the satellite radio industry, gets tips from readers all the time. Ryan explains

> *Customers reach out and say, "Can you bring this to light? There's a bad firmware update on this receiver." These are passionate consumers that hope I publicize an issue and get it addressed.*

It's likely that customers who have had a problem and gotten it resolved are more loyal than those who've been treated flawlessly. A crisis resolved well creates more confidence in the relationship than if everything had been done correctly in the first place. This is especially true if you had "bent" the rules a bit to make the customer happy.

But being responsive is about more than customer service.

It wasn't a great day for marketing at McDonald's when the movie *Super Size Me!* debuted. Someone documented the impact on his health from eating at McDonald's for 30 days. Whether the movie was fair or not, they needed to handle it. But McDonald's didn't respond effectively. They withdrew their trademarked "super size" meals but claimed that the movie had nothing to do with it. Nothing else they did made a ripple in the negative public perception.

Contrast McDonald's inaction with another big company in crisis. When several people died after ingesting tainted Tylenol back in the 1980s, the company swung into action, recalling all bottles from store shelves, investigating their factories, and preventing future problems by instituting tamper-resistant packaging. The public was thrilled. The Tylenol brand took a huge leap forward for responding to a problem that the company had no fault in causing.

How do companies use the Internet to handle a crisis? DuPont provides an educational example with its Teflon® product, a non-stick coating used in cookware. In 2005, the US Environmental Protection Agency found that an obscure chemical used in the process of manufacturing Teflon is a "likely carcinogen." The final manufactured coating contains barely a trace of this carcinogen, but people who heard the story were understandably concerned.

DuPont used the Internet to defend its product's safety reputation. It posted detailed information on both teflon.com and its corporate Web site. DuPont also took the clever step of running print advertisements with an invitation to its customers: "So let's start a conversation" by going to Teflon's Web site to learn more about the controversy. After all, customers are *going* to have conversations about this kind of story—it might as well be with you instead of about you. DuPont's approach was responsiveness at its best.

Other big companies have dealt with negative publicity. It goes with the territory—when you're big, you're a target. The Internet makes big companies an even bigger target, but small companies can be targeted, too. It costs almost nothing for your company to be criticized online these days, so you must be ready to respond and be part of the conversation, whether your company is big or small.

In the old days, the negative story had to be interesting enough for the media to cover it. Nowadays, any blogger can put your company in the stew. Almost anyone can create a Web site called "yourcompanysucks.com" and fire away. And even if the story is false or uninteresting, your customers might see it. You'll need to respond. You'll need to be part of the conversation.

In Chapter 3, we'll talk more about how to listen to your customers to be responsive. In Chapter 4, we'll cover how you can listen in even deeper ways, not to what they say but by analyzing what they do.

In the new world of Web marketing, your message must be relevant to your customers' needs at the moment. You must be authentic (real), and you must be responsive to customer feedback. Don't be caught with a 20th century marketing program for new millennium customers. If you aren't ensuring your message is relevant, real, and responsive, your customers will tune you out. Marketers who heed the "Three Rs" will get the all-important fourth R—*relationship*.

Brands are no longer owned by companies as much as by the people who use them. Coke drinkers screamed at the change of the time-honored formula to "New Coke," but Coca-Cola saved the brand by switching back in response. Apple has a community of evangelists using their Macintosh computers and iPods—they say, "Once you go Mac, you never go back." These brand-loyal customers are becoming rarer than in times past but are just as valuable to the companies that attract them.

A great product is important for brand loyalty, but so is good marketing. Coca-Cola is the king of old-style brand marketing, while Apple is staking out a unique brand image for cool technology using Web marketing along with traditional marketing tactics. Some people won't drink any soda but Coke. Some won't use any computer or MP3 player except Apple's. That sense of shared brand ownership between company and customer is a relationship.

On the Internet, you can attract customers who will buy and buy again, if you don't waste their time, if you earn their trust, and if you jump when they call. When you do all of these things, a relationship will naturally begin to form—a different kind of relationship than with old-style marketing because online marketing is *personal*. We'll talk about that in Chapter 5, "The New Customer Relations."

The New Marketing Is Not So New

OK, we've talked about the new wine—how interactive marketing is different in several ways from old-style marketing. Now it's time to look at the old bottles. How can we understand these new marketing tactics in light of traditional marketing promotion?

It isn't as much of a stretch as it might seem at first. Promotion has always been about advertising, direct marketing, and publicity—interactive marketing tactics can be broadly characterized in those terms, too.

Danger bells go off whenever you tightly categorize anything new as just being more of the same old thing, but it can be helpful to generalize about these new tactics so you can apply your existing knowledge to what's new. So make the connections but remember that these tactics all differ from the old techniques in both big and subtle ways, so don't use the mapping as a substitute for learning more.

We'll spend the rest of the book examining how these new marketing tactics are different from what's gone before, but we'll spend the next few pages treating them as new wine in old bottles. If you've got a firm grip on the new Web marketing approaches, you can safely skip ahead to Chapter 3. However, if you find blogs, wikis, and podcasts to be inscrutable (they cannot be, uh, never mind), then keep reading. We'll take a look at some time-worn categories of marketing techniques and see how the old labels fit the new tactics.

Advertising

Someone once described advertising as the science of arresting the human intelligence long enough to get money from it. This cynical outlook is a holdover from the bad old days, however, because it's changed a bit on the Web. You can continue to interrupt people in certain demographic groups with random messages, but you'll find more success with new tactics that emphasize relevance.

The first appearance of ads on the Web mirrored print ads. Known as *banner ads* or *display ads*, as shown in Exhibit 2-1, they appear mainly on popular sites such as Yahoo! and MySpace. Banners are typically purchased for particular pages of a Web site, often rotated for viewing with other ads each time the page is displayed to a new person. That Web site is carefully chosen to reach targeted demographic segments, the same way magazine advertising is purchased. Marketers pay each time the ad is displayed (called an *impression fee*), hoping the customer will click the ad and be taken to the marketer's Web site, where the marketer can deliver a deeper message and maybe get a sale.

Anyone who clicks on the ad is taken to Citibank's Web site.

Exhibit 2-1   A typical banner ad as shown on the Yahoo! portal

Banner ads have become less popular with marketers due to so-called "banner blindness"—eye tracking shows less than a second spent on traditional graphical banner ads by customers when they view a Web page. This banner blindness explains why less than half of one percent of banner ads are clicked by customers.

As click rates for banner ads decreased, misguided marketers became even more intrusive in their quest to interrupt customers. They began using pop-up ads that open a new Web browser, window covering up whatever the customer was doing—forcing the window to be closed before continuing to use the browser. Others started experimenting with *adware* (a more benign form of *spyware*), where the customer (often unwittingly) downloads a program that can show ads when the computer is being used.

Stay far away from pop-ups and adware—these are the online equivalents of the door-to-door salesman sticking his foot inside the house to prevent the door from closing. These hyper-aggressive intrusions are no way to start a relationship.

Banner ads and their more aggressive cousins are simple translations of old-style interruption marketing to the Web—most are shown on traditional Web sites, but they can also appear on blogs or even games. Banner ads can be an effective part of some Web marketing campaigns, but flee all pop-ups and adware opportunities, no matter how tempting they might seem.

Paid search is the other major form of Web advertising spending, with search spending increasing at a much faster rate than banners. Paid search ads, as shown in Exhibit 2-2, are typically textual, and they get far higher click rates—sometimes 10 percent or more.

When a searcher looks for "life insurance," Google shows paid ads above and to the right of the organic search results on that topic.

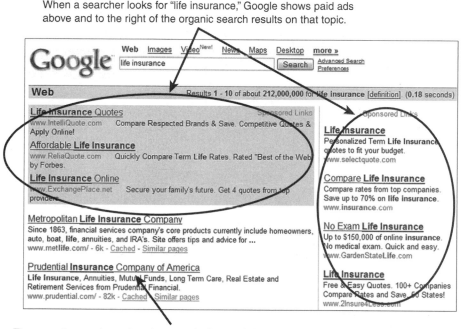

The organic search results, shown at the bottom left, are Web pages Google believes to be the best (unbiased) matches.

Exhibit 2-2   Sample paid search ads displayed by the Google search engine

Why do customers click these boring-looking ads while ignoring the glitzier banners? Because the search ads are relevant to what they are looking for. Search engines, such as Google and Yahoo!, sell the ads based on the words the customer enters, so ads for "life insurance" are displayed when the searcher is interested in that topic (unlike banners that are shown at random).

Marketers pay for search ads only when they are clicked (called a *per-click fee*), in contrast to banner ads that are paid when shown. And the amount you pay is set by an auction—each search word has a separate auction running all the time. Marketers bid how much they are willing to pay for clicks on their ads for "life insurance," for example. The ad from the marketer with the best combination of a high bid and a high click rate gets shown first by the search engine.

Most businesses can benefit from paid search ads because they sell far more than it costs for the advertising. But Coca-Cola probably has no reason to buy ads from Google—no one is going to buy more Coke after a visit to their Web site, and as we'll see later, Google will display Coke's Web site in its organic search results anyway. Most businesses benefit from paid search, however. In Chapter 3, we'll delve deeper into how to assess paid search for your business.

So, then, banner ads interrupt people while paid search ads meet people at their point of need—a stark contrast. Betwixt these polar opposites lie *contextual ads*, which offer the ubiquity of banner ads without seeming completely random. Google and other search engines offer contextual ads to Web sites to display on their pages (just as those sites can display banner ads), but those ads are selected based on the topic of the Web page. The search engine analyzes the page and shows an ad that is relevant to the information on the page, as shown in Exhibit 2-3.

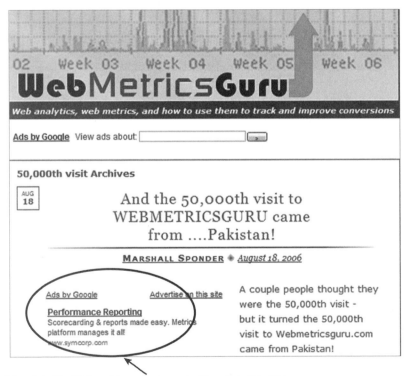

Ads related to Web metrics are shown by Google in this blog.

Exhibit 2-3   Standard contextual ads displayed on a popular blog

EXPERIMENTING IN COMMUNITY BUILDING

Some marketers are going beyond social networks into more aggressive community building. "Communities" can take many forms, from overgrown message boards to areas of specialized content to consumer generated content sites.

Despite the differences in communities, marketers who succeed at creating them would probably give similar advice:

- **Focus on a niche**—Communities work best when they create rabid followings. Few companies of any size can excite customers about their entire product line. IBM's developerWorks community focuses only on software developers—and further breaks its content down by specific technologies of interest to particular groups of programmers. Similarly, Pontiac Underground focuses only on the owners of Firebirds, GTOs, and other sporty cars.

- **Take a low-key approach**—Communities don't grow because they are heavily promoted—word of mouth works much better. You might almost say that communities succeed in inverse proportion to their marketing budgets. Communities grow because they are cool and exclusive—advertising might disrupt that.

- **Befriend community elders**—Converseon's Rob Key notes that many communities are "not open democracies, but oligarchies with their own social intricacies and hierarchies." The most influential Wikipedia editors, Second Life residents, or Diggers are relatively few in number. By getting to know these powerful individuals, marketers can increase their influence in the community. But be careful—the big dogs can bury your brand as easily as they can praise it. If you approach the elders with humility and an interest in helping the community first, you may find that one day they will help you.

- **Start small**—Marketers can create the conditions that allow communities to form, but most attempts fail. If you start small, you can try many community ideas so that you're likely to get a few hits. Pontiac experimented with communities on MySpace and Second Life before teaming up with Yahoo! on Pontiac Underground.

Marketers benefit from communities because they offer opportunities to sell products, but they can be more important for creating loyalty. Communities offer your best customers a chance to interact with each other and with information on their favorite subjects.

What subjects can inspire communities among *your* customers?

Marketers bid for contextual ads, just as they do with paid search ads (paying their bid when the ads are clicked), but those ads show up on Web site pages, including blogs and other consumer-generated media, instead of on search result pages. A contextual ad is, at heart, an interruption, so it doesn't yield the high click rate of a paid search ad, but it garners far more clicks than a banner ad.

Most contextual advertising is text-based (just like paid search ads), but some graphical ads and even audio ads (for insertion into podcasts) are cropping up. Large advertisers are stepping into contextual ads in a big way, even in new media such as podcasts. As high-speed broadband Internet access becomes more common, more audio and video will be created and consumed on the Web, and advertisers will look for ways to be part of that new media.

Other forms of offline advertising have migrated online as well:

- **Yellow Pages**—If your business attracts many new customers through the advertising in printed phone directories, you'll want to list your business in Web phone directories too. Besides Web directories offered by phone companies, Yahoo! and other companies also offer popular directories.

- **Product Placement**—The Internet offers many opportunities to show off products in action, especially as a part of online games. Pioneered in films, online product placement can help raise the "cool" factor for your product, especially with younger audiences.

- **Sponsorship**—Your company can sponsor YouTube videos or *Webinars* (online Web seminars) that attract the target audience you have in mind. Some companies have even taken on the producer role and created their own content just to show associated ads. Coke (mycokemusic.com) has gone in this direction with music, for example.

None of the tactics we've discussed are radical departures from traditional offline advertising, but expect that to change as the Web gets more inventive. As one example, take a look at social networks, such as MySpace, FaceBook, and LinkedIn. Millions have posted profiles of themselves on these sites and use these virtual places to connect with (offline or online) friends and colleagues. Depending on the site, profiles can be private (seen only by those invited by the owner) or public (viewable by any member of the networking site).

Some marketers are experimenting with social networks. Burger King, for example, has created a MySpace profile for the scary King character in their commercials, and he has attracted thousands of MySpace friends linked to his profile. Why do people link to the profile of a fictional character? I don't know because I'm neither young nor hip. (I'm actually more likely to need an artificial hip.) Regardless, lots of people are linking to our buddy, the king. How many burgers this sells, no one knows, but expect marketers to look for more ways to use social networks.

Anheuser-Busch, America's largest brewery, is encouraging beer drinkers to congregate at the MingleNow social networking site to post photos of "clinks"—two or more people tapping together bottles or glasses of beer. Will this campaign provide any buzz (beyond what you get from drinking the beer)? Perhaps not, but at least the brewer is allowing photos of any brand of beer, which increases their odds of success because brand-fixated campaigns have not fared well.

Successful social network marketing might need to be less blatant and more cheeky than traditional advertising—if it's fun, then people will tolerate it. Burger King, for example, gave away free viewings to online videos of popular TV shows to attract MySpace friends. Social networking is not cheap, however, as MySpace charges big brands hundreds of thousands of dollars for their profiles.

Perhaps that's why Anheuser-Bush partnered with a little-known social network. Other big brands, such as Nickelodeon and Disney, have created their own child-oriented social networks, eschewing partnerships with the big players.

Web advertising is not monolithic—it's more like a game of Monopoly. Paid search is Boardwalk, while banner ads are more like Baltic Avenue. Contextual advertising and other tactics fall somewhere between St. Charles Place and Marvin Gardens. (No, I don't know what Community Chest represents, but I'll work on it.) Any of these Web advertising tactics can pay off for you if done well. If you want to do it wrong quickly, start with paid search and branch out from there.

Direct Marketing

Each time I open my e-mail inbox, I can see how well direct marketers are targeting me. They think I am trustworthy enough to manage large sums of money from people in Nigeria, which is a bit odd because they also believe that I'm very interested in gambling. Oh, and they have no doubt that my favorite body part is too small. (Who told?)

OK, so maybe wading through the spam in your inbox each day might turn you off to Internet-style direct marketing, but truly targeted e-mail marketing doesn't irritate your prospective customers. Relevant and authentic e-mail works. Spam is among the most annoying interruption marketing *because* it is irrelevant and impersonal. Spam is precisely the opposite of what you want to do.

We touched on direct marketing in Chapter 1, "They're Doing Wonderful Things with Computers," but now we'll talk about the new ways that Web marketers can use direct marketing techniques. Direct marketers have always mailed letters and catalogs to their customers, but the Internet provides new ways to deliver messages.

While some estimates place spam e-mail at over half of all e-mail, marketers can still use e-mail properly and profitably. In fact, of all the companies that do marketing, 95 percent use e-mail in their marketing mix and many companies are increasing their e-mail spending. In particular, e-mail is becoming *the* way to alert customers to catalog updates—and four out of every five catalogs are *online* catalogs.

E-mail need not be the online equivalent of the "cold call." Increasingly, e-mail is used to send offers to existing customers. Airlines and travel Web sites love to send last-minute vacation offers to frequent flyers, for example.

E-mail can also be combined with other marketing tactics for even greater effectiveness. Some marketers report great success in using search marketing to attract new subscribers to e-mail newsletters. Still others are using social marketing to build their e-mail lists. Girls Learn to Ride, a Web site targeted at women who enjoy extreme sports, sends daily MySpace *bulletins* (private posted messages) to its 50,000-strong list of friends, soliciting subscriptions to its e-mails.

E-mail is also one of the marketer's best relationship management tools. Auto dealers prompt you to service your car, with messages personalized to you and the car you bought. Doctors remind you about upcoming appointments. Your B2B suppliers ask if it's time to replenish your supplies. (The most-common e-mail relationship tool is the newsletter, which we'll cover later when we discuss publicity.)

If you aren't currently using e-mail to remind your customers to reorder or to provide a newsletter to solve some of their problems, it's a great opportunity to do it wrong quickly. Pick just one kind of communication that you can do by e-mail and start sending it out. See what your customers think.

Just as with snail mail, you can use e-mail for your direct response campaigns. And it's free—kind of. Unlike advertising, where you have to pay someone to deliver your message, you pay nothing to send an e-mail. But as with all "free" marketing techniques, you'll find that it costs money to execute and manage your marketing campaign. For e-mail campaigns, you must maintain mailing lists, you need people to write the messages, and you must hire an e-mail service provider (or get your own folks and your own computers) to send out the e-mails and track response. Despite these costs, direct e-mail marketing can be hugely profitable.

But the rise of spam has caused problems in legitimate direct e-mail marketing. Customers are less likely to provide their e-mail addresses than ever because that is one way to stay off the spammers' lists. Even after they do provide you their addresses, your message can be erroneously caught in well-meaning spam filters—never to be delivered. Or the onslaught of spam in your customers' inboxes causes them to miss your message or to fail to recognize that it's safe to open.

For all these reasons, new delivery methods are needed—needed by both customers and marketers. Customers want a method that they can turn on and off easily, and marketers want a way to ensure their message is delivered to any customers that want it.

Enter *Web feeds*. A Web feed is a blanket term for several different ways of delivering subscribed information from an information provider (such as a marketer) to a reader. *Really Simple Syndication (RSS)* and *Atom* are two popular types of Web feeds, but expect other similar techniques to arise. The differences between these techniques are not important because it's easy to send and receive information using any or all of these methods. What is important is what they do for customers and for marketers.

Customers can subscribe to any Web feed without revealing any personal information about themselves (such as an e-mail address) and can cancel the subscription at any time. Once they cancel, the publisher of the Web feed has no way to contact them—unless they subscribe again. Contrast this to e-mail where the customer must trust the publisher not to pass along email addresses to others and where the publisher can continue to hound people years after they have unsubscribed.

Marketers love Web feeds, too. Because customers have no worries about spam, Web feeds require no spam filters, so legitimate subscribed messages never get lost, and customers are not swimming in a sea of spam to find those messages. The result is that more of the messages are read and acted upon.

But marketers beware! The "Three Rs" of online marketing are critically important when you deliver your messages through Web feeds because irrelevance, hype, and unresponsiveness are met with your subscriber canceling your feed. You then have no way to contact a canceled subscriber for a second chance.

So what can you send in a Web feed? Just about anything. If you can e-mail it, you can feed it. Web feeds exist for coupons, for hot deals, for products, and even housing, as shown in Exhibit 2-4. Some of these companies offer the information using both feeds and e-mail, allowing customers to choose the delivery method.

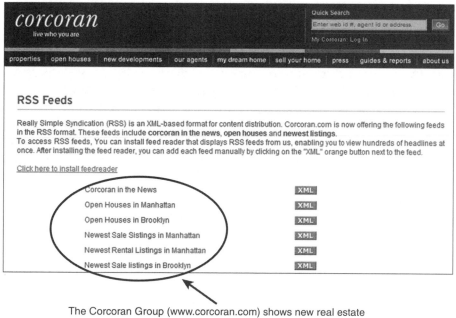

The Corcoran Group (www.corcoran.com) shows new real estate listings and open house schedules, all using Web feeds.

Exhibit 2-4 Web feeds can be used to deliver almost any timely information.

WEB FEEDS ARE NOT JUST FOR BLOGS

It started small, but Al Hurlebaus knew it was working quickly enough. The Senior Director of e-commerce for CompUSA decided to try out the use of RSS Feeds to alert customers about product news.

In November of 2006, CompUSA began offering Web feeds for specific products on a limited basis but soon allowed customers to subscribe to "new technology," "unadvertised specials," and more feeds. In just one month, CompUSA attracted over 3,000 subscribers.

You might imagine that having a way to identify the interests of 3,000 customers is valuable enough, but Al also noted an "increase in Web traffic and in clicks to the unadvertised specials area" among other benefits.

Your Web site should be full of interesting, changing content. Allowing your customers to *subscribe* to that content brings you more value for the same content investment.

Feeds also can be customized. Instead of feeding customers every deal they have, Deal of the Day offers feeds on specific product categories to allow customers to see just what is relevant to them.

Adoption of Web feeds is still small compared to overall Web usage, but it will grow dramatically in the next few years as newer Web browsers make subscribing easy. But if your target customers have not yet made the switch to Web feeds, you can combine the power of Web feeds and e-mail—services such as FeedBlitz allow you to distribute feeds to customers through e-mail. That way, you create one Web feed that your customers can subscribe to either as a Web feed or as e-mail, depending on their individual preferences.

E-mail and Web feeds are the main ways that direct marketers can translate direct mail and catalog marketing to the Internet. Just about any interactive marketer can use these techniques as part of a successful marketing mix, but the Internet provides many more marketing tactics. Next, we'll look at how interactive media is transforming traditional publicity.

Publicity

The word "publicity" might call to mind stunts—and the Web allows whole new classes of publicity stunts, such as Alex Tew's "Million Dollar Home Page," where he sold each of one million pixels to sponsors for a buck apiece. But most publicity is not about such stunts, on or off the Web.

Publicity covers a broad range of marketing tactics calculated to spread your message, differentiated from advertising because these activities don't require paying anyone (although like e-mail, they aren't completely free). Traditionally, publicity has been about attracting media coverage without payment. As we'll see, numerous Web "media outlets" make the distinction between free and paid marketing a bit harder to draw. (Actually, I am not enough of an artist to draw a distinction even if it *were* easy.)

Traditional public relations methods center on the venerable *press release*—a news story written by a company in the hope of getting newspapers to print it, or at least to write about it. As media has expanded beyond print to radio, TV, and beyond, targets for press releases have broadened. A PR person hits the jackpot when many media outlets "pick up" a press release.

You want the Web to pick up your press release, too, and you're in luck. If you submit your press release to PR Newswire or another service that distributes releases to traditional media outlets, you'll see that they already publish them on the Web also. In addition, some companies even distribute press releases using Web feeds, a practice that will expand. If you don't currently include links to your Web site in your press releases, that's an excellent way to do it wrong quickly. You can make your press releases Web friendly in many ways, but start with links.

Press releases, however, are typically rather bland. They don't communicate well with your customers. More polished marketing communications, like a newsletter, improve your message delivery to customers. While many companies once printed newsletters that they mailed to customers, the advent of e-mail has caused an explosion in the number of e-newsletters. No printing costs and no mailing costs make it easy to afford an e-mail newsletter. Some are simple, text-only affairs. Others, such as the Procter & Gamble HomeMadeSimple.com newsletter, shown in Exhibit 2-5, are beautifully done and front entire Web sites full of friendly information. Because customers *subscribe* to newsletters, you have a chance to speak to them every month.

Exhibit 2-5 E-mail newsletters provide favorable publicity for your products.

A relatively new publicity technique is the *podcast*, an audio file downloaded from the Web and played on demand using an Apple iPod or any MP3 media player. Many podcasts are just for fun, but marketers are discovering this new way of delivering their marketing messages. Some marketers treat podcasts almost like audio newsletters, as shown in Exhibit 2-6.

In a sense, there's no difference from what you can do with a podcast than with radio air time. You can record a speech, an interview, a commercial, or any other audio, but podcasts are used differently than radio because of their immediacy, their low cost, and their flexible time duration.

First off, podcasts can cover the most unusual subjects—if you want to target a few hundred people, it's cheap enough to do with a podcast, whereas a radio broadcast or a mailed CD would be unaffordable. Go ahead and do a podcast interview with a famous photographer about digital cameras. Mention your company a few times as the sponsor—maybe you'll sell a few digital cameras to serious photographers. Used this way, podcasts are another form of sponsorship of content produced by the advertiser, as just described.

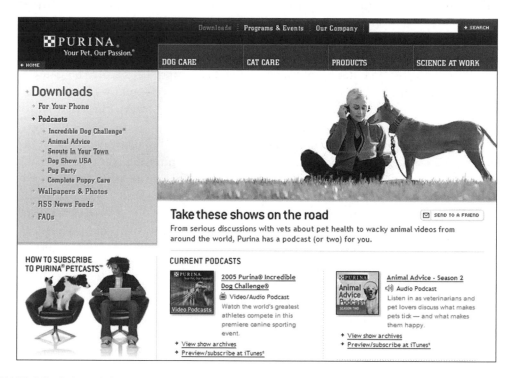

Exhibit 2-6   Podcasts help marketers reach target markets through audio.

Many marketers use podcasts to reach the seemingly unreachable. Folks walking their dogs are now listening to iPods. Train passengers listen to iPods when they used to sleep away their daily commute. At times when consumers are beyond the reach of most advertising media, people are listening to podcasts. In addition, podcasts are favored by folks under 30 years old, who are becoming harder to reach through traditional print and broadcast advertising.

Podcasts also provide long-form messages that were formerly possible only with infomercials or public relations opportunities, and you can do them quickly. Record it today, stick it on your Web site, and your message is out there. For these and many other reasons, podcasts are the cool new way to deliver your marketing message.

Video forms are appearing also, but they don't have a cool name like *podcast*. Variously known as *video podcasts*, *vidcasts*, or even *vodcasts*, some iPods can play them, but more videos are viewed on computers at sites such as YouTube. Some marketers sponsor entertainment videos, while others are using the video newsletter approach, creating a branded message designed to speak for itself to their markets.

If you already send DVDs or video tapes to your customers, a great way to do it wrong quickly is to simply post them on your site. If nothing else, you'll save some mailing and media duplication costs, and you just might attract more customer inquiries. Don't set up a task force to consider this—just do it and see what happens.

But all the tactics we've discussed so far remind us of communication techniques that predate the Web. Press releases, newsletters, audio, video—we've seen them all before, although the Web does put a new twist on each one. Let's shift the game a bit to look at techniques that are distinctly new for the Web—many of these are the talked about Web 2.0 techniques. We'll try to compare them to the tried-and-true when possible, but it's more of a stretch.

We'll start with one with a funny name: the *blog*. Blog is actually a nickname for *Weblog* because blogs began as online diaries written by individuals—logs kept on the Web. Marketers can compare blogs to press releases. Your company can write a blog post or a press release to try to attract attention, and both are free.

But that's where the similarities end. Press releases are usually sanitized to the point of lacking any personal point of view—they are literally the voice of a faceless company—while blog posts must have an intensely personal approach to be interesting. Also press releases don't directly reach their audience—they are filtered through mainstream media—while blogs are read directly by subscribers and even commented upon out in public.

Blogs are more credible than press releases in part because your customers can comment on what you say, so that keeps you honest. And that commentary makes blogs very different from other forms of communication. Each blog post written by your company can begin a conversation.

But just as most newspapers won't publish press releases verbatim, expect to see the equivalent of Web reporters who will write independent stories about your press release or your blog post—maybe a highly critical one.

Welcome to the *blogosphere*.

Beyond comments on your blog post, bloggers might write posts of their own, citing yours, which elicit comments and other blog posts in response...and on and on. If your subject is interesting enough, the conversation takes on a life of its own.

As we explained in the "Three Rs," blogs must be written by a real person. Blogs must sound authentic, yes, but they actually must *be* authentic. Admit mistakes when they happen. Be personal. Offer tips. Above all, don't assign blogs to your PR person. The blogosphere tortures anything that sounds like spin.

So far, only a small percentage of Web users read blogs, and an even smaller percentage write them. But those bloggers are far more influential than the average person—you are better off treating bloggers as media rather than customers because you never know what they will say and how many people will listen to them. Savvy marketers seek product plugs in influential blogs the same way they do in traditional media.

CASE STUDY: THE INFLUENCE OF BLOGS

Not every company believes they should be writing blogs, but that doesn't mean they don't find blogs important. Just listen to Steve Swasey, Director of Corporate Communications for Internet video renter Netflix: "We don't have a Netflix blog by design—our philosophy is to let our customers speak."

Netflix has over six million members, some of them bloggers, and the company pays close attention to what they write. Mike Kaltschnee, author of a blog he calls Hacking Netflix, has the company's attention, according to Steve. "We have people dedicated to reading Hacking Netflix every day. We treat him with equal importance to the *Wall Street Journal* and the *New York Times* because he knows more about Netflix than anyone else."

Mike agrees that he gets treated as a full-fledged member of the media—he was one of just five reporters to get a sneak preview of the Netflix "Watch Now" download service, along with the *New York Times*, *Forbes* magazine, and the *Reuters* and *Associated Press* news services. Like many reporters, Mike says he has a direct line to Steve for story corrections: "Once, Steve responded from Taiwan with his Blackberry."

Steve summed up the Netflix blog philosophy: "Rather than creating our own blogs, we harness the energy of someone who's independent." The "let others blog about us" approach is risky because you don't tell your own story, but for Netflix, the risk is low—research firm ForeSee Results has named Netflix the #1 site for customer satisfaction several times running.

Maybe delighting your customers is the only real key to getting positive publicity in the blogosphere.

Despite the small penetration to date, most experts believe blogs are taking off. *Business Week* has called blogs "simply the most explosive outbreak in the information world since the Internet itself." About one in three large companies have a blog, and an equal number are planning one. And it's not just high-tech companies. Bob Lutz, Vice Chairman of General Motors, contributes to GM's FastLane blog. Federico Minoli, CEO of Ducati, publishes his blog in both Italian and English, as shown in Exhibit 2-7.

How do you do blogs wrong quickly? You can start by simply subscribing to blogs to read—that will get you familiar with the form (and might even show you the conversation about your company already underway). If you or someone at your company feels confident writing a blog, check out Blogger or TypePad or another hosted blog service. They're easy, and they're free. Join the conversation.

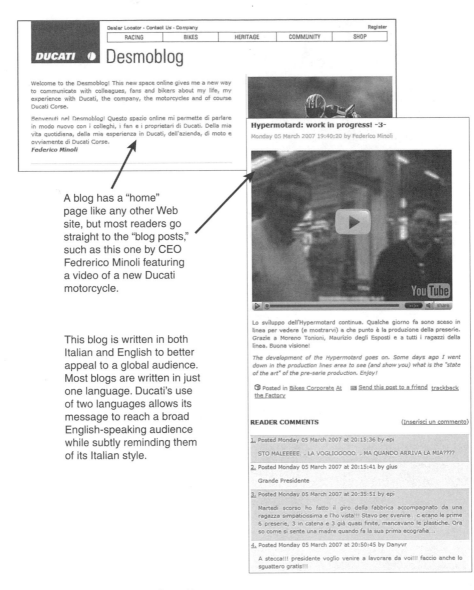

A blog has a "home" page like any other Web site, but most readers go straight to the "blog posts," such as this one by CEO Fedrerico Minoli featuring a video of a new Ducati motorcycle.

This blog is written in both Italian and English to better appeal to a global audience. Most blogs are written in just one language. Ducati's use of two languages allows its message to reach a broad English-speaking audience while subtly reminding them of its Italian style.

Exhibit 2-7   Well-known marketers are turning to blogs.

For proof that the blog concept is hot, just check out the explosion of blog variants. CBS Sportsline offers *glogs* (game logs) with running commentary from a sports reporter as a contest progresses. Amazon is challenging readers to assemble *plogs* (personal logs) of their favorite Amazon bloggers. Some bloggers are now pursuing *vlogs* (blogs in video form). But if all these ersatz words are giving your brain a *clog*, don't worry—learn how to use regular blogs, and you'll know plenty. These new words just show that blogs are trendy. Wait and see whether any of these variants become important in their own right.

Other new Web tactics are clearly becoming important, however, so let's talk about the next one. If you think about blogs as being documents that draw feedback, what would you call a document that can be changed by anyone at any time? A *wiki*, that's what. Derived from the Hawaiian word wiki-wiki, meaning "quick," wikis can be likened to a group word processor whose documents are always available for viewing and updating.

The most famous wiki is Wikipedia, an encyclopedia created and maintained by the public. Proponents laud the wiki's wealth of information from the wisdom of crowds. Some question the accuracy of information compiled in this way, but others say wikis are self-policing, with erroneous material quickly corrected.

The truth undoubtedly lies in the middle. Wikipedia has more information than a printed paper encyclopedia and has over 30,000 contributors, but just two full-time employees. That's a lot of information without a lot of author costs.

As you can see, wikis can be used for much more than marketing, but marketers need to pay special attention to wikis for their customers, as shown in Exhibit 2-8. Wikis can be used to discuss product plans, to solve support problems, to generate ideas for the company's direction—and so much more. Sometimes you'll want to use wikis for more private discussions—you can limit access (to your most loyal customers, for example) when needed. Wikis are limited only by your imagination and your comfort in discussing the information in public.

OK, so we've looked at documents with feedback (blogs) and living documents with many authors (wikis). How about a conversation among many people at once? The Internet has those, too. Variously called *news groups*, *forums*, *message boards*, and other names, customers start *threads* (conversations) about a particular topic—perhaps by posting a question or an opinion—and others join in to elaborate, explain, encourage, debate...you get the idea. It's a conversation.

What does this have to do with marketing? Plenty. Prospective customers often visit message boards to see what problems a product has before buying it. They also get an eyeful of how the manufacturer jumps in to fix the problem. (Or doesn't.)

Marketers can use message boards and their cousins to find out what their customers really think. As you read, you'll be asking yourself some questions. How many problems do your products have? Are you honest about them? Are you fair about fixing them? Do you go the extra mile? Do you promise to make the next version better? Do you follow through on that promise? Your customers are asking those questions and answering them, too. Your reputation on message boards might affect your sales more than you realize.

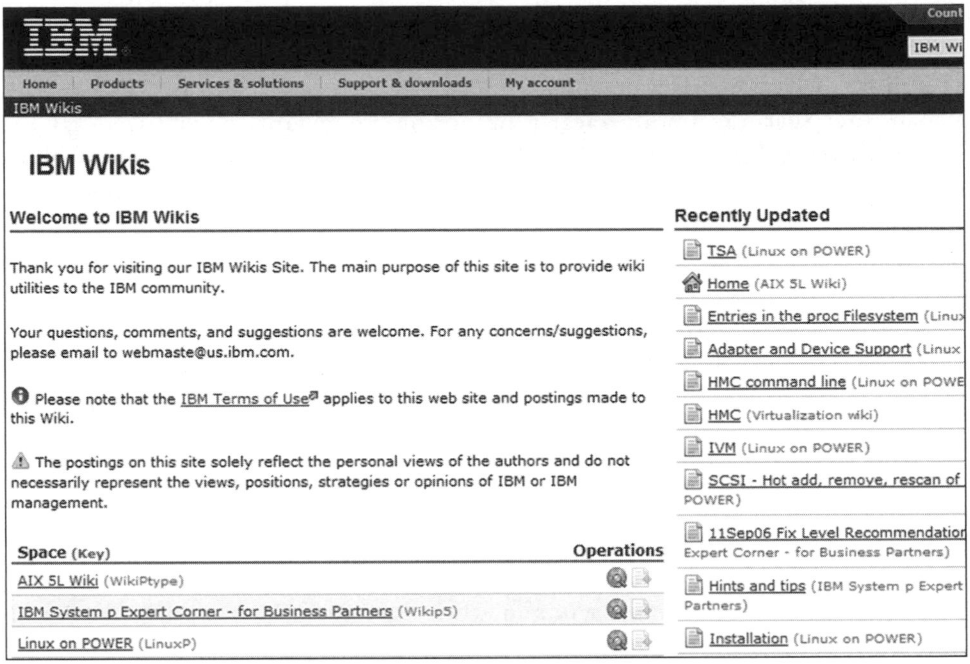

Exhibit 2-8 Wikis allow customers to interact with marketers.

Other message boards might provide ways for you to promote your company if it is pertinent to the conversation. If someone posts a question about finding a consulting firm, it's reasonable to suggest your company if you qualify. Be careful not to be too commercial, however—different boards have different codes of conduct. The worst impression you can make is to ignore those cultural norms. It's usually OK to sell a little bit as long as it is factual and pertinent to the conversation. (Gee, there's that "real" and "relevance" stuff again.) Read the board's rules before you post so you know what is acceptable.

As with blogs, the best way to do message boards wrong quickly starts with reading them. See what people are saying. Encourage your colleagues to answer questions when possible. If you're ready to start your own message board, several easy hosted message boards (such as Yahoo! Groups) are available for free. Put yourself out there and start learning what your customers want.

Before we leave the subject of publicity, you should know that we've skipped two forms of publicity unique to the Web: attracting links to your site and appealing to organic search engines. These two techniques are different from the others because they amplify everything else that you do. You can use link and search campaigns in concert with every publicity technique here—we'll cover them both in Chapter 3.

Remember, above all, that publicity is effective for the simple reason that it has credibility. Except for the costs of thinking it up and producing it, publicity costs nothing, or it at least *appears* to cost nothing. Some cheat the publicity system by paying for things that are expected to be free. People expect that links are freely given, but some can be bought. People expect that blogs are independent, but some bloggers might be paid to write favorable stories. When these arrangements are found out, the value of the publicity disappears. In fact, it becomes negative—bad publicity. So scurrilous marketers go to great lengths to conceal these arrangements.

None of this is new. Newspaper reporters have been bribed in the past. Radio disc jockeys were known to accept "payola" to play certain music. Tricking the system in new ways on the Web is new wine in old bottles, too.

Summary

Whew! That was a lot of wine—maybe you're feeling a bit tipsy. Before you take complete leave of your senses, let's review what we talked about:

- **Web marketing requires a new approach**—The way your father sold Oldsmobiles just won't work online. You need to speak personally to your customers—to use the "Three Rs" to be relevant, real, and responsive. Anything else will be ignored or criticized.

- **Web marketing is not totally new**—What you know about advertising, direct marketing, and publicity is still valid. The Internet offers new twists on these old approaches, but the basic goal is the same. You want your company's message to be accepted by your customers because that leads to a relationship with customers—leading to more sales.

So now that you know the basics, let's see how to use these tactics. In Chapter 3, you'll learn how to start the marketing conversation, how to listen to customers, and how to get your customers to introduce you to others. Let's go!

3

Marketing Is a Conversation

"For a list of all the ways technology has failed to improve the quality of life, please press three."

—Alice Kahn

Chapter Contents

- Starting the Conversation   57
- Learning to Listen   74
- Getting Introduced to Others   90
- Summary   101

A few of my friends stopped into a diner after a night of revelry (a polite way to describe sloppy drunks). When the waitress came to take their orders, Wally said, "I'll have the special." The waitress informed Wally that there was no special, so he should just tell her what he wanted. Nonplussed, Wally persisted, "I'll have the special." The waitress again insisted that there was no special and asked Wally to order from the menu. Wally looked up from his menu and repeated, "I'll have the special." Frustrated, the waitress turned to Bill and asked for his order. Pointing to Wally, Bill responded, "I'll have what he's having."

Marketing would be easy if it weren't for the customers. When you talk to customers, you never know what they'll say. Some of them, such as my friends, will turn out to be lunatics that you wish you never met, but most of them will be people you are happy to take money from.

Marketers have always been about taking money from their markets—that's the job. But the relationship between most marketers and their markets has always been a bit distant—like ordering fast food at the drive-through.

"Welcome to Jack in the Box. Speak directly into the clown." Often the person on the other end of that clown microphone can't hear anything the customer says, or the customer can't hear the employee. But even when it goes well, the customer has only a few choices. Even if the customer knows exactly what she wants to eat, she can't say, "I'll start with the lobster bisque"—that isn't one of the choices.

Old-style marketing doesn't offer customers many choices, either. If the customer is offended by your ad, she can change the channel or turn the page, or she can simply avoid your product. But those are really the only choices open to her. Of course, she *could* write a letter of complaint, if she were willing to take the time to figure out to whom to send it, but almost no one does. We marketers sure don't make it easy to provide that kind of feedback because we don't really want to hear it. When we *do* get complaints, we brush them off, citing as justification just how few complaints we got.

Old-style marketing is most decidedly *not* a conversation. It's a monologue from the marketer. Anything the customer says has been explicitly relegated to areas outside of marketing. "Contact customer support" or "You really must take that up with your account manager" are two phrases that marketers use if they ever have the misfortune of talking to a real customer. (It's a rare situation, but accidents sometimes happen.)

Web marketing is totally different. Web marketing really *is* a conversation. Between real, breathing people. Our message can't merely be "targeted" at a market segment. Yes, we still need to think about our customers in groups, and *market segment* is a perfectly fine name for those groups. But we can't stop there.

We need to remember that we are talking individually to each of our customers. No matter how we've categorized them, they might not fit into our tidy little segments all the time. So just because our research tells us that moms of teenagers are more likely to drive minivans and dads are more likely to drive SUVs, it doesn't mean that any particular mom or dad does either one. Maybe one mom and dad live in Copenhagen, and their family car is a bike.

One of the problems with market segmentation is that it tends to be oversimplified, by necessity. If you split the parents of teenagers into moms and dads (by the single dimension of gender), then split those groups by geography, and further try to subdivide by age and income, now you've got a lot of segments—too many for people to keep in their heads when thinking about strategy and messaging. But computers, don't cha know, are pretty good at that.

Computers are so good at targeting tiny segments that online marketers can personalize messages for as many segments as we need—we can even let customers segment themselves, as we saw in Chapter 1, "They're Doing Wonderful Things with Computers." So we can use technology to start conversations. And when we do customize our messages to the people we're talking to, they tend to answer a lot more often—more than if our marketing message is about as personal as a public announcement made over a loudspeaker.

That's what we'll talk about next—starting the conversation. Before the end of this chapter, we'll learn how to be better listeners when our customers respond, and we'll see how we can get introduced to others—to start even more conversations. But first things first (which sounds like something Yogi Berra should have said)—let's start with the start.

Starting the Conversation

Remember dances in junior high? The boys were lined up on one side of the room and the girls on the other. For a boy to cross the room to ask a girl to dance was a big commitment. He had to think of just what he'd say. And, if you're as old as I am, you recall that no respectable girl would ask a boy—she had to wait to be asked.

The old days in marketing were a lot like the old junior high school dance. The marketers lined up on one side of the room and the customers on the other. For marketers to send a message was a big commitment, but they had no choice because the only way to generate customer demand was through marketing.

Those were the good old days, when you had a new campaign each year. You'd kick around a dozen ideas for the campaign ("How can we sell this puppy?"), pick ones to discard ("That dog won't hunt"), merge the other ideas into three that you'd test with focus groups ("Will the dogs eat it?"), and you'd pick the best one ("Which dog wins best in show?").

Then you spent loads of cash developing it. That's why it was such a big commitment. You'd plaster it on everything in sight, which cost even more money and made it an even bigger commitment. Then you sat back and waited for your Cleo award.

(Or prayed that the campaign did not turn out to be a "dog.") At least you hoped that someone liked it—your boss, if you were lucky.

You listened to anecdotal feedback because you didn't have solid measurements to see if it worked—your focus groups were the closest thing you had to hard data. People just decided that the campaign was good or it was lousy, and then you argued to say it really wasn't your fault if it was lousy, or it was all your idea if folks thought it was good. Then you strapped yourself back into your seat to do it all again the next year.

Just like junior high—if she danced with you, you were a hero, and if she didn't, you'd explain to your friends why it wasn't your fault. (I remember "She's really stuck up" being a favorite expression for a girl that no boy could unstick from her seat.) Then you tried again with someone else.

Well, we're not in junior high anymore. We've grown up, and marketing is growing up, too. We've talked about how marketing is moving from a monologue to a conversation, but now let's talk about who *starts* the conversation. Sometimes it's the marketer, but increasingly, it's the customer.

When Your Customer Starts the Conversation

In Web marketing, nothing much happens until you get someone to come to your site—by definition. (I always wanted to write "by definition" in that oh-so-scholarly way.) So how do customers come to your Web site? We can argue about the categories, but let's split them into three broad activities:

- **Type a URL**—Your Web site's URL (Uniform Resource Locator, in geek-speak) is the address of a Web page—your home page's URL is www.yourdomain.com (or .org or .co.uk or dot something else). If your customers know your URL, they can type it in, and they can *bookmark* it in their browsers to return to later.

- **Follow a link**—If another Web site links to yours, then every reader is exposed to a piece of your message and might even follow the link to learn more.

- **Search for a word**—Perhaps they are searching for the name of your company or one of your branded products, but they might just be looking for a generic product name or even researching a problem, not knowing what kind of product can solve it. If your Web site's page pops up in the search results, they might visit your site.

So how do you make sure your Web site is the one these customers visit? When customers are ready to start a conversation, how can you make sure it is with you?

You start with your offline marketing and do it wrong quickly. To get more people to learn your URL and to remember it, plaster it on anything you can think of. Put it on every print and TV ad. Say it at the end of a radio spot. If you use billboards, put it up there. Put it on your employees' business cards. Use it in the recording for your voice response system ("If you can't stand listening to elevator music, visit www.ourdomain.com..."). Slap it on the product itself if you can. As shown in Exhibit 3-1, IBM even puts it on the signs outside its buildings. Any company can try these ideas. Don't have a meeting about it—if you're not doing all of them, just get started.

IBM shows its Web address on signs outside its buildings.

(Photo by Madeline and Marcella Moran)

Exhibit 3-1 Plaster your Web address everywhere.

If your company is well-known, and your URL is short enough and easy to spell correctly, some people will remember it and type it in when they need it. But that's not enough. You need to provide an impetus for people to go to your site—to "drive them to the Web" as marketers like to say. (To me, it makes our customers sound like cattle, but oh well.)

So does your offline advertising drive people to *do* something on your site—not just visit the home page? Post (a division of Kraft Foods) uses its cereal boxes to send kids to play games on its postopia.com Web site—secret codes printed inside the cereal boxes give kids an edge in the games (which raises Post cereal purchases). Unilever raised traffic to its Web site 1500 percent with just one product placement on the popular TV show "The Apprentice" for its Dove soap. General Motors' Pontiac divisions used ads for its cars to tell people to "Google Pontiac."

You don't have to tell people to Google you, however. They do it anyway. But your advertising can give them a hint of which words to use. Instead of just listing your product's name and your Web site's URLs in print and TV advertising, why not include several unique words that describe features of your product? As an example, some print ads for the Toyota Avalon included great search keywords, such as "dynamic laser cruise control" and "smart key system"—those words bring up Toyota's site in a search engine. You too can clue your customers into the search words that will bring up your site.

If your offline marketing is not driving people to your Web site, where they can learn more about your story, you might be missing out. As the previous examples show, the Web can serve as an extension of your offline marketing campaign by delivering your marketing message when customers are interested in receiving it.

Let's repeat that—when customers are interested in receiving it. That's the key. If kids didn't like Post's games, they wouldn't visit Postopia no matter what offline advertising was done. But a good story motivates people to find out more or to do something at your site.

Having an interesting story helps you even more when you go beyond the reach of your offline marketing. After all, the defining characteristic of the Web is the *hyperlink*. If you can somehow attract *inbound links* from other sites, you'll soon find customers coming to your Web site from the most unexpected places.

Most sites find that their less commercial content draws more links than their sales-oriented product pages. Procter & Gamble sells multiple brands of laundry detergent, but its pages on treating stains are more popular than any detergent product page. So all those interesting blogs, podcasts, and wikis serve an additional purpose for your site—they offer the kind of interesting content that attracts links from other sites.

How do you do *this* wrong quickly? Pick just one good story and post it on your site. Don't set up a committee to choose your *best* story. Yes, the one you pick might be the wrong story; it might not be the one that turns out to attract the *most* links. Who cares? Just pick one and try it. Then pick another story and write that one. Keep measuring how many links you get for each story—the more you get, the better. Over time, you'll attract lots of links to your site.

Don't overlook off-beat sources of links. For example, if you create a needed software tool and make it available on your Web site, you will draw links. Just make sure that you're drawing *qualified* visitors. A digital camera manufacturer won't be helped by adding a tool for planning retirement, but offering a scrapbook for digital photos might be very enticing to their target market.

To create "link magnet" content, keep a few ideas in mind:

- **Reinforce the topic**—To attract links, you must know the subject of your page. Why should people link to you? Why should visitors follow the link? Remember that the visitor to that page could have been anywhere on the Web before reaching you. Smooth the visitor's transition to your site through clear titles and copy that show what your page is about. Cutesy headlines and clever introductions might not work as well as copy that uses the same words your customers use to describe the topic.

■ **Deliver excellent content**—Your page must be well-written and high-quality in every way. If you have a well-known brand name, use it. The people whose links you must attract have many choices of pages to link to—yours must be the *best*, or you will draw far fewer links. The better your page is, and the more it completely fulfills the visitor's need, the more links you'll attract. The single most important tip to attracting links is to make your landing page one that sites *must* link to—if they don't, their visitors have missed out on a gem. Create that gem, and the links will follow. But don't worry about doing it all at once—you can gradually improve a page to eventually make it the best.

■ **Use link-friendly URLs**—Make sure your URLs are short and easy to spell and remember. If a great page on your site is saddled with a URL the size of a small Latin American country (such as www.domain.com?id=36253454345prod= 54635432&rate=87), expect to draw much fewer links than for the same page with a short URL.

■ **Take down the roadblocks**—If you think people will link to pages that immediately pop up a registration page or a "choose your country" page, you're wrong. You'll drive away many more links than you attract. We know that the marketing department wants to collect the e-mail address of everyone who downloads a case study, but forcing entry before viewing just won't fly. You might coax some people to comply, but you'll see many more visitors abandon. Worse, you'll drastically reduce the number of sites willing to link to you in the first place. Take down the roadblocks for all link landing pages.

Experiment with directories. Take advantage of any directories willing to link to your site. If you have podcasts, register them with a podcast directory. Link your site with industry directories. Apply for a listing with Yahoo! Directory and Open Directory. Every link sends more traffic for your site.

Beyond the traffic they provide, links have a huge impact on search marketing. Google and other search engines raise a page's *authority* based on its incoming links—pages higher in authority (the ones with better links to them) tend to rank higher than other pages in organic searches. The more links to your page, the better, particularly if those links are from other pages, which themselves possess high authority.

Search engines are especially fond of pages that have high-authority links containing the searcher's word—when the searcher looks for "cameras" (for example), the search engine looks for pages that have the most high-authority links using the word "cameras." For keywords that match many pages on the Web, a page's authority is often the most important determinant of where it ranks.

Now let's turn our attention to search, which is a fundamentally different behavior than other ways customers come to your site. When customers type your Web site's URL, it's because they remembered it from somewhere, and when they click a link, it's because another site is recommending yours. But with search, your customers are usually interested in an *idea* rather than a specific destination.

People sometimes *do* search for company names to get to a company Web site, but searches are often more complicated than that. Search, in fact, can be so complex that you could write a whole book on search marketing—but don't bother, because Bill Hunt and I already did, called *Search Engine Marketing, Inc.* (You should buy three copies each for your 100 closest friends.) That's the book you need to excel at search marketing.

In *this* book, we won't cover everything you need to know about search marketing, any more than we do so for blogs, e-mail, or any other Web marketing technique. But you'll learn at least enough to get started.

Search marketing is not for everyone, but it's for *almost* everyone. It is a key way to do it wrong quickly. Even if you're not ready to jump into every tactic covered in this book, you ought to investigate search marketing. Exhibit 3-2 shows why.

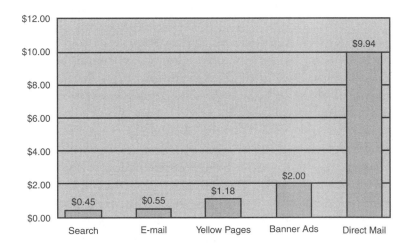

Source: Piper, Jaffray & Co. (March, 2003)

Exhibit 3-2 Conversational marketing generates the most cost-effective leads.

Internet marketing is vastly more cost-effective than offline direct marketing—because of zero printing and mailing costs. Also the more conversational the tactic, the more cost-effective it is. Search marketing and properly-used e-mail marketing reach customers in action, while a banner ad is merely a new way to interrupt people. Later in this chapter, we discuss effective use of e-mail, but let's talk now about search marketing.

Search marketing helps you reach customers who are interested in what you're selling at that precise moment, which makes them more qualified leads for a sale. Search marketing also helps you maximize all the public relations work you learned about in Chapter 2, "New Wine in Old Bottles." If you optimize blogs, wikis, and plain old Web pages for organic search, those pages will get much more attention, as searchers find them again and again in Google.

What happens if, instead, you continue to ignore search marketing? Lagging behind your competitors can damage your career, as the chief marketer of the florist delivery company, FTD, learned after the 2005 holiday shopping season. A bad fourth quarter was attributed to the lack of search marketing—and the marketing head was replaced.

As you consider how to get people to type your URL, follow a link, or search for your site, remember that you want conversations with the right people on the right subject—people who are interested in what you offer. It's useless to get traffic from people who don't care about you or your products—they'll never buy. As you think about all of these tactics, don't forget that relevance is still important. You want the right people to come to your Web site, not zillions of the wrong people.

We spoke earlier about how traditional marketing communication can now be used to invite your customers to start a conversation, but sometimes you need to make the first move. If your customers don't start the conversation, it's up to you.

When Marketers Start the Conversation

Marketers are not used to starting one-on-one conversations—that's for salespeople, right? Well, not anymore. Marketers have always blanketed messages to target markets, but the Web demands starting individual conversations with each customer.

When marketers think about starting conversations, however, they usually think about buying a mailing list because that's how direct marketers work. While laws in each country differ, in most locales you are permitted to purchase e-mail addresses and send out your message if the list seller has permission from the customers in the list. The technique might be legal and can be ethical, but it's not terribly effective. This way of starting a conversation is the online equivalent of a cold call. Even if it's legal, you might still look like a spammer to customers puzzled by why you are sending mail—which will be many of them.

Almost any other use of e-mail is more effective. When you buy an e-mail list, you're communicating with people who told the list seller they wanted messages from "partners." You're better off contacting people that *you* already know. For conversations with strangers, it's more effective to use the techniques we've previously reviewed to coax the customer to start the conversation with you.

You can also persuade the customer to start it. Beauty retailer Sephora has used print ads in Oprah's "O" magazine to ask readers to go to its Web site to opt in to its e-mail. The International Thriller Writers association attracted opt-ins for its mystery newsletter by giving away a set of 150 books to the lucky winner—that's a lot better offer than the standard (and irrelevant) iPod. Creative marketers can find a way.

One of the more creative ways to start a conversation is with a wiki. You seed the wiki with content and invite your customers to improve it. *Executive Travel* magazine created city guides and other information for its Web site, with a big button that says "You can contribute to this site." The result? More engaged customers and better information.

THE FOUR STEPS TO SEARCH SUCCESS

In Chapter 2, we discussed the difference between organic and paid search, as shown in Exhibit 3-3. Paid search is basically advertising. You pay Google or another search engine to display your ad when certain words are searched. Organic search requires no payments to search engines because it shows the best Web pages for each search entered.

Although organic and paid searches require somewhat different approaches, you can use four similar steps for each:

1. **Choose your keywords**—The words that searchers enter into the search engine are called *keywords*. You need to anticipate what words searchers will use to find your Web site. You can use keyword research tools, such as Wordtracker, to show you different combinations of words that searchers use together—and see how many times they use each combination. To be successful, you must choose (as your target keywords) the most popular words that match your products. Remember, you won't drive much traffic with words no one uses. Conversely, choosing popular words that don't match your site won't help you sell anything. Instead, you need the middle ground—the most frequently used keywords that are also strong matches for your content.

2. **Get your content shown**—Once you know your target keywords, it's time to get your Web site into the results. First, you choose a *landing page* for each keyword you've chosen. (Go back to the tips for good link landing pages and they will serve you well here, too.) With paid search, once you

The key to success for any of these tactics is to know your purpose. We'll talk about that more in Chapter 4, but as you think through these conversation starters, you need to distinguish between whether you are using content to create a community or using a community to create content. *Executive Travel* wants to use a community to create content because the better their content, the more traffic their site gets (and the more ad revenue they pocket). In contrast, IBM uses its developerWorks content to attract a community of software developers so that its marketing message can get through to a segment that's hard to reach any other way. Conversational marketing can be a way to overcome the divide between manufacturer and customer because there's no distribution channel in between.

Whether it's a wiki entry, a blog post, an e-mail offer, or something else, you first need people to look at it before you get anywhere. If your e-mail has a great title, it

> pick your per-click bid and write your copy, then your page shows up in the paid search results. Organic is a bit tougher. You need to make sure your landing page is placed in the organic search index (ask your Webmaster to check on this) and make sure you've included the chosen keywords in the text on your landing page.
>
> 3. **Get your content ranked**—It's not enough to be somewhere in the results list—you need to be near the top for your targeted keywords, or you'll get few people coming to your site. To get close to the top of the organic rankings, you need to optimize your content (by using the target keywords frequently in the body and especially in the title) and get numerous links to your landing page from well-respected sites. For paid search, you need a high bid, but you also require a high clickthrough rate, which we talk about next.
>
> 4. **Get your content clicked**—Who cares if you have the #1 result if no one clicks on it? People click on results that have titles and descriptions (the words under the title in the search results) that mention the keywords—they look like the right places to click. Working over this content to raise the percentage of people that click (the *clickthrough rate*) is the only way to get searchers to your site.
>
> Now, you might be thinking, don't we care about actually making sales, rather than getting content clicked? Well, yes. But we'll wait until Chapter 4, "Going Over to the Dark Side," to dive into that. Before we're done, we'll focus on sales, lifetime customer relationships, and return on investment—but those concepts go beyond starting the conversation.

Paid

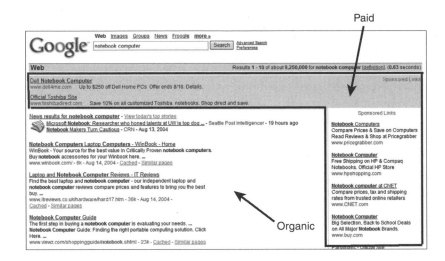

Exhibit 3-3   Search engines show both organic and paid search results.

THE COMPANY BLOG

Companies are no longer ignoring blogs as a way to reach customers. Two-thirds of large companies planned to have a blog by the end of 2006, according to JupiterResearch. Why? Because they work. One-third of all Web users read blogs, including 80 percent of Business to Business customers and research shows that customers value this content when making decisions—above almost all other.

So if your company is ready to get into the game, you might be asking yourself, "Who should be blogging at my company?"

Not top executives, right?—Wrong. Jonathan Schwartz, President of Sun Microsystems, writes an acclaimed blog that directly reaches his company's core audience of software developers. His blog has higher readership than many of the trade magazines his PR people try to get Sun's message into.

Well, that's only for high-tech companies, right?—Wrong. Bob Lutz, head of car maker General Motors, has a highly successful blog. He goes straight to his customers instead of being filtered through the press, as he said in his very first blog entry: "In the age of the Internet, anyone can be a journalist."

OK, but those blogs are written by the PR people, right?—Wrong. They are the authentic writings of a real person—that's why they are successful. Despite how busy they are, these executives have prioritized blogging in their jobs.

might get opened. If your podcast is clever and informative, it might get linked to. If your blog is optimized for popular search keywords, Google might rank it highly. If you concentrate on being interesting, your message might get noticed.

Blogs offer unique ways of attracting attention. Like any content, if you write something attention-getting—it's real, relevant, and responsive—you'll attract links from other sites. But blogs allow you to give *yourself* a link, using a technique called a *trackback*. A trackback is a comment that you make about someone else's blog, except the comment is actually stored on *your* blog, with a link to it from the blog you are commenting on. The trackback might be read by many people who don't see your blog regularly—now they will come to your site and might learn more about you.

Beyond trackbacks, the blogosphere offers other ways to get attention. Comment on other blogs. Link to other blogs. Get involved in conversations, and others will start paying attention to what *you* say. Bloggers are very generous with their attention. They like to talk, but they also like listening to others interested in the same subjects. In their book on blogging, *Naked Conversations*, Robert Scoble and Shel Israel provide succinct advice, "Talk, don't sell." If you take part in this discussion, *your* message will get noticed.

Sure, but only big companies have such good communicators at the top.—Size doesn't matter. Dave Winer, then head of small software maker UserLand, was one of the world's first bloggers (starting in 1997). Steve Rubel's Micro Persuasion blog helped to make his former PR firm, CooperKatz, as well-known as far larger competitors. Historically, small companies have adopted blogging much faster than large ones have.

Yeah, but my top exec can't even type.—It doesn't have to be your chief executive. Organic yogurt maker Stonyfield Farm has a Chief Blogging Officer because they've committed to the importance of blogging in their marketing strategy. Likewise, over 10% of Sun employees are blogging, not just their company president.

Just about anyone can be an effective blogger if they follow the real, relevant, and responsive rules and they follow a well-constructed company policy on blogging (which we'll cover in Chapter 8, "This Won't Work Where I Work"). If it's interesting to you, it will be interesting to other people, too.

But don't wait to develop a blogging policy before you get started. Do it wrong quickly by getting interested employees in front of your customers. Over time you can get the policy in place. Start by picking responsible people with a passion for your customers and improve from there.

So did you hit the jackpot? Did you get your message noticed? Great. But it only matters if you get someone to *subscribe*. It's nice that someone might read your e-mail or listen to your podcast, but you need a relationship before you make any real money. When customers start the conversation, you need to get permission to keep talking to them. You need your customer to "opt in" so that you can start another conversation later—you need your customers to subscribe to your message.

Once they subscribe, you can start many conversations over the life of your mutual relationship. Whether you want them to subscribe to e-mail newsletters, Web feeds of your blogs, or delivery of your weekly sale offers is not important. Getting that first "opt in" from your customer is what's important. Once you get permission to contact customers, you will have plenty of chances to talk to them.

So how do you get permission? What motivates people to sign up, and what stops them?

People subscribe when the offer clearly provides value to them. "Get our free e-mail with our weekly specials" offers value; "Sign up for free weekly e-mail" doesn't. (No, people really aren't trying to get more mail in their inboxes.) Tweak your copy or improve your offer until it is appealing to your potential subscribers.

THE "OPT IN" STRADDLE

What do you do when a new customer makes a purchase? Do you automatically check that box and make the customer remove the checkmark? You know the box I mean: "I agree to happily accept all future offers to flood my in-box with spammy stuff I am not interested in." OK, it doesn't really say that, but that is how people interpret it.

Some marketers say they'd rather be known for respecting their customers' privacy, so they don't check that box. (And their customers, in turn, rarely check it themselves, and so those marketers have very short mailing lists.)

Aggressive marketers check the box and try to hide it at the bottom of the screen in small print so that the busy shopper doesn't notice and leaves it checked. They get large mailing lists but also many unhappy customers who have no idea why they are getting e-mail—so they unsubscribe.

What do you do? It sounds like a difficult choice.

Live Nation, a leading Broadway show and concert event company, takes a middle ground by automatically checking the box but sending a gentle introductory e-mail to start. That "welcome" e-mail stresses the value of receiving future e-mails and provides an easy way to opt out. Guess what? Linda Villwock, Live Nation's head of Internet marketing, reports they get very few opt outs. Why?

People take action when time is of the essence. Is it a limited time offer? What will be missed if the offer is passed up now?

People run away if it's too hard to subscribe. You can decide to ask 15 questions in your subscription form, but it doesn't mean they'll get answered. It's hard to answer that many questions, and the questions themselves might be perceived as nosy. In addition, potential subscribers flee if your policy is to sell their e-mail address to others.

Regardless of whether it takes the form of e-mail or a Web feed subscription, customers must understand and appreciate your offer and believe that it's worth whatever privacy they are giving up.

Once you've got them signed up to receive e-mails or Web feeds, what do you send? Yes, the tried-and-true monthly newsletter can be effective, and the several-times-a-week blog feed can be compelling, but don't stop there. Use subscriptions to send overstocks or price specials or new offerings. Let customers know when information they care about has changed—if someone has updated the wiki they read or their warranty has expired.

First, the welcome e-mail is sent quickly after the purchase, when customers still remember why you're allowed to contact them. More importantly, that e-mail explains the benefits of being on Live Nation's mailing list. Why does this work better than explaining everything up front?

Perhaps this success is explained by the moment of purchase not being the best time to ask the "opt in" question. People are focused on what they are trying to do—purchase—so it's easy to sneak something by them. But it's wrong and it will backfire. What Live Nation does is sneak that first opt-in by them but then openly explain what they did and ask if it was OK—at a later time when the customer can really make a good decision on that separate question that has nothing to do with the original purchase.

Your welcome e-mail is the single most-opened piece of e-mail you'll ever send—75 percent of recipients open it. However, according to research firm Marketing Sherpa, Live Nation is part of just 48 percent of companies that even send a welcome e-mail for an "opt in." Even fewer, only 10 percent, go further by sending a special offer in that welcome e-mail. If your company pays attention to that welcome e-mail, you'll form more relationships with your customers, just the way Live Nation has.

An extremely effective technique is called a *recontact*. If a customer responded to a previous offer but did not buy, try sending a sale offer for the same product a few days later. You might be amazed at how many sales result from a recontact campaign. Chapter 5, "The New Customer Relations," describes how to pull this off.

Subscriptions and recontacts are important techniques due to the nature of Web marketing itself. The low switching costs of the Web, coupled with a seemingly unlimited choice of stores, has created a situation where more than 20 percent of shoppers have *no* stated preference for any particular store—up sharply in recent years. In fact, some say there are no more "customers," only "prospects." By that they mean that you can no longer count on your customers to return to buy from you again. You need to win them back to your business each time they are looking to buy. To some extent, of course, that has always been true, but it has never been more true than today.

That's why smart Web marketers use recontact techniques to turn prospects into customers and why it's so important to turn single conversations into ongoing subscriptions. But you need to do it in an appropriate way.

How *Not* to Start a Conversation

Back in junior high, where we learned at the dance how to start a conversation and the commitment that it entailed, we also learned what *not* to do to start a conversation. Lying about yourself might make get you a date, but eventually you'll be found out. So most of us learned that honesty really is the best policy. (That makes dishonesty the second-best policy, as comedian George Carlin correctly points out, but it doesn't advance my point, OK?)

Some similarly simple rules apply to Web marketing. Don't misrepresent who you are, or who *you* represent, or what you want to talk about. And don't do anything that was not requested. (You might get your face slapped.)

Despite the hubbub over spam and various brouhahas over privacy policies, respecting your customers isn't more complicated than what we learned in junior high. If you think about the other person's needs before your own, you might end up with a great relationship, instead of just a date.

But you paid good money for this book, and you won't let me get away with giving you advice on dating. And while some forms of bad behavior are illegal in certain countries, don't expect my advice here to keep you out of jail. (I am not a lawyer and I don't even play one on TV.) Seek real legal advice if you're contemplating starting conversations with your customers.

The advice I *am* offering is to go beyond what's required by the letter of the law. Think about the code of conduct that your customers are demanding from you:

- **Don't misrepresent who you are**—Customers hate spam e-mail, in part, because spammers are always lying about their identities. (How many ex-presidents of Lower Slobovia are out there, anyway?) If you misrepresent your identity, expect that it will eventually be found out. When it is, you'll become the new unethical behavior story to sweep the blogosphere. (It might also violate the law in some countries, including the U.S.) So, put your company's name in the "from" line of your e-mails. Make sure your message includes both your address and phone number so recipients can verify it's really you. Forego tricky e-mails, ersatz Web sites, fake blogs—you get the idea. Just be yourself, and your customers will love you for who you really are.

- **Don't misrepresent who you represent**—If you have a relationship that customers should know about, reveal it. If you're being paid to provide a link to another company or paid to write a complimentary blog entry, or you're providing an affiliate link, it's best to say so. And make sure your partners follow the same code of ethics when they recommend you. Everyone's reputation is at stake.

- **Don't misrepresent what you want to talk about**—E-mail spam is often about tricking people. The ex-president of Lower Slobovia doesn't really need your help in hiding his money from the authorities—he is actually trying to hide *your* money from *you*. But outright scams are just a drop in the bucket (or the tip of the iceberg, if it's below freezing). Spam search techniques try to fool the search engines to find the spammer's page when they shouldn't—and your customers end up on the spammer's site when they ought to be at yours, all because the spammer misrepresented the subject of the page. Further, the U.S. and other countries require by law that your e-mail subject lines clearly articulate the purpose of the message. Just be clear about what you want to discuss—no tricks.

- **Don't do anything that was not requested**—Obviously, you know by now not to send any unsolicited e-mail to anyone. In many countries, it's illegal, but it's also just dumb marketing designed for a sale rather than a relationship. You similarly should not compromise your customer's privacy by selling e-mail addresses or revealing other personal information. That's not how you treat someone you have a good relationship with, and it is also illegal in many locales. Post your privacy policy and stick to it. And, on the off-chance that you do send something that someone doesn't want, make it incredibly easy to opt out.

If you're thinking, "Gee, this is rather draconian" (followed by, "Gee, Mike is using a thesaurus"), you're right (about both). *Could* you get away with less than this? Won't some of your customers let you slide if you pay a blogger without telling them or fail to disclose affiliate links? Yes. *Some* of your customers will just chalk it up to human nature, but others will place a black mark in your permanent record. You alone can decide between a fleeting advantage and permanent damage to your reputation.

As time goes on, you'll likely be making more and more decisions on ethics because each new Web marketing technique that emerges poses new ethical questions. A few years ago, no one thought to pay Web sites for links, but now we have clearinghouses where links are bought and sold.

Are paid links and these other tactics wrong? Not necessarily. Many of these techniques are no more nefarious than any form of paid advertising, so long as they are *disclosed*. If you'd prefer not to disclose something, ask yourself whether you are trying to slip a fast one (or even an off-speed pitch) past your customer. Only you can make that decision, and only you can explain your decision to your customer when you are called on it—and someday someone probably will call you on it.

THREE SURE-FIRE WAYS TO EMBARRASS YOUR COMPANY

Many of us fancy ourselves as being clever, but don't try to trick Google. Yes, it's true that some people make a living out of fooling Google, but odds are you're not one of them.

You don't need to cut any ethical corners for your site to be ranked where it belongs. If you put your nose to the grindstone, you'll get the organic search rankings you deserve (along with a scratched nose). Note that we're not talking about guaranteeing #1 rankings. If your site is a market leader, you'll be at the top of the search results, but if you're not, you'll be ranked lower. Earlier in this chapter, we reviewed the ethical techniques to use to improve your search rankings.

But a few people who want better rankings than they deserve go further. These folks resort to some less-than-ethical practices known as *spamdexing* or *search spam*. Spamming search engines is not only unethical, but it is also punished severely by search engines who remove spam sites from their search indexes (so their pages won't be found for *any* search queries).

You need to understand search spam so that you can ensure that no one at your company is breaking the rules—your company's reputation is at stake. Three basic forms of bad behavior predominate:

- **Tricky Content**—Some people go beyond optimizing their pages for search—they perform *keyword stuffing*, in which they litter their pages with potential search keywords, sometimes hiding them so that the search engine sees them but people don't. Search engines rarely fall for these tricks, but spammers keep trying.

But ask yourself some questions. Is there anything you're doing that you wouldn't want your customer to find out about or wouldn't want posted in a blog entry? A yes answer to these questions might be a red flag waiting to become a black mark. Obviously, every company has trade secrets, such as customer lists, financial records, and the recipe for a secret sauce, but if you have secrets that would embarrass you if revealed, take this as a wake-up call to reassess your practices.

OK. Enough about bad behavior—let's review where we've been. Now you see how Web conversations start. The customer usually initiates the conversation, but the marketer can restart a conversation with a willing customer—as long as the customer's interests are kept in mind. And when you talk to people, a funny thing sometimes happens. They talk back. Are you listening? That's what we tackle next.

- **Tricky Links**—Because search engines rank pages higher when other pages link to them, some people place links to their sites in spurious blog comments or create fake blogs (called *splogs*) full of links. Some spammers go so far as to fabricate hundreds or thousands of Web sites that link to each other (known as *link farms*), just to raise their search rankings. Google and the other search engines usually detect these spammy links.

- **Tricky Pages**—Perhaps the most elaborate trick of them all, *cloaking*, shows the search engines different Web pages than human visitors are shown. Software on the spammer's Web site detects when it's a search engine that is accessing pages and feeds it different pages (pages designed to rank highly in a search) than customers get. So the search engine ranks the pages it saw, and when the customer clicks through, a different page is shown. Search engines often catch this trick, too.

You need to understand these sleazy practices, not so you can perform them, but rather to spot them—and to prevent your site from accidentally running afoul of the rules and suffering the consequences. You can also use this knowledge to discover lapses on a competitor's site so you can justifiably turn them in to the search engines.

When search engines detect these techniques, they take action. In 2006, car maker BMW was banned from Google for cloaking its pages. In addition to the lost revenue from disappearing from searches, the company suffered public embarrassment as bloggers and the mainstream media picked up the story. Don't let this happen to you.

Learning to Listen

U.S. President Calvin Coolidge believed that "No one ever listened themselves out of a job." You're unlikely to become the first one. No, *failure* to listen is far more likely to lead to unemployment, especially when the people you don't listen to are your customers.

Most traditional marketers actually *do* listen to customers, but they do it in the traditional way—with *focus groups*. Focus groups find out what your customers think by placing a few of them into one of those rooms with a two-way mirror. Or is it a *one*-way mirror? Regardless, your focus group moderator can ask your customers whatever you want, and you can see how they respond.

But that doesn't mean you really find out what your customers think. Focus groups, like any information-gathering technique, suffer from many flaws:

- **Dishonesty**—People don't always answer truthfully in focus groups. People might lie to please the moderator or to avoid embarrassment, depending on what questions you ask.

- **Wishful thinking**—Sometimes, people might tell the truth, but they'd actually do something different when placed in the real situation. They say what they *think* they'd do, so people might tell you that they'd pay $5000 more to buy a fuel-efficient car, but in real life, maybe they won't. They honestly believe they would, but that doesn't help much—you're still getting the wrong answer to your question.

- **Lack of interest**—Focus groups might force customers to express an opinion when they don't necessarily care. Moderators attempt to overcome this problem by asking how strongly participants feel about their answers, but that only helps so much.

- **Group think**—Sometimes participants influence each other unduly. One strong personality can bias the thought process of an entire group. Moderators are trained to control big mouths, but some are easier to harness than others.

- **Selectivity**—The focus group methodology is even more flawed by the selection of the very questions asked. You might not know which questions are critically important to your success, as opposed to side shows that miss the point. If you ask questions about minor issues, you'll get answers on minor issues, but they won't be the answers you need.

- **Sample size**—Focus groups are expensive and necessarily small. Rarely do even multiple focus groups contain enough participants that the results are statistically significant. ("Results are qualitative in nature," the practitioners like to say.) So sometimes the conclusions you reach might turn out to be wrong because you didn't ask enough people.

Focus groups are not the only kind of market research possible. Solo interviews, phone interviews, shopper surveys, and other techniques are heavily used also. Some of these techniques allow cost-effective studies that are quantitative in nature—they have a large enough sample size—but they all suffer from creating an artificial situation. Your customers just don't always do what they say they'll do.

That doesn't mean these techniques aren't useful. In fact, *online panels*, also known as online focus groups, can be a far more cost effective way to gather information than traditional focus groups. You can even amass quantitative results because it's cheap to ask many participants the same questions. Del Monte foods operates the "I love my dog" site to gain deeper consumer understanding and to generate new ideas. The company tries its own ideas and also asks for ideas from the panel. Companies, such as Vision Critical, offer services to help marketers easily create online panels.

Online panels and other customer research tools answer the "why" behind what customers do—and those questions can be critically important. Unfortunately, some marketers use these survey mechanisms to answer the "what" questions—as we've seen in real life, customers don't always do what they say they will in an artificial panel situation.

To see what customers *really* do, you must observe them in the wild. That's easier said than done, however. Most consumers don't let you into their home to watch them use your product, nor do businesses permit observers behind their badge-accessed doors. Even if they did, the simple act of observing people often changes their behavior. Nor can marketers find out which commercials are best-received by hanging around TV sets in use.

So how do we normally collect feedback from customers in the real world? Our sales force reports what customers tell them. Our phone operators get calls. Customers write to us. But these sources of information are almost as flawed as focus groups. Our salespeople filter what they pass on, perhaps leaving out important information, such as if customers want to buy direct on the Web (thus reducing the need for salespeople). Phone operators might not be familiar with the substance of the consumer complaint, inadvertently misinterpreting it when reporting it. But the biggest flaw in these feedback mechanisms is people angry enough to take the time to contact you might not be representative of your average customer—you don't know how widespread that particular problem is.

Just because focus groups and traditional market feedback mechanisms are flawed is no reason to ignore them. All of these techniques provide useful information, and a careful professional can tease out the news from the noise in most cases. But the Web helps you listen to customers in a whole new way. In fact, the Web *demands* you listen to customers.

And some of us need to hear that demand. Honestly, we don't make it easy for customers to talk back to us. Think about how hard it is to even find an address or phone number to address a complaint to most companies. Maybe, at some level, that's intentional. As comedian Dick Cavett says, "It's the rare person who wants to hear what he doesn't want to hear."

Why is that? When customers complain, it often means that someone working at your company has made a mistake. Maybe even you. And none of us wants to be called on our mistakes. Depending on the size of the mistake and your company's attitude toward mistakes, it could cost you your job.

So it's natural that we'd want to filter out the bad news or be defensive when someone criticizes us or to dismiss complaints as coming from only a few. In the old days, you could get away with that. Oh, once in a while a really persistent complainer called on friends in high places or handed a powerful story to the media, but most complaints withered away when ignored. The complainer eventually gave up and moved on in life—and no one lost a job.

This sounds good, except for what unhappy customers do next, which is to tell everyone within earshot what happened to them. You lose the unhappy customer, yes, but also many others with him. Sometimes the experience is embellished as well, making the listener more aggrieved with the company than the one who experienced the problem first-hand.

Regardless, no business can make every customer happy, and bad experiences have always driven away some customers and always will. The Web, however, magnifies the secondary impact of failure to listen. Your unhappy customers can far more easily complain to you—they just press that "Contact Us" button on your Web site. Your customers can also tell others about their experiences more easily—total strangers are now within virtual earshot. The Web provides a megaphone with its megabytes so that anyone can post a message that takes your company to task for any situation at any moment.

And anyone can take issue with your marketing message itself. On the Web, your message is filtered, changed, critiqued, amplified, rebutted, exaggerated, and misconstrued by your customers (and once in a while applauded), just like any conversation. It has always been happening, but now it can happen a lot more because the Web lets it happen. The Web almost *forces* it to happen.

These Web customers talk back. You don't just see stories about your company in the newspaper. You get comments on your blog. You get others blogging about you. Your wikis get changed. YouTube videos parody your commercials.

In response, all businesses must learn to listen, and they must listen in different ways, depending on the source of the feedback and the situation. Let's start with the everyday listening that all companies must do to improve themselves.

Listening in Daily Life

Humorist Oscar Wilde once described a man with "his mouth open and his mind closed." More and more, customers are ignoring marketers with open mouths in favor of those with open ears.

Let's recall how the Web is providing a voice to our customers in ways that never existed before. Customers comment on what you say and do—in their blogs, on your blogs, and elsewhere. They expect to review and rate your products. They discuss your offerings on message boards and other community sites.

This is not theoretical. Over one third of all Americans created Web content by the end of 2005 (and this trend is growing worldwide also). Moreover, these opinionated customers spend more than the quieter ones.

Perhaps more important is that the rest of your customers, the ones who don't create content, are reading the content and being influenced by it. Three-fourths of online shoppers rely on product reviews and ratings, according to one Jupiter Research report, while another reveals that 90 percent of companies believe customer recommendations influence purchase decisions.

Web 2.0 technologies take consumer participation beyond commentary and ratings. Some companies are putting their ideas into wikis and letting customers change them if they are not explaining it right. The data and functions of other companies are used in mash-ups because their customers need more than what they're getting.

So how do companies cope with these new, more vocal customers? It goes back to being relevant, real, and responsive. Provide everything you can to help your customer answer questions and take action. Do it in an authentic way and respond to what they need—which requires a new-found skill in listening.

But knowing that listening is important doesn't make it easy. When people say things that you don't like—maybe even things that you feel are blatantly unfair or demonstrably wrong—you *still* need to listen.

The ABC television network learned a hard lesson in 2006 with a blog they started about their mini-series "Path to 9/11." The blog posts from mini-series writer Cyrus Nowrasteh drew a wave of negative comments for conservative political bias. ABC publicists were understandably upset at having created a blog overrun with critical comments before the show even aired.

ABC's initial reaction was to remove the blog (and thus all the negative comments), but that was a mistake. Instead of being part of the conversation—by responding to critics on its own blog—ABC now forced the conversation to shift to other blogs on other sites. And ABC's removal of the blog stoked the fire with charges of censorship.

To their credit, the leadership at ABC learned quickly. They quickly restored the blog (including all the negative comments) and responded to critics on the facts. They certainly didn't win over their detractors, but at least they were listening and responding, creating a more favorable impression with people who had not yet made up their minds. Some even said that the firestorm drew more attention to their show and helped raise its viewership when it aired.

Other companies have navigated similar waters. The computer company Dell started blogging in 2006 with a rather lame post that mentioned that dell.com was ten years old. Dell's poor reputation for customer service made its new blog the subject of ridicule in the blogosphere, with Jeff Jarvis saying on his BuzzMachine blog, "Yes, I think I spent about ten years on hold with you guys."

Jarvis wasn't alone. Dell was flamed mercilessly about their customer service and taken to task for thinking a blog would fix any of that. So given this embarrassment, you'd expect Dell to shut down the effort and lick their wounds. But Dell stuck with it. They chose to listen to the feedback of the marketplace and to adjust.

Dell's blog began to honestly take on its customer service issues, admitting their problems and describing what Dell was doing to fix them—all in a personal and

THE MARKETING TACTIC THAT GETS FIVE STARS

Quick: Which online marketing technique is used by 70 percent of the top Internet retailers and is the most influential factor in purchase for over one-third of all buyers?

The answer is customer ratings and reviews. So why aren't you using them on *your* site?

For most online marketers, it's all about fear—fear of negative reviews. David Seifert, Director of Direct Marketing Operations for outdoors retailer Bass Pro Shops, sums it up: "As a retailer, you never want to say anything bad about something you sell." But the fear is overblown in that "Only seven to eight percent are negative reviews," according to David.

The negative reviews are a small price to pay for some impressive results. Customers want to see negative reviews—it makes all other reviews more credible. The Senior Director of e-commerce for CompUSA, Al Hurlebaus, notes that after the U.S. technology retailer added product reviews to its site, "Every single [product] category improved its conversion rate."

Customer reviews and ratings are moving beyond products into services. U.S. telephone company AT&T has launched reviews on YELLOWPAGES.COM, allowing consumers to rate any business, from a local plumber to a global retailer.

down-to-earth way by the customer service executive herself. And Dell was widely praised by bloggers for doing so, blunting its negative reputation.

Now these same bloggers will take Dell to task at some point if the problems are not truly addressed, but Dell is handling its first foray into the blogosphere by being real, relevant, and responsive—which makes all the difference.

Listening occurs outside of blogs, too. Even a well-loved brand, such as Apple, is not immune to criticism. Casey Neistat, a longtime Apple customer, posted a video to YouTube showing him defacing an iPod poster with a complaint about the iPod's unreplaceable battery. As the video's message spread, Apple decided to inaugurate a battery replacement program, showing that good marketers are good listeners.

Marketers must constantly scan the digital world to hear what customers are saying. Your customers will post complaints to message boards. They'll give your products bad reviews. Often they will do this anonymously.

But sometimes you can respond to customers after you listen to them because customers identify themselves when they complain, using e-mail, for example. It's easier

You might be getting more convinced that offering reviews is a good idea for product retailers and service directories. After all, if one listing gets bad reviews, maybe people will buy other items from you. What takes real guts is for a product *manufacturer* to post reviews; negative ratings might send customers to your biggest competitor instead.

Meet a manufacturer with guts. Sun Microsystems, manufacturer of computer servers, has put product ratings and reviews for all of Sun's products on sun.com—a sign of supreme confidence in what they sell.

Curt Sasaki, Vice President of .SUN Web, found that for every bad review they get, they get several good ones. Curt approached the project believing that "...the more folks that did reviews, the more it would balance out—it's self-correcting."

Product ratings and reviews are proven to lead to higher conversions, but they also provide an invaluable listening post for customer feedback. David Seifert says Bass Pro monitors the top-rated and lowest-rated items and "we fix things not designed correctly." And Al Hurlebaus says, "It gives [CompUSA] information about what's important to them."

But do reviews change customer perceptions? According to Curt Sasaki, "If you read and respond to what people say, people think, 'Hey, Sun actually listened.'" In an era with so little trust in marketing, that might be the biggest benefit of all.

LISTENING ADVICE FROM A BLOGGER

Ryan Saghir is a force in the satellite radio industry. With a quarter million visitors to his Orbitcast blog each month, his words influence satellite radio customers and industry decision makers alike.

Ryan says that "Both XM and Sirius [the two leading North American satellite radio companies] do a good job of treating me like press," but he offered advice for marketers in other industries as to how to treat bloggers who write about them.

"Companies have the wrong impression of bloggers," Ryan believes, because they treat bloggers as some kind of second-tier journalists. Ryan says "the press is taught to be an unbiased source trying to read between the lines and interpret something [in a] negative [way]. They're trying to create buzz and sell papers."

Bloggers are different, Ryan asserts. "Bloggers are usually not trying to make money. Bloggers are fans of the product and of what the company does. We love the product more than anyone else does, and we foster an environment where other fans can rally around."

Clearly not all bloggers are cast in Ryan's mold, but many industries have bloggers just like him. As he says, "Satellite radio is what I am passionate about and what I evangelize." A little nurturing makes that passion a huge positive for XM and Sirius.

Ryan also advises marketers to use the blogosphere as an early warning system: "PR people I've spoken to have noticed that there's a reaction in the media after I've written something." If you have powerful bloggers in your industry, addressing the issues they raise may ameliorate later coverage in the mainstream media.

Ryan believes that marketers have a huge opportunity to win over bloggers. "If they speak like human beings (without the corporate-speak), they'd be amazed at the response they'd get from bloggers. Bloggers are on your side."

for your customers to send you an e-mail than it is to send a printed letter, first of all, but the Web makes it simpler to find the right place to send it. Your "Contact Us" link on your Web page allows you to hear more feedback then you ever got by mail.

When you have an opportunity to respond to negative feedback, whether it is in a private e-mail, a public message board, or any other way, remember that your response need not stay private. Your e-mail can easily be forwarded to others or be posted in a blog or on a message board for many others to see. Treat every interaction with your customers the same way you would if it were in full public view—because it might be.

America Online learned the hard way in 2006. AOL customer Vincent Ferrari recorded a conversation with an AOL representative in which he tried to cancel his service, but the representative raised objection after objection, making it uncomfortable for Ferrari to cancel. Ferrari was so irritated by the experience that he posted the recording first on his blog and later on YouTube. The representative's arm-twisting tactics struck such a cord with others trying to cancel their AOL service that it gathered thousands of links and was picked up by NBC's *Today* show and other mainstream media. (Then the *Today* show interview was itself posted on YouTube, and the cycle continued.) The videos received hundreds of comments, most of them supportive, many with AOL horror stories of their own.

Ferrari's anger is an important point to remember, too. Sometimes you are dealing with confused customers that just need a clear explanation to make them happy, but often, you are listening to people who are angry. They're upset about something, and they blame you for it—rightly or wrongly. And your first job in that situation is to listen, not defend, even if they are wrong. You don't need to agree with the angry person, but you do need to show that you understand the problem.

If publicly posted information is factually, beyond a shadow of a doubt, wrong, then you should ask for a correction, a retraction, or (best of all) a removal of the erroneous information. But you should ask for this only when you can prove your facts. Often, someone who posts erroneous information will take corrective actions when the error is proven.

If the information is correct, however, then your customer has every right to be angry. When you realize that you are dealing with someone who is angry, it is sometimes helpful to change the venue. (I couldda been a lawyer, mom.) Written words are far easier to misinterpret than spoken words. When someone is angry, your best bet is to try to move the conversation to the phone or in person, if possible. The more intimate your communication method, the more you can defuse the situation.

When the angry person feels heard, you can take the next step by asking what it would take to make things right. Your goal is to make the person happy, but you might have to live with mollifying him—at least he might not go out and tell other people that you stink.

Perhaps you are able to do what the person wants, but even if you don't have that authority, you've taken a good step by asking. Make sure that you understand exactly what the person wants—repeat it back to him if you need to. If you need to ask higher-ups to approve, tell the customer what you are going to do and then do it.

If you're lucky, your angry customer will agree to talk by phone, but you might be forced to converse in a public forum in front of the rest of your customers. That's the way it goes. By staying calm, by listening, by showing that you really are making an effort, you impress everyone else, even if you can't win over the unhappy one. Some of them might agree with the customer, especially if you don't get permission to give him what he wants, but others will be won over by your behavior. Some bystanders might even rise to your defense. If he's really a nut, expect others to see that, too. Or you might find that lots of your customers are annoyed by the same issue, which is extremely valuable information. Go fix it!

Contrast that with what happens if you don't listen. If you don't answer the customer's e-mail. If you don't respond to the message board post. If you ignore the blog entry. What happens is that your customers see only the angry side of the issue—they don't see you. And because the angry person does not feel heard, he is more likely to find other public ways to vent.

Listening can be a competitive advantage. Listening shows you to be responsive in front of your customers, but it also gives you critical information about what you need to change that you can't gather any other way. If you listen to customers—really listen—and act on what they say, it's amazing how smart you'll look after a while. Most of your customers will root for you to succeed if you just listen to them.

OK, time for a cleansing breath—this listening stuff is not easy, especially for those of us that have spent our lives delivering messages rather than receiving them. But a few of us see opportunities for horseplay with our competitors because they have to learn to listen, too:

- **Flogs**—If your public relations firm suggests starting a blog to criticize your main competitor or to boost your own products without revealing your involvement, it's up to you to have the morals to say no. Payperpost.com, for example, features a service where companies pay bloggers to "shill" their products. Famous brands, such as Wal-Mart and Sony, have already been caught "flogging" their products.

- **Feeviews**—When you pay people to post good reviews, or when your sales team brags about giving your competitors' products bad reviews online, you need to put a stop to it. Microsoft ended up embarrassed when they gave top bloggers laptop computers with their new Windows Vista operating system. It looked like they were trying to buy favorable reviews.

- **Astroturfing**—A few of our ethically-challenged marketing brethren are fomenting conversation by planting stories and comments without revealing their true sources. "Astroturfing" is so named because it is "fake grass roots" uprisings. The situation resembles a public outcry when it is actually carefully staged by an interested party.

These shady tactics have serious consequences. If the retail site detects a seller playing with reviews or ratings, it will take drastic action to rectify the situation, which will hurt the seller's reputation enormously. Similarly, if a company is found out as the real source of flogs or Astroturfing activities, the public embarrassment will not help, as Wal-Mart learned to its chagrin. (No one likes *chagrin*.) Fake conversation is not worth listening to.

Are *you* listening, or are you still spending months testing your message to make sure you have it "right," instead of doing it wrong quickly? If you do it wrong

WAL-MART EMBARRASSED BY ITS "FLOG"

Wal-Mart has a customer-friendly policy of allowing recreational vehicles to park overnight in its parking lots, so when a blog appeared from two RVers that took advantage of that policy, it got some attention. The pair was taking a trip across America, stopping at Wal-Marts overnight and blogging about the people they met. And naturally, some of the posts were complimentary about Wal-Mart, describing an employee who went "the extra mile," for example.

So far, so good. But the pair of travelers identified themselves only as "Jim and Laura" on their blog, so the anti-Wal-Mart crowd and the press grew interested in who they were, exactly. Inevitably, they were identified. Jim Thresher, a *Washington Post* reporter, and freelance writer Laurie St. Claire were "Jim and Laurie." But that wasn't the big revelation.

BusinessWeek magazine disclosed that the entire trip was sponsored by Working Families for Wal-Mart, an organization run by Wal-Mart's public relations firm. WFWM paid for the whole trip, including the RV itself. And nowhere was it disclosed that WFWM was a paid sponsor for the trip or the blog. It's not known whether anyone at Wal-Mart knew about this or had anything to do with it, but they were blamed for what their PR firm did. The PR firm eventually admitted to creating two other "flogs" for Wal-Mart, too. The usual firestorm ensued, and the flames were fanned because Wal-Mart has so many detractors in the first place.

For you, this should be a cautionary tale. Businesses take a huge chance when they hide the identities of bloggers. But more importantly, all paid relationships must be revealed. If you say to yourself, "Well, if people *knew* it was paid, then it wouldn't work very well," then don't do it at all. Moreover, your customers and critics will hold you responsible for anything done on your behalf, so you need to watch not just your own behavior but that of anyone you hire also.

In the end, what could have been a feel-good story connecting Wal-Mart to RVers ended up being a fiasco. By getting real (as we discussed in Chapter 2), you can avoid this fate for yourself.

quickly, you can adjust your message based on what your customers tell you—if you are listening.

If you *are* listening, are you acting on what you hear? If not, customers will talk *to* you less and talk *about* you more, poisoning your brand image with others. You'll be seen as increasingly out of touch and impersonal, and you'll be rightfully viewed as unresponsive. If you're not careful, you could find yourself in a full-blown crisis. Let's address crisis management next.

Listening in a Crisis

If you think plain old garden variety listening is tough, wait until the chips are down. It's difficult to listen in a crisis. You'd probably prefer to pick up those chips instead. Listening in a crisis is the first step to defusing the crisis, so it's a skill worth developing.

What differentiates crisis listening from everyday listening? The skill is the same, actually, and everything you know about everyday listening applies. It's just a lot harder to do. Let's walk through a case study to see how crises unfold differently now with the Web.

Our crisis began in September of 2004, when the popular Engadget blog ran a story about the Kryptonite lock company. It's not the kind of story that you're looking for when you make locks because the gist of it was that Kryptonite's locks could be picked. Well, you might say, most locks can probably be picked by someone skillful, right? Yeah, but Kryptonite's locks could be picked by a ballpoint pen. You don't need to be Harry Houdini to see the problem here. "Get picked by a Bic" is not anyone's idea of a strong slogan.

No sooner had the blog exposed this problem than a video was posted demonstrating a lock being picked. If anyone doubted the original blog, the video was a real convincer.

So there's a story about Kryptonite in a blog, now accompanied by a video, and the company has no choice but to recall the locks. What's interesting about this crisis is that no traditional media is yet involved. Kryptonite knows the story and knows what it has to do, but most of its customers don't know. If this had happened before the Web, Kryptonite would have been called for comment by a reporter right before the story ran, and the company would have had no time to react before its customers heard the bad news.

Kryptonite had a chance to talk to the bloggers, to post comments on the blogs with the company's position, and to issue its own statement on its Web site. But Kryptonite did not do any of these things; instead they waited three days to respond. To the company's credit, they announced a lock exchange program just five days after the post, which was operational three days after that.

But the silence of the first few days let the story go viral, as blogger after blogger retold the story. Because today's customers find traditional marketing messages suspect, bloggers have far more credibility than an ad. By allowing the bloggers to tell the story and not providing a response, Kryptonite allowed years of marketing messages to be wiped out in a blink.

Without picking on Kryptonite (pun intended), the company was aware of the discussions going on in the blogosphere and in public forums but chose not to respond for days. Kryptonite's PR person later explained that these blogs are read by a relatively small part of the company's customers, but, gee, that's true of any single media outlet. Kryptonite had been talking to print reporters who called, but was not responding to the bloggers who posted. The real point is that ignoring this blogosphere story gave it legs (and underarms). The longer it raged out of control, the smellier it got for Kryptonite.

This is a difficult situation, for sure, but Kryptonite could have used the same Web that caused the crisis to alleviate it. What if Kryptonite responded to the crisis by admitting its lock was flawed and pledging to replace it? Kryptonite could have allowed customers to opt in to an e-mail alert list that would keep them apprised of its steps to replace the locks. Kryptonite could have set up its own blog to keep the information flowing—whatever they could tell reporters could be posted.

Instead, the company allowed the conversation to happen without them, and the damage done is incalculable. Many prospective customers to this day know nothing about Kryptonite except this story.

You might be reading this thinking, "Gee, three days is a rather quick response." Not anymore. Kryptonite tried to think through the proper response and do it right, but doing it wrong quickly would have been better. Responding rapidly with the best information you can—and with apologies and promises to make it right somehow—is better than silence.

In Kryptonite's defense, few companies were savvy enough back in 2004 to respond appropriately to a blogger-induced crisis, so consider yourself blessed that it didn't happen to you and be ready for the day that it does. If you respond well, you might find that a crisis actually improves your standing. If you respond badly or not at all, sometimes a crisis can turn into all-out war.

Listening in a War

Rocker Henry Rollins once remarked that "Nothing brings people together more than a mutual hatred," which can be very dangerous to your business. Just as people will sometimes get angry with you, on rare occasions people will get so royally ticked off that you just can't tick them on again. They develop a full-fledged hatred for your company.

Start with a hating ex-customer, then add the Web, and gently stir. The results are not pleasant for your company. We've talked at length about how customers can embarrass you in public, how they can trash you on their blogs, post nasty comments on yours, or take you to task on a message board.

But that's just the beginning.

The ultimate declaration of war against your company is a *hate site* (www.yourdomainsucks.com). These sites are run by individuals or, more commonly, groups that are out to damage your business. They have an axe to grind, and they will use it to chop your profits if you let them. These groups want to attract attention for their message, and the Web is an easy, low-cost way to do so.

Sometimes these groups are scrupulously honest, and they are doing a public service by shining a spotlight on corporate bad behavior. Often, however, they are ethically challenged themselves, run by hotheads that shade or exaggerate the truth about your company. Even when they are technically truthful, they often deliver a biased version of the facts designed to put your company in the worst possible light.

As distasteful as it might be, these organizations are usually well within their right of free speech to produce these hate sites. And as we've discussed so many times in this chapter, you need to listen to them. You need to listen to them because they often are making a good point—you should carefully examine their points and change your behavior if their criticism is valid.

But even when their criticism is *not* valid, even when they are totally off-base or are printing outright lies about your company, you still need to listen. You need to listen so that you know what is being said—so that you can defend yourself in the court of public opinion.

Hate sites thrive on publicity for their point of view. They post controversial and highly newsworthy stories, hoping for pickup by bloggers to spread the word. When a hate site targets a large, well-known company, it hopes that traditional media will pay attention. Whether the target is big or small, hate sites depend on Google and other search engines, as shown in Exhibit 3-4.

With reputations at stake, how do companies listen to everything? How can your business know when hate sites pop up or when a hater posts a nasty blog entry or message board post?

It's not easy, but it is possible. Fortune 1000 firms with deep pockets can hire a consulting firm that specializes in reputation management. These consultants can be pricey, but big companies have billions riding on their reputations, so it's worth it.

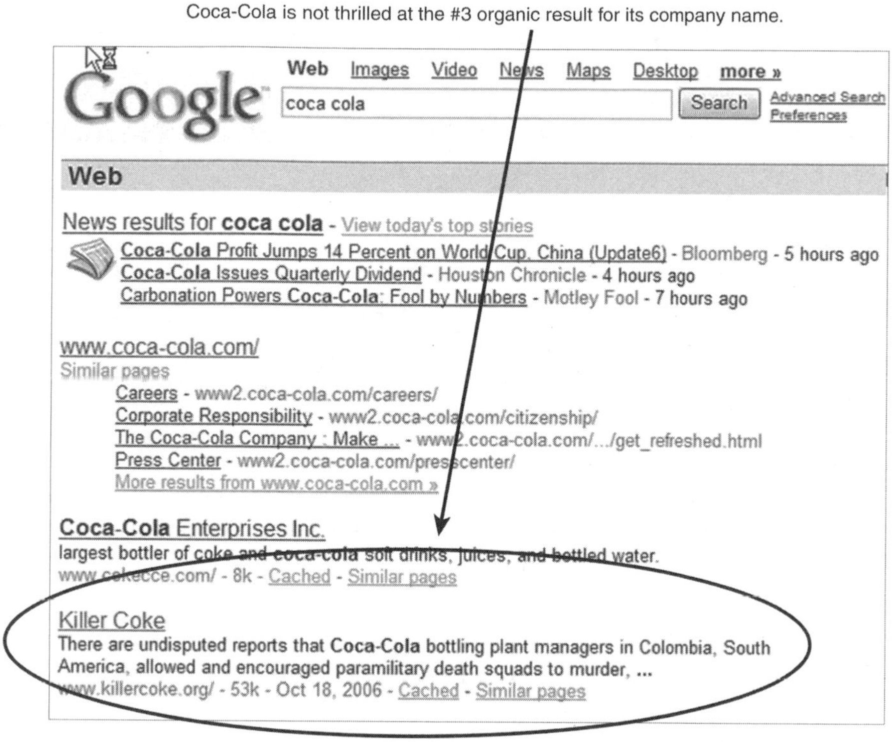

Coca-Cola is not thrilled at the #3 organic result for its company name.

Exhibit 3-4   Hate sites target specific companies through search marketing.

Small companies, by necessity, take a more do-it-yourself approach. Google and other search engines offer e-mail alerts for any search words that you specify. You can set up these alerts (for your company's name, its brand and product names, and those of its top officers) so that the search engine notifies you when it finds matches on Web pages, blogs, or message boards. Technorati and other blog search engines can create custom Web feeds that send you any blog posts that contain the search words you specify. You can also monitor your competitors' Web pages using tools such as Website Watcher and WatchThatPage.com.

So, if you do find a hate blog or a hate Web site, what do you do?

If the hate site is misusing your trademarks or has lifted copyrighted material from your Web site without permission (such as product images), you can pursue legal remedies. Sue 'em.

MONITORING YOUR GOOD NAME

Whether you are a big company or a small one, your reputation is extremely important and you should be taking steps to listen to the ongoing conversation. But whether you hire a fancy consulting firm or just fire off a few Google Alerts, what does reputation monitoring listen for?

- **Visibility**—How often are you talked about? Is it more or less than your competitors? If no one is talking about you, that might not be good.

- **Speakers**—Who is talking about you? Are they customers, employees, activists, or unidentified people? Which individuals seem the most influential for and against your brand? You can't evaluate what is being said or choose a proper response without considering where each speaker is coming from.

- **Tone**—Are the comments positive, negative, neutral, or mixed? Is your marketing and customer experience working or not? The sentiments expressed toward your brand may be more important than any particular issue.

- **Topics**—What subjects are they discussing? Is it always the same few or do some catch fire and die out? When the same things come up over and over again, it's probably something to highlight in your marketing (if it's positive) or correct (if it's not).

Converseon's Rob Key recommends a benchmark report for his new reputation management clients—30 days retroactively and the next 30 days going forward—"to generate baseline metrics and to create quantitative goals," such as a certain percentage increase in positive comments on a particular topic in the next 90 days. You can't control your reputation, but you can certainly monitor it and influence it.

But what if there are no grounds for a lawsuit? Let's examine a specific example of a company under attack. A Colombian labor union filed suit in 2001 against Coca-Cola for intimidating its leaders, which prompted some U.S. colleges to ban Coke sales on campus. Protesters also created a hate site (www.killercoke.org), which provides details of the union's claims.

When, in 2006, a U.S. federal court dismissed the labor union's claims, Coke went on the offensive, buying search terms such as "killer coke," showing ads that trumpet "Coke Lawsuit Dismissed" (with a link to the full story at Coke's Web site) as shown in Exhibit 3-5. Coke could have waited until the search engines found news stories about the dismissal, but they decided to act quickly, instead. Expect more companies to use the Web itself to blunt the attacks of Web protesters.

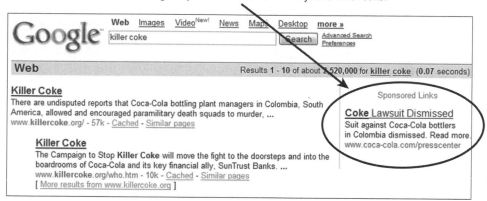

Exhibit 3-5   Companies fight back against hate sites with search marketing.

Many companies use search marketing to blunt the attack by crowding hate sites out of the search rankings. Search results never contain more than two listings from any one domain, but you might be able to get a little help from your friends. First, make sure your pages are optimized so that you get your legitimate two listings. (Spots #1 and #2 are what you are shooting for.) Next, if your company has multiple domains (for subsidiaries, international affiliates, and so on), you can ethically optimize those sites for your company's target keywords.

Your vendors, business partners, and other friendly companies might also have pages on their sites that legitimately speak of their relationship with your company—you can assist them to optimize those pages. Never do anything unethical to divert searchers to places that are not relevant, but you should cultivate the help of friendly sites. If your friends provide more relevant results than your enemies, the hate sites will be pushed down in the list so they don't draw as much attention.

You might also be able to enlist your friends to speak out in your defense when inaccurate stories circulate. If you go this route, however, be sure that your allies are telling the truth—don't *prove* your opponent's charges that you are unethical by deceiving or lying.

Responding to the charges of a hate site is messy, no matter how it pans out (or how much they pan you). Better yet is to avoid hate sites in the first place by striving for the utmost in ethics, treating every customer with respect, and listening every day and in crises so that problems don't turn into wars. If that sounds too tough to do, you had better buy the domain name "yourdomainsucks.com" before someone else does.

Getting Introduced to Others

If you excel at starting conversations, and you're a good listener, then you'll be a popular conversationalist—people will talk about you and will introduce you to others. And while that will often happen naturally, it occurs more frequently when you craft your message to be passed on to others.

With all the work you've put into starting a conversation and listening, there's no reason for it to stop there. Sure, you want those customers you've talked up to buy from you (and we'll spend all of Part 2 of this book talking about *that*), but they can help you now—maybe before they've bought anything—if you know what you're doing.

As important as it has always been for people to recommend your company to others, the Web brings new dimensions to getting introduced to others. And the first place to start is with *who* can introduce you to other people. Customers and prospective customers are the biggest group, but before we're finished we'll show you how to engage your employees and your business partners too.

Introductions by Your Customers

Eighty percent of companies rely on customers to evangelize other customers. Just like other marketing tactics, *word of mouth* marketing has moved to the Web.

Viral marketing, as it has been christened (or sometimes, *word of Web*), is different in some ways from traditional word of mouth but only because of the speed at which the word can move. In the old days, publicity was aimed at media outlets because one good magazine story could move a product faster than talking to hundreds of ordinary customers. Word of mouth marketing was more likely to occur spontaneously, when a good story just begged to be told.

The Web changed that. Some talk about *word of e-mail*, in which e-mail messages are forwarded to dozens or hundreds of people—e-mail containing a message or maybe drawing attention to a YouTube video. Others call out *word of IM*, as instant messages are quickly passed among friends.

Web 2.0 ups the ante. Now that any customer essentially has a printing press, word of mouth marketing takes on new power. Any customer can write a blog, can create a Web site, and can link to marketing messages they like or assail ones they don't. Web 2.0 makes every one of your customers a media person.

What you're looking for is a recommendation. A recommendation from someone trusted is one of the most powerful spurs to action, which is no different on the Web than it ever was. So, how do you get your customers to recommend what you sell to other people? Recommendations are based on noteworthiness. You need to give your customers a story that they can tell and make it easy to tell that story.

Some people tell you that certain products are never noteworthy and you're wasting your time if you think you'll get recommendations for them. If that's true, you're selling a pure commodity, and it's hard to make a living as a marketer that way.

Often the lack of a story is actually lack of imagination. If you have nothing to say, you need either a new product or a new job. Not convinced? What are the products that you think never have a story?

- **Toilet paper**—"Scott's tissue is safe for septic systems" or "Charmin is squeezably soft" are obviously things some people care about. Others want their paper free of dyes or made from recycled paper.

- **Paper clips**—"Our vinyl-coated paper clips come in bright colors and leave no marks on your documents" or "These high-quality American-made paper clips hold their grip even with repeated use" might be noteworthy to some people.

- **Sponges**—"Our natural sea sponges are better for bathing and cleaning because they soak up and hold more water without dripping" or "Our premium sponges withstand repeated sanitizing in the dishwasher without deteriorating" might convince someone to buy.

You get the idea. Something about your product is probably unique—that's why you make it. Look, I had a great dinner one night in a restaurant in Copenhagen called *Salt*. With each course, they explained several different kinds of salt that you could use on your food. Geez, if people can make a living explaining how salt is made, you must be able to explain what you make.

Whether or not people care about what you make will determine how good the story you have to tell is. But those stories need to be on your Web site, probably in greater detail than they are now. Tell how to use your product on your blog. Provide tips for getting the most out of your service. Give customers something to talk about.

Once you've settled on your story, you must make it easy to pass on. That's where the Web comes in. Can your customers easily pass along the stories you tell on your Web site? The Web can make your story easy for others to tell:

- **Print this page**—Do you make it easy for people to create a nice printed version of your page to give to someone else?

- **E-mail this page**—Can someone press a button on your page and send it to a friend?

- **Link to this page**—Some sites provide code for linking to their pages.

- **Blog this**—Can bloggers embed your content in a post by pressing a button?

- **Digg this**—Do you make it easy to use social bookmarks and tags on your content?

If you have a story to tell and make it easy to pass on, more people will provide that recommendation you crave.

Many viral marketing successes are accidental. When videos were posted of Diet Coke bottles turning into gushers after Mentos candies were added, people rushed to tell their friends about it. No one at Coca-Cola or at Mentos had anything to do with it, but their brand names were certainly bandied about. Coca-Cola was guarded in its

WHAT EXACTLY IS SOCIAL BOOKMARKING, ANYWAY?

Some call it *social bookmarking*, others *social tagging* or *folksonomies*, and maybe a new name will crop up by the time you read this. Whatever you name it, marketers need to understand and use this growing means of gathering attention for your message. In essence, social bookmarking systems let your readers categorize and vote for your content.

Let's take a new blog post that you are writing. We already saw how you'd want to think carefully about the words you use so that searchers find your content. Social bookmarking allows you to explicitly call out those words as *tags* for your post, allowing the bookmarking service to show your post to anyone looking for information on those subjects. The most popular example might be del.icio.us, owned by Yahoo!, which lets you set and share bookmarks (links) to any Web content, along with your annotations about that content.

So if your blog post is about a new service you're offering to streamline hospital check-in procedures, you can tag it with words that allow others to find it, such as "hospital" (duh), "check-in procedures" (difficult, huh?), and maybe "registration" and "new patient." You might also want to add "cost reduction" or "consulting"—if those words accurately describe what you do.

But more important is what everyone else does with your blog post. Do your readers also tag your content? Do they use the same words you do, or different ones? Perhaps they view your offering differently than you do and would categorize it under "re-engineering" or "training."

As numerous people bookmark your blog post, the bookmarking service might send more and more people your way for information on those tagged subjects. Social bookmarking services provide special search facilities to find bookmarks tagged with certain subjects—the search results are often ranked by the number of times a story has been bookmarked with the right tag. Many bookmark

enthusiasm ("We would hope that people would prefer to drink [Diet Coke] more than do experiments with it.") while Mentos was thrilled, even featuring the video and background information on its home page, as shown in Exhibit 3-6.

So while some viral successes are pure chance, others are the result of hard work seeding stories that beg to be told. Google introduced its free Gmail offering with no advertising, instead offering a trial period by invitation only. People were so hot to try Gmail that these free invitations were being sold on eBay. Exclusivity gets jaws to wag.

---

services produce Web feeds based on their tags so that someone interested in "hospital consulting" might subscribe to a feed that would contain your post.

Some social bookmarking sites emphasize voting on the popularity of content in addition to tags. Digg, for example, allows readers to highlight a good story or bury a poor one to indicate their interest, which Digg uses to guide others to the most newsworthy stories out there. Enough votes for your story can land it on Digg's front page, at least for a while, until the next hot idea comes along to gather its own support. It might seem tempting for you to Digg your own stories, but it's risky—readers will bury stories submitted by authors because it's considered bad form within the community. My advice is to play by the rules of each community.

Social bookmarking systems aren't perfect. Some complain that we'd be better off allowing readers to use a standard set of tag names to improve quality, rather than having someone tag posts with "hospital check-in" and others "in-patient registration"—they both mean the same thing. But social bookmarking provides a better alternative to search in many areas, such as for images and pictures, and it seems especially well-suited to brand new subjects in the news that no standard set of subject categories can keep up with.

A few marketers have started tagging mechanisms on their own Web sites. Texas Instruments, for example, allows customers to tag any page on their site. Eventually, TI expects customers to view and manage their tags on a personal page on their site.

So the radical idea behind social bookmarking is that the public determines which stories get publicity. To those of us who've tried to raise traditional media interest in covering our stories, this might sound liberating, but the public is a tough audience—at least as tough as any reporter you've dealt with. If you have something genuinely interesting to say, social bookmarking will help you, but don't expect your boring press release to be the top story on Digg.

Exhibit 3-6   Successful viral marketing is often accidental.

DOES YOUR CONTENT DEMAND TO BE PASSED ON?

Making it easy for customers to pass your message on to others is important, but how do you create content that practically compels them to do it? What makes someone decide to take the step of introducing your content to someone who trusts them?

Seth Godin, in his excellent book *Unleashing the IdeaVirus*, advises marketers to focus on the *sneezers*, those idea-passing folks that are always looking for a new insider tip to confide. These idea spreaders have huge social networks that they constantly pass ideas to.

But why? What motivates sneezers to "e-mail a friend" your Web page? Reputation. They like to be seen as "in the know" or "on the cutting edge" or (add your own cliché for "trendy" here). Sending good ideas to others is the main way they enlarge and strengthen their social connections, whom they call when *they* need help. If you can tap into the kinds of ideas that spreaders want to spread, they'll do the work for you.

First, it helps if you show your sneezers they're special. Can you offer them an "insider" status that provides early peeks into your strategies and ideas? Many customers might be interested, but sneezers certainly will be.

Affiliate links are the simplest example of special treatment—let your customers refer other customers and get paid to do so. Likewise, when Bass Pro

Some refer to the ideas that people pass around as *memes*, with the strongest memes spreading the fastest. While memes are being spread all the time—we humans do like a good story—they are not always easy to engineer. Car maker General Motors, for example, tried to spread its message for the Chevy Tahoe SUV using viral techniques. GM announced a contest for TV viewers to create their own commercials for the SUV using video clips and tools on a GM Web site.

GM was caught by surprise, however, as their site was overrun with negative ads that mocked the SUV's environmentally-unfriendly gas mileage and its danger to occupants of smaller cars. Other "contestants" contributed sexually explicit or profane commercials as their entries. GM responded well under the circumstances, removing the offensive ads but allowing the negative ones to remain on their site.

Could GM have avoided the negative publicity? Possibly. GM might have tried enlisting satisfied Tahoe customers for their contest rather than recruiting random TV viewers.

But others argued the campaign was a great success because so many more people heard about it. They reasoned that the detractors weren't going to buy anyway, but that

Shops introduced customer reviews, it randomly awarded $100 gift cards to reviewers to get the contributions started—those early reviewers are your sneezers.

Six Apart, a leading blog software company, has introduced a blogging service at vox.com for *private* blogs—the authors control which people are allowed to read them. Marketers can easily take advantage of this kind of private channel to hold trusted conversations with influential customers.

Do you offer a wiki for your best customers—your sneezers—to shape your strategy? If you do, they are far more likely to talk about your strategy because they helped create it. Do you provide message boards that help them talk to each other? Help sneezers meet other sneezers so that your message flows faster among their networks.

As we discussed earlier, make it easy. Put the buttons on your site that help sneezers to introduce your content to others, such as "Digg this" and "print this page." Make sure your e-mail forwards easily without getting scrambled by e-mail software. These simple ideas are the essence of "do it wrong quickly."

But most of all, value the relationship you have with your sneezers. Let them know how important they are. Make them feel special. And never (never!) compromise their relationship with their social network. If you decide that it would be a great idea to send an offer to every e-mail address that you got from sneezers who e-mailed a friend, then expect the sneezers to drop you like a hot potato. Or give you the cold shoulder. Look, they won't like you anymore, OK?

more prospects came to the site than otherwise would have. Could GM have executed this campaign better? Perhaps, but give them credit for doing it wrong quickly. They learned something for their next campaign.

As with so many other tactics we've explained, you can fake introductions if you want to. It's dumb because when you get caught, you'll look like the fraud you are, but it's done all the time. You can ask your employees to haunt the message boards and pretend to be customers raving about how good your products are. You can pay people to provide good reviews.

But the new favorite form of fake flackery (Holy alliteration, Batman!) afflicts social networks, such as MySpace, allowing anyone to pretend to be Ordinary Joe when he is really Mercenary Moe. You can pay people to back your products while pretending to be just plain folks, and it might even work, but beware the backlash when you're discovered, especially if you target the kids and teenagers that are everywhere on MySpace.

Traditional media and even Web pages make it clear which content is sponsored and which is not. You should do the same on social networks, too. Instead of pretending to be someone you're not, just keep it real, bro. (I still don't sound cool, do I?)

So if you shouldn't ask your employees to pose as customers, what should you do with them? Stay tuned.

Introductions by Your Employees

Our employees are our greatest assets. That's what it says on the coffee mugs we got from HR, anyway. But most companies waste those great assets—our employees *can* be great ambassadors to our customers if we let them.

Yes, I know that we've trained all of our "customer-facing personnel" to be "customer-centric" and that we started that "friends and family" program that allows our employees to pass on company discounts. That's good, but the Web offers more opportunities. *All* of our employees can represent our companies, not just the ones in customer support—all of them.

And these employees influence more people than ever—even total strangers. The Web allows them to introduce our message to *anyone* on the Web, not just friends and families, but *anyone*.

If we let them.

But mostly, we don't. Mostly we're fraidy-scared—afraid of what they'd say and scared of what they'd do. What if they do something really dumb? What if they promise something they shouldn't? What if we get sued? What if they accelerate global warming? (OK, OK, you probably aren't worried that they'll do that last one.)

Inhale slowly now. First, your fears are somewhat warranted. You are taking a chance whenever you clean up your employees and let them meet the public. There are some that you probably shouldn't let out of that asylum you call corporate world global headquarters (and grill), but most of your employees are smart, and they know how to conduct themselves. And you can train most of the rest.

Let them out. The easiest way to be real in front of your customers is with real people, and you have a whole bunch of them on your side already—or at least you should have them on your side. If you are concerned that your employees hate the company so much that they won't help you talk to customers, that sounds like time to start treating your employees better. But if you're like most companies, your employees stay with you because it ain't so bad. In fact, showing employees that you trust them to speak for your company might tip some fence-sitters onto your side.

So what can your employees do? Blogging is one idea. Set up a corporate blogging policy and train employees to be careful not to offend anyone or to give away company secrets or whatever else you are afraid of. And take away the Blogger account of anyone who can't follow the rules.

Besides blogs, how else can employees introduce their company to customers? Participate in the community. Actually, on the Web, it's more like participate in the commun*ities* because one of the most striking characteristics of life on the Web is how many different communities exist.

Whatever you sell, there's a community somewhere that is talking about it. Maybe they talk about other subjects, too, but some of the time they are talking about you. There might even be communities that talk about nothing but you—they exist just so your customers can share tips and secrets about how to use your products better. You could actually set it up yourself.

Communities form around message boards, wikis, and Web sites. The venue matters little. What *does* matter is that your customers spend their time there and that they talk about you. What they say can make or break your marketing.

Depending on your business, communities might be the ideal way to reach your customers. More than half of American moms say they use recommendations to make home purchase decisions—and even more do so for decisions about their children. That's a big reason why moms use the Web and use consumer-generated media in particular in such large numbers. These online communities help them make purchase decisions every day.

Your employees are the best way to reach out to these communities. Encourage them to participate. Your customers will congregate whether your employees are there or not, but if your employees are there, several things will happen:

- **Your employees will help you listen**—This helps you adapt what you say and do in response.
- **Your employees can be real, authentic voices**—They can help your customers to hear your message or that say "I'm sorry" when your product doesn't work or that suggest something that can be done to make a bad situation better.

- **The community will grow faster**—Your employees often provide better, more credible information than customers, improving the value of the community. When your employees make the community more valuable, it grows faster.

Customers notice whether your employees are on public groups, for example, or whether your policy is that all communication comes from the PR department or the official tech support site. This is something you can do wrong quickly. If your employees join to answer questions, it shows they care about your company. What's more, in a crisis, an employee who has been part of the community has more credibility than one who shows up after the crisis hits.

So far, small companies have allowed employees to reach out to customers more than large ones have, with more small companies encouraging blogs, for example. Large companies tend to be slower to free employees from muzzle policies that prevent embarrassment and lawsuits (and prevent the kind of positive stories that word of mouth depends on).

Allowing employees to be your best ambassadors is important, but equally important is avoiding negative word of mouth from disgruntled employees. When an employee is terminated or quits, make sure that you offer an exit interview to allow him to feel heard. Frustrated employees are more likely to turn to public venues, such as the Web, to tell their stories.

You've seen how customers and employees can introduce your company to new potential customers, but don't overlook your business partners—they have loads of contacts and will sometimes be the easiest to convince to help.

Introductions by Your Partners

For some reason, we often overlook our company's existing relationships when we turn our attention to the Web. Every company has business partners it can call on to make introductions to customers.

Most companies, especially large companies, have an extensive set of partners that they do business with. Resellers, dealers, affiliates, retailers, suppliers—it doesn't matter what you call them. If you are a manufacturer, work with your resellers. If you are a retailer, use your affiliates. Every organization has relationships with other organizations. Use yours!

You'll remember that earlier in this chapter we called on our business partners to deal with hate sites, but they can be used for so much more. Your business partners are constantly communicating with *their* customers—see if you can get them to pass along your message when they do. You might be able to do the same for them in exchange.

Recommendations from your partners are valuable because they are from neutral parties—any of these companies can freely decide to recommend you or not. If their relationship with your company ends, the recommendation will, too. These companies are independent from yours—that's what makes an endorsement from them so valuable.

What form can these recommendations take? Just about anything you can think of might work under the right circumstances—it depends on the nature of your relationship.

Perhaps you can introduce a new product in a partner's mailing list—make it an exclusive offer that they see before you make it generally available. Solicit feedback for the product you manufacture from your retailer's customers or just get your partner to link to your Web site—you remember how well links can start a conversation. You can do any of these things now. Don't set up a conference call to discuss it. Try it!

Start by making your list. What companies will want to recommend you? Do you manufacture a product they sell? Are you a reference customer for a supplier? Do you have a deal to sell another company's product? Will your customers provide testimonials on their Web sites? Stop and think. What relationships exist between your company and others?

Depending on the nature of your company's relationships, you might be in a commanding position. If your suppliers want your reference, you can insist upon a link. You can require that all affiliates include your detailed product information. Examine all of your relationships and see if you are in a position to request recommendations that they are very likely to agree to.

Links to your Web sites are often the easiest recommendations to get. But even if your company already has plenty of links from your partners, you might still have work to do. Frequently, large companies have an abundance of links to their home pages but not enough links to interior pages. Links to your individual products, for example, get your customers closer to buying something (and they help your search rankings for those product-related keywords).

In large companies, sponsorships are often a missed opportunity. Whenever corporate largesse funds a non-profit or industry activity, it is customary for the funded Web site to thank your company by providing a link back to your site and mentioning your name in announcements. If your company sponsors research at a local university or endows a chair, get links to your site. Perhaps your company sponsors an external organization or one of its programs or events. Because you probably don't need any more links to your home page with your company name, ask instead for a link to an interior page of your site that is focused on the event topic. Instead of settling for the company name to be mentioned in the announcement, see if you can have the event sponsored by a specific product.

IBM's Globalization team, for example, sponsored the Localization Industry Standards Association (LISA) conference, which dutifully placed a sponsor link on their site to IBM's home page. A quick e-mail from IBM got the sponsor link pointed to the

IBM Globalization page—a much more relevant link that attracted more qualified visitors as well as improved search rankings. Your site might have similar opportunities.

Don't overlook trade associations. Your company might be a member of one or more of these industry organizations. Each trade association has its own Web site, and most have a member list page, as well as other pages on the site that might link to member Web sites. Make sure that your organization is listed in the member directory of each trade association you belong to and that its Web directory entry includes a link to your site. Investigate whether there are other opportunities for your company to provide news or information for posting on the site (along with a handy link back to your site, of course). These links are especially helpful in establishing your company's credentials in searches for the name of your industry and other industry terms.

With all of these possibilities, you can see that your business partners should be a critical part of your recommendation strategy. Customers and employees can make introductions for you, but don't forget to ask your friends in other businesses, too.

AFFILIATES: A SPECIAL KIND OF BUSINESS PARTNER

Affiliate marketing is a new name for an old practice: paying another company for sending you a sales lead. Your affiliate attracts interest from potential customers, sends them to your Web site, and collects a commission if they make a purchase. Many companies have affiliate programs—you should look into establishing one if you don't.

If your company already runs an affiliate program (acting as a *merchant*, in affiliate-speak), you're actually paying other companies to recommend you, by cutting them in on the sale. Although we've talked over and over again about being wary of these paid relationships, affiliate marketing is completely ethical as long as you are not hiding the nature of the relationship.

Affiliates send traffic to your Web site every day, using Web links. As they do, tracking systems ensure that the leads passed to the merchant are counted so that the affiliate's commission can be paid if a lead turns into a sale. Unfortunately, many affiliate tracking systems use complex ways of linking that search engines don't give any credit for. You might be getting traffic from your affiliates, but you aren't improving your search rankings with those links. Insist on a "search-friendly" affiliate tracking system for your merchant program.

Search marketing is the major way affiliates attract people to their sites, but many merchants are ambivalent about the way their affiliates use paid search. Some companies are happy to get the leads from their affiliates' paid search marketing campaigns, but others have sought to restrict their affiliates' activities in

Summary

You can see that, as with any kind of marketing, it's easy to get caught up in the specifics of each new online marketing technique and miss the broad lessons of the changes in our industry. As important as it is to know the details, it's less important than the way you *think* about what you are doing.

Keep in mind that your marketing needs to be conversational, which means that you must understand how online marketing conversations start, how to really listen to your customers, and how to get yourself introduced to new prospective customers. Staying above the details will keep you focused in the future, as new techniques are born and old ones fade in importance.

So don't focus on blogs. Focus on personal ways to communicate with your customers. Don't get caught up with wikis. Instead, find ways to collaborate with your customers. Don't obsess over podcasts. Concentrate on how to put your customers in

---

this area. Some merchants have added new terms to their affiliate agreements, banning the use of the merchant's trademarks and other brand names in any paid search marketing campaigns by their affiliates.

These merchants argue that searchers using trademark names have already made a brand decision and should be brought directly to the merchant's site. They see no reason to pay an affiliate a fee for bringing them a customer who was trying to come to the merchant in the first place. These merchants are happy for affiliates to conduct paid search campaigns using generic keywords devoid of brand and trademark names—those keywords are bringing the customers to the merchants that might have gone to competitors.

Some merchants see this as short-sighted, however. No matter what a merchant does to block its affiliates from buying branded keywords, competitors can't be blocked because the merchant has no control over them. Although the merchant might have the top paid spot, who has the rest of the spots? Randy Antin, Search Marketing Manager of Travelocity, notes that when his company restricted its affiliates from bidding on branded keywords, "...the spaces in the bidding were soon replaced by our competitors' affiliates." Searchers clicking anything other than Travelocity's single ad might end up buying from a competitor.

Whatever your position on your affiliates' search marketing activities, an affiliate marketing program can provide the right incentives to get your company introduced to customers you'd have never otherwise met.

control of when they listen to your message. Don't fixate on e-mail or Web feeds. Do emphasize techniques that let your customers subscribe to your message.

As time goes by, new tactics will emerge—if this book had been written a few years ago, we wouldn't have been talking about Digg or wikis, for example. As new techniques emerge, ask yourself, "Is this a good way for my customer to start a conversation? Is it an opportunity for me to listen? Does this tactic lend itself to getting me introduced to others?" Your answers will tell you how to think about each new technique.

Remember that the secret of good conversation is to always think about the other person. The less you make the conversation about you and the more you make it about your customer, the better the outcome for you and the more your customers will introduce you to others to start new conversations. Make every conversation the beginning of a relationship instead of just a quick sale.

That's it for Chapter 3, and that's it for Part 1 of this book. You've learned how the Internet has turned marketing into a conversation—and how you get in on the talk. In Part 2, we'll go beyond the conversation and look at the customer relationship. How do we go from a conversation to a sale? And how do we build on one sale to create a lifetime customer? Read on to find out.

PART **2**

That Newfangled *Direct* Marketing

Chapter 4 ■ Going Over to the Dark Side   105

Chapter 5 ■ The New Custom Relations   149

Chapter 6 ■ Customers Vote with Their Mice   211

E ngaging your customer is about more than just listening. If actions speak louder than words, then how can you watch the actions your customers are taking?

The Internet allows you to observe everything they do and count how many times each person does them and under what circumstances. It's the most powerful market research tool you've ever seen—if you know how to use it.

Part 2 teaches you how to measure what your customers do, how to choose from the options available for improvement, and how to adjust your marketing in response.

Chapter 4, "Going Over to the Dark Side," brings us face to face with customer activity metrics. You learn to identify the purpose of your Web site and to track your site's success in fulfilling that purpose. If you can count everything your customers do, you'll be amazed at the information you unearth to fuel improvement. Don't worry if Web measurements never made sense before. You'll learn to do the math.

Chapter 5, "The New Customer Relations," explains the tools you have at your disposal for creating an interactive marketing experience. You learn online design, messaging, and segmentation—even personalized targeting. You can do a lot more online than with mass media—online marketing provides an edge to those who understand it.

Chapter 6, "Customers Vote with Their Mice," shows you how to collect the feedback available from customer activity and what to do with it. You learn how to choose the first area of improvement, how to measure effectiveness, and how to speed up your pace so you can change things over and over again.

By the end of Part 2, you'll be able to observe what your customers are doing, en masse, and decide which experiments to conduct to boost your marketing results. You'll understand the full inventory of new marketing tools at your disposal and know how to choose which ones to use. Most importantly, you'll be equipped to examine any aspect of your online marketing and improve it quickly.

Now turn the page quickly!

4

Going Over to the Dark Side

"Old statisticians never die—they just get broken down by age and sex."

—Anonymous

Chapter Contents

- Find Your Purpose   109
- Measure Your Customer Activity   125
- Measure Your Customer Relationships   142
- Summary   147

We've made marketing very complex.

There's only one purpose for marketing—to evoke a response from a potential customer. But to read all the marketing books, it's a lot more complicated than that. We need to raise brand awareness. We need to make an emotional connection. We need to create mind share—and about a dozen other things that aren't very easy to understand.

What *is* easy to understand, however, is what all of these fuzzy marketing concepts have in common. They matter only if they result in sales.

A sale is the most-desired response from a potential customer, obviously, but it's not the only good response from a customer. Customers can call you, they can e-mail you—they can contact you in many ways. Those are all *responses*, as any direct marketer will tell you. They'll also tell you that all responses are good because they often lead to sales. Direct marketers have built their businesses on responses to their catalogs and their direct mail campaigns.

In contrast, dyed-in-the-wool brand marketers have lived in a world starved of response. (I don't know exactly when their wool was first dyed, but work with me here.) They inhabit a very quiet world of mass media delivering their marketing message with no reply. At least there's no *direct* reply because brand marketers can't hear people saying, "I *hate* this commercial" to their family while they're gathered around the TV.

The Web changes all that. Web marketing tactics encourage response. Banner ads and search results demand to be clicked. Blogs entice commentary. Wikis want to be changed. In short, the Web is about participation.

In the early days of the Web, marketers did not understand this. We thought we'd attract attention for passive brand advertising just the way we do in mass media. We bought banner ads that looked a lot like print ads and tried to attract attention by interrupting folks from what they were really doing. We counted the number of "eyeballs" we attracted to an ad (although we seemed to always count just one eyeball per person). How many saw it? How many clicked it? The more eyeballs, the better the ad.

But, as Microsoft's Harrison Magun points out, you can't take eyeballs to the bank. That's what caused the great Internet "dot-bomb" era. Sure, there are a few successful businesses based on eyeballs because they sell advertising based on the number of people that look at their sites. So if you work for CNN, or ESPN, or the kids' game site Neopets, then your business model is about eyeballs. But alas, most businesses have to sell something more than advertising.

So we all resolved to change our ways. No more eyeballs. No more fluffy statistics on brand awareness on the Web anymore—we're all sales, all the time. Does that mean that there's no such thing as brand awareness or that brand awareness is merely an excuse for a bad campaign? ("Unclicked banner ads still increase branding"—that's our story and we're sticking with it.) Well, not really.

Brand awareness is very important for some businesses. Coke isn't the best-known (and one of the most profitable) brands on the planet by accident. But eventually, brand awareness wants a response, too. (See an ad for Coke, then drink a Coke.) Response can be measured, and the Web demands measurement.

All marketers are now jumping on the measurement bandwagon. (It must be quite a large wagon to fit all marketers, I guess.) The growing Marketing Performance Measurement (MPM) movement is focused on measurement, as the name implies. So whether you talk to the MPM gurus or the Web gurus, only responses really matter—it's all about sales. You can't split marketing and sales anymore, and if you aren't selling, all the brand awareness in the world won't save you.

But where do sales come from? What do we do to get customers to buy? If we focus our efforts only on sales, we miss the *relationship*. So we'll talk about more than sales. We'll talk about what your customer is trying to do, visit by visit, and how we know if your customer succeeded. But first—a warning. I will take you to the dark side (cue ominous music)—MATH!

OK, I know that many marketers are completely comfortable around a spreadsheet, but the truth is that for more than a few of you, the sheer idea of statistics gives you an adrenaline rush. Some of you would far prefer to do creative work than hunch over a calculator, but Web marketing demands that we measure what we are doing so that we know what's working and what's not. That way we can improve every day.

If, for you, math has always been the dark side of the force, fear not. The math itself is not complicated—it's simple arithmetic. You can handle it if you can punch keys on a calculator. Numbers won't hurt you—if they start to make you queasy, just press the OFF button on the calculator and they all go away. You *can* do the math.

What *is* complicated is the metrics themselves. Just as marketers have made marketing too complicated, likewise have metrics gurus provided us with a wealth of statistics that try even a mathematician's soul. Mathematicians don't mind the arithmetic—that's not what's complicated. They detest the multiple names and multiple meanings.

One source of confusion in Web metrics comes from too many names for the same measurement. When a banner ad is displayed, we count an *impression*. When an e-mail is shown, it's an *opened e-mail*. When a Web page appears, it is counted as a *page view*. They all mean the same thing—the customer saw your marketing message.

Web metrics also include too many ways to *measure* the same thing. For example, several different ways exist to measure page views, none of them totally accurate. Multiple names for similar concepts and multiple formulas for measuring them—they both drive a mathematician to reach for the Alka Seltzer.

Now before you mutter to yourself, "Problems for our heroes," just know that it doesn't have to be complicated. You *can* stake out a simple system for counting what's important in your business and not get tied up in all the complexity.

When it comes to designing your metrics system, you should do *that* wrong quickly, too. Start with the basics and add to it only when you are convinced that the additional complexity is worth it. Put together a simple set of metrics that measures what you need to make decisions about and change it when it needs changing.

You might be asking yourself why we should go to all this trouble—because without measuring results:

■ You don't know what's working.

■ You can't convince anyone that you are doing a good job.

■ You can't get more money to do your job.

If you're honest with yourself, you'll admit that you've had all of these problems in the past. Maybe you are having them now. These problems seem to come up whenever you have to deal with people who aren't marketers. They don't understand brand awareness, and they don't buy that it has any value. When it's your colleague in sales, that's annoying. When it's your CEO, that's scary.

You see, marketing has always set its own rules. Marketing is something we've done because, deep down, we *believe* that it works. We can't prove it, no, but we fervently believe in marketing's effectiveness. We have faith in it. But that's treating marketing as a religion instead of a business. If you believe, if you *really* believe, clap your hands three times and say, "I know that the metrics will prove the value of marketing."

And they will. The metrics will even prove the value of marketing to *you* because you will understand the metrics. You'll understand them because they are about people, about who your customers are, and what they do, and what it's worth to you. It's that simple.

Please understand that I believe in marketing too. Marketing really *does* work. No need to convince me. But more and more, we'll need to persuade decision makers not about marketing's effectiveness in the abstract but about the effectiveness of *this* particular marketing tactic to drive *that* sales result. With offline marketing, as effective as it has been—and it's been extremely effective—it has been difficult to always tie sales back to the marketing tactic.

It's much easier to prove the value of Web marketing—if you know what to measure.

Exhibit 4-1 lists a number of different measurements you can use. It's not important that you understand what each of them means yet. What is important is that you see that measurements answer three distinct questions: who, what, and how much. In this chapter, we look at who your customers are and what they do. We'll wait until Chapter 6, "Customers Vote with Their Mice," to talk about what it's all worth.

In this chapter, we start with a sense of purpose—both your purpose in having a Web site and your customer's purpose in using your Web site. Then we examine how you measure your customer's activity—what they do *before* they come to your Web site, *while* they are there, and *after* they leave. We'll wrap up by learning to measure your online customer relationships.

Who Are They?	What Did They Do?	How Much Is It Worth?
Anonymous visitors	Opened e-mail	Revenue
Registered members	Clicked	Profit
Customers	Viewed page	Lifetime value
Subscribers	Downloaded	
	Contacted us	
	Purchased	
	Returned to site	
	Commented	
	Subscribed	

Exhibit 4-1   So many metrics, so little time

So if you're ready to try something new, something that really works, then come over to the dark side with me. Let's bring on the numbers. But before we dive into the digits, let's start with people. We start with two people you know well. You and your customer. You as a marketer have a purpose and so does your customer. Unless we start there, there's no reason to count anything.

Find Your Purpose

You have a Web site. There's a *reason* you have a Web site, and there is a reason that customers come to that Web site. The goal of Web marketing is to bring the purpose of your Web site together with the purpose of your customer.

If your purpose is to sell a consulting engagement, you must identify customers whose purpose is to solve their problems—and you must persuade them that your firm does it best. If you own a restaurant, you are trying to sell food, which can solve several customer problems. Some are hungry, while others are entertaining a new client. Others are just trying to feed their kids something they'll eat. Restaurants that solve *multiple* customer problems can be more successful.

Your Web site must negotiate the difference between what you want and what your customers want. To do so, we must first focus on what *you* want. What is your Web site's purpose?

Your Web Site's Purpose

The purpose of any business is selling something at a profit. Your profits are higher when you sell in higher quantities, when you have the lowest cost of sales, and when you resell to the same customers over and over. The Web helps you do all of these things. But that's rather vague.

How *exactly* does your Web site sell for your business? Do you sell online? Maybe, instead, you have a research site that persuades customers to buy but sends them offline to actually close the deal. Or perhaps your site is mainly for information purposes, sending customer *leads* to other sales channels relatively early in the sales process.

It doesn't matter whether your site is built for online sales, offline sales, or leads—or some combination of all three. When you focus on your site's purpose, you can continuously improve your customer experience so that you'll sell more.

We'll spend the next three chapters looking at how to make these improvements, but for now, let's closely examine these three broad purposes—online sales, offline sales, and leads—so that you can identify *your* Web site's purpose.

If your site has a shopping cart and sells directly to visitors, then *Web sales* is one of its goals. Amazon.com might be the best known example of a pure Web sales site, but it's one of many Web sites that sell directly to customers. Did you know that there are two kinds?

An *online commerce* site allows customers to purchase items on the site, but it delivers the items, such as books or clothing, offline. In contrast, a *pure online* site *delivers* its products electronically, too—there's no physical package sent to the buyer. Your business might be squarely in one of these camps, or it might be a hybrid, where some of your products are delivered online, and some are delivered offline. So while we contrast online and pure online commerce, keep in mind that in real life businesses fall on different points of a continuum, not always at the extremes.

Many successful Web businesses are pure online businesses. Charles Schwab sells investments—the buyer makes the purchase online and might receive a mail confirmation, but the asset is owned immediately. Other financial services businesses, such as insurance, are moving to pure online models also. Downloaded software and music are other examples of pure online businesses.

In contrast, online commerce businesses sell physical goods—books, packaged software, CDs, clothing, and so many other things. Every day, something new is available for sale on the Web, to be shipped to the buyer's address. In many ways, Federal Express and other shipping companies are the biggest winners in the e-commerce revolution.

But why is this distinction between online and offline delivery important? It's because online delivery leads to far more impulse purchases. Instant gratification causes buyers to shorten their research and planning. In addition, the lower cost of electronic delivery leads to more impulse purchases because people do less research when something costs so little.

Impulse purchases differ from a well-researched purchase in important ways. Satisfying impulse purchasers requires a better Web experience—it takes very little irritation to dampen the impulse.

PROFITING FROM IMPULSIVENESS

Impulse purchases are rising because Web sites become more convenient each year because customers grow more confident in Web purchasing and because product delivery keeps improving. Pure online businesses, where delivery is immediate, inspire the most impulsive purchases.

Think about how online trading has rocked the securities industry in the past ten years. Time was, buying or selling stock was a big decision, one not made very often. Advice was frequently sought from a stock broker, a financial advisor, or even friends and family. Buying or selling an investment usually received careful consideration.

What happened when investments could be bought and sold online? Everything changed. Competitors began battling over the lowest fees charged for each sale, the simplest customer experience, *and* the trustworthiness of the electronic broker.

But that was just the beginning. Completely new needs began to emerge. Brokers began to compete on the information available—real-time quotes, investment analysis, and portfolio management tools.

And then day traders emerged—the ultimate impulse purchasers in the electronic brokerage business. They are highly sought-after customers because the churn in their accounts brings in large fees. They are the high rollers of the brokerage business.

This kind of change is underway in music today, as *brick-and-mortar retailers* that first came under attack from CDNow and other Web retailers now also fear Apple iTunes, the music download store. Digital commerce and digital delivery inexorably result in more impulse purchases at lower prices. Where someone formerly thought a bit before trooping to the store to buy a $15 CD, today they think nothing of downloading a single song for 99¢. You can guess that the advent of e-books might cause upheaval in that industry, and you can imagine effects in many other industries as the years go by.

What does this shift to more impulsive purchasing mean for Web marketing? First, it means more of your business shifts to the Web, but it means much more than that. Impulse purchasers want different things. A day trader is not looking for the same brokerage features as a conservative investor. People buying CDs are more likely to choose by artist and by album, while folks downloading tunes for their iPods are choosing a song.

As your business moves from offline to online to pure online commerce, you might see similar shifts in customer needs that drive your Web marketing strategy.

Whether your business is ripe for a rise in impulse purchases or not, you might be seeing more and more of your customer interactions move to the Web and more of your sales closing directly on the Web.

But while it's true that more transactions move online each year, studies show that customers frequently make the actual purchase offline. Searchers for consumer goods, for example, research their purchase on the Web but purchase at brick-and-mortar stores about half the time.

It can be trickier to measure *offline sales* than sales that ring the digital cash register. You might be trying to get people to come into your store or buy over the phone. Perhaps you sell direct on the Web also, but you find that people often ask questions before buying. Or maybe you don't have any e-commerce capability at all. You might be a forklift manufacturer, a car dealer, or you might sell other big-ticket items. Your site encourages research and comparison because most of your sales close through more traditional channels. Your company might be a product manufacturer or a manufacturer's representative.

If this sounds like your business, then your primary goal is offline sales. As we have discussed before, however, your goals might not be so black-and-white. You might have a mix of products, some of which are conducive to online sales and some that are better served with an offline approach.

For products where you do emphasize offline sales, you need to work hard at your *call to action*, which is sales-speak for the thing you are trying to get someone to do. Where the call to action for Web sales might be as simple as a shopping cart icon next to a sales pitch, your offline sales site must move the customer to the sales channel where you will eventually close the deal. Depending on your business, that channel can take very different forms:

- A toll-free telephone number
- Directions to your store
- A list of locations of stores that carry your product
- A link to a retailing Web site that sells your product online

Many Web sites have multiple goals, even for the same product. Manufacturer W.L. Gore & Associates, maker of GORE-TEX®, explains its benefits on their Web site but directs customers to retailers (both online and offline) to purchase GORE-TEX products. They also suggest that customers "send to a friend" or "print product info." Some companies have even more elaborate ways of shifting people to the channel to close the sale, which we'll see later.

Similar to offline sales, Web sites looking for leads attract visitors that eventually buy elsewhere, but those visitors tend to switch channels far earlier in the sales process.

When someone walks into your home improvement store with a printout of the Web page with the snow blower's model number and price, you're making an offline sale. Someone who downloads your article on the difference between snow blowers and electric snow shovels becomes a lead. Many corporate sites exist entirely to generate leads, such as consulting firms, construction contractors, or other companies that normally bid a custom service for each customer.

Regardless of how the sale is closed, the main distinction between a lead and an offline sale is at what point in the sales process the customer switches to the offline channel. Customers who do online research and immediately switch offline are leads, while customers that know the model number and the sale price walking into the store produce offline sales.

What if your Web site has multiple purposes, even for the same offering? Perhaps your company manufactures home theatre components. You can sell online, you can direct people to retailers for offline sales, or you can hand leads to full-service firms that design and construct home theatre setup with your components. You might think that you'd want to direct customers to the channel that delivers the most sales or the highest profits, but you'd be wrong. You need to help the customer find the best choice for *their* purposes—that's how to create sales and happy customers. That's what we look at next.

Your Customer's Purpose

A global electronics components manufacturer noticed that their distributors were closing far fewer orders in Japan than in other countries, so they started analyzing what was going wrong. In their business, customers come to their Web site to find parts to be used in consumer electronics products. When customers find a part that looks promising, they order a sample to test in a product prototype. If the part works, customers will use it in their product design, later ordering thousands or even millions of parts from distributors for full-scale manufacturing.

After a little analysis, the components manufacturer discovered the problem. Their Web site in Japan did not allow customers to order sample parts. The Web site handed customers off to their distributors' Web sites, who took much longer to ship those samples than competitors did.

The reason for the hand-off was for better measurements—to accurately track which sample shipments eventually resulted in large-quantity orders to the distributors. Because the distributors shipped the sample parts orders, they were able to tie them to the larger orders that came to them later.

Unfortunately, as a result of the hand-off process, customers ordered 30 percent fewer parts in Japan, preferring to try sample parts from competitors who were easy to order from and who shipped in just a few days. Guess whose parts ended up in the electronics products? Right, the competitors'. That's why Japanese customers were not placing those big orders with the component manufacturer's distributors.

Sadly, the same result could befall you if you place measurement above your customer's purpose. The components manufacturer realized the error and changed the Web site to express ship parts anywhere in Japan, even though it no longer could accurately track the eventual orders placed with its distributors. Satisfying your customer's purpose is much more important than metrics.

So that's why we're talking about your customer's purpose. Before we think about metrics, we need to think about the sales process from your customer's point of view.

The traditional sales process is often depicted as a "funnel," which demonstrates that many people must be contacted to get a sale. The concept of a funnel is a bit odd—it's really a leaky funnel because many people leak out of the funnel before some consummate a sale. Salespeople try to *qualify* prospects and to *close* leads (when they complete sales). Sales managers analyze how to make the funnel more efficient so that fewer potential customers drop out of the process along the way—that way you book even more sales.

But the Web turns the sales funnel on its ear (OK, I know a funnel has a mouth but no ear). Look at the actions from a customer's point of view, rather than a sales standpoint—look at the *buying* cycle rather than the selling cycle. After all, customers don't think of themselves as being qualified by your salesperson—they are learning about what you offer and deciding whether it fits them. Both activities (qualifying and learning) occur at the same time. By looking at things from the customer's side, we improve our understanding of your customer's purpose.

If you bought my first book, *Search Engine Marketing, Inc.* (co-authored with Bill Hunt), you learned how to model your customer's behavior on your Web site—many of the examples here are taken from that book. Let's take a simple behavioral model as shown in Exhibit 4-2.

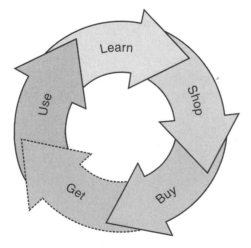

Exhibit 4-2   A behavioral model for your customer relationships

One aspect of a behavioral model is that each activity can lead to another one in sequence. Customers might set out to Learn more about a problem and its possible solutions. Once informed, they can narrow their choices to Shop for a specific product, comparing prices and features, perhaps. Once they identify the best product, they are ready to Buy the product and then wait to Get it before they can Use it.

Not every product fits this model, but let's look at one that does—a personal computer. Customers start out not really knowing what to buy—there are laptops and desktops, and there are even different kinds of desktops that actually sit on your desk or "towers" that go under your desk. Most people need to Learn more about what's out there before they even know what category of computer is right for them.

When the customer has chosen a particular category, such as a laptop, then she needs to decide which one. She must analyze Dell versus ThinkPad versus Apple, and she must also make decisions about operating systems, weight, battery life, screen resolution, memory, disk space, and lots of other features. She can get definitive information straight from the manufacturers and can compare prices from retailers.

Once she's narrowed her choices down to just a few, she begins thinking about whether to Buy. She starts to think about where she can get the lowest price and the fastest shipping for one of the models that she wants. The Web is a great place for customers to do this if you've designed your site for easy price comparisons (including shipping) and if you explain shipping options and special offers.

After purchasing, she wants an email confirmation. While waiting to Get her computer, she can check the status of the order at any time. You can help her track the package delivery. (Because the Get step happens mostly offline, it's depicted on the chart using dotted lines.)

The moment she receives her computer, she can begin to Use it. She can install it and get right to work. As she does, she can get answers to her problems on the manufacturer's Web site. She might sometimes have trouble throughout the life of the computer and return for technical support. If the manufacturer has done a good job helping her, she might at some point want to upgrade her computer by adding more memory, or she might want to replace her computer with a new model, in which case she begins to Learn all over again as she considers a new purchase.

Some of you might be wondering what all this has to do with marketing. Most of it sounds like sales. You need to remember that one of the changes ushered in by the Web is the merger of sales and marketing. In the offline world, it's easy to draw a hard line between marketing and sales, but the Web offers no such clarity. Just as with traditional direct marketing, when there's no salesperson, everything is marketing right up until someone buys from you.

OK, you might be thinking, "But that technical support stuff isn't even sales, so why should marketers care about it?" It's because support is a critical part of your customer experience, and that customer experience *is* your brand.

This way of thinking might seem foreign to your company's culture. Your support team might be considered a cost center, where every improvement they make is justified by lowering costs—they might have beefed up your Web site's support capabilities merely to lower the cost of customer phone calls. But that's short-sighted.

Take this challenge. If your company values investment in support based solely on cutting costs, why not stop doing support? Think about it—your support costs drop to zero! What could be better than that? You can't have a bigger cost reduction.

By now, you might be howling, "You can't do that! Our customers would be so upset that they'd leave in droves!" Then the value of technical support *must* be part of marketing. If you're treating technical support as a cost of doing business rather than a strategic marketing weapon, then you are under-investing. The same is true of customer support activities, such as order status and other "My Account" functions.

Your model of your customer's behavior must include *all* of these interaction points—every part of the customer's relationship with your company. Customer loyalty can develop based on a great product, a great support experience, or dozens of other factors. Make sure that you look at the whole experience when you model your customer's behavior.

Speaking of *your* customer's behavior, perhaps it doesn't resemble the personal computer sales model. Let's look at some examples of customer behavior in different businesses with the goals we looked at earlier: Web sales, offline sales, and leads.

Some Web sales sites have customer models that look just like the one we've already examined for PC sales. But what if you have a pure online business, where the customer downloads the software that you sell? Your model might look like the upper-left picture in Exhibit 4-3, which is very similar to the personal computer model, where customers need to Learn, Shop, and Buy (and get support when they Use it), but there is no truly distinct Get step—the software is downloaded to their computer as part of the Buy step. Therefore, there is no order status needed because no package is being physically shipped.

It's also possible that your model might not require any substantial post-sales support, such as an e-book store. In that case, it might resemble the upper-right picture in Exhibit 4-3, where (after the Buy step) your customers don't return to your Web site until they need to consider their next purchase.

The lower-left picture in Exhibit 4-3 shows how a Web bookstore might operate, where you ship a physical book (requiring a Get step) but usually have no post-purchase customer interactions until the next buying opportunity.

You might actually have a very different model for your Web sales business, such as a content subscription site, as shown in the lower-right picture of Exhibit 4-3. The first step for this site is taken when people Discover the site, possibly from a search query. They later return to the site for free content and discover that premium services are available, eventually paying to subscribe. On espn.com, for example, "Insiders" can view exclusive content not available to others. These premium stories are shown alongside the free stories, with a sales pitch for ESPN Insider shown each time a non-member clicks them.

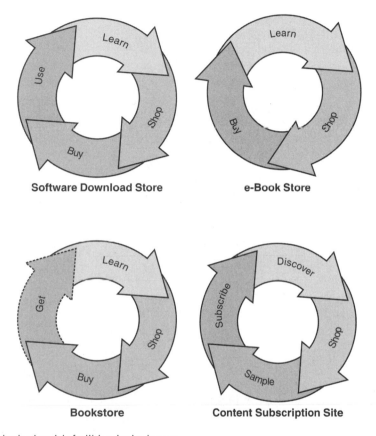

Software Download Store   **e-Book Store**

Bookstore   **Content Subscription Site**

Exhibit 4-3   Behavioral models for Web sales businesses

You can see that different Web sales sites elicit different customer behavior. But what about offline sales sites? Can you model them, too? Sure you can. (You thought I'd say no?)

Offline sales businesses have behavior models that closely resemble those of their Web sales competitors, except that some steps occur offline—often through face-to-face interaction or by phone. Exhibit 4-4 uses the example of an automobile manufacturer, and offline interactions with the customer are depicted with dotted lines.

For offline sales, just as we saw for Web sales, the customer needs to Learn about what kinds of cars are available because so many choices exist (and they increase each year). People don't buy cars every year, and they typically do a lot of research on the Web before making a decision.

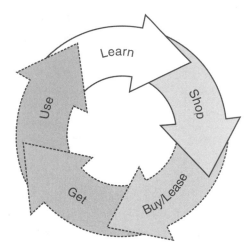

Exhibit 4-4   A behavioral model for an offline sales business

Increasingly, people are starting to Shop for a new car on the Web as well. Auto manufacturer Web sites allow customers to choose the exact model they want, the exterior and interior colors, and options packages and can see the manufacturer's suggested price. If your customers typically walk into a dealer showroom with a Web printout of exactly what they want, they have actually completed the Shop step on the Web.

If your Web site doesn't offer this "build your car" capability, then *your* model would show the Shop step with dotted lines because your goal is to shift your customers to offline channels following the Learn step. But just as we noted the trend for offline sales to shift to online, likewise offline Shop steps are increasingly moving online, with car shopping being a great example.

Relatively few cars are actually purchased on the Web, so the model in Exhibit 4-4 shows the Buy/Lease step in dotted lines, emphasizing that it happens offline. It is possible that this step might shift to the Web at some point in the future, with customers dropping by the dealer to Get their new car, but most customers still haggle and purchase in person today.

Customers still Get their cars at the dealer and return to the dealer (or elsewhere) for maintenance while they Use their cars, with relatively little interaction with your Web site, so these steps are shown as offline as well. (Some car dealers allow customers to make service appointments online, so the Web site is involved even for some steps that occur offline.)

Lead-oriented sites can be modeled also. Let's first examine a typical behavior model for a leads site, in this case a swimming pool dealer, in the left-hand picture of Exhibit 4-5.

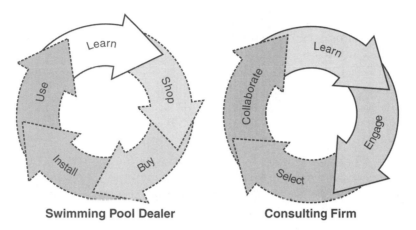

Exhibit 4-5   Behavioral models for lead-oriented businesses

The first thing that you notice is all those dotted lines! For the typical lead-oriented site, customers Learn on the Web site but tend to do everything else offline. For a customer looking for a swimming pool, he wants to get information about whether to choose an above-ground or in-ground pool on the Web. But when he begins to Shop for a specific in-ground pool, for example, he needs a dealer to come to his house to draw that kidney shape in his backyard. Similarly, the Buy, Install, and Use steps usually occur offline, although some dealers might offer do-it-yourself pool maintenance tips on the Web.

If your business is not based on product sales, you might need a different model. Consider how a consulting firm might model visitor activities, as shown in the right-hand picture of Exhibit 4-5. This model is very different from product-oriented businesses—your customer doesn't exactly drop a consultant in a shopping cart (unless the consultant really ticks off your customer, I guess).

In product-oriented businesses, the products are largely offered as-is (or can be somewhat customized), while a customer requiring consulting services is focused on explaining the problem to suppliers so they can solve it. Consulting customers need to Learn about their problem so they can understand what kinds of solutions can be provided, but they quickly move to Engage with a few possible consultants.

The Engage step typically includes a Request for Proposal (RFP) where customers describe their specific situations. The Engage step is being more frequently executed online, as customers describe their problems and provide contact information in Web forms.

The Select step, where the customer receives written responses to the RFP and selects a consultant to work with, is almost always done offline, as is the engagement itself, where the consultant and the customer Collaborate to solve the problem.

And while your consultants are solving the customer's problem, don't you think that they take the opportunity to point out three other areas where the customer could use some consulting? You bet they do. And then the customer typically shoos them away ("Just finish the job we hired you for without any more sales pitches…"). What happens next? In private, where there's no sales pressure, the customer probably starts looking at your company's Web site to Learn about these new potential problems, and the cycle starts all over again.

But maybe your Web site doesn't fall into any of these common categories. Can you still model it? Of course you can. (You guessed that, huh?) You just need to think clearly about what people do on your Web site. Sometime it's enough to model what customers do on your Web site and ignore modeling their offline behavior.

Exhibit 4-6 shows a specific example of a market awareness site for a children's cereal. The Web site is promoted on the cereal box itself and in TV ads for the cereal, leading kids to Discover the Web site. Once there, they Engage by reading stories and playing games that reinforce the brand as fun for kids. The goal of the site is to get kids to Enroll in a club by providing their mailing addresses. Club members are mailed a monthly newsletter with fun games for the kids, action figures to buy, and cereal discount coupons for mom. Because most cereal companies sell multiple cereals, the Enroll step might also trigger mail solicitations for other kids' cereal clubs, starting the cycle again.

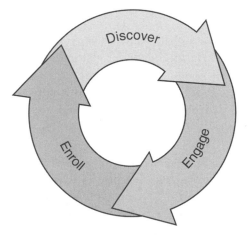

Exhibit 4-6   A behavioral model for an influencer site

If you're getting the idea that you can do whatever you want with behavioral models, you're right. Do it wrong quickly—draw your model for your business *now*. You don't need to hire a consultant. With a little creativity, you can identify what your customers are doing on your Web site.

And while I'm sure you've been enthralled so far by this chapter, you might be wondering exactly why I'm working so hard to identify the marketing and customer purposes of our Web sites. Don't worry. I'll spend the rest of the chapter showing you what you can do with this new-found knowledge about your site and your customers.

A Common Purpose

We've looked at your goals for your Web site, and we've looked at your customers' goals. Are marketers and customers working at cross-purposes, or is there common ground? (Hint: There *is* common ground.)

We should keep in mind that the tension between marketing goals and customer goals is nothing new. It's existed as long as marketing has existed.

The customer wants to walk into the store and buy milk, but the supermarket marketer (that was hard to say) decides that by putting the milk in the back of the store, it forces the shopper to walk past a passel of other items that might provoke a purchase. That's good marketing, right?

Well, maybe. It's good marketing right up to the day that your customer decides to go to the convenience store instead of walking to the back of your supermarket. Of course, hind-sight is 20/20 (or 20/15 with LASIK)—if you knew that moving the milk to the back of the store might lower sales, you might have decided against it.

The key idea here is that marketing can be successful only when customer needs are given top priority. In the end, what your customer wants wins. Your goal is to sell something along the way.

TOO MUCH OF A GOOD THING

Mark Hurst, in his excellent newsletter *Good Experience* (www.goodexperience.com), told a cautionary tale of marketing run amuck. One of Mark's customers, an auto research Web site, began to devote more and more space on its page to advertising and other revenue-generating purposes, leaving less space for the actual editorial content.

As Mark tells it, eventually so much advertising was being plastered on the home page that any relevant content was shoved to the lower-right of the page—the last part of the page that a reader's eyes will roam. The primary purpose a customer had for visiting the site, to find car prices and reviews, had seemingly been forgotten.

It didn't take much research to find out what customers thought of the changes. They hated how the site was little more than advertising and would gladly go to a competitor that gave them more of the content they were looking for.

Mark's client heeded his advice to refocus on the core purpose of the site to improve the customer experience. Only by helping customers reach their goals do marketers reach theirs.

Good marketing meets customers at their point of need. That's the common ground. In a world where marketers can no longer push messages indiscriminately at customers, your message must be found at the moment customers are interested.

Let's use search marketing as an example. Using your customer behavior model can help you target specific search keywords for your campaign. Imagine that you are the marketing manager for TurboTax for Intuit Inc. (the very successful maker of Quicken). Some prospective customers are clearly looking for a solution to the problem of filing their income taxes and might enter the search keywords "income tax return." These searchers are in the Learn activity. You can then imagine the search engine providing several different types of answers to that query:

- **How-To Information**—Advice from the government or other well-respected sources on how to fill out tax forms, usually in laymen's terms.

- **Tax Services**—Descriptions of accounting firms and tax preparation firms, such as H&R Block, that will fill out a tax return for a fee.

- **Tax Software**—Reviews of computer programs, such as TurboTax, that complete your tax return using a personal computer.

- **Comparisons**—Articles contrasting the approaches of doing it alone, using accounting and tax preparation firms, and using tax software to determine the best way to complete tax returns.

As the TurboTax marketing manager, you have undoubtedly placed pages on your site that explain the workings of computer tax software. Even better, you *could* place pages on your site that compare the advantages of tax preparation software versus having it prepared by professionals (or doing it by hand). Both types of content will help you get high rankings in search engines for the query "income tax return" (and related searches, such as "file tax return" or "income tax help").

But some searchers will be further along in the buying process. They might be searching for "computer tax software" because they have already decided how to solve their problem and are shopping for exactly the right solution. This kind of search is looking for the product category and is typical of those in the Shop activity. The pages you created on tax software to satisfy Learners will also serve you well here. In addition, pages devoted to the features of TurboTax might also rank well when searchers enter "tax software for businesses" or "macintosh tax software."

Other searchers know exactly what they are looking for. They are in the Buy activity—"buy turbotax" might literally be what they search for. For these queries, you'll want pages on your site that clearly show how to buy the product and perhaps display some special offers that might help people decide now. Because the customer has already decided on your product, your search marketing here is focused on selling directly from your site rather than having a retailer or other distributor make the sale.

Other searchers need help with your product. They are in the Use activity, which is a very common reason to visit a software manufacturer's Web site. Technical support issues trigger queries such as "turbotax printing error." And don't forget Intuit's favorite Use query: "turbotax upgrade" (which for tax software comes along every March). That's the kind of query that can close the loop in the cycle and return the customer to the Learn activity.

Why are we talking about all this stuff? Because this is the common ground between marketing and customer need. It makes no sense to try to scream "Save 10% on TurboTax!" when customers search for "income tax return." They aren't ready to buy yet, so they don't care about getting a bargain for something they don't know they need. Likewise, someone who enters "buy turbotax" doesn't want a comparison of using computer tax software versus H&R Block. *They* want that "10% off" coupon.

Meeting the customer at the point of need is Web marketing that works. You're not interrupting people trying to do something else. You're not trying to distract them with a canned marketing message. Finding the common ground between your customer's purpose and yours is the secret of marketing on the Web.

Look at Exhibit 4-7, for a different take on a behavioral model used by the marketing firm Digitas. Here you see the same kinds of steps we've been looking at, except the steps don't stop when the customer uses the product. The right marketing and product experiences lead customers to grow loyal—bringing them back around to the Learn step—but it does more. It allows you to sell other things to these loyal customers, too. You could imagine expanding the model to include customers recommending your product to others—unleashing the word of mouth marketing we discussed in Chapter 3 "Marketing Is a Conversation."

(Source: Digitas)

Exhibit 4-7   An extended behavioral model

By now, you might be eyeing these nice, neat models and saying to yourself, "If only things really went this smoothly!" And you are correct—people don't proceed in orderly fashion from one step to the next (in single file). As Sir Arthur Conan Doyle once wrote, "Depend upon it, there is nothing so unnatural as the commonplace." Real life is rarely as clean as shown here, but a simple model helps you analyze what is going on. Sometimes people really look for something and buy it when they find it, but purchases are often spread over several sessions on the Web, sometimes weeks apart for large purchases.

Let's look at a realistic scenario of how your customer model might work. With less than two months before the kids' winter break at school, Bill Payer wanted to get away. He and Molly couldn't afford a vacation the previous year, but they thought they could swing it this year if they did it on the cheap.

Bill fired up his Web browser and started surfing the travel search sites. Expedia, Orbitz, and Travelocity all had different prices for flights to warm places, but after half a dozen searches, Florida and Jamaica seemed to be the lowest-priced. Some of the flight times were more convenient than others, so Bill jotted down a few possibilities and talked it over with his family.

A week later, the family settled on Jamaica, and Bill hit the travel sites again. He found a low price for a flight from Hot Airways, known for its flights to warm climates and for hype-laden marketing. Bill decided to check the Hot Airways Web site to see if there was a lower price. Bingo! But he decided to double-check with Molly before buying, and she'd already gone to bed. The next day, Molly asked Bill if he checked the travel search sites for bundled deals that charge one price for the airfare and the hotel.

Bill got really busy at work, so it took a few days before he dutifully checked the bundle deals. He found a very low-priced package, but he checked a Jamaica travel Web site and found the hotel had mixed reviews. At that point, Bill checked again with Molly, and she nixed the bundle.

The next day Bill returned to Hot Airways and booked the reservations, although he was annoyed the tickets were $10 higher than when he looked originally. He then turned his attention to the hotel and rental car as the vacation planning continued.

So what's the moral of the story? Another purchase was made. The customer is marginally happy. It took a couple of weeks, and for most of that time, Hot Airways was blithely unaware that Bill was even in the market, and Bill would never even be able to reconstruct all the steps he took. Douglas Adams could have been describing a Web purchase when he said, "I might not have gone where I intended to go, but I think I have ended up where I intended to be."

Studies show, however, that Bill Payer was very typical of travel buyers. They tend to start their planning within eight weeks of their travel date. They go to a few travel search sites and perform an average of six searches, motivated by finding the lowest price, and they typically find the flight they ultimately buy two weeks before they book the tickets.

It's not only travel buyers that behave this way, however. High-risk and big-ticket purchases follow a "long and winding path" according to research by Yahoo! and the ad agency OMD, who found four typical paths to purchase:

- **Quick paths**—Little or no research, often for impulse purchases
- **Winding paths**—Comparison shopping with multiple vendors
- **Long paths**—Slow shopping to wait for new products or price drops
- **Long and winding paths**—Multiple vendors and delays for high-priced items

Because your customers would prefer a shorter, simpler purchase process, buying cycles that include long and winding paths would seem the ripest for marketing opportunity with better offers and a streamlined experience. Now, honestly, it's nice to quote research, and perhaps it is arbitrary to divide all Web purchases into four distinct paths, but this does make sense, doesn't it? People follow meandering, sometimes tortured paths when they make purchases, not some straight line through our sites, no matter how well-designed they are. So as we (perhaps simplistically) analyze customer activity through a site, remember real customer paths are messy.

Whatever the path, the Web offers a unique opportunity to discern your customer's needs by paying attention to what they do—that's where the numbers come in. Now that we have a model for what customers do, we can learn how to keep track of customer activity.

Measure Your Customer Activity

"You need to check your open rate and your bounce rate," advises an e-mail marketing expert. "Subscribers and comments tell you the most about how well your blog is doing," opines another wizard. "Until something better comes along, podcasts are best measured by download counts," a third guru offers.

Now, if this advice were wrong, it would be easy to tell you to ignore it. The problem is that all the advice is good, as far as it goes. As with any new area, Web marketing tactics are emerging (and changing) faster than anyone can figure out how to measure their effectiveness. And each new tactic seems to drag along its own measurement language, which can make things more precise for an expert but leave ordinary people "confuzzled."

So if you are stuck between confused and puzzled, don't worry. We can simplify things for clarity. If we end up *over*simplifying things a bit, that's the price you pay. As mathematician John von Neuman observed, "There's no sense in being precise when you don't even know what you're talking about."

Just as Einstein and others pursued the Unified Field Theory of Physics, we need to think about a Unified Field Theory of Metrics. (And when they give a Nobel Prize for

Web Analytics, I'm all set.) All of these competing metrics are just too confusing. Each of them has its place, but each relegates analysis to the realm of the expert instead of the practitioner. Let's look at metrics in a unified way across all marketing tactics to be able to easily analyze anything. Remember, every day new marketing tactics show up—the Web doesn't stand still. We need some organizing principles that help us think about any tactic in the same way.

To do that, we need to think about the basics of what we are measuring:

- **Did they see it?**—The first thing we want to know is if our content was viewed by the customer. Was the ad shown? Was the e-mail seen? Was the blog post viewed? We call this measurement the *impression*.
- **Did they choose it?**—If seen, was it acted upon? Did they click our message to go deeper? This one is called the *selection*.
- **Did they do it?**—What did we want the customer to do? Buy something? Fill out a contact form? Call our toll-free number? This metric is called the *conversion*.

Get ready for a little math. Here's why you care about these metrics. Suppose your Web page is seen 100 times (that's 100 impressions), and 40 of those people click deeper into your site (40 selections), with two people eventually buying from you (two conversions). Your job is to improve your results. What do you do?

You try to raise *everything*.

You try to raise impressions. Send out more e-mails, increase your paid search bidding, improve the rank of your organic search results, produce better copy to attract links, and anything else you can think of. Do whatever it takes to increase the number of impressions for your message. In general, the more your message is seen, the more conversions you'll get.

You try to raise selections. You improve your Web page and blog titles, write better copy, improve and personalize your offers, target your offers better, and anything else you can think of. Do whatever it takes to increase the number of selections for your message. In general, the higher the number of selections on your message, the more conversions you'll get.

You try to raise your conversions. You improve your copy, simplify your site navigation, upgrade your design, improve and personalize your offers, and anything else you can think of. And yeah, the more conversions you get, uh, the more conversions you get (and the more money you get).

We're going to spend Chapter 5, "The New Customer Relations," on how you improve all this stuff. But before we do, you need to understand how you *know* you're improving. It's not enough that the writer says the copy is better or the designer has a good reputation or that this is better than the offer that worked last year.

Changing is not the same as improving. The way you know any of these changes are actual improvements is by measuring the results. You count stuff. You count impressions, selections, and conversions, as we just discussed. Conversions are the most important of the three—wouldn't a store owner rather know how many sales were made than how many keys the cashier pressed? So counting conversions is up first.

Count Your Conversions

It all goes back to purpose. Depending what your goal is and what your customer's goal is, there are different ways to measure success. We will call these successful outcomes *conversions*. After we take a close look at what conversions are, we'll explore which conversions make sense for each kind of business.

Conversion is a traditional sales term that refers to converting prospects into customers. We can use the concept of conversion more broadly than just for sales. There is no reason you can't apply the same kind of conversion rate calculation to *any* goal for your Web site. Instead of discussing only sales conversions, you can track *Web conversions*—any Web event that fulfills your and your customer's purposes.

Earlier in this chapter, I showed that every Web site has a goal for its customers to achieve, which we are now calling a Web conversion. Now, let's measure the effectiveness of each site by *counting* its Web conversions. For example, your Web site's purpose might be creating as many leads to an offline channel as possible. Perhaps you've placed a form on your Web site that allows visitors to provide their contact information, which gets routed to your offline sales force. You can treat each completed contact form as a Web conversion.

Now that you've got the concept of Web conversions, we can examine the same list of Web site purposes that we covered earlier to see how Web conversions can be measured for each one.

If your site's purpose is Web sales, then one conversion metric you should count is the number of Web orders taken by your site. To analyze what a visitor is doing on his way to becoming one of your "conversions," we again turn to the behavior models we discussed earlier in the chapter. But we can think of them differently now—we can think of them as *Web Conversion Cycles* because they illustrate the steps your customers take on the way to conversions.

Some Web sites truly engage in online sales, but they might not offer the classic shopping cart experiences. Shipping company DHL, as shown in Exhibit 4-8, optimizes the customer's task of scheduling a pickup for a package. Yes, that is, in effect, a sale for DHL, but it's more than that. Simplifying the "schedule a pickup" Web task raises customer satisfaction and lowers DHL's costs compared to scheduling done by phone. DHL can use its Web Conversion Cycle to model customer behavior whether it calls the task "Buy" or not.

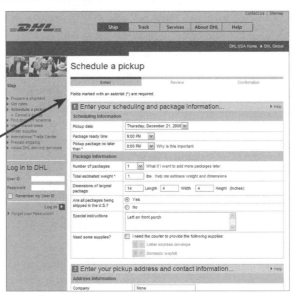

DHL recognizes that marketing is about more than selling—it's about helping their customers get what they want. Customers can find their task, such as "scheduling a pickup," right on DHL's home page.

DHL can be confident that customers who click on "schedule a pickup" want to complete that task, and DHL can measure how many people actually do complete it.

DHL can redesign their form to reduce the number of people who abandon the page, and measure whether the new designs improve the completion rate. Each completed form is one less phone call to their call center.

DHL can measure the confirmation page as its Web conversion. Its effectiveness in converting customers drives sales and lowers cost of sales from phone scheduling.

Exhibit 4-8 A sale by any other name rings the same cash register.

Regardless of which version of the Web Conversion Cycle is right for your Web sales business, it is very simple for you to calculate your success. The same e-commerce system that takes your customer's order can count the number of sales that you make from your site. As you improve your site, you'll see the number of orders go up.

But even if your Web site's primary purpose is Web sales, the Web might drive a significant number of offline sales. As we discussed earlier, various studies make it a safe bet that half of all sales driven by Web sales sites actually close offline. So let's tackle offline sales and leads.

If the purpose of your Web site is offline sales or leads, you have more thinking to do about which events comprise your Web conversions. It's easy to count the purchases on your Web site but difficult to identify when a customer starts on your Web site but then buys offline. No matter what you do, you will never have perfect measurements, but there are some very basic ways to tie offline sales to the Web:

- **Provide a special phone number**—If your goal is to shift Web visitors to your call center to take the order by phone, you can use some simple tricks to tie the call to your Web site, such as displaying a phone number that appears only on your Web site and is not used in TV or print ads or any other materials. That way, anyone who uses that number must have come from your site. A variant on this is to call your regular number but advise them to "Ask for Operator 123" or "Ask for Alice." (Not all of your visitors will do this, however, so you might have them "Ask for Alice to receive a free mouse pad with your computer.")

- **Contact me**—If you can entice your customer to complete a request to be contacted (usually by e-mail), you can tie any resultant sale to the Web.

- **Call me**—You can provide a form on your Web site that lets Web visitors complete their contact information so you can call them. IBM has had success with a "Call Me Now" button. When the button is pressed, the customer is prompted to supply a phone number, and an IBM telephone salesperson calls the customer within a few minutes.

- **Pass to another company**—If you're an affiliate marketer or you pass your customers to other companies to close, doing so online allows you to track them. Your partner's site will know where the customer came from and can let you know whether they buy or not.

- **Bring this printout**—As discussed, automakers encourage customers to select the color and options for their car before coming to the dealer. The dealer can note any customer who brought in that printout for tracking purposes. Customers will do almost anything to spend less time with a car salesman, but if customers actually *like* your salespeople, you might have to offer a discount coupon or something else that is more motivating. If your product does not require extensive customization, it makes more sense to offer an online coupon for a freebie or a discounted price the customer can print and bring to the store.

- **Request for quote**—Some automaker sites also offer an RFQ capability, where the car the customer "built" can be shown to a local dealer who prices it. The customer needs to fill out contact information to receive the quote, so any sales made to this customer can then be accurately tracked as assisted by the Web site.

If, as you read this list, you are thinking that these techniques are excellent choices for your Web conversions, you're catching on! If you're not currently using these techniques to tie offline sales to the Web, here's a chance to do it wrong quickly.

WHAT IF I CAN'T TRACK MY OFFLINE SALES BACK TO MY WEB SITE?

Not to worry. If you don't have any systems in place that let you track your offline sales back to your Web site, all is not lost. First, it isn't that hard to set up special phone numbers or print discount coupons, but maybe you can't get your organization to take even those minimal steps. If you truly can't track actual sales instigated by the Web, the next-best thing is estimating them. How to go about estimating depends on your business (as always), but there are a few possibilities:

- **Ask customers when they buy**—If you close most of your sales on the phone, add a question to the call center script to ask the customer if they used your Web site before calling. U.S. technology retailer CompUSA has surveyed customers at their store checkouts to prove that their product Web feeds truly drive sales in physical stores.

- **Update your warranty cards**—If your product already requires the return of a warranty card, change your questions to ask about use of your Web site.

- **Add a question to a survey**—Your business might regularly survey your customers. Add one question to the survey to see whether they used the Web site before their last purchase.

Are these methods perfect? Nope. It's another example of doing it wrong quickly. None of these methods are as scientific as tracking actual sales, but they are better than nothing. If possible, however, you should try to eventually implement systems that accurately track sales back to the Web.

But your Web conversions might number far more than those listed here, especially for lead-driven businesses. Suppose you offer a consulting service on globalized supply chains. You can't sell that on the Web. What's your Web conversion?

Well, it could be several of the things in the list, but maybe you have a terrific white paper that explains why your consulting is so valuable, or maybe you have several case studies from satisfied customers. If you do some market research, you might find that many of your engagements come from people who downloaded those Adobe PDF files from your site. Maybe those downloads are important Web conversions, and you should be highlighting them on your site to drive higher sales.

You might need to think even more expansively about your conversions. If you know that customers who receive your monthly e-mail newsletter buy twice as much as those who don't, might it make sense to highlight the newsletter much more?

Suppose a significant number of your customers come to your Web site to check their order status or to see if their last check was received. Each of these activities can be tracked as conversions, too. Sites that satisfy all of their customers' various purposes are more likely to engender loyal customers. Each successful experience builds your brand. (Guess what happens when your site thwarts your customer's purpose.)

Once you know what your conversions are, you must figure out how to actually count them as they occur. Your e-commerce system should have no problem counting Web sales, but you might have to work harder at counting other conversions. Soon, we explain how Web metrics software works and how it can count conversions and lots of other things.

Identifying all of your Web conversions helps you see which customer outcomes are worth counting. Your next step is to understand the conversion process so that you know what else to count.

The Conversion Process

I talked earlier about how Web metrics can sometimes confuse people who don't do it for a living, so I am oversimplifying them here to get the basics straight. If you master this level and you want to wade in deeper, there's no shortage of information available, some of which is highlighted in Chapter 9, "This Stuff Changes Too Fast."

Exhibit 4-9 diagrams a simple "Bert and Ernie" level conversion process, highlighting all the activity that can occur on and off your Web site leading to a Web conversion. Let's walk through that chart and understand the basic conversion process.

At the top of the chart is the box labeled *marketing impression*. (I made this name up, so if your metrics experts don't recognize the term, don't question their expertise.) We discussed what an impression is—a count of whether a customer saw something. A *marketing impression* counts something your customers saw to drive them to your Web site.

So the first thing you want to count is impressions that can lead to your site. You want to know how many times that banner ad was shown. How many e-mails were seen? How many blog posts were sent to feed readers? You get the idea—they're all marketing impressions of one kind or another. As was mentioned earlier, you'll generally get more conversions if you have more marketing impressions, so count them to ensure they're increasing over time.

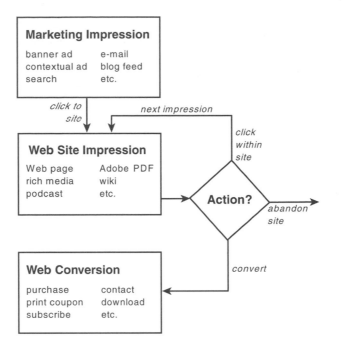

Exhibit 4-9   The "Bert and Ernie" conversion process

Usually measuring marketing impressions is straightforward, but not always. Marketers that use ad networks such as Google's DoubleClick sometimes find that their Web metrics software can't trace a customer who clicks on a banner ad all the way to a conversion, so consult with your ad network and your Web metrics vendor to ensure that they can work together.

The next thing you want to measure is the *selection*, which most people call a *clickthrough*. Customers decide whether or not to click every marketing impression. You want to know how many times they clicked. The reason I usually favor the term *selection* in this book, rather than always calling it a *clickthrough*, is that selections can occur without a click, when you use Ajax technology (or Flash). If you can remember that a clickthrough does not always demand an actual click, as shown in Exhibit 4-10, you can call it whatever you want.

For each selection, a *Web site impression* occurs. (I made that name up, too, in case you are wondering.) A *Web site* impression is something your customers saw when they came to your Web site. Most metrics systems call this a *page view*, but rich media (such as Flash and Ajax) are creating customer experiences outside of traditional Web pages (which metrics systems don't count as page views). Regardless of whether techies think of it as a page view or not, you want to know what your customer saw.

With Ajax user interfaces, your customer can mouse over a link and get a content impression. So, *selections* don't require clicks—we need to measure these content impressions, also.

Exhibit 4-10   Selection without clicks

Now, in this chart it appears as though everyone who comes to your Web site started with a marketing impression, but it's not so. Some have bookmarked your site, others guessed your URL, and still others followed a link from another site. You can even think of print or TV ads as marketing impressions, but we just can't measure each time one is shown to someone. In truth, many customers can come to your site (causing a Web site impression to be tallied) without your being able to count any marketing impression that preceded it.

And every time a customer clicks something to see more from your site, that action racks up another Web site impression. So if someone lands on your home page and clicks four other pages before leaving, that's registered as five Web site impressions.

Not all clicks are created equal, however. If your customers are participating—updating your wiki, commenting on your blog, or adding a review to your product page—rather than merely consuming information, they are demonstrating more engagement. Some Web sites track those clicks separately from the run-of-the-mill clicks that merely display a new page. (Why running the mill is so boring, I'll never know.)

As the chart shows, clicking within your site to see another Web site impression is not the only possible customer action. Rather than clicking to view new content, the customer might abandon the site by going somewhere else, or, more happily, your customer might complete a Web conversion—by purchasing a product online or completing other tasks that fulfill the marketer's purpose for the Web site. (Do keep in mind, however, that many sales occur offline with no Web conversion, which looks like the customer abandoned the site.)

By thinking about the conversion process in this way, you start to view your content differently. Each marketing and Web impression must entice selections—clicks to intermediate content and clicks to final Web conversions. You can think of the job of each impression to be to persuade the customer to take the next step—the click to deeper content or to a conversion. The consultancy FutureNow even describes the design of content as "persuasion architecture," to highlight this point.

If you take on your customer's experience impression by impression, striving to raise the percentage of people that click through each piece of content (commonly called the *clickthrough rate*), you'll gradually raise your conversions over time.

That's your "Bert and Ernie" tour through Web metrics. You want to count when people are exposed to your marketing message (marketing impressions) and when they see your Web content (Web site impressions). You also want to count which ones they click (selections), and you want to know when they convert (Web conversions).

Once you have that information, you can discern which content seems to be working—it gets a high clickthrough rate when it is shown, and it is associated with higher conversions. You can also make decisions about which of your changes actually worked, by examining metrics before and after each change. That's part of doing it wrong quickly—you need to measure results to see how wrong it is. That way you can fix it. If you then change the content, and the clickthrough rate goes up, for example, that's probably good. By keeping track of clickthrough rate and other metrics, you can grade your successes and failures.

So how do you collect your Web metrics?

You need software that tracks your customers' activity on the Web. Most Web sites have software that tracks *Web metrics* (which they sometimes call *Web analytics*), such as WebTrends, Omniture, CoreMetrics, and many others. Most metrics systems can count any Web event as a Web conversion. (You'll have to change your offline processes to track your offline sales conversions back to the Web.)

If your site doesn't have a metrics system, get one. If you think you can't afford one, start with Google Analytics—it's free. It might not be the best metrics system, but it's better than flying blind. (Yes, yes, do it wrong quickly.)

You might wonder why you need these fancy metrics systems to spot what's important. After all, your Webmaster says, "I read the server logs every once in a while, so if there's something you should know about, I'll spot it." Unfortunately, the "scan the logs" approach is akin to feeling confident you'll spot your luggage on the arrivals carousel because you know it's black and has wheels. You're more likely to miss what you are looking for than you are to find it. A computer is much better at tracking the minutiae than any human being, but the computer won't analyze what the metrics *mean*. For that you need people.

You might have someone at your company that counts this stuff already—a "Web Analyst" or a "Web Metrics Analyst" or the "Director of Web Analytics." There's no standard name yet. When you meet your metrics guru, you'll understand why Nietzche said, "There are no facts, only interpretations."

Metrics experts understand statistics in a very deep way and might find it challenging to explain things simply. Certainly, many exceptions exist, but some numbers people are not strong communicators. They also might not be comfortable interpreting what they find, leaving it to you to understand this deep stuff and make sense of it.

If so, you might need to fight a battle over simplicity. Your metrics experts might be appalled at how impressions, selections, and conversions oversimplify their sainted metrics. Try to negotiate a truce: The gurus can count in as complex a fashion as possible as long as they simplify it when they explain it to you. That way business people can understand the data and make informed decisions, rather than rely on a metrics guru because no one else understands. (If your metrics person calls this oversimplification "the last straw," tell him to drink straight from the cup.)

Web marketing should *not* be run by the IT department any more than your telesales should be run by the guy who maintains the telephone wiring closet. In Chapter 8, "This Won't Work Where I Work," we'll talk in more detail about how to create a working partnership with your metrics experts. If you have no metrics experts at all, that's a very different problem, but I'll explain how to encourage a metrics culture within your company in Chapter 8 also.

If numbers and technology give you the willies, feel free to skip the next section. But if you can stand it, hang in for the explanation of how Web metrics are collected. You'll especially appreciate the way that knowledge helps you communicate with your Web metrics guru.

Count Your Impressions and Selections

First, the good news: Counting selections is usually not very difficult. Your Web metrics software can count the clicks made on any Web page on your site. They can also count selections that get people *to* your site by examining the *referrer* for each page view. The referrer is the actual URL of the Web page viewed prior to your page.

Clearly, referrers can be used to see whether people followed links to your page from other pages within your site or from pages on other sites. Your metrics software provides special support for search referrals—referrals that come from a URL known to be a search engine (such as www.yahoo.com)—by capturing the search keyword the searcher used. So you can accurately count the number of searches that come to your site from each search engine for each individual keyword. Your metrics expert can explain how counting these *referrals* help you measure the selections for almost any impression.

Now for the bad news. You were warned that Web metrics can be complicated and that we've been oversimplifying things here. Now, let's go just one level deeper to expose some of the ways that sometimes something as simple as an impression can be difficult to accurately count.

The first complexity starts with the names used by metrics experts. We've used the name *impression* to denote any display of content, but the experts don't always do so. Sure, they use the word *impression* for advertising—banner ads, contextual ads, and paid search ads. But where's the sport in that? They need new names for impressions, such as *page views* for Web pages and *opens* for e-mails. Despite the experts' nomenclature, page views and opens are nothing more than impressions.

The multitude of names is the easy part, though. What's truly complex about impressions is how hard they can be to count. Take the *page view* as an example. Because Web pages are assembled from many different pieces of content, Web metrics software requires one more piece of content to each page that has no use except to count that the page was shown. Variously known as *single-pixel tracking* or *Web beacons*, this technique depends on your Webmaster adding a one-pixel image file to each Web page on your site. When each page is shown, the metrics software notices that the image file was displayed and counts that as a surrogate for a page view. Because the image is just one pixel, your customer never notices it. That way, Web page impressions can be counted using this technique for tracking page views.

But it gets even tougher. Let's take Web feeds, such as RSS, that are used whenever someone subscribes to a blog. Your customer is using a reader (sometimes called a blog reader or RSS reader or feed reader), such as Bloglines, to look at all subscribed blogs. When a particular blog is selected, your customer can read the individual blog posts from within the reader, as shown in Exhibit 4-11.

The problem is that no metrics can be easily gathered from within blog readers, so no one knows for sure how many posts are actually read. You can take a guess that every subscriber sees each post, but that surely overstates the number of impressions. Geeks are working on adapting the single-pixel tracking technique to register a page view when blog posts are displayed within the blog reader, but until then we have to estimate based on *subscribers*.

Customers can use Bloglines or another feed reader to quickly scan the posts sent to them for each blog they subscribe to. If they prefer, customers can click through to the blog's Web site to look at the post, but they don't have to.

Exhibit 4-11   How blog posts are read in blog readers

Some metrics experts suggest that you send short excerpts of your blog posts in your blog feed, rather than the full posts. Doing so makes it easy to count impressions of the full post because customers click through to your Web site to read it, thus making it as easy to count as any other Web page view. But many usability experts decry this practice because customers prefer to read everything in their feed readers, without bouncing back and forth to your Web site. Don't annoy your customers just to solve a measurement problem—just accept that blog feed impression counts are not terribly precise.

E-mail is even more complicated to measure than blogs because so many steps happen before your customer clicks through to your Web site, as shown in Exhibit 4-12. When you send out a group of targeted e-mails for your campaign, you can count how many you sent. But that doesn't mean that each one was received. To know how many are received, you must monitor how many e-mails *bounce*—get returned to you as undeliverable. So the number you send less the number bounced tells you the number delivered.

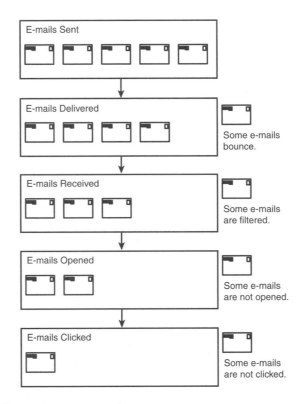

Exhibit 4-12 How e-mail campaigns are measured

Unfortunately, all delivered e-mail is not received. E-mail spam filters block many messages from reaching their recipients, even when those messages are *not* spam. Some are blocked by mail servers; others by spam filters on each individual customer's personal computer. Usually, spam filters do not return flagged e-mail to the sender, so you'll never know how many e-mails you sent were never received.

You can estimate the number received by subtracting bounced e-mails from sent e-mails, but you know it is an overestimate. You can use that number as the e-mail "inbox" impressions—that's the number of e-mails that were seen in customer inboxes.

Some of those e-mails are opened—this is usually referred to as the *open rate*, but it isn't any different from a clickthrough rate on any content. If you deliver a lot of e-mails but few of them are opened, you might not have the best e-mail subject line.

If you're wondering how anyone can measure how many e-mails are opened, remember that e-mail can be sent in the form of a Web page, and the single-pixel tracking technique can be applied to it as long as the customer is connected to the Internet when opening the mail. Unfortunately, the anti-spam technology used in some e-mail systems is beginning to block images from being displayed, defeating this measurement technique. Measured open rates dropped 16 percent during 2005, but because click rates remained the same, experts believe the open rate drop is caused by image blocking technology.

Once the e-mail is opened, this is *another* impression—this time of the contents of the e-mail itself. If your e-mails are routinely opened, but you get few selections to your Web site, then you need to work on your e-mail design, copy, and offer.

E-mail is complicated, huh? You can measure two impressions (seeing the subject line in the inbox and seeing the entire mail message), with neither of them actually called impressions by the experts. And the measurements themselves are not the most precise either, as an example can demonstrate.

Take a simple e-mail campaign. Suppose you send out 1,000 e-mail messages, but 200 of them bounce, leaving 800 messages delivered. Let's further suppose that of those 800 delivered, 400 of them are opened, and 80 of them are clicked. What's the click rate for that campaign? Eight percent (80 divided by 1,000)? Ten percent (80 divided by 800)? Twenty percent (80 divided by 400)? It depends on whom you ask. Make sure that you understand the calculation behind any measurement you need to rely on and standardize the definitions of these measurements within your company. Which definition you pick isn't important as long as everyone understands it and consistently uses the same one.

Neither is measuring podcasts simple. Podcasts must be downloaded from a Web site and listened to on an iPod or a personal computer. Your metrics expert can tell you if your podcast was downloaded but not whether anyone ever listened to it. Metrics gurus are experimenting with using voluntary surveys of podcast listeners that install software to track what they listen to (similar to how television ratings are measured), but it's not clear how widespread or accurate such an approach will become.

Perhaps the toughest impression of all to measure is the organic search impression. Search engines display the title of your page in the search results, along with a "snippet," made up of text extracted from your page that contains the searcher's keyword. How do you know when search engines show your Web page in its results?

It's not that easy to tell. Some search engines offer keyword tools that tell you how many searches it performed for popular keywords in the last month, but you can only guess at how many times your site was shown.

You could decide to count an impression for any result on the first page of search results (the top 10), although this is a very wild guess. Moreover, search results change frequently, so it's not very easy to estimate organic search impressions. Even simpler might be to treat every search as a potential impression because whether your page was not shown or not clicked, it's still a missed opportunity that you'd want to address.

In the future, when search is personalized so that each searcher gets results tailored just for them, only the search engines themselves will know what search results were displayed. It's possible that the search engines will sell this information to hungry marketers to settle the question of organic search impressions once and for all.

I warned you that this stuff was a wee bit complicated, so it's summarized for you in Exhibit 4-13. The Web keeps changing to make it even more complex, unfortunately. Even Web pages, which we thought were relatively simple, are getting harder to measure. Increasingly, Web pages are being personalized, with different content being displayed for different customers. When you personalize, you really want to track what content was displayed, not what *page*. You want to know how many times the offer for "free shipping" was shown rather than the one for "10% off"—you want those impressions counted individually, not rolled up into one number for all the ads shown on the same page.

Personalization isn't the only factor complicating measurements of the Web page. More and more, Web content isn't made up of Web pages. Rich media content, including video, Flash, and Ajax don't lend themselves to be counted as page views—they're not pages. Even Adobe PDF files aren't that easy to count, especially when they consist of many physical printed pages.

These complexities are not the marketer's problem. Make friends with your Web metrics experts and let them solve the problem. You just want to know whether the customer saw your message, chose your message, and converted. Insist on getting that answer for every piece of content you create, and you'll be fine. To get that answer, work closely with your metrics guru.

You've undoubtedly noticed that many of these answers are not terribly precise. As you were reading this section, you probably noticed how often we had to guess at something or assume something else. That's because even though the Web allows you to measure everything, it doesn't always allow you to measure everything *precisely*.

For most marketers, that's not a big issue. Marketers know that numbers are rarely precise, and getting a good idea of what the numbers mean is close enough. After all, as imprecise as online metrics might be, they are typically far more accurate than offline ones. But this lack of precision might be very troubling to your metrics expert. Remember that anyone interested enough in numbers to specialize in metrics holds precision dear—maybe too dear.

Content	Impressions	Comments
Web pages	Page views	Page views don't tell you exactly which content appeared on the page, nor does it tell you how much of a Flash demo was shown.
E-mail (in inbox)	E-mails delivered (e-mails sent less e-mails bounced)	The number of e-mails delivered overstates the number of e-mails viewed in the inbox because spam filters hide some delivered e-mails before the customer can see them.
E-mail (full message opened)	Page views	Page views can be tracked for opened e-mails only when the e-mail is sent in Web format (as an HTML page) and only when the customer is online when opening the e-mail.
Wikis	Page views	
Banner ads	Impressions	
Contextual ads	Impressions	
Paid search	Impressions	
Organic search	Keyword volume for pages ranked in top 10	Organic search impressions are the most imprecise metric in this table. Most metrics experts don't track them.
Blog feeds	Subscribers	The number of subscribers overstates this metric because not all subscribers see each blog post.
Podcasts	Downloads	No reliable way yet exists to measure whether the podcast was actually listened to after being downloaded.

Exhibit 4-13   Web metrics, simplified

You need to help your numbers person get over the lack of precision by explaining that it's better to make decisions based on imprecise numbers than on no numbers at all, the way marketers did in the bad old days. Admittedly, that's a low bar to jump over, but that's why we can live with imprecision.

Jim Sterne, a world expert in Web metrics, likes to say that "Web analytics are not precise, but they are true." What he means is that they are close enough to make decisions on. The reason for this magic is the *trend*.

The trend is your friend.

Let's take an example. You already know that the number of impressions of blog posts read in feed readers is nothing more than a guess using the number of subscribers. For various reasons that are discussed later, it's hard to know the exact number of subscribers. And you know that some subscribers don't look at every post (just because a certain percentage of any population fails to do whatever you are measuring). So you're *really* shooting in the dark when estimating blog feed impressions.

But suppose you know that you have 10 percent more subscribers this month than last month and that you're up 23 percent in three months? That, dear reader, is a trend. You *still* don't know precisely how many subscribers you have. And you still don't know how many subscribers actually read each blog post sent, but whatever errors creep into the numbers are probably the same errors month after month. So the trend of how subscriber counts are changing over the last few months is a trend as well—and it is plenty good to make a decision on. (In this case, you want to give your blog writer a raise and see how you can do even more of what's working.)

If, after reading this, you think this is common sense, good. Just know that you might have to convince a few experts along the way that are not comfortable with lack of precision. Experts who should know better, such as *BusinessWeek,* have declared Web metrics to be "a crapshoot" because different experts count the numbers differently. That's not unlike questioning time measurement because you found several clocks that disagree. To be fair, the magazine found *large* discrepancies between estimates, but what was ignored was the power of the trend.

Make sure your metrics guru understands how critical it is to estimate, guess, and just plain "take a shot." That's the essence of "do it wrong quickly." Remember the advice of sports writer Damon Runyon: "The race may not always be to the swift nor the victory to the strong, but that's how you bet." Bet on the trend.

Measure Your Customer Relationships

Impressions, selections, and conversions are about activity, not about people. Web marketing is about relationships, however, so we need to measure them, too.

Depending on your business, you might have a rich set of relationships with your Web customers. They might start out as anonymous visitors to your site, but they might register their identities to become members. They can sign up for Web feeds and newsletters to become subscribers, and of course they can make purchases to become true customers. When they buy from you over and over, they've marked themselves as loyal customers.

We've thoroughly covered purchases so far, so let's check out how to count subscribers. E-mail subscribers are simple to determine—whatever program you use to send out your e-mail will have a list of all intended recipients. When you try to count the subscribers for Web feeds, however, it gets tougher.

Most blogs and other feeds allow the subscriber to choose the format of the feed (providing buttons for XML, RSS, or Atom, for example), which makes it harder for the feed owner to count the number of subscribers. Feed aggregation companies, such as Google's Feedburner, have arisen to solve this problem. Feedburner and its competitors provide a single subscribe button for you to place on your site, with

Feedburner providing the best format to each subscriber's individual feed reader. Because all subscribers go through Feedburner, the feed owner can be provided with statistics to show the number of subscribers, for example.

But it gets even *more* complex. Yahoo!, AOL, and other companies often aggregate feeds for their subscribers so that when an AOL user subscribes to a feed, AOL might provide that feed from its own cache of feeds rather than alerting Feedburner. While an efficient way of providing feeds to subscribers, it guarantees under-counting of subscribers—possibly by 25 percent. This is a good time to remember the wisdom of trends—use whatever feed subscription metrics you can lay your hands on. (Repeat after me, "The trend is my friend. The trend is my friend.") Do metrics wrong quickly.

Now let's focus on the difference between visitors and members—the difference between anonymity and identity.

Web marketing is no different than any other kind of marketing in its quest to learn more about customers. When your local supermarket gives its customers a discount card to present at the cash register, its purpose is to determine identity to build up a purchase history. Customers give up a little privacy to get the discount, with the marketer calculating that the increase in customer knowledge is well worth the cost.

The Web equivalent of a discount card is the user identifier, or *userID*. If you can convince your anonymous visitors to register with your site, you can be sure of their identities. You can ask for names, e-mail addresses, demographic information, and anything else you want to know. You require anyone coming to your Web site to "sign in" with their userID so that you can track all of their activity, knowing who they are.

Sounds easy, right?

Well, it is, as long as you can convince people to do it. The supermarket offers discounts for people to apply for a card and to show it at each purchase. You need to provide sufficient incentives for people to register and sign in. Most sites don't offer enough to convince customers to sign in every time they visit. Some people are concerned about giving up privacy, and others are in too much of a hurry to sign in.

Because we can't depend on every visitor to sign in to tie their activity together, most sites rely on less intrusive means of identifying visitors. For example, up until now, we've counted Web site impressions (which are typically called page views), but we've paid no attention to just who exactly is viewing those pages.

Most Web metrics software can identify a series of pages that have been viewed by the same visitor by using *cookies*. The Web metrics software "drops" a cookie file on each visitor's computer when she enters the site. This file contains a unique identifier not shared by any other computer's cookie. The metrics software reads the identifier from the cookie file each time a page is shown and remembers which computer viewed that page.

HOW THE COOKIE CRUMBLES

Cookies are used by nearly all Web sites, if only by their Web metrics software. Cookies tell your metrics software which computer is taking the action it is counting (seeing an impression, making a selection, or a conversion). So, by using cookies, your metrics software can trace the path taken through your site, and customers don't need to sign in with their userIDs.

So what's not to like?

Well, the first thing is that cookies measure computers, not people. If several people use the same computer, your metrics software can't tell who's who. Likewise, if one person uses multiple computers, your metrics software won't detect that either. So while we act like cookies identify which people come to our Web sites, they only identify which computers do.

But don't worry—it gets worse. Some people set their browsers to block cookies so that they always surf the Web anonymously. Your metrics software can continue to count impressions, selections, and conversions, but it can't determine which computer is behind them.

Relatively few people block cookies. *Many* erase cookies. Many people delete cookies for privacy purposes. Anti-spyware programs eat cookies also.

When cookies are blocked or dumped, anyone using that computer becomes anonymous again. Metrics software has no idea what those computers have done in the past. That's why you really do want to get people to register and sign in. Registered, signed-in users are people, not just computers. They can move from computer to computer, and metrics software will still know them. They can share computers with others, and the metrics software will still know them.

If you can establish a trusted relationship with your customers and provide real value in return, you can entice them to register and to sign in. If not, cookies are a lot better than nothing.

Identifying visitors allows metrics software to provide you with better information. Now, instead of merely counting Web site impressions, you can count the number of *visits* to your site. Visits, called *sessions* by some metrics software, let you see how many people are coming, not just how many pages were viewed by all people.

For example, two Web sites might each show 100 Web site impressions, but one has four visits with 25 impressions each, while another might have ten visits that average ten impressions each. If you count just impressions, all you know is that 100 pages were viewed. If you count visits, you know that one site got four visits, but they stayed and looked around for a while, while the other site got ten visits from people who looked at fewer pages in each visit. This information is critical because you can't directly get more conversions from more impressions—you get more conversions from more visits.

In addition to identifying visits, you can also track the number of visitors (sometimes called *unique visitors* or *traffic*) because you can track whether the *same* visitor has returned to your site multiple times. So the metrics report could show 100 Web site

WHEN MORE IS NOT MERRIER

Web metrics software accurately counts impressions, selections, and conversions, but to accurately count visits and visitors, you must use a *single* metrics facility across your entire site. While small sites would undoubtedly do so, very large Web sites with hundreds of thousands of pages might implement different metrics software for different parts of the site. If you are in this situation, collecting accurate measurements across your entire site is impossible.

To see why, imagine that you have two metrics systems, one used in the sales part of your site and the other in the support area. In this situation, you can't just add up the number of visitors in each system to get your total because each system drops a visitor cookie when it sees a new visitor, so any visitor whose visit crosses both sales and support pages will be double counted. It will seem like two separate visits when it was, in fact, only one. If you have more than two systems, the problem is worse. Double-counting your visits lowers your reported conversion rate and makes your efforts appear less effective than they are because sales are reported accurately, but the number of visitors that created the sales is artificially high.

If you must live with a situation where multiple metrics facilities are used for the same Web site, just keep in mind that the visit and visitor numbers will not be accurate when added up for the total site. It's *still* better to use those inaccurate numbers than to ignore them. Remember that you can perform trend analysis on even inaccurate numbers because the inaccuracies are relatively constant. For example, if you add up visitor totals across three separate metrics systems, they won't be right because some of those "visitors" are actually the *same* people who headed into different parts of your site. Regardless, if you see that you added up 30 percent more visitors this month than you added up last month, you can probably conclude that *something* good is happening, even though you really can't be sure that the improvement is actually 30 percent as opposed to 22 percent or 45 percent. It's definitely worth the effort to get to a single metrics system so that your numbers *are* accurate, but do use whatever data you have, no matter how imperfect. It's better than nothing.

impressions in ten visits by eight different visitors because a couple of those eight visitors had more than one visit. This is important also because, for many Web sites, people tend to visit multiple times before they convert, so knowing the number of *new* versus *returning* visitors can tell you even more than tracking visits alone.

Before concluding this chapter, we must tackle a metric that is often discussed but is of far less importance than is usually assumed. You might often hear about a business raising its *conversion rate*, the ratio of "lookers" to "buyers." For a Web sales business, you can think of the conversion rate as the number of orders (counted by your e-commerce system) divided by the number of visitors (calculated by your Web metrics software). Raising the sales conversion rate means that you book more sales with the same number of customers coming into the "store" (your Web site).

People talk about conversion rate a lot, but different people calculate it differently. Some argue that conversion rate should be based on conversions per visit, others on conversions per visitor because you can't convert every visit—people return multiple times for a single purchase. But the right calculation might depend on your business—if I come back three days in a row to amazon.com, I might have made three purchases, but if I did likewise at Honda.com, it is unlikely I really might have bought three cars in three days.

Regardless of how it's calculated, you'll see so-called experts fixate on conversion rates. They'll focus on a drop in your conversion rate as the most salient fact about your site. It's not. After all, George Washington's brother is the uncle of his country, but who cares?

Conversion rate is, well, *overrated*. Remember that whatever your business, you are not trying to maximize conversion *rate*—you are trying to maximize *conversions*. If you lowered your conversion rate, but raised your conversions, that's a good thing. Likewise for clickthrough rate versus clicks and profit margin versus profits. It's OK to raise your clicks and profits while rates go down.

So what are conversion rates good for? Projections. You can use conversion rate to project increases in conversions. For example, if you improve your search marketing so that a thousand more people come to your site each day, you can multiply that increase by your conversion rate to project your rise in conversions. If your conversion rate is four percent, you can multiply 1000 by four percent to project you'll get 40 more conversions.

For that reason, it's worthwhile to watch your conversion rate, but not to fixate on it. Obviously, if you increase the number of people coming to your site and also improve your conversion rate, that's fantastic, but often bringing greater numbers to your site means you're being less selective. If you are drawing from wider markets, your conversion rate might drop because your new visitors might not be your perfect target market. As long as you raise conversions, who cares about conversion rate drops?

Conversion rates also fluctuate because many visitors to your Web site have no interest in converting. At ibm.com, for example, 60 percent of visits to the site are for support for products already owned. A small percentage of those visits might be converted to sales—perhaps to add memory to a server or to buy a new one—but the vast majority of technical support visits won't end in a sale even if IBM does everything right. So IBM is better off looking at its conversion rate within the 40 percent of people who might buy something because an increase in support visits might lead you to conclude your conversion rate is dropping (and something is wrong) when maybe what is happening is your Web support improved, and fewer people are calling on the phone to solve their problems.

This is a good way to end this section on measuring customer relationships. You need to think about what relationships you have with your customers and how to improve them. If you focus on what your customers want to do and help them achieve their purpose each time they come to your Web site, they'll be far more likely to buy from you.

Summary

And that's a wrap on this chapter as well. We've covered a lot of ground (although I'm not sure why we want ground to be covered), learning the three major steps to measure your online marketing:

- **Find your purpose**—Every Web site has a purpose, and every customer has a purpose for using yours. Your business might be devoted to Web sales, offline sales, lead generation, or all three. When you find the common ground between your purpose and your customer's, that's when you build your brand and your business.

- **Measure your customer activity**—A sense of purpose is not enough. You need metrics. Only with metrics can you measure how well customers are succeeding at your Web site. By identifying these customer success events—conversions—and measuring the frequency of their occurrence, you can assess the benefit of changes made to your marketing and to your Web site. Remember, too, that 100 percent accuracy is a fool's errand but that understanding your model and the power of trend analysis is what's important.

- **Measure your customer relationships**—Conversions are powerful events because they lead to sales, but conversions pack even more power over relationships. Many conversion events are relationship changers. Conversions denote an increasing level of engagement from anonymous visitors to identified registrants to subscribers to customers to repeat, loyal customers.

As we conclude, it's worth remembering why we are focusing on metrics in the first place. In *Good to Great*, author Jim Collins quotes former U.S. Vice Admiral Jim Stockdale's advice: "Confront the brutal facts of your current reality, whatever they might be." In marketing, the metrics we collect and analyze are the keepers of our most brutal facts. Only by understanding what they mean can we determine which areas to improve.

But how do you design your marketing and your Web site to attract loyal customers? What changes do you make to improve your customers' experience and your bottom line? That's what's teed up for Chapter 5.

5

The New Customer Relations

"A common mistake that people make when trying to design something completely foolproof is to underestimate the ingenuity of complete fools."

—Douglas Adams

Chapter Contents

- The Look and Feel   153
- The Sights and Sounds   175
- The Touch   186
- Summary   208

"Why did the chicken *not* cross the road?" asked my daughter. When I gave up, she answered, "To ruin my joke." Too often we treat our customers like the chicken in that riddle. We are so focused on what *we* want them to do that we lose track of what *they* want to do.

When you put so much thought and effort into designing a Web site, it's hard not to take it personally when the chickens won't cross your road to get to a conversion. Even though you know that customers are not refusing to cross the road merely to spite you, what you really want to know is what to do about it.

Everything counts in getting your customer to take that next step across that road—the way your site looks, the choices you offer, the words you use, even the pictures you show. Everything.

That's what we explore in this chapter—the elements of your Web site and of other online marketing. But we won't dissect them and preserve them in formaldehyde to observe. Each one is important only in the context of what it means to your customer. Each element makes an impression on your customer in some way, positively or negatively—often subconsciously. Pulling these elements together to form a positive customer experience is the new customer relations.

I'll be very specific about the specialty skills that go into creating this experience, all the way from usability experts to graphics designers to information architects and more. Large businesses have people on staff (sometimes dozens in each specialty), but small businesses use these skills as well—they just might roll them all into fewer people.

For a small business, a single "Web person" may choose the graphical design, the information architecture, *and* write the content. That person might work for an agency rather than for the small business itself. That's not important. What *is* important is that you understand the roles for each of these specialties, whether they are performed by one person or many. Then you'll know what goes into creating online marketing experiences.

If you already understand the basics of online marketing creative material and Web site design, content, and personalization, feel free to skip to Chapter 6, "Customers Vote with Their Mice." This chapter is a thorough introduction for those who don't. It's a long chapter (sorry), but it helps if you know where the dials are before you can decide which ones to turn and where to set them. For those who want even deeper coverage of these subjects than what's provided here, you'll be pointed to more resources when we get to Chapter 9, "This Stuff Changes Too Fast."

Perhaps you've heard the story of the psychology class that decided to experiment on their unwitting professor. As the teacher lectured the class each day, the students sat in rapt attention with smiles on their faces whenever the professor ventured closer to the windows, while feigning loss of interest and boredom when he moved near the door. The students practiced this for weeks until finally the professor was conducting his lecture while sitting on the radiator under the window.

A cute story? Sure. (I like to start a chapter that way to make a good impression on *you*.) There's a lesson in there, however. The reason this practical joke was so effective was that the professor was paying attention to his students. He really *cared* whether they were attentive and happy. He did not even realize what he was doing to get the feedback he desired, but that didn't matter. His attitude was what made the trick work. Another professor who didn't care about his students might not have changed his behavior at all.

What about you? Do your customers smile at you? Do you notice? And if you do, do you know *why* they are smiling?

Notice when your customers comment on your blog. When your customers respond to a change on your Web site, pay attention. If your customers want you to sit on the radiator to deliver your message, it's best to get over there now.

So what are the Web equivalents of sitting on the radiator? What are the elements in your customer's Web experience that you can change? Precisely *because* the Web is an experience, we'll examine the elements in terms of our physical senses.

We start with the *look and feel*, a layman's term that describes how the experience looks to the customer and how it feels to use it. For the Web, it includes everything from the visual design (colors, typefaces, layout, and white space) to the way customers interact with the information (how the site responds to a mouse, how the site is navigated, and what customers are expected to know). Some people limit the term "look and feel" to merely the visual aspects of the site, but online marketing, and the Web in particular, is so interactive that the navigation and structure of the customer experience provides much of the usability, which I think of as "the feel." To me, the term "look and feel" is much more than making the site look pretty—it's the entire *user experience*, as the professionals would say.

I also cover the sights and sounds, what Web-heads call the *content* of the site. How do you write the copy for an e-mail? What exactly is your marketing message? What kinds of pictures should you use? Whose voice is best for that podcast?

Last, we consider the touch. It's that personal touch that often distinguishes a great experience from a good one. I talk about both how you set a personal tone and how you personalize the content and the experience for each customer. The right personal touch leaves your customers feeling each experience has been individually selected for them.

Before we do all this, however, we must confront a paradox. Your customer's actual needs might differ from what you think they need. Like baseball fans who expect an umpire to start out perfect and improve with age, your customers want two opposing qualities from your Web site.

First, they expect your Web site to be like everyone else's. The title of Steve Krug's excellent book, *Don't Make Me Think*, sums up what customers want. They want to immediately understand what is expected of them for every click. It should work just the way they expect it to.

At the same time, your customers want your Web site to keep improving. And *you* want your Web site to be better than your competitors'. But how can you make your site the same as the rest while being better at the same time?

You pick your spots.

Most of your site should be straightforward, predictable, and unremarkable, in that customers "just know" what to do. If you think you have a better name for the link to your home page than "Home" (or you think you can improve on the words "Contact Us" or "About Us"), you can give it a try, but using the standard names is what customers expect. Doing what people expect usually makes your site easier to use, but you don't have to make it look *exactly* the same. Just consider it a serving suggestion.

You *can* innovate in certain areas where it makes sense. To do so, you need to use the listening skills you've picked up in previous chapters. You must listen to what your customers say, and you must watch what they do. Every time you change one of the elements on your Web site, you should be consciously moving toward standardization (working the way the rest of the world does) or to innovation (a better mousetrap). When your site is different but not better, that's when customers get frustrated. Your job is to identify that situation and fix it.

Warning: Another cute story ahead. When my family bought our first minivan, it was an entirely new form of car that required many decisions for its designers. ("Should we use a sliding passenger door to make it easier to get in and out?") We learned how it worked, and that became our mental model for minivans...until seven years later, when the day came to replace it with a new minivan.

My wife and I sat in the driveway in our brand new minivan, unable to find the latch to unlock the rear hatch. We looked everywhere. We pored over the owner's manual. We got more and more upset with the situation. How dumb can these people be that they don't make it easy to open that rear hatch? The words "rear hatch" are not even in the index of the owner's manual, for Pete's sake. (And Pete wasn't around to ask.)

Finally, exasperated after several attempts to figure this out over the course of a week, I broke down and called the dealer. The woman on the phone listened patiently for a minute but then broke in, "You just need to unlock the doors."

Well, color me stupid. Our old minivan treated the rear hatch the way sedans treat the *trunk*, with a little lever that you pull to open it. Our new minivan considered the rear hatch to be the rear *door*—when you unlock the rest of the doors, you've unlocked that one, too. We'd never tried just opening the rear door to see if it was already unlocked.

As we marketers consider every element we can change on our Web sites and consider changes we can make in our Web marketing, just remember that nothing works unless your customer understands it. Eventually, my wife and I came to agree that the new minivan's approach really *was* simpler and better, so it was therefore an innovation rather than an annoyance.

You need to make sure that your Web site's differences are truly improvements and not just differences. Marketers know better than anyone that a difference is a differentiator only if the customer cares about it. As the great automotive engineer Ferdinand Porsche once said, "Change is easy. Improvement is far more difficult."

So if you're the creative type who's been gritting your teeth waiting for the good stuff, here is your chapter. Finally, we're going to talk about creative things—the elements of the customer experience that you can craft. But maybe you're not the creative type, and you're vaguely suspicious of all this newfangled "experience" talk. Don't be— it's not so new.

Some companies do no brand advertising yet have powerful brands—Google is a well-known example. How does this happen? Because the experience *is* the brand, so says Web usability guru Jakob Nielsen, and who are we to disagree?

This has been true long before the Web, however. Another advertising-free company, American cataloger L.L. Bean, has long focused on their customer's experience in receiving the catalog, looking it over, choosing an item, calling them by phone, and placing the order—and then getting and wearing the clothing. This experience is exactly what brings folks back to them. Even the ease with which they return unwanted clothing is part of why they come back to L.L. Bean year after year. L.L. Bean knows that *everything counts*.

This chapter talks about what *everything* is. So let's come to our senses, starting with a look at look and feel.

The Look and Feel

When you call a company's telephone number, what do you expect? You probably don't expect to have a person answer—you know that you'll get the dreaded voice response system asking ridiculous questions. ("If you're indecisive, please press 1 *and* 2.") You know you'll be placed on hold. ("If you think the recorded music will improve, please press your luck.") You hope that you'll talk to someone who knows the answer to your question, but you don't expect a lot.

Expectations are much higher on the Web.

The place to start to fulfill those expectations is the "look and feel." It might seem hard to believe, but customers make up their minds about your Web site in as little as one-twentieth of a second. They're not reading your whole page—they are getting an impression of how it looks. If your site doesn't pass, they bang the "Back" button in the browser and look at another site.

If your site passes that snap judgment, customers start scanning your page for what they are looking for. It could be the words they searched for, the name of a link to perform the task they have in mind, or something else entirely. Their expectation is that they'll find what they are scanning for *fast*.

When customers come to *your* Web site, their expectations have been set by every other Web site they've ever been to. They expect the experience to be good because when they visit Amazon, eBay, or Google, they get what they want. Their expectations are, in fact, more specific than getting a "good experience."

Retailers must match Amazon's experience—personalized offers, quick, reliable delivery, e-mails every step of the way, and customer ratings. Your Web site search engine must be as relevant as Google's. Your selection should seem unlimited, the way eBay's does. That's what customers are starting to expect.

But you obviously shouldn't copy every element of a successful experience on your own site. Besides a little thing called copyright infringement, it's better to focus on *your* customer's needs. Those needs will inevitably differ in some ways from the needs of the customers of those successful experiences. So how do you know which parts to imitate on your site and where to part ways? You need to learn more about your customers.

Some of us might be perfectly happy thinking about the Learn, Shop, and Buy tasks in the Web Conversion Cycle, but technical people might be appalled. "Where is the *evidence* that these tasks are what our users are actually doing?" (Like drug dealers, techies always call customers "users.") Now, being a gear head myself, I actually agree that we might want to get some facts about what our visitors are doing before we go off and redesign the whole Web site.

As luck would have it, a methodology exists to do exactly that, brought to us by the *User-Centered Design (UCD)* professionals. (While UCD pros are passionate about making everything more accessible and usable, you might note with some irony that they haven't worked very hard at coming up with an easy-to-understand name.) As the name implies, UCD places the user at the center of the design process. UCD types are scientists of human behavior—sometimes Ph.D.s in cognitive psychology possessing both analytical and sociological skills.

Marketers and UCD people have not traditionally traveled in the same circles, but that's starting to change, as marketers are open to designing sites around tasks. Devashish Saxena, Manager of Worldwide Internet Marketing for Texas Instruments, says, "We have gone from a site that was more a reflection of our organization—'Here are our products!'—to organizing our site around tasks the customers perform."

We know from Chapter 3, "Marketing Is a Conversation," that customers are becoming participants in an experience, rather than passive receivers of your marketing messages. User-centered design focuses on what customers do, rather than merely what they say.

One of the most important activities in user-centered design is *user testing*. Real customers sit down in front of your Web site and try to complete their tasks, with varying degrees of success. When your UCD people have done enough testing, they can develop a set of *use cases*. Use cases are detailed depictions of each step that your visitors take to complete a task—a task such as buying your product. Use cases are incredibly complex at times, but there's a simple one shown in Exhibit 5-1.

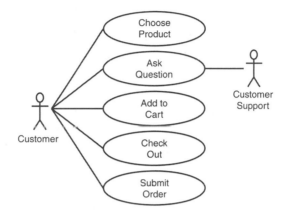

Exhibit 5-1 Sample use case diagram

If you don't have any spare UCD people lying around, here's a head start on your use cases—it's a way to do use cases wrong quickly. Once you get down to this level of detail, some of the use cases for vastly different products and services can start to look similar. Here are the most common use cases:

- **Browsing**—One strategy your visitors employ to find what they are looking for is to navigate—often by category. They look for the link that helps them get closer to their goal.

- **Filtering**—Visitors narrow down a large set of possibilities into a smaller set. Entering words into a search engine is one example of this, but so is drilling down into any list of items.

- **Viewing details**—Clicking a search result to see more information is one example, but any action that reveals more about an item in the list fits the bill.

- **Viewing context**—Visitors frequently need to explore surrounding information so that they understand what they are reading. This is an especially important behavior after viewing details from a search result—when a visitor "parachutes" into your site from a search, understanding context can be very important.

- **Compare**—Visitors often need to see several items in a list side-by-side so that they can see their similarities and differences, helping them make choices between them.

- **Buy**—Depending on your site, this use case might entail dropping an item into a cart and checking out or could encompass myriad offline connections (such as pressing "Call me" buttons, starting a text chat, finding stores or dealers, filling out contact forms, and others, just as we discussed in Chapter 4, "Going Over to the Dark Side").

Customers have a lot of strategies they use to find what they need and buy it. Try some of these use cases on your site and use your measurements and user testing to gradually improve.

Exhibit 5-2 shows the look and feel of Become, an up-and-coming shopping search site. In the first split second of viewing a page, customers see that Become is a well-designed, attractive site, which makes it seem trustworthy. Look a few seconds longer and you can see that Become's customers have two main use cases: researching products and shopping for products. (Sounds a lot like Learn and Shop, huh?) Become divides its pages into research content (reviews, user forums, and other product background) and shopping content (product specs and price comparisons). The site feels responsive because mousing over items displays deeper information—customers click only items that are of interest.

Everything about Become's site provides impetus for the customer to move deeper into the experience and eventually buy. The look and feel of the experience is a key factor in driving customers to conversion.

The Design

Product designers have argued for years over whether form should follow function or the other way around. Regardless, the *form* of your marketing experience—its visual design—is a key piece of your customer's overall experience.

Exhibit 5-3 shows three different landing pages from sites that review digital cameras. At one point these three pages were all listed on the first page of search results for the query "digital camera" on Google. The pictures show, however, that they have three radically different designs. At a glance, the sites evoke different responses that might attract different target markets—news hounds, fun-loving types, and the more analytical. None of these designs are necessarily better than the others—each site is very successful with its target audience.

Become splits its page into "Research" and "Shop" to support its two main use cases.

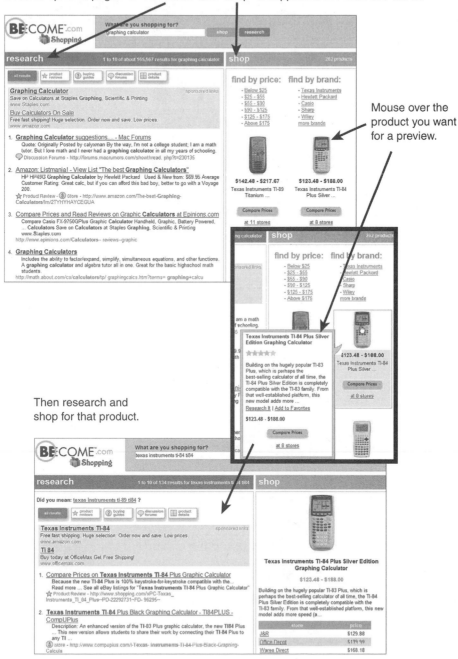

Mouse over the product you want for a preview.

Then research and shop for that product.

Exhibit 5-2 Successful design based on use cases

Our first digital camera site has a design reminiscent of newspapers or magazines—customers may expect to find unbiased coverage here.

Our second site has an airy feel, with images that evoke fun and games.

Our final site has a clean style that emphasizes facts, appealing to analytical customers.

Exhibit 5-3   Same product, three different designs

Each of the pages shown in Exhibit 5-3 is a *landing page*, the first page seen by someone coming to your site—in this case, someone coming from the Google search results page for "digital camera." Landing pages are not confined to search marketing, however. Each time you buy a banner ad, the page that customers reach when they click the ad is a landing page. Every link in an e-mail message brings your customer to a landing page.

Landing pages are important because they provide the first impression of your site. Once in a while, your landing page can be your conversion page. If someone searches for your software download or your e-mail newsletter, the page they land on could allow them to complete the conversion right there. But that's the exception.

Most of the time, the purpose of the landing page is to get your customer to click to another page on your site to continue the experience—eventually leading to a conversion. So what that means is that *each* of those pages along the way to conversion is just as important as the original landing page. In fact, most pages on your site would benefit from the same care that landing pages get. Ultimately, as more and more of your customers use search to enter your site, almost any page could be a landing page.

It's not that easy to put equal effort into every page, but there's one thing that you can apply to every page on your site—your *visual design*.

Visual design encompasses a range of concepts including color, typography, the amount of white space, and many others. Good visual design evokes emotion. (Actually, bad design evokes emotion too—just not the emotion the designer was hoping for.)

Think about the image that you want to convey to your customer, which might be different based on your product. Microsoft's Zune needs to be cool and fun, while its Exchange e-mail server software might need to appear more serious. Your design can set the tone—more white space and more pictures (and less text) convey a sense of fun. More text and a tighter, information-packed display seem more serious. Boxes are serious, and circles are fun.

Are these rules? No, just examples. A good visual designer brings skills, creativity, and experience to each situation. A good designer also brings an individual perspective that you need to match with your target audience. One interesting study by the University of Glamorgan (Wales) shows that female customers seem to prefer Web sites designed by women—and men prefer those by men. If your agency or your in-house team is staffed with both male and female designers, that may give you the flexibility to appeal to all of your customers.

Color matters, too. Bright colors are associated with fun, while pastels and grays with a more sober approach. But different colors have different meanings in different countries. Western countries associate white with weddings, while in India it is the color of mourning. Does this matter on the Web? Not necessarily, but if you have a global site, you need designers that understand differences in each of your markets, and you need to test in those markets. You probably won't change the colors in the company logo you've had since 1974, but you can choose secondary colors based on your company's style and your customers' preferences.

In fact, limiting the number of colors you use might be the single most important step toward a professional look. Selecting just a few colors for your palette doesn't preclude using full-color images, but it assures that you won't go overboard with every color in the rainbow.

When selecting colors in your palette, remember that some combinations just look better together than others, such as green and yellow, blue and orange, or purple and pink. It's especially important to avoid clashing colors, such as red and blue right next to each other—*color vibration* can result, which causes eye fatigue. If you don't have the services of a Web designer, you can use Color Schemer (www.colorschemer.com) or Kuler (http://kuler.adobe.com) for ideas.

You should also keep in mind that *color deficiency* (sometimes called *color blindness*) affects as many as eight percent of males in some countries. Don't design your site so that the only way to distinguish information on your site is its color—especially red, green, or any color that contains reds or greens. ("The features shown in purple are available only in our Professional Edition.")

People with color deficiency also struggle with text that is inadequately contrasted with its background color, but it's uncomfortable for all readers. In general, if you use dark text on light backgrounds, your text will be more readable. If you really want to use white text on a blue background, make sure you make the text large. The smaller the point size of the text, the more that color contrast matters.

While we are at it, make sure that your site is designed to be *accessible* so that customers with disabilities can use all the major features of your Web site. It's the law in some countries, but it's just plain good business. Interactive marketing is a good way to reach people with disabilities because some tend to be less able to leave their homes. Moreover, they'll sing your praises instead of bashing you in the Internet conversation about your company—the American retailer Target became a target of a highly-publicized lawsuit brought by the National Federation for the Blind. To avoid similarly negative publicity for your company, check out Web site accessibility guidance from the Worldwide Web Consortium (www.w3.org).

Let's get back to basics. Why is design important? Because it affects customer trust. If the Web site for your nursing home has a wild typeface with a dark background and pictures of pretty nurses, that might not convey the sense of professionalism and responsibility that attracts your clientele. Similarly, MTV might benefit from that kind of look more than from a staid, gray, boxy layout with ordinary fonts. Your design, in large measure, defines your brand image.

Designers are the people that think through these kinds of issues to help you project the right marketing image for your site as a whole. Designers also make decisions on each tiny element of individual pages, such as how much space to leave on a tab so that its name can be translated into German (whose words are often longer than those in other languages). If your customers find your pages easy to scan to find what they are looking for, it's in part because your designer thought through how that page should be laid out and how to visually separate its parts.

We've talked about design exclusively in the context of Web sites so far, but you should know that most e-mail messages sent these days are formatted as Web pages, so all of the design techniques that apply to individual Web pages can be applied to e-mail marketing also. It's important that your e-mail messages be designed to look similar to the landing pages they lead to. That way, when someone clicks the call to action in the e-mail, the Web page that shows up next doesn't cause a break in the experience. You want it to feel like a continuation of the e-mail experience, so use similar design, common images, and the same tone in your text.

THE MAIL MUST GO THROUGH

All the creative content in the world won't matter if your customer never sees your marketing e-mail. You must design your campaign to get your content in front of your customer, passing several hurdles:

- **Bounces**—E-mail addresses are notorious for changing without notice. In Chapter 6, we look at how you can get software to carry the bulk of load through list management functions. But you can prevent many bounces with a "double opt-in process"—requesting subscribers to opt in at your Web site *and* to click the confirmation link in an e-mail you send them.

- **Spam Filters**—Many bounces have nothing to do with bad addresses, but rather are caused by spam filters. Most e-mails must run two spam gauntlets, the mail server's spam detector and the one in your individual customer's e-mail program. Test your e-mail messages against popular server filters, such as SpamAssasin, to make sure they get through. In addition, consider *authenticating* your e-mail so that you are identified as a trusted sender. To beat each customer's spam filter, provide instructions during your opt-in process for customers to specify that e-mail from your e-mail address is allowed to pass through.

- **Image Blockers**—Many e-mail providers routinely block all images from being shown in e-mail, to thwart those sending pornographic offers. That could seriously affect the persuasiveness of your message. Consider using an e-mail delivery service such as Goodmail to get your pictures through.

Delivering e-mail is much tougher than delivering direct mail letters to snail mailboxes, but luckily it is far cheaper. It's worth the time to analyze these tools and techniques to get more of your mail through.

Another tool in your visual toolbox is your *grid layout*. A professional-looking design uses the same grid everywhere so that similar information appears in similar places. Using the same grid does not mean that pages can't have different layouts—it does mean that you won't have the right column start a half inch further to the right on some pages than others.

Another technique in Web page design is *liquid design*, which allows Web pages to dynamically change their layout when the browser window is resized. Exhibit 5-4 shows how Dutch airline KLM uses liquid design techniques on its home page.

More and more, however, the Web experience you offer your customers is not defined totally by Web *pages*. In fact, Bryan Eisenberg, co-author of *Waiting for Your Cat to Bark*, likes to say that "The Web page is dead." Your customer's Web experience is a lot richer than reading a page in a book.

First, Web pages are far more interactive than a printed page. Your customers choose the order in which they consume content by clicking links of their choosing, not merely turning to the next page. But more importantly, Web pages are increasingly composed of far more than HTML and text.

Podcasts and video are very different experiences than pages. Likewise, Flash content and other rich media are far more engaging than the average Web page. And even Web pages themselves are much more interactive now than they once were, with Ajax and other techniques making Web pages as responsive as personal computer software. As these technologies become commonplace, your use of them will communicate the "feel" of your site, perhaps even more than the visual design does.

Beyond your Web site, the same principles of design apply to banner ads, e-mail messages (which more and more are constructed the same way as Web pages, in HTML format), blogs and wikis (which are merely specialized Web pages), and many other marketing techniques. The design of each one affects customer trust and affects the persuasiveness of your message. An *integrated design system* for all your customer communications provides a unified brand image.

While you're integrating your marketing, maybe you should think about integrating your budgets, too. If most marketers devoted even a fraction of their offline marketing budgets to interactive marketing, they could dump the standard stock photography and improve their interactive look and feel. Would it result in bigger sales? It's certainly an experiment I would try.

Some marketers are creative enough to do a good job designing their Web sites and their Web marketing messages, but most need to find someone with strong design skills—variously called graphics designers, Web designers, art directors, or creative directors, depending on how skilled and experienced they are. In Chapter 8, "This Won't Work Where I Work," we look at how to work with your designer.

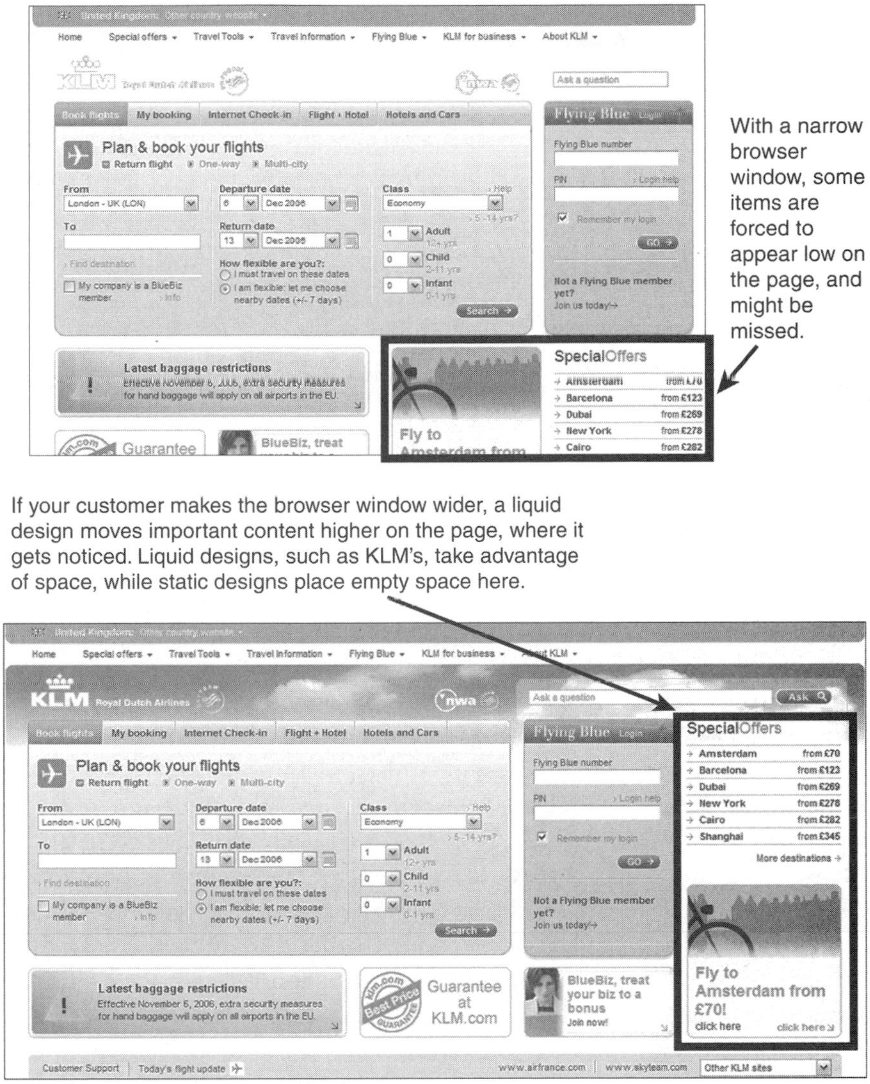

With a narrow browser window, some items are forced to appear low on the page, and might be missed.

If your customer makes the browser window wider, a liquid design moves important content higher on the page, where it gets noticed. Liquid designs, such as KLM's, take advantage of space, while static designs place empty space here.

Exhibit 5-4 Liquid design uses space effectively.

You probably appreciate the need for your site to *look* good, but next we examine something more subtle—whether your site seems easy. That depends in part on the structure of your site's navigation. Applying a spiffy visual design to a poorly-structured site is like buying the wrong house and then vowing to redecorate. Let's look at how to lay out the floor plan of your Web house now.

The Navigation

The Christmas shopping season in the United States traditionally kicks off on the Friday after Thanksgiving, which for many brick-and-mortar retailers is the biggest sales day of the year. Electronics retailer Best Buy chose this high-volume day to start using security cameras in a whole new way. Instead of merely checking for shoplifters, they watched where the crowds were gathering.

Which areas were jam-packed with lines? Send more personnel there. Which areas of the store had little traffic? Move the displays around so that more people notice the special offers there. Best Buy moved promotions and personnel from place to place to make their customers' experience better. By doing so, they jammed more shoppers into their finite floor space and they highlighted more offers to each person, resulting in both happier customers and higher sales.

As you can imagine, it's expensive to employ people to monitor cameras and redeploy personnel and promotions. Best Buy can afford to do it only a few shopping days each year. Most retailers can't afford to do it at all. But it costs a lot less to rearrange your Web site's navigation—you need only a couple of people to make changes, unlike Best Buy's army of floor managers, camera scanners, cashiers, and stock clerks. You can tweak your Web navigation and change your offers to see how they work. Then you can change them again.

The Web specialists who think about your Web site's navigation are called *information architects*. They are specialists in (wait for it) *information architecture*, which deals with the findability and understandability of information. Information architects define the structure of a Web site, working closely with designers on its visual appearance.

Lou Rosenfeld and Peter Morville, authors of the seminal book *Information Architecture for the World Wide Web*, describe information architecture as "The combination of organization, labeling, and navigation schemes…to help people find and manage information." In other words, your customers should think your information is *easy*—easy to find, easy to understand, and easy to act on.

So where better to start than the folks whose marketing campaigns are built around the "Easy button." American office supplies retailer Staples has taken a user-centered approach to its information architecture, as shown in Exhibit 5-5. Take a look at the tabs across the top of Staples' page. They show a "Products" tab followed by the "Ink & Toner" tab, instead of the typical approach that would bury ink and toner under "Products." A library sciences person would run screaming into the night ("Ink and toner are not products?!!"), but this is clearly based on Staples' user research that shows what helps visitors the most. Your information architecture is not some scientific taxonomy, nor a corporate Dewey Decimal System.

Your site navigation must be about the simplest path for your customers. Obviously Staples realizes that a high percentage of their customers are looking for ink and toner—by designing their site around that, they make it easier for people to find what they are looking for.

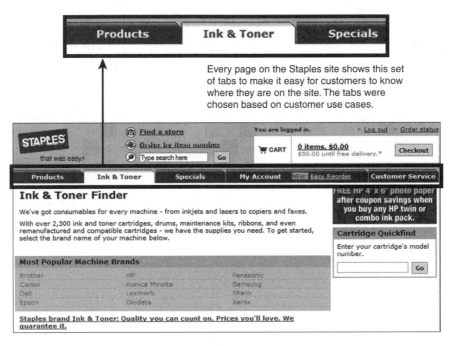

Exhibit 5-5   Successful navigation keeps the customer in mind.

What your customers find easy, however, depends on your customers. Look at IBM's home page in Exhibit 5-6. IBM customers can use the home page to select the task they want to perform if they find that easier than choosing a product or service. Your site might need yet a different approach to make its information easy.

What qualities seem to make information easy?

- **The right names**—Our information architects talk about nomenclature, controlled vocabularies, allowed values, and maybe they have other terms, too. What they mean is that you need to use understandable names for things—not names that *you* understand, but names that your customers do. Customers are happy when they see the name of a link and they accurately predict what they'll find after they click it. Testing the names you use with customers is the only way to know if they can accurately predict what is behind the link with that name. Staples could have used "Printer supplies" instead of "Ink & Toner," but they must have found that more customers were scanning for "ink" than "supplies."

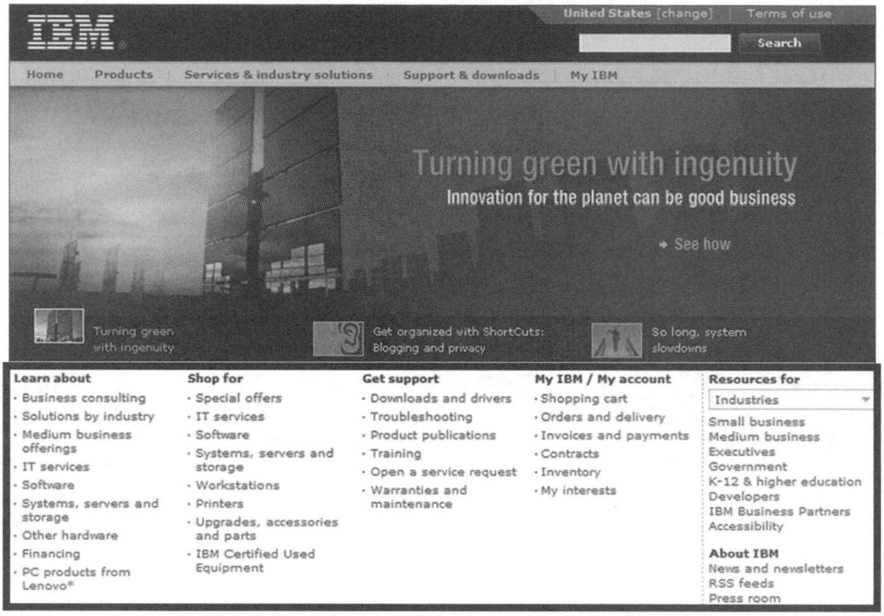

IBM shows different tasks on its home page to help its customers quickly accomplish their goals.

Exhibit 5-6   Some Web sites organize by tasks.

- **The right structure**—Customers must understand how your site is organized, and it must make sense to them. Customers have a mental model of their tasks. If your site matches their model, they will find your site easy to use. You must test your site's navigation structure to ensure that customers think it's easy. In the past, information architects created hierarchical taxonomies, the way librarians do, but social bookmarking (as described in Chapter 3) now allows customers to tag content to create their own organizations, known as *folksonomies*.

- **The right help**—When your site fails a particular customer—and it's inevitable that it will—can your customer recover? Can customers find what they are looking for using your search facility? Can they contact you by instant message? E-mail? Phone? The right help can turn failure into success.

Information architects especially focus on *findability*—the ease with which customers locate the information they need. Their focus on names, structure, and help each assist customers in finding what they need when they need it. They use the names that customers expect and structure the site the way customers expect, also. Your customers will love your site if they never feel lost.

One way to do your navigation wrong quickly is to choose the shallowest structure that you can get away with. In general, having seven top level categories with just one lower level is better than having three top categories with two levels below. Why? Because customers do better at scanning a somewhat longer list and making one choice than they do making two choices.

Information architects know how hard it is for customers to make a choice—the fewer the better. That's one reason that Staples made "Ink & Toner" a top-level category. Is a shallow structure right for your site? You won't know until you try it. But starting with a shallow structure lets you observe which choices are *not* being selected—it's harder to figure out how to subdivide a choice than it is to merge two.

Information architects spend their lives trying to choose the right names, the right links, and the right help to make your information easy. Sometimes they work closely with your designers on individual pages, especially on the page layout. Sometimes they're thinking about your *entire* site. When they do, they typically split your site into two kinds of pages, *navigation pages* and *destination pages*, as shown in Exhibit 5-7.

Navigation pages are the streets in your town. You need them to get around, but you don't want to live in the street. Destination pages are the houses—nice places to live, which you get to by using the streets.

The sole purpose of a navigation page is to get the customer to *another* page. Your home page is a navigation page, as is the main page for your best-selling product. Your navigation pages are the most-used pages on your site, but customers don't convert there. Customers don't complete their tasks on your home page.

They complete them on your destination pages. Your product specification page is a destination page—it contains enough information that some customers decide to drop that product in the shopping cart. Most of the pages on your site are destination pages. Even destination pages contain *some* navigation, but it's not their central focus.

Why do we distinguish between navigation pages and destination pages? Because they pose different information architecture challenges. Exhibit 5-8 shows how these pages differ—they have different purposes and require different approaches. Navigation pages often share a similar design across a site, providing context and offering choices of where to go next. In contrast, destination pages come in many forms: product specifications, a case study, the price list, product reviews, and many others. The information on a destination page should provide what the customer needs with a simple layout and effective writing.

Exhibit 5-7 Navigation pages and destination pages have different purposes.

	Navigation Pages	Destination Pages
Page's Purpose	Provide orientation to the topic, and reveal structure and choices	Help complete task by providing detailed information about the topic
Traffic	High	Low
Customer Question	"What is the scope of this topic?" "Where do I go next?"	"Is this what I wanted?"
Customer Actions	Finding, navigating, searching, locating	Scanning, reading, consuming, using
Challenges	What are the use cases? What is the natural navigation flow?	What are the document types? What makes each type unique? What related content should be linked to?
Page Emphasis	Context, branding, clear presentation of choices	Text, images, details, persuasion, call to action

Exhibit 5-8   Navigation pages and destination pages pose different challenges.

Usability expert Jakob Nielsen describes the process of "progressive disclosure," in which each step the customer takes allows more and more information to unfold, as the customer is ready for it. A well-structured experience feels like the information becomes available as it's needed. Look at how online retailer Buy.com offers a layered view of product information for an HDTV in Exhibit 5-9.

We've talked about visual design and navigation, but Web sites can also be thought of as software. Even the simplest Web site uses Web server software to present its pages to customers, and leading-edge designs are now quite interactive. How does your Web site respond to what your customers do?

The Interactivity

All Web marketing uses some kind of software, even if it is just a simple Web server to display pages and respond to clicks. So in a sense, all Web marketing is interactive to some degree. The question is whether your Web site and your Web marketing respond the way your customer wants it to and whether it responds better than your competitors'.

Your *Web developers* are the programmers of your Web site. They might install commercial software packages or might write their own software, but what they do affects the interactivity of your Web site. If you have an e-commerce site, you've got a shopping cart and a checkout process—it's driven by software. Your designers and your information architects design the interactive experience working with the developers, who implement that experience in software.

Your site might not require much software. If you provide supply chain consulting services, your site might consist of a number of informational pages that describe your services, talk about a few satisfied clients, and contain buttons on the right side to fill out a form to be contacted by a consultant. And that might be exactly what your customers want and expect. But even that form requires some programming—even if just to check the information entered for correctness and to send an e-mail to someone to follow up with each person who fills out the form. Even the simplest sites sometimes use JavaScript programming to make the site more interactive—when the customer's mouse moves over a menu item, it automatically shows the items in the menu without requiring a click.

One image is displayed, along with thumbnail previews of the rest for selection.

Detailed product information is organized by tabs for easy access.

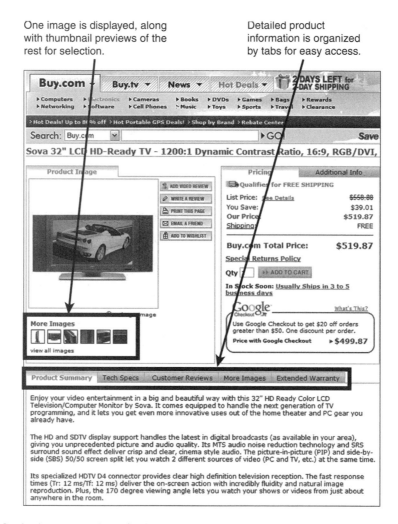

Exhibit 5-9   *Destination pages use layers for simplicity.*

Exhibit 5-10 shows how an e-commerce site might use software for its site search facility and for its shopping cart. Your programmers typically buy software packages, install them, and configure them to operate with your content and product catalog.

Searchers for 32-inch LCD TVs at CompUSA are using search
software to find what they are looking for.

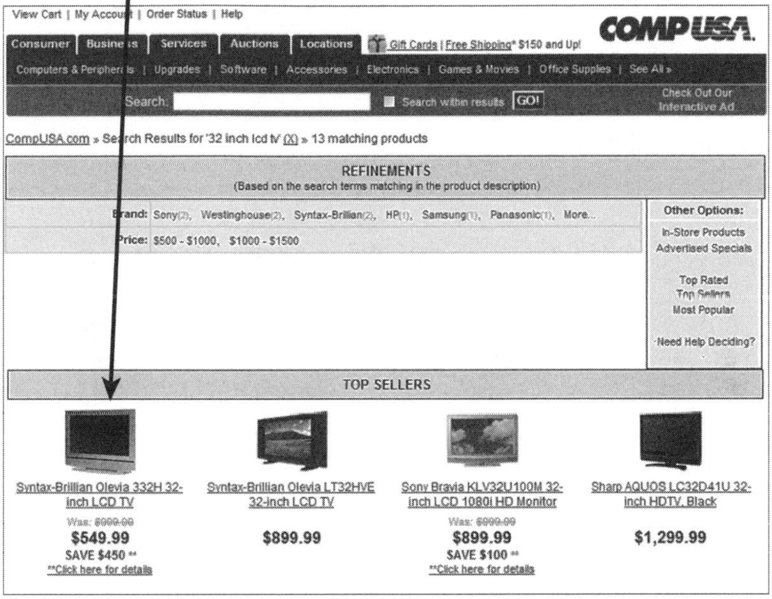

Customers also use e-commerce software to drop the TV in
their shopping carts and buy.

Exhibit 5-10   E-commerce sites require more interactivity.

You've seen many uses of software to provide interactivity over the years, but let's
look at some Web 2.0 examples. We've talked previously about how marketers are

beginning to offer ratings and reviews on their sites—that level of interactivity requires software also. Exhibit 5-11 shows how Sun Microsystems does it. You'll notice that Sun shows the brief product rating on its main product page and allows the customer to click through to the more detailed product reviews on a separate page.

In Chapter 4, we examined how Netflix increases interactivity using Ajax techniques. In Exhibit 4-10, we saw how a customer can mouse over a movie title to pop up more details. You'll see more and more of these highly interactive pages as Web 2.0 developers work with designers and information architects to make the Web experience as smooth as one found in PC software. (Not that PC usability is a high bar to jump over, but it's more interactive than the average Web site.)

You can use Ajax to streamline your shopping cart experience, too. Clothing retailer Gap, Inc. eschews the standard experience of dropping an item into an unseen shopping cart and having to click to a new page to view the shopping cart. Instead gap.com shows the shopping cart (which they refer to as a "bag") overlaid on the screen as the customer continues to shop. It's reminiscent of taking a shopping bag around a physical store as shopping continues. It might be better had they used the standard name "shopping cart" but maybe their testing shows they need a new name for a new experience.

Exhibit 5-12 shows another Ajax shopping cart, this one at panic.com, another clothier. Notice how the shopper simply drags the desired item into the shopping cart area at the bottom of the page. The shopping experience can continue by adding more items to the cart, or the shopper can check out. Ajax can help marketers to take distracting Web page transitions out of the user experience, which might lead to more completed conversions.

Rich media, such as Adobe's Flash, is a few years older than Ajax, but it's another very effective technique for injecting interactivity. You can combine images, graphics, and animation to provide an interactive customer experience, all contained in a nifty Flash module on your Web site. As with Ajax, Flash can respond to mouse-over actions as well as to clicks, so a Flash experience can seem as interactive as one on a desktop computer. Flash is often being used in banners and other ads in place of still images, to provide a richer (and more attention-getting) experience. While Flash modules are technically software applications, most are developed by designers rather than developers.

These examples give you a glimpse into how software can be used on your site to provide interactivity. Your Web developers make the software work, but they do so under the tutelage of designers and information architects who provide the right look and who make it easy for the customer.

Take care not to be fooled by all the fancy techniques like Ajax and Flash. Interactivity, when done well, provides the polished finish to a great Web experience, but good content still matters more than glitz. Pasting Ajax on top of a poor Web site is like polishing a cardboard box. It might be shiny, but it's still just a cardboard box.

While common for retailers, Sun Microsystems is the rare
manufacturer that shows product ratings by customers.

Customer
reviews
are also
shown for
Sun's
products.

Exhibit 5-11   Product ratings and reviews increase interactivity.

Drag and drop the shirt to the shopping cart at the bottom.

Shoppers are less distracted than when a new page loads and they must re-orient themselves to where they are and what to do next.

Exhibit 5-12 A more interactive shopping cart

Additionally, it's best to reserve Flash and other rich media for situations where regular old Web pages don't do the job. Flash has at times been used in place of standard Web navigation, which makes the content nearly unsearchable. Flash is great for an animated banner ad or that 3D tour of your latest product, but it should not be used in place of boring old Web pages just to spiffy up your site.

The attention you pay to the look and feel of your pages will pay off in more customers finding what they are looking for—and converting. After all, most poorly-designed sites *do* contain the information customers are looking for. If only they'd use your site map and carefully read your pages, they'd find it. But they don't.

Four out of every five customers *scan* your Web page, with just one reading it word-for-word. Navigation pages, especially, must be clearly laid out, well-organized, and emphasize images and color over text. Destination pages, by nature, have more text. Customers are more willing to spend time reading destination pages, but those pages also need to be written to be scanned. That's what we look at next.

The Sights and Sounds

Marketers have forever been obsessed with "the message"—and for good reason. We know that our marketing message is a key tool in persuading our customers to buy.

In Web marketing, the message is usually called "content"—the text, images, and (increasingly) audio and video that get the message across. The way that messages are conveyed to customers online differs from previous media. In Chapter 2, "New Wine in Old Bottles," we examined how your message needs to be real, relevant, and responsive. Let's get more specific about how you deliver that message.

The Web is unusual in its capacity to deliver large amounts of information—you can argue that it has the capacity to deliver the most information of any medium. You can provide books worth of text, albums of photos, oodles of sound and video—and the cost of distributing all of this content online is quite small.

And the Web has demonstrated its ability to present deeper information to people than other media—that's one reason that the Web is used so frequently to research purchases. Complex purchases that require research are well-suited to presentation on the Web.

But this information needs to be presented in bite-sized chunks. Marketers learned in the Web's early days that the long direct mail letters that work so well offline don't pack the same punch online. Web readers want it short and sweet. They want it to be punchy. They want to scan it, not read it.

Therein lies the rub (perhaps one that rubs you the wrong way).

People expect to get more information—*all* the information available—on the Web, but they want it to be carefully organized and findable so that they can swoop in on just the nugget that answers their question and spend as little time as possible.

People want all the information in none of the time.

Meeting your customer's desire requires effort because there's nothing harder than making something simple. Remember, the universe is simple; it's the explanation that's complex. Your marketing message might also seem complex when you first start working on it. Next we look at how you simplify your content so people pay attention to your message. Because the Web is such a writer's medium, we start with Web copywriting.

The Words

Maria Veloso, author of *Web Copy That Sells*, says, "Selling on the Web is text-driven," and she's right. No matter what else you do in Web marketing, you need to get the words right. And her number one rule for getting it right is "Don't make your Web site look like an ad."

It's simple, but it's true. People have been trained by old-style interruption marketing to ignore ads. The more your Web copy reads like editorial content from a magazine or newspaper, the better the odds that it gets read. Let's look at an example to see how important these informational pages are.

Suppose your company sells software to combat credit card fraud, with the catchy name DataMiner Pro. Now, it might be hard to accept, but relatively few people search for "DataMiner Pro"—they start farther back in the Web Conversion cycle, in the Learn phase. Those searchers are looking for "credit card fraud" instead.

They have no idea what they need to buy. They just know that they have a problem. If you provide editorial-style content that explains the dangers of credit card fraud and reviews the alternatives, searchers will find it and pay attention. Why? Because it answers their need—their need to understand what they can do about credit card fraud.

To the extent that you can deliver straight, factual information that answers your customers' questions, you can persuade them to take the next step to solve their problem. You must reinforce that you understand their problem, and you must explain what it's costing them, what their alternatives are, and why they should choose yours.

As we saw in Chapter 4, you have to work hard for every click. Your e-mail might be received, but it might not get read. Your page might be found by the search engine, but the searcher might not even select it to view. You need a hook—your *title*.

Whether it's the title shown on the search results page, the subject line of your e-mail, or the title of your latest blog post, you need to provide a compelling reason for your customer to look closer. If you're not sure which headline is compelling, try several different variations. You can test them on a few people you know at first, but eventually, you'll want to try the promising ones on real customers to see which ones garner the most clicks.

E-LOAN, the Internet lender, ran one such customer test for an e-mail marketing campaign. They tried three variations for the e-mail's subject line: "Your first payment is on us," "Your first payment is free," and "Skip a payment." By sending a small number of customers e-mails with different titles, they picked the winner within three days. (Turns out more people responded to "Your first payment is on us.")

When you write a headline, consider what will appeal to your audience. Think like a headline writer at a tabloid newspaper—entice people to read on with proven approaches:

- **Ask a question**—People tend to want the answer: "Do you have these symptoms of sleep apnea?"

- **Appeal to emotion**—Strong feelings cause interest: "Is fear of public speaking killing your career?"

- **Raise curiosity**—Only clicking will satisfy it: "Three Secrets to Successful Relationships"

- **Offer compelling value**—Target the right people with the right offer: "Master Spanish in 30 Days or Pay Nothing"

Don't limit yourself to these techniques. Experiment with what you believe will work with your target market and measure your success. Your title must drive clicks, especially for your ads. If you have a well-known brand name, test whether including your name in your title attracts more clicks—studies show that it might.

Text ads don't have many more words than a title does. The kind of ads displayed by search engines, as shown in Exhibit 5-13, are excellent examples of how a few words make all the difference. Remember that search engines rank their paid results based on the per-click bid *and* the clickthrough rate. The ads shown on the first page of search results are far more likely to have high click rates than lower-ranked ads. Because the words in the ads prompt those clicks, the text you see in these first-page ads might make excellent title words for e-mail subject lines or Web page titles.

One aspect of a Web page title that you shouldn't overlook is its importance in search marketing. By now you know that searchers see your title on the search results page, so you know it makes sense that better titles draw more searchers to click on your pages. But titles also must appeal to the search engines themselves.

Your title is the single most important place that search engines look for keywords on your page. If you want your page to be found by search engines for the phrase "personal color copiers," you'd best include it in your title.

But what about the rest of the content, beyond titles?

Each piece of content must be crafted to draw clicks so that the *next* message can be seen. And what qualities should that message have? Jakob Nielsen, all the way back in 1997, showed that Web copy is most successful when it is concise, scannable, and objective. We've talked about how content must avoid the marketing hype and fluff common to other media—you need to at least *sound* objective.

And you must keep it brief. That doesn't mean that you can't explain everything in its glorious details because some of your customers will want that. Just make sure that each page has a single focus, with your whole story diced into digestible chunks.

These ads use different approaches that may all be successful.

One emphasizes price and a guarantee.

Another stresses automation and a complete system.

This one flogs its ease of use and scalability.

An easy, bargain shopping experience is this claim.

The text emphasizes the brand name.

Exhibit 5-13 Text ads can be copy laboratories.

How do you make information easy to scan? Here are your tools of the trade:

- **Get to the point**—Write in newspaper style, with the most important points at the top. Do the same in each paragraph—keep them short with the important stuff first. Copy edit ruthlessly. Remember the words of Blaise Pascal: "I would have written a shorter letter, but I did not have the time." Take the time to make your copy shorter.

- **Break it up**—Paragraph after paragraph of unremitting text is deadly online. Use headings, bulleted lists, and highlighted text (including color). Stick a one-sentence paragraph in the middle that poses a question. Use a frequently-asked question approach. Each of these techniques helps your readers to scan the page for the words they are looking for.

- **Highlight the next step**—Once you have them convinced, don't make them read everything to divine their next move. Make sure that the next step is abundantly clear.

SEARCH ME

One of the factors search engines use to decide which pages are listed first is the text on the page. Craft your text for top rankings and high conversions:

- **Emphasize your keywords**—Use them several times on a page (but not to excess) and use them in prominent places—in the title, near the top of the page, in headings, and in bold or italicized text. Don't stuff keywords into every nook and cranny (if Web pages have crannies). The search engines won't put up with it. If you write naturally, you'll use the right amount of keywords. Some writers like to read their copy out loud so they can listen to it as well as read it. They say that if it sounds stupid, it is.

- **Write with variety**—Using variations of your keywords in your copy helps both rankings and conversions. Because searchers do not use the exact same keywords each time they search, peppering your text with both singular and plural forms, varying verb tenses, and using different word orders helps your page be found no matter what searchers type. Moreover, writing with variety overcomes tendencies toward the stultifying, repetitive prose that marks amateurish search optimization. Because your writing is easier to read, you'll attract more links to your site and higher conversions as well.

- **Think location**—Search engines are increasingly taking searchers' locations into account. If you are a local business, make sure that all of the variations of your place names are woven into your content so that search engines know where you're located. Search engines increasingly attempt to match local searchers with local organizations.

- **Think local**—Global marketers routinely translate pages into local languages, with translators choosing each word in the local language with a similar meaning to the original word. But that standard approach to translation can endanger your search marketing. Don't settle for translating for the proper meaning—you must do your search keyword research over again for each country and language. (Think about whether you'd want your computer product called a *portable computer* or a *laptop*—they both share the same meaning, but searchers look for *laptop* far more often.) The difference between a semantically correct word and the *best* keyword could cost you a lot of conversions. And insist that translators pay attention to the same writing techniques listed here.

The challenge of writing good copy with these tips in mind underscores how difficult it is to optimize a page for more than one keyword phrase. These tips limit the number of keywords you target—they can't *all* be the first words on the page. In general, it's best to optimize your page for one or two closely related keywords and no more. So don't try to use the same page for keywords such as "supply chain management" and "automotive supply chain management"—those searchers are looking for somewhat different things.

People might tell you that they'll read every word on your page to find that important link at the bottom, but in real life they don't. Check out Exhibit 5-14 for a great example of Web copywriting that's scannable. Flickr doesn't overwhelm you with information, but it shows you everything you need to know. If you saw this screen in color, you'd find the pink and blue contrasted with the mainly black text makes it even easier to scan.

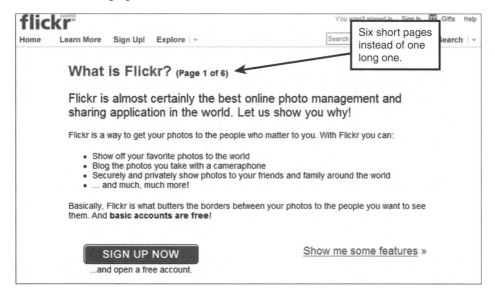

Short + Bullets + Highlighted text = Scannable

Just two choices about what to do. Sign up or learn more.

Exhibit 5-14   Web copy must be easy to scan.

In Chapter 4, we talked about measuring your impressions, selections, and conversions to assess how well your content is doing, but you also want to get customers to introduce your content to other people, as we discussed in Chapter 3. What can you do to improve the viral marketing qualities of your content?

Luckily, most of what we've already discussed works for viral marketing, too. Editorial-style content—with catchy headlines that truly provide help—works best to get customers to pass the word. That page will get them to press the "Digg This" button, and it will attract links from other Web sites. That e-mail will be sent to friends.

You can do even more:

- **Tell a story**—Human beings love to hear about other human beings. No matter how interesting your product might seem, how people *use* it will usually turn out to be more interesting. Or *why* people use it. Or how they heard about it. Or how your founder thought of the idea. People like stories and retell them.

- **Be a resource**—The best way to get links is to *give* them. If your page links to the very best resources on a subject, then others will link to you. Always give your customer pointers to more information so that you'll be seen as an expert to be consulted—and talked about.

- **Fine-tune your offers**—Some offers work and some don't. Offers that demand to be passed on must be compelling and noteworthy. Free shipping is interesting, but giving your product away to the first 200 who come to the site might bring thousands of people there. Whether you persuade each one of the latecomers to buy is up to you, but word of mouth will work for a while.

While it makes sense for e-mail messages or Web landing pages to get this kind of attention, you might think it's impossible to provide this level of care for every page on your site. The truth is that, although it is hard, every page on your site needs to have a purpose, and you need to devote time and resources to that purpose according to each page's relative value. Each piece of content on your site must be designed to get the customer to take the next step.

If you can't devote this kind of attention to each page on your Web site, maybe you have too many pages. Don't laugh. It's better to have fewer high quality pages than a whole bunch that leave a bad impression.

Companies that have pursued this approach have benefited. Disk drive maker Seagate found that just 20 percent of their pages yielded 80 percent of their page views. Now, it's always true that your navigation pages will garner many more page views than other pages, but designer Calvin Klein found an even more extreme situation: Less than six percent of their pages accounted for 80 percent of their page views. So they cut their 8,000-page Web site down to 3,000 pages.

That goes for e-mail also. If you send mediocre e-mails, you are training people to ignore them. No matter what your content, spend the time to make it high quality (whatever that means to you), even if it means sending fewer e-mails. You'll reap the benefits of an improved brand image, which will lead to more people reading your content (and acting on it).

You can apply this "cut the clutter" approach to each individual piece of content also. Experiment with making your content simpler and shorter, even if it seems like it is working well already. Gerry McGovern, author of *Killer Web Content*, reminds us of how precious our customer's attention is:

Every time you add a word to a Web page, you take something away. You take away the ability to focus on the words that are already on the page. Every time you add a link you offer a choice. What you also do is impact on the ability to choose the links already on the page.

If you're global, keeping things short also saves you translation costs. Each word costs money and time.

Web marketing has more than just words, however. Listen up for the best way to produce podcasts.

The Sounds

Sounds that accompany Web pages tend to be annoying because they are following the old-style intrusive approach, so you'd best use them sparingly. The best use of audio in Web marketing is for podcasts because your customers actually *want* to hear something from you.

As with textual content, your best approach is to make editorial podcasts, not ads. Yes, podcasts allow you to put out a longer version of your radio commercial, but you'll probably draw more customers with information than with a sales pitch. You're better off emulating radio programming rather than radio advertising.

A few successful podcasts are amateurish in quality, but customers expect more from marketers. Most companies will find customers compare their podcast quality to that of radio shows, so use that as your standard.

Fortunately, any PC can be outfitted with a professional microphone and headphones for acceptable sound quality. You can edit your podcast using inexpensive software and post it to your blog or Web site. In short, quality audio is not terribly expensive to record or distribute.

The harder part is the content itself. Here are some tips to get you started:

- **Decide your schedule**—Are you doing a ten-minute interview each month? A roundup of headlines every day? You'll build a following faster if you keep to a regular schedule. Many successful business podcasts come out once a week—their listeners subscribe to a Web feed and get it each week at the same time.

- **Choose your length**—Can you really create 30 high-quality minutes *each* week? Keep in mind that it might take you two hours every week to produce those 30 minutes. Does your customer listening on an iPod on a commuter train want to listen to 30 minutes, or would something shorter be better?

- **Select a format**—Think in terms of short regular features, such as news headlines, a commentary, or an interview, or combine several of them into a longer show.

- **Cast your podcast**—Decide who will be your regular host and contributors and bring in guests for variety. In general, multiple voices in conversation make for a more interesting production than a one-person monologue. You can overcome geographical boundaries by using Skype for free phone calls—the quality is quite good.

Consider the tips above but use your judgment, too. If you can't find a partner who will add to the show, then do it solo. If you just can't post on a regular schedule, at least make it worthwhile when you do. If your audience responds to long podcasts of speeches you make at conferences, who cares if they are 45 minutes? You need to figure out what works for you and your customers, not follow a set of rules. "Please your customer" is always the most important advice.

To improve your sound quality, pick a regular recording "studio" that's quiet and free of echoes. If you record on location, always perform a sound test before your first real "take" so you don't waste your efforts on a full show before discovering you were inaudible.

If you do "soundseeing" podcasts ("This week, we'll tour our Des Moines factory floor with our Quality Control Supervisor, Les D. Fects..."), you'll undoubtedly have a higher background noise level than in your studio. Make sure that you and your guests talk as close to the microphone as possible so you can be heard clearly.

If possible, break up your full show into segments that can be recorded separately. That way, re-takes can be limited to the segment with the error, rather than having to "take it from the top" if you mispronounce your guest's name in the last 30 seconds of the show. Exhibit 5-15 shows a sample podcast outline.

Timeline for 3/10 podcast			
Time	**Segment**	**Cast**	**Comments**
0:00	Cue Intro Music		
0:08	Intro	Larry	Talk over music to announce the name of show with today's guest. Introduce Sheila and Rick.
0:20	Welcome and News	Sheila and Rick	
1:50	Transition Music	Larry	Talk over music for company name.
2:00	Guest Interview	Sheila and Guest	
12:00	Transition	Larry	Talk over music for brief company message. Followed by Rick's intro.
12:30	Rick's Commentary	Rick	
14:30	Wrap-up	Sheila	Thank our guest and preview next wook's show.

Exhibit 5-15 Planning podcasts leads to higher quality

Don't write out a full-blown script. It sounds more natural if you have no more than talking points jotted down. You don't need to be religious about the timing—unlike radio, if this week's show is 15 minutes and 30 seconds, and last week's was 14 minutes, it's no big deal.

Using music gives it a more professional sound, but don't forget to get permission from the copyright holder—popular music usually requires a royalty payment. While we are on the subject, you'll need to get permission from anyone you record (and from venue owners when you record on location).

Podcasts are great for posting to your blog because customers can subscribe to them and get them the moment they are available. You can also post them to podcast directories (such as podcast.net). Just as with a text Web page, make sure you use a good title for your podcast and provide textual notes with the highlights of the show. This text will help searchers find your podcast and will cause people seeing the page to want to actually listen to it. (It also helps to list any Web links you refer to in the podcast so your customers don't have to write them down while they listen.)

Podcasts are more likely to be consumed by younger customers and by people who use mass transportation, so if your product skews to these audiences, podcasts might be an especially important way to reach them.

Some companies find that podcasts break through the everyday marketing clutter. Enterprise security firm Arbor Networks created a dozen four-minute podcasts patterned after the TV series "24"—each one advancing the story of a fictional financial institution whose computer network was threatened by cyberterrorists. Twenty-four thousand episodes were downloaded, spurring the company to launch a second "season" of podcasts.

But why stop with sound when you can have pictures? They're up next.

The Pictures

Although words are the most important part of Web marketing, your pictures count, too. The Web has long been a place where still pictures convey powerful emotional branding messages, and now video is increasingly part of interactive marketing messages. Let's take each one in turn.

Image selection is an art, not a science. Regardless, your judgment must be based on your brand image, just as your copy and your Web design is. Only you know which pictures advance your brand and which ones detract—and even you're not always sure. Your brand image sets the tone for pictures that are professional, edgy, light-hearted, innovative, or whatever emotion you want to convey.

Certain guidelines cross any brand, however:

- **Treat the pictures and the words as one message**—They should reinforce each other or play off each other, but not conflict with each other.

- **Show off your products**—If you sell something that can be seen, show it. If you don't, show the most tangible thing you can—pictures of employees, delivery trucks, or whatever your customer associates with you.

- **Develop a theme**—Use a similar look among all the pages for a single product rather than several individual pages so that the experience feels cohesive. Pay special attention to transitions—from e-mail to Web site, from ad to Web site, or between pages on your site—because jarring changes at the transition points lead to customers abandoning the experience. Your images are a key part of convincing them they are still in the right place.

- **Don't forget your customers**—Show them using your product or at least *needing* it. Unless your brand image depends on idealized people, consider showing normal-looking people on the Web—even if on TV your customers look beautiful. Most cultures like to see people smiling, but make sure that your people look real rather than posed or stereotypical.

Global marketers should consider cultural sensibilities. GalaxoSmithKline found that Asian cultures prefer group images, while Western ones favor individual photos—Middle Eastern cultures sometimes prefer pictures of buildings. So should you take the people pictures off your Saudi Arabian site? Not necessarily. You can use this information as a jumping off point and test what works and what doesn't on *your* site with *your* customers.

Another study shows that men prefer to see shots of products alone, while women prefer to see them in the context of being used. If your target market skews to one gender or the other, you can tilt your photo selection to maximize appeal, or you can play it down the middle and show each product with multiple pictures to better attract both genders. As always, you still need to test these ideas in *your* situation to really know what works.

But still pictures are *so* 20th century. We want video!

Videos that you post on YouTube follow all the same rules you'd apply to videos you distribute to your customers on tapes or DVDs. You can shoot it with an amateur video camera and edit it on your PC, but your customer might expect higher production values, so consider hiring professionals.

Video podcasts are a different game, with different rules than DVDs. Some companies are creating audio podcasts with a software product demonstration or a Flash animation that isn't really video at all, but others are producing full-blown video podcasts.

Video podcasts benefit from the same tips provided for audio podcasts. Plan ahead, think in segments, use multiple people for variety, and all the rest. Beyond those tips, you need to take a different approach to making the video itself because iPods are not TVs.

So how do you go about making your own video podcast?

- **Keep it short**—Battery life continues to improve, but iPods are not the best way to watch hours of video. Your customers are on the run with their iPods, so deliver your message in small doses over time. Moreover, movies as short as ten minutes might take up to 50MB of space. Some popular video podcasts are five minutes long, and many are ten. Don't make yours 30. Better to do a weekly 10-minute show than a monthly hour.

- **Get ready for your close-up**—Ever see the screen of an iPod? It's tiny compared to a TV. So when you shoot your video, get *very* close to your subjects. And forget wide-screen mode—stick with standard mode.

- **Stay still**—Talking heads work best. Many fast-motion sequences will be lost on the iPod's small screen.

- **Write big**—When you add on-screen titles to your video, remember that text that looks fine while editing your video on your computer could be unreadable on the small iPod screen. Use text judiciously and in a large point size. Test everything on a real iPod before posting it.

- **Think viral**—If your video is well done, people will share it, which is great. But if you don't watermark it, people won't know where to go for more.

Make it easy by using a *digital* video camera. If you have an analog video camera, you can convert the footage to digital format, but doing so adds another step to the process. If you'll be doing this a lot, choose efficiency.

The Touch

Interactive marketing is *personal*—in more ways than one.

It's personal in *tone*. Web copy requires a personal style that differs from the breathless hype your customers dealt with in the past. Web customers don't want sales-y; they want authentic. They want an authentic, personal voice that helps them make an emotional connection to what you're selling.

Web marketing is also personal in *message*. The Internet has brought information overload, infoglut, data smog, and information anxiety—choose your own favorite term for the same phenomenon. More information is chasing less time for everyone. We know that when people feel overloaded, they engage in classic coping strategies.

In the 1970s, psychologist Stanley Milgram studied people's reactions to those overloaded feelings brought on by life in the city. He identified how people shut down their ability to absorb, by adopting strategies of blocking or filtering inputs, disregarding inputs, and spending less time on each input. In 2006, computer scientist Peter Demming noted how these same strategies are employed by people suffering from Internet overload—similar techniques have been adapted by your customers to their e-mail inbox.

As a marketer, how do you break through the clutter? How can yours be the message that your customers will spend their precious time on?

Be relevant to each person—personalize to their needs. The difference between a successful e-mail marketing message and spam or between just another offer and one that is accepted is relevance. Your message must be personally relevant to the receiver.

This used to be called *sales*. One-on-one communication was always the domain of the sales team. Marketing always stopped short of being personal. But it doesn't matter whether we call one-on-one communication marketing or sales. What matters is whether you are doing it well. You must listen to what people say, watch what they do, and act on it.

Remember, however, that sales are different now. In the old days, salespeople might have succeeded by hoodwinking their customers or by merely promising a lot more than was delivered. We talked about how the overblown bombast is losing steam with today's customers. But what do you do instead?

Be real. Be relevant. And be responsive. Those are the three Rs discussed in Chapter 2. That's the way you form a real relationship with customers, which is the biggest "R" of them all. You must be relational.

This is what makes sales different today. In the old days, the mantra for sales was ABC: Always Be Closing. But selling online requires a new approach, a more relational approach. Michael Port, author of *Book Yourself Solid*, advises consultants trying to grow their businesses to reframe the traditional ABC approach as "Always Be Communicating." That advice works for more than just consultants.

It's through that communication (marketing is a conversation) that you carve out the perfect niche (or multiple niches) for your business. Michael further advises consultants to go after only the perfect customers for them. This advice seems counterintuitive because you'd think that a struggling consultant would want to take on every customer possible. In fact, taking on just the clients that are a perfect fit (even turning down other opportunities) causes consultants to do their best work, which in turn causes clients to sing their praises. That attracts more clients.

Does this remind you of anything? Yes, it's viral marketing for consultants. But Michael's advice rings true for any business. The mass media interruption model focused on getting your message out to anyone and everyone. ("Throw it against the wall and see what sticks.") The new media rewards relevance.

Identify the perfect search keywords that define your offering for your ideal customer. Design your marketing message to speak to the hearts and minds (and pocketbooks) of your ideal customer. And make it personal. Speak to each customer in a relevant way. Provide the right individual customer experience.

To do so, you must target ideal customers, get to know them as individuals, and design your marketing to reach them—one customer at a time.

Deciding Which Customers to Target

"My play was a complete success. The audience was a failure." When author Ashleigh Brilliant made that remark, he could have been talking about the perils of market segmentation. It's easy to have a good product or service targeted at the wrong market—or more likely, targeted at a less-than-optimum market segment.

An even more common error is targeting a good marketing promotion at the wrong segment. "Free shipping" is a great offer for someone almost ready to buy who needs just *one* more reason to do it now, but it won't move someone who isn't ready yet. Similarly, many of your offers will work wonders with your *best* customers but might appear to be poor campaigns when unleashed on a larger target market segment— your typical customers. The question is how to tell who your best customers are.

Traditional direct marketers identify their best customers using the *RFM rating*. RFM stands for Recency, Frequency, and Monetary. You can use these three metrics to target *your* very best customers:

- **Recency**—The more recently that an action has been taken, the sooner it is likely to recur. So your most recent purchasers are the ones most likely to repurchase soon. Those who visited your Web site yesterday are more likely to visit again today. Those who listened to last week's podcast are more likely to listen to this week's.

- **Frequency**—The more frequently an action occurs, the more likely it is to be repeated. Your most frequent purchasers are most likely to repurchase soon. Those who visited your Web site every day last week are more likely to visit tomorrow. Those who have listened to the last four podcasts are more likely to listen to this week's.

- **Monetary**—The higher the value of the action, the more likely it is to be repeated. Customers with the largest orders are more likely to repurchase. Those who have purchased a subscription to your Web site's premium information are more likely to visit tomorrow. Those who paid for your Webinar are more likely to listen to your free podcasts.

When catalog marketers first discovered this technique, they were overjoyed (or at least sufficiently joyed). By targeting customers that had bought most recently, most frequently, and with the highest order sizes, they were able to mail catalogs more frequently to that group (and less frequently to less valuable groups). They increased their revenue while decreasing their costs (which everyone seems to like).

Why did this work? Because RFM is a measurable proxy for customer interest. Your most interested customers—the ones who are most valuable to you—have purchased recently (they are *current* customers), have purchased frequently (they are *regular* customers), and spent a lot of money (they are *profitable* customers). These customers are the most interested in what you sell, and they are the most responsive to your marketing message and your offers.

RFM is a rating system that you customize for your own business, so you might need to experiment to find the optimum formula. (You might need to do it wrong quickly and then fix it.) A car dealer calculates purchase Recency in years, while Apple rates iTunes customers in days. Frequency is often calculated over a period of months, but seasonal businesses might want to use one year. Monetary ratings vary widely based on the cost of your product or service. Regardless of how you calculate RFM ratings for your business, the point is to start doing it now so that over time, you will home in on your very best customers. You don't have to do it perfectly from the start, but make sure you *do* start. If you have none of this data on your customers, then start by collecting it, as discussed in Chapter 4.

If you're getting a bit impatient wondering what RFM has to do with your online marketing efforts, don't get unruly. (I think you need to be "ruly," whatever that means.) RFM has everything to do with how you personalize your Web site. Using this rating, you can decide who your best customers are and show them your best offers.

For example, if a customer with a high RFM rating visits your Web site, you *know* that free shipping is a relevant offer because they frequently purchase from you. You also know that promoting other products you sell might be relevant offers too because the more they buy from you, the more likely it is that they'll buy more yet.

Don't limit your use of RFM to purchases alone. Remember what we learned in Chapter 4—your Web conversions take in more than purchases. People who read your blog frequently are more likely to read your next post—what do your most frequent readers want to read about? People who have read your most recent white paper will probably read the next one—what do they respond to? People who have paid for your Webinar might pay for more—what do they want?

Getting feedback from the customers with the highest RFM ratings for purchases (or any other Web conversion) gives you insights into what is causing that high-value behavior—and helps you do more of it.

But what about those customers who do not have high RFM ratings? Most are simply not in your sweet spot—they are not the best matches for what you do. A few were once highly rated in RFM, but are no longer your best customers—at least right now. Your job as a marketer is to try to get them back into that "top customer" segment:

- **"Not so Recency"**—Customers who've had high RFM ratings who have suddenly stopped visiting your Web site (lowering their Recency rating) might now be frequenting the competition. Maybe you should send them an e-mail with an offer.

- **"A bit lower Frequency"**—Customers whose Frequency rating suddenly drops might no longer need the same amount of your products. Perhaps you might want to offer them a discount for referring a friend or expose them to other products you sell.

- **"A little less Monetary"**—Customers whose order sizes plunge (lowering their Monetary rating) might have found alternatives for some of your products. Perhaps offering them discounts based on raising their order size might bring them back into the top segment.

You'll find that providing different offers based on RFM ratings will not only increase your conversions, but also raise your average order size and lower your promotional discount costs (because you can selectively offer discounts only in those situations where it raises your overall profits). You might also find that different marketing approaches (e-mail versus search marketing) might prove more effective for your best customers or that different areas of your Web sites are best at attracting new high-RFM customers.

But suppose you can't keep track of all these variables or you don't know how to sort them out? Do it wrong quickly by fixating only on Recency. For most businesses, that's the strongest individual predictor. With every day that passes without your customer performing an action (visiting your site, logging in, reading your blog, or making a purchase, for example), it's less likely that the customer will do it again. Your customer's Recency rating is the single best predictor for future behavior.

What's more, this means that your customers with the highest Recency ratings are also the ones most likely to respond to your promotions.

Let's look at a Recency example to see what you can do with it. Suppose you send two different e-mail messages to two similar mailing lists, the "Trusted Provider" message and the "Free Shipping" message. When you first ran these campaigns, you found that two percent of the "Trusted Provider" recipients made a purchase, while four percent of the "Free Shipping" customers did. It's pretty simple to see that the "Free Shipping" message was the better performer.

That is, until you look at it again a few months later and calculate your Recency. Suppose that you find that only two percent of the "Free Shipping" recipients have purchased in the last 30 days, while five percent of the "Trusted Provider" ones did. The "Trusted Provider" campaign seems to have attracted a greater number of loyal customers than the other did. Such is the power of Recency—you can use it to determine the relative value of campaigns to attract higher Lifetime Value (which we discuss in more depth in Chapter 6).

Using RFM, or even Recency alone, is a great way to target your highest value customers without knowing anything else about them besides their activity metrics. But you can do more if you know more. Next, we look at what else you might want to know about your customers and how you find out.

Getting to Know Your Customers

Who exactly are these people reading your newsletter e-mails, coming to your Web site, and listening to your podcasts? In the old days, it was the salesperson's job to get to know the customer. Marketers focused on target market characteristics as shown in Exhibit 5-16 but didn't focus on individual customers.

Business to Consumer		Business to Business	
Characteristic	*Examples*	*Characteristic*	*Examples*
Demographics	age gender geographic location income	Firmographics	company size industry geographic location revenue
Psychographics	aggressive vs. conservative trendsetter vs. laggard	Organizational Psychographics	fast vs. slow decision making innovator vs. laggard
Behavioral	heavy vs. light usage gift vs. purchase for self	Behavioral	heavy vs. light usage repurchase vs. new purchase

Exhibit 5-16 Traditional market segmentation methods

Online marketers can still use any of the traditional segmentation methods that prove useful, but those methods are more powerful when applied to individual customers. Rather than slotting your customer in a bucket with other customers, computer technology offers the promise of true one-to-one marketing. As we'll see, we're a long way from that promise becoming reality, but we should begin to think this way so we can take advantage of opportunities that make sense. Some kinds of one-to-one marketing are worth the costs.

Beyond the traditional segmentation methods, needs-based segmentation is easier online than ever before and provides a rich supplement to demographics- or firmographics-based segmentation. With old-style marketing, you didn't know who was interested in your product, so you used these characteristics as a stand-in: "We don't know who exactly buys diaper services, but obviously they are new mothers, so let's advertise where they are—pregnancy magazines and young baby magazines."

Now you can find out exactly who these folks are because they search for "diaper service"—no wasted advertising there. You might find that these mothers are more ecologically-minded than most parents—they also care about breast feeding, so perhaps you can cross-sell a breast-feeding book. You can try out these kinds of relationships and test to see if they are true.

To get your offers accepted, they must be relevant. The more you know about each individual customer, the more you can fine-tune your relevance for each one. So how do you get to know your customers? Three main techniques can get you the information you need to know:

- **Ask them**—It sounds easy, but it's not because they mostly won't tell you. You need to offer something of value in exchange for the information and you must earn more information through the strength of your relationship.

- **Watch them**—Because so much of what customers do online is measurable, you can observe their actions and discern meaning from them. If this sounds tricky to do, there's a good reason for that—it *is* tricky, but we'll talk about the basics.

- **Do both**—Often, the best approach between two extremes is to go for both. Watch what people do, takes guesses at what it means, and then offer them the ability to correct what you got wrong. This can provide the most customer insight.

Let's begin with how you go about asking customers for information. If you've never read Seth Godin's book, *Permission Marketing*, go do that right now. (I'll wait right here for you.) One of Seth's many insights in that book is the value exchange between customers and marketers—you need to offer something in return for the information you seek.

And what you ask for must make sense. It's the rare customer that will enter an e-mail address to download a case study. If you make people do something stupid like that, they'll just enter "billgates@microsoft.com," or some other made-up address. People just won't provide information that you don't need to deliver the value you promise.

You also need a *privacy policy* that discloses what you'll do with personal information, but you need more than that. If you can explain in simple terms, right on the entry form page, that you won't sell personal information and that you won't provide it to anyone else, you'll lower customer resistance to provide it to you.

So what kind of value can you offer to get customers to enter their personal information? E-mail newsletters entice e-mail addresses because the request makes sense. If

PRIVACY IS THE BEST POLICY

Your company probably has a privacy policy posted on its Web site, but what's in it? Does it comply with the regulations in each country you serve? Does it contain each of the following provisions?

- **Disclosure**—Customers can read your policies on what information you collect and how you use it.

- **Control**—Customers must agree to disclose information before it is collected. Once collected, they may change any information disclosed or revoke your right to use it at any time.

- **Safety**—Customers have a right to expect that the information disclosed to you will remain with you.

- **Sensitivity**—Customers can see that you comply with heightened security laws to protect information about children, about a person's health, or someone's finances.

a customer fills out a contact form, providing a telephone number is reasonable. Depending on your business, other information exchanges will also work—check out Exhibit 5-17 for a very successful one.

Scotts makes a compelling offer—free personalized lawn care advice based on your zip code and grass type. Scotts asks for very little information and explains its privacy policy right on the form. Subscribers get advice based on the local weather and pests, delivered on the Web or through an e-mail newsletter. Scotts shows that personalization doesn't have to be complicated to be effective.

But wouldn't it be wonderful to be able to create a quality personalization experience without having to ask your customers anything? You might be able to do that by watching what they do. The most famous activity-based personalization experience is Amazon's—the product category navigation is augmented by product links based on recent purchase and navigation activity.

Most companies, however, don't have the level of activity that Amazon does, with repeat visits and purchases providing a wealth of information to fuel personalization. What can the average site do? Here are a few ideas:

- **Geographic location**—You can look up a visitor's IP address (a computer's unique network identifier on the Internet) and determine its physical location.

- **Company name and industry**—Medium-to-large companies own their own computer servers (rather than renting them from a hosting company), so their IP addresses can be used to look up the company's name and industry.

- **Interests**—What's your newsletter about? Do you have subject categories for your blogs? Every customer who subscribes is divulging subject interests you can use for promotional offers and other purposes.

- **Responsiveness**—Customers should receive rapid responses to questions, especially if it is suspected that personal data was inadvertently disclosed to the public.

In addition, make sure that your privacy policy is written in simple language—it's more credible when your customers understand it.

Privacy policies have become more and more prevalent in recent years due to customer demand. Customers have responded with an increased interest in exchanging personal information for a personalized experience, with a 2006 study by software maker ChoiceStream showing over half of Web users willing to do so.

Make sure your privacy policy measures up to the law—and to what your customers expect.

Exhibit 5-17 Customers provide information in return for value.

Are these observations foolproof? No. IP addresses are not reliable sources of information about visitors that use multiple computers or who share a single computer with others. And a French citizen could be surfing today from Germany, but you might mistakenly think he's from Germany. These kinds of observations lead to correct inferences the great majority of the time.

There's more you can do. Each search visitor to your site has entered a search query that reflects a strong interest—John Batelle, author of *The Search*, calls the aggregated list of search keywords and clicked pages the "database of intentions." This collection of information is interesting to many parties, but marketers should be at the head of the line. You can choose frequently-occurring keywords as triggers for special offers related to what the searcher is looking for.

You can use your blog feed subscriptions to discover more than customer interests—you can determine behavioral tendencies. Continental Airlines, Delta Airlines, and Pheedz each offer vacation deals for regular customers who subscribe to their Web feeds. What can you do with this information? Maybe the free spirits who subscribe to these feeds are the right people to offer to "bump" when their flights are overbooked. Or perhaps they'd give permission for your hotel partners to contact them with last-minute resort vacancies, too. You can test to find out. If you put on your thinking cap, you can put almost any piece of information to use.

You can go much further, however. Want to identify customers based on psychographics? Maybe you should start a blog that appeals to the people in your target segment. Both Ford and BP are pursuing green initiatives to soften their environmental images. Should they start blogs on the subject? The blog subscribers might respond to vastly different promotions than their other customers—a prime use for personalization.

You can also design the navigation of your site to collect information. Business to Consumer (B2C) companies can separate their Web experience based on country. If a customer consistently visits a particular country site, you can conclude the country of residence. Will you get a few wrong? Sure, but if you get almost all of them right, the personalization value is worth it. If your customer consistently visits your France country site *and* comes from an IP address located in France, that evidence seems fairly conclusive.

Business to Business (B2B) marketers have even more navigation design options. In addition to identifying countries, B2B sites often employ extranets—special Web sites designed for use by a single customer company. Each employee of that company typically must register and be approved before accessing that site. The attractiveness of the content on that extranet site will drive large numbers of customer employees to register, revealing the company they work for.

Hewlett-Packard has designed the large business area of its Web site around industry solutions, as shown in Exhibit 5-18. Wanna bet that people who click on a particular industry actually work in that industry?

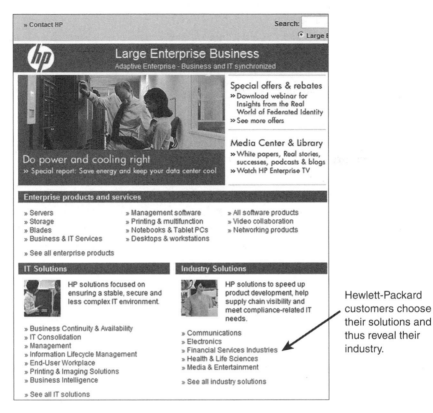

Hewlett-Packard customers choose their solutions and thus reveal their industry.

Exhibit 5-18   Your site navigation can reveal firmographics information.

Sometimes, it's most effective to combine the technique of guessing based on activity with the technique of asking the customer directly. IBM uses visitors' IP addresses to deduce their companies (and their industry), utilizing the information for personalization. Sometimes the guess is not correct, however, so the customer is always prompted to change the industry if it's wrong. You might think that merely asking customers to divulge their industries might be equally effective, but customers are actually more likely to correct an error than to fill in an omission.

No two businesses are the same, so these examples are merely food for thought. As you think about what information you need to improve relevance to customers, consider how you can entice customers to reveal it or to design your site to guess it. Once you're armed with the customer information you need, you have to figure out how to personalize your site with it.

Designing Your Experience for Each Customer

Today, you segment to attract customers and define segment messages and approaches. Tomorrow, the segmentation can be much more granular, and the conversation extends all the way through sales and beyond. This is the real Customer Relationship Management. Andreas Weigend, the former Chief Technology Officer at Amazon, says the industry is moving from "e-business to Me-business."

Any salesman worth his salt (or even pepper) knows how to personalize the sales pitch to the customer. The more that is learned about the customer, the more the pitch can be tailored to fit the customer's needs. In fact, the very products selected to be pitched are based on knowledge of the customer. Technologists promise that computers can do the same thing through a Web site feature called *personalization*. But just because they've promised it doesn't mean that it is easy or even possible. (Marketers should be able to relate to this.)

Personalization, at its simplest, is about each customer getting an individual experience, which sounds really expensive and hard to do. So the trick is to make people feel special without it being quite as much work as it seems. It reminds me of something I say to my four kids, "You're unique, just like everyone else."

How *do* you offer individual attention to thousands or even millions of customers, while making each one cost the same as everyone else?

You start with those User-Centered Design folks discussed earlier in this chapter. They'll help you develop *personas*—shorthand caricatures of your real customers. Maybe one of your target segments is represented by Adam, a twenty-something college-educated professional who pores over the details of every electronics product you sell and will pay the price to get what he wants. Perhaps Juanita is another persona for your business—she's a single mom in her mid-thirties who buys the hottest designs (but only after you mark them down to clear them out for the new stuff).

Author Bryan Eisenberg advises using "four to seven personas for each business unit," but some companies use considerably more—W.L. Gore employs about 30 personas. ScottsMiracleGro, the U.S. lawn care company, has three main personas for which they tailor their marketing experience:

- **Confident masters**—They take pride in their lawn. They're enthusiastic and interested in learning more about lawn care. They're experts interested in advanced techniques, such as thatching and lawn aeration.

- **Challenged optimists**—They are frustrated and anxious to have a good lawn. They want the nuts and bolts explained: "How do I make my lawn greener now?"

- **Minimum maintainers**—"I'm happy so long as no one notices my lawn is the worst in the neighborhood."

Your mileage may vary, and so will your personas, but developing concrete personas will make your varied market segments real. Some companies have made life-sized cardboard cutouts of their half-dozen personas and scattered them around their offices. Having your customers "in your face" helps everyone remember *why* you do everything you do. As you make each decision, you can ask yourself what Juanita would think—it changes what you decide.

Carphone Warehouse Plc, a European mobile phone retailer, has taken personas one step further by estimating the *value* of each persona, so they know which ones are more important than others. You can experiment with the right metrics for your situation, but if you want to do it wrong quickly, just prioritize based on the size of each target segment and the average profit (or even revenue) per customer.

Beyond personas, you can design your navigation for self-segmentation, as discussed in Chapter 1, "They're Doing Wonderful Things with Computers." As you recall, self-segmentation allows customers to choose the exact product that interests them by progressively refining what they want. To allow customers to segment themselves, you need your Web site to support *dynamic navigation*—the links and other choices on each page must be assembled as the page is shown to each person so that different choices can be shown based on what your customers are doing. The technical magic behind this technique is called *multifaceted search*—each selection executes a new search behind the scenes, even though the customer might not be aware it's happening.

Exhibit 5-19 shows how Radio Shack uses multifaceted search to help customers select the perfect camcorder. Customers can choose *facets*—their preferred price range, brand preference, media format, and optical zoom capabilities—to narrow down the list of camcorders to choose from. You can even take into account your on-hand inventory, so that you show only products that are in stock. Customers don't think of this experience as search, but this search technology quickly revises the results and the features left to choose from each time a customer makes a selection.

Product manufacturers use multifaceted search to help customers choose from their product line, while retailers use it across product lines from multiple manufacturers. Multifaceted search allows self-segmentation based on needs—you can think of it as allowing deep customization of products or choice among near-infinite selection. Chris Anderson, author of *The Long Tail*, explains that the Internet is frequently about "selling less of more"—selling lower quantities of vastly more different items. Multifaceted search makes it easy for a customer to find the right item among this seemingly boundless selection.

Multifaceted search also helps marketers collect information—Radio Shack might get some insight into brand preferences of customers who start their selections with the *brand* facet. Customers loyal to Sony, for example, would be likely to choose "Sony" first. Radio Shack can use that information to personalize later visits to the site by emphasizing ads for Sony products.

Radio Shack customers can choose the features important to them to narrow down the selection of camcorders.

Exhibit 5-19 Self-segmentation through multifaceted search

Other businesses can design different information collection experiences. If you offer case studies that can be selected by industry and company size, you can bet that customers who select "insurance" and "large business" probably work for a large insurance company. Similarly, if customers choose a location for in-person training, it stands to reason that they live there.

Such is the beauty of multifaceted search—every facet selected is used immediately to refine the information displayed but can also be saved in a personalization profile for later use. You should design your multifaceted experiences to elicit the information you want to know, in addition to designing for customers to find what they want.

Multifaceted navigation is perfect for customers who know exactly what they want, and works well for customers that figure out what they want from being prompted with the available features on the screen. As you can see from the example from Radio Shack, customers who don't understand any of the media formats and never heard of "optical zoom" need more background information before multifaceted search is effective. Your information architects can help plan paths that assist customers of varying skill levels.

You might be wondering at this point what is required to provide multifaceted search capability for your site. Besides the technology itself, you need to have *structured* information—an e-commerce catalog or some other computer database will do just fine. *Metadata*, such as the subject or the author of an HTML page or of an *XML* file, can also be used as facets. Ask your Web developers to check into whether your data is already in the format you need.

Understanding just enough of the technical details will vastly improve the navigation of your Web site—your marketing depends on it. Each *field* in your database (or every tag in your XML file) can be a facet. Your information architects and your User-Centered Design folks can help decide what the right facets are for your customers and the task at hand.

Just as with everything else, you can experiment with an initial set of facets to see what works and then refine them based on which ones result in clicks and conversions. Yes, you can do it wrong quickly and then fix it. Pick the ones that seem best to you and put them in the order that makes sense. Then mix them up and see if customers convert at higher rates.

Despite how useful personas and multifaceted search can be, experts do not consider them to be true personalization techniques because every customer can get the same experience. Experts reserve the term *personalization* for an experience in which different customers do the same things (come to the same page and click the same links) but see different content. Amazon, for example, shows different content on its pages to each customer based on their navigation and purchase history.

Web sites are traditionally organized using a *location*-based information architecture, which operate based on a sense of place. ("*Where* am I? On the consumer electronics page.") Personalized sites use a *view*-based approach. ("Who am I? If you are not Jerry, then click here.") At Amazon, customers see their personal store, full of items Amazon believes they are interested in, based on their previous browsing and purchases. At Netflix, each customer sees their personal queue of DVDs scheduled to be sent, which they have chosen. Each customer gets a different view of the site even when they perform the same actions as other customers.

Most personalized sites, in fact, are a hybrid of location-based and view-based architectures. IBM's site, for example, is heavily location-based, with separate areas for products, services, and support, for example, but IBM also provides extranet sites tailored for the view of a particular company. As shown in Exhibit 5-20, IBM's home page can offer separate views of tasks and promotions picked for a customer's company and industry. If you compare these personalized screen shots against the standard home page shown in Exhibit 5-6, you can see that IBM not only personalizes the main image, but also adds links for industry-specific consulting, solutions, and services.

Exhibit 5-20   Using a customer's industry for personalization

Navigation pages are the aisles in your store, and destination pages are the shelves that contain your products. Personalization lets you change the aisles, the shelves, and the products you stock on those shelves—for each person.

Amazon is the most famous example of personalization—and the most misleading. Amazon makes it look easy, but it's not. Amazon has made an enormous investment in the technology behind its winning experience—and that's only part of the story.

Amazon's business is unusual in that huge amounts of activity data can be analyzed. When Amazon began the world's greatest bookstore, it benefited from book buyers' propensity to buy multiple books from the same author or on the same subject. When

Amazon customers buy a book on choosing a college, it's likely that they'll buy other books on that subject, and it's even more likely that they'll buy more books of some kind.

Your business might not be able to emulate the personalization approaches of Amazon. If your customer buys a new car, it's not terribly likely she'll buy another next week, much less a similar one. So, the way Amazon personalizes won't work for most businesses because their transactions are too few and far between.

Most businesses are left trying to automate the decisions that their best salesperson makes. They create simple *business rules* based on their experience—"If a customer places a digital camera in the cart, show offers for a leather case and a larger memory card." If you don't currently take advantage of these cross-sell opportunities, that's a great place to start.

Later, you can improve your cross-sell rules. Bass Pro Shops, the outdoor retailer, developed successful simple business rules to cross-sell accessories and similar items on a product page but found some customers were confused by the promotions. David Seifert, Director of Operations for Bass Direct Marketing, replaced the simple business rules with a metrics-based approach, working with analytics vendor CoreMetrics. Seifert said his buyers were initially skeptical because some of the promotions selected based on purchase history "don't look logical, but when we showed the buyers the conversion rate, there was no question." Bass saw a 50 percent increase in cross-sell revenues.

Metrics-based personalization works well, just as metrics-based approaches work well even when no personalization is involved. Personalization approaches that rely on simple business rules are better than nothing (do it wrong quickly), but metrics can improve your results.

Your Web metrics package ought to be able to break your customers into market segments to show you which products, messages, and offers provide more conversions than others, segment by segment. It's one thing to see that your conversion rate has dropped, but quite another to know which segments have plummeted the most. Your experimentation should start with personalized messages for *those* segments to see if conversions can be increased.

So how *do* you personalize your Web site? Several elements must be brought together into a single experience:

- **Identity**—Your Web software must be able to identify who the customer is. Often this involves use of a *cookie*, a special file that Web browsers employ to uniquely identify the computer being used—usually when identifying the same computer for multiple visits means it's the same person. Many customers block or erase cookies, so most personalization software also uses a *profile*, which stores information you've gathered about each customer. Personalized sites often require registration with a user identifier and password.

- **Dynamic Pages**—Your site must be able to show different content to different customers—software must generate your Web pages "on the fly" (at the moment they are displayed). Personalized sites use different technical approaches to display dynamic content, with *portal servers* providing the most built-in support for personalization.

- **Business Rules**—As we've discussed previously, your site must be able to present different content on the page based on what you know about your customer. The rules specify how to do that, such as "Provide a link to small business information for each customer who works for a business with fewer than 50 employees" or "Show the free shipping offer to customers with the highest RFM ratings that have previously used expedited shipping."

- **Content**—Obviously, if you intend to show different content to different customers, you must develop multiple versions of that content. For example, when Scotts personalized its lawn care information, it committed to create and maintain a long list of tips categorized by zip code and grass type. Usually, personalized sites employ a *content management system* to keep this varied content organized.

Creating and maintaining all that content is the hardest part of many personalized experiences. It's one thing to provide a personalized view of order history—that requires not much more than a database of each customer's orders. Providing personalized messaging might require multiple versions of what used to be standard content. Each customer may see just one version of your page, but you must create *all* of them. Most companies can't afford production of that much content. As comedian Steven Wright says, "It's a small world, but I wouldn't want to paint it."

Personalization can be very helpful for some businesses, but many Web sites have struggled to improve their experience with personalization. Some ideas are nearly universally useful, such as providing a "My account" page that shows recent orders, bills paid, and other service information. But most personalization ideas need to be tested on your site to see if they work—and if they are affordable. Some ideas that produce good results might require too much expensive content to be worthwhile, such as crafting a different sales pitch for every industry. Test what works for you.

Some kinds of personalization don't require extravagant investments in content. For example, prices needn't be one-size-fits-all. (One size never really fit all, anyway—it should have been called "one-size-is-all-we-make.") You can use business rules to reduce the price for certain kinds of customers (such as those that deliver the highest revenue) or in certain situations (such as customers that looked at this item three times without buying or those that have over $100 of other items in the cart).

Other personalization techniques can be implemented without high content costs. B2B marketers can set up extranet sites designed to serve just one company. You can provide a product catalog containing just the products that company buys from you, at their negotiated prices.

Some of your customers might want you to go further by sending them a data feed of your products to use in their procurement systems. Web feeds, the same technique that distributes your blog feeds to subscribers, can be used to send updates of your product catalogs. A great use of personalization is to send different feeds to each customer—you can provide each customer with their negotiated prices.

But why stop at personalizing your Web site when e-mail might be the most important marketing method for personalization?

Personalized e-mail is nothing new, but it's critically important. In a sense, all e-mail is personal in that it's personally addressed subscriber by subscriber. The problem is that

NEITHER PHISH NOR FOUL

Legitimate e-mail marketers have struggled for years to avoid association with spammers, but *phishing* might constitute an even more dangerous threat. Your customers have probably developed some confidence that they can tell spam from your legitimate messages, but phishing attacks are designed to fool recipients into believing the messages come from *you*.

Phishers impersonate legitimate companies, stealing their company names, e-mail addresses, logos, visual design, and anything else they can think of, all in the hopes of fooling your customers with a counterfeit message. Phishing attacks often come under the guise of a message from customer service, asking the recipient to log into their account after clicking a link in the message.

Those fooled by this ruse are redirected to a rogue site (which looks just like yours) that happily collects their passwords, allowing the phishers access to their accounts. Most phishers parlay several of these break-ins to amass enough information to pile up fraudulent credit card charges or a larger scale identity theft.

If your company is targeted, your customers are being defrauded, and customers will be understandably wary about responding to your legitimate messages. As phishing becomes more recognized, your customers will be less inclined to click on *any* marketing e-mail, regardless of whether your particular company has been impersonated.

What's a legitimate marketer to do?

Rule one is to avoid looking like a phisher yourself—avoid the foul smell associated with techniques that phishers use. Never send an e-mail requesting your customers to log in, to update their expiring credit card number, or to provide

we often send the same message to everyone—or essentially the same message. (Changing "Dear Mike" to "Dear Hector" doesn't count.) Sometimes, such as when you send out your monthly newsletter, sending the same message to everyone is reasonable, but truly personalized e-mail can be more powerful in spurring conversions because it is more relevant to your customer.

Relevance is the coin of the realm in e-mail marketing. Despite all the talk about how spam kings get rich, the truth is that hardworking, legitimate e-mail marketers enjoy a far more lucrative and customer-friendly existence. Jupiter Research notes that conversion rates for carefully targeted e-mails reach nearly four percent, while traditional broadcast e-mail techniques barely approach one percent. Moreover, using these

---

any personal information. Beyond this basic advice, you should keep three other points in mind:

- **One source**—Use a single domain as the source of all your e-mail. Don't set up cutesy domain names for each campaign—it teaches your customers that they'll never know from whence your legitimate messages come. That provides an opening for phishers to pick their own cutesy domain names to impersonate you. Instead, force the phisher to impersonate your single source of e-mail—that makes it tougher on them.

- **One destination**—Clean up your customer records so that you send all e-mail from your company to one e-mail address per customer. Because customers typically have multiple e-mail addresses, if they know that all e-mail from you comes to only one of them, they can spot phishing attempts easily when they come to other addresses.

- **One contact**—When customers aren't sure if a particular e-mail is legitimate or is a phishing attempt, they should be able to easily contact someone at your company to find out. Your contact should be the central clearinghouse of all e-mails being sent and should be able to quickly provide the correct answer. This might sound easy, but large companies with far-flung marketing groups might have no single focal point with knowledge of all e-mail campaigns. Nothing will doom your credibility more quickly than being unable to verify whether you sent an e-mail to your customer.

By now, it's probably clear that you can't avoid being swept up in the phishing mess merely by avoiding the practice yourself. If you're sending out e-mail, you must eliminate that foul phish smell by avoiding all association with phishing techniques and by helping your customers when they need it.

techniques to deliver relevant offers yields 18 times more profit than the simple-minded blast approach.

Wal-Mart sends out personalized e-mail to moms based on the birth date of their babies. "Baby Connection" is a weekly e-mail designed around the milestones that infants reach at certain ages and of course contains appropriate products available from Wal-Mart. Simply learning a baby's birth date makes Wal-Mart's program effective.

Personalized e-mail can be assembled and sent automatically if you have the right software. Using everything from CRM systems to Web analytics, marketers can identify the right message for just about anyone. Your CRM system might know which customers might be ready to replace their laptops (because they were purchased three years ago)—and might also know their e-mail addresses. Do you sell supplies on a recurring basis? Send a timed e-mail with a replenishment offer. Staples, for example, sends customers e-mails offering accessories for products it recently sold them.

But how do you generate unique offers for each of these highly targeted groups? It's incredibly expensive to create custom pages for so many offers.

Multifaceted search comes to the rescue. If you've already loaded up your product catalog in a multifaceted search engine, you can use multifaceted search queries as your URLs in your e-mail marketing campaigns (such as www.store.com/camcorders.jsp?brand=sony). Beverage supplier BevMo.com and Northern Tool, for example, send e-mails that can drill into their product catalogs for just the right product or category of products, allowing shoppers to then drill yet deeper to find what they want.

Your CRM-based e-mail can do the same. Why not send those laptop owners e-mails pointing them to the top catalog page of your current laptops? Every feature is listed so that drilling to the best one is easy.

Some companies are going even further, sending personalized e-mail on a one-to-one basis. Wouldn't it be great if you could make a special offer to a customer who is thinking about buying something but hasn't pulled the trigger yet? That's what a "recontact" e-mail can do.

If you think about it, it makes sense that an e-mail sent to someone who has already been to your site to look at your product will be more likely to lead to a sale than someone you've targeted for other reasons, no matter how smart your targeting. Continuing our example, which group of customers is more likely to buy, the ones whose laptops are three years old or the ones who looked at the laptop pages on your site last week? Clearly, you'd like to be able to contact the ones who visited last week, but how do you do that?

First, you need to be able to identify customers when they come to your site. If you use cookies and profiles to identify registered customers, then you'll know when they visit your site, and you'll know which pages they look at.

Second, you must know your customers' e-mail addresses. If you've offered an e-mail newsletter, they've provided their addresses. Or if you send an e-mail confirmation with each order, you have their addresses. Any legitimate service you can provide through e-mail allows you to collect a customer's e-mail address.

Last, you need permission to contact your customer with an offer—knowing an e-mail address doesn't allow you to contact your customer whenever you want. You should ask for permission to send offers anytime you request someone's e-mail address. If you can convince people that the special offers will be targeted to exactly what they are interested in, rather than blanket e-mails to all customers, you'll persuade more folks to opt in. If you really provide valuable offers, very few of your customers will later opt out.

If you pull together all three of these elements, then your Web metrics system can trigger your marketing e-mail system to send out special offers under certain circumstances, such as for customers who abandon their shopping carts. In truth, you don't need to use e-mail—some banner ad networks can show a special message of yours to customers who've already visited your site—but e-mail is the most common way to recontact.

Bass Pro Shops sends one kind of e-mail to customers who abandon their carts and another kind to those that browse several product areas without buying, as shown in Exhibit 5-21. Bass sends its e-mails between three to five days after the Web visit, offering a few products in the same price range as what was viewed at the site. While most companies provide discounted pricing with their offers, Bass found that they get about the same conversion rate regardless of whether they discount.

Other companies are moving away from e-mail to personalized Web feeds. If you have a site search engine, your customers can register search queries that provide new results each day in a Web feed. Perhaps your customer is just waiting for every new case study for a particular industry—a personalized Web feed can provide that. On top of the benefits that the personalization itself provides, individual feeds for each customer also ensure that you overcome the metrics challenges of counting the number of subscribers accurately—no aggregators are redistributing your feed if it's designed for just one customer.

Every business must experiment with different approaches to personalization to find out what works best. You must constantly review new ways to make both your message and your offers more personal and more relevant. That added personal touch is more and more the differentiator that marks a lasting relationship between you and your customer.

This email was sent to you by Bass Pro Shops.
To ensure delivery to your inbox (not bulk or junk folders), please add basspro@BassProNews.com to your address book.

Shopping

Select your favorite category:

Freshwater Fishing
Fly Fishing
Saltwater Fishing
Hunting
Camping & Auto
Marine & Electronics
Apparel
Footwear
Gift & Home

GREAT OUTDOOR GEAR FOR YOU

Bass Pro sends "recontact" e-mails with products individually selected for each customer, based on their recent activity on their Web site.

Stacy, Here are several great products we have selected just for you.

SALE Rapala® Giant Lures Replica Decor
$39.99

Special Offer Bass Pro Shops® Enticer Spinning Reel and Rod Combo
$39.88

Bass Pro Shops® Deluxe Rod Rack
$39.99

SALE Bass Pro Shops® Corner Rod Rack
$44.88

Giant Heddon® Torpedo or Spook Lure Replica Decor
$49.99

SALE Bass Pro Shops® Floor Rod Rack
$49.88

FREE Offer Shakespeare® Ugly Cat SC20 Rod and Reel Combo
$39.95

Exhibit 5-21   Recontact e-mails raise your conversions.

Summary

Jakob Nielsen likes to say that "The experience *is* the brand." What's more, your customer's experience defines the *new* customer relations. Your relationship with your customer rests more on your online marketing than ever before.

In this chapter, you learned the three big areas that comprise that online customer experience and the considerations you should have in designing yours:

- **The look and feel**—It all starts with use cases—the tasks your customers perform when they come to your Web site. Your visual design, your navigation, and the interactivity of your experience affect customer perception of your brand based on how well they assist completing each task.

- **The sights and sounds**—The content is what delivers your marketing messages. Your copy must be both bite-sized and engaging to be persuasive, but it needs help from pictures, audio, and video to break through the clutter of words your customers are exposed to each day.

- **The touch**—Your marketing can be adaptive and personal to each customer. You can use RFM ratings to decide which customers to target with your messages and create a safe and inviting environment for customers to share personal information. Once they do, you can combine personas with the right content and technology to design a personal experience for each customer.

We covered a lot of ground in this chapter, and we are ready to move on. Now that you understand all the elements you have under your control, which ones should you change first? How do you know when you've made enough changes in one area for now, and should begin to focus on something else, and how do you get any of these changes made quickly?

Chapter 6 talks about the value of everything you do, so you can decide which problems to attack first—and see how far off your first attempt is. This next chapter also helps you speed up your company's metabolism so you really can do it wrong *quickly*.

6

Customers Vote with Their Mice

"You can observe a lot just by watching."

—Yogi Berra

Chapter Contents

- Where Do You Start?   215
- How Do You Know How Wrong It Is?   224
- How Do You Speed Up?   240
- Summary   252

Imagine that you are responsible for your company's product catalog business. It's your baby. (You rock it.) You have spent weeks on the project, and you've finally completed it. So now it's time to tell your boss what you've done. And this is what you say:

We completed the catalog on time and under budget. We redesigned it from the ground up, which was long overdue, and we used a completely new printing process that provides better quality than ever. We also used a new binding process that lets the catalog lay flat when it's opened—that makes it far easier to use. And the customers love it—they say it has never looked better. We are following up with a survey of all catalog customers to confirm that this is our best catalog yet, but it looks very good so far.

What do you think your boss would say? Maybe something like "Get out! Get out! What are you, crazy? That's the dumbest status report on a catalog I have ever heard in all my years in the business! You better well have shipped it on time and under budget! Who cares how you produced the $^#% thing? And who cares what customer surveys say? What are the *sales*? Better than last year at this time? How many inquiries are we getting? How many orders? What are the *results*, you twit?"

That was a silly story, wasn't it? No sane catalog marketer would ever talk to his boss that way. But suppose I change the story just a little bit. Suppose you are reporting to your boss about a slightly different project:

We completed the Web site re-launch on time and under budget. We redesigned it from the ground up, which was long overdue, and we used completely new software and servers that provide better quality than ever. We also used a new content process that lets us have different navigation bars for each part of the site—which makes it far easier to use. And the customers love it—they say it has never looked better. We are following up with a survey of all Web customers to confirm that this is our best design yet, but it looks very good so far.

Hmmm. Why doesn't that sound just as dumb as it did for the catalog? It's because we are accustomed to thinking about Web sites as some kind of technical project that we're proud just to complete. But who cares how we produce the #^$% thing? And who cares what customer surveys say? What are the *sales*? Better than last year at this time? How many inquiries are we getting? How many orders? What are the *results* (you twit)?

Results. That's what we are in business for, but too often we are working through some kind of technological tour de force, and we forget why we are in business. I have personally provided that kind of status report for a redesigned Web site and been given an award for a job well done. (I am slightly ashamed, in retrospect, but I *did* cash the check.)

Maybe you can get away with giving that kind of report, too. Today. But that's going to change. The only question is whether you figure it out before your boss does.

In Chapter 4, "Going Over to the Dark Side," we reminded ourselves what our Web sites are for. In Chapter 5, "The New Customer Relations," we reminded ourselves that the customer is in control. In this chapter, we'll talk about results. What are the results of all this technological investment? And, more importantly, how can results improve?

It all goes back to satisfying your customers—and your customers vote with their mice. Every e-mail you send, every Web page you show, every move you make, they'll be watching you. But will they click you?

That's what *you'll* be watching, using the techniques covered in Chapter 4, and you'll be changing what you do in response, using the knowledge you picked up in Chapter 5. This chapter talks about how to do it wrong quickly.

Some of you might be uncomfortable with the idea of doing it wrong at all, much less *quickly*. It just feels better to deliberate and slowly decide the right thing to do. You're more comfortable with a style of "do it right slowly."

Except that you probably *don't* do it right, certainly not all the time and maybe not even most of the time. At those times, when you get it wrong despite your best efforts, your philosophy turns out to be "do it wrong slowly." Gee, that doesn't sound comforting. We're getting it wrong, but we make up for that with a plodding pace. Not good.

It's actually worse than that, however, because the slow, deliberative style often results in watching your competitors do things before you, giving them the advantage of being known for something that you can only copy. Once Dell became known for allowing customers to build their own computers, no one else got any credit for doing so. Once Starbucks changed what people expected from coffee, Dunkin' Donuts could only match them.

Maybe you had the idea first, but if you didn't *do* it first, you've forever lost the advantage of making your mark. To your customers, it doesn't appear that your philosophy is "do it right slowly." To them, it seems like "don't just do something—stand there."

Maybe you're still not convinced. Ask yourself: Is there a company whose marketing you truly admire? Coca-Cola? Apple? It doesn't matter exactly which company it is, really—just think about them for a minute. Think about what it is you admire about them.

Now think about what it's like to work there. Do you have this idealized vision that everything just goes oh-so-smoothly? That the people there somehow *know* what to do? Coca-Cola famously dumped their market-leading product in favor of New Coke. Apple struggled for years until it realized that it should be selling music.

Why am I dwelling on mistakes made by these great marketing companies? Because mistakes are the point. One of the reasons these companies are great is that they try things—even dumb things, sometimes. And their employees often have no idea what the right thing is to do—just like in your little screwed-up corner of the world.

We're all screw-ups.

Not one of us knows what we're doing all the time. You'll take a step forward if you admit that and reach out for experimentation instead of correctness.

Do you have a clear goal? Do you have what it takes to do it? And, finally, are you ready to adjust *all* your means to that end? That's what doing it wrong quickly is all about—knowing what you want to achieve, knowing how to do it, and changing, changing, changing until you get results.

Naysayers tell you that change is complicated. There was no greater naysayer than social critic H.L. Mencken, who liked to say, "For every complex problem, there is a solution that is simple, neat, and wrong." It's a nice quote, but isn't that simple, neat solution still the first thing to try?

Of course it is.

Especially when *no one* knows what the right answer is. When you are dealing with something as new as online marketing, you are always experimenting, whether you like it or not. Trying all kinds of ideas is the only way out.

If you keep shooting at the sky, eventually a duck will fall. I'm not advocating that you shoot randomly—but we're all more likely to spend a lifetime aiming at ducks without shooting, just to avoid the embarrassment of a single miss. Instead, we need to keep shooting, even if we aren't sure of our aim. Each time we shoot, we can assess how far off we are before the next shot. (Those poor ducks...)

You don't need to be a nuclear physicist to see the logic of experimentation, but if it gives you more confidence, nuclear physicist Richard Feynman once said, "...it doesn't matter how beautiful your theory is, it doesn't matter how smart you are—if it doesn't agree with experiment, it's wrong."

Are you experimenting? Are you making mistakes? How far off was that last try? How do you know? That's what we are going to talk about. You should be able to change a font on a page at 9 am and know by 5 pm whether it was a mistake or not. Exaggeration?

Let's look at a real-life example as told by Andreas Weigend, Amazon's former Chief Scientist. Amazon.com is famous for its personalized customer experience, but personalization is not the real secret of its success. Its real secret is doing it wrong quickly. As Andreas tells it, some Amazon designers thought the shopping cart panel should be on the left. Others thought it should be on the right. At many companies, these designers would have argued back and forth until some manager, who knew even less about the issue than the warring designers, put his foot down (or in his mouth) and made a decision.

Not at Amazon.

At Amazon, the customers decide. They vote with their mice. Amazon tested each design with a random set of customers. The shopping cart panel on the right yielded one percent more revenue than the one on the left. So on the right it went. Controversy ended because the customers had spoken.

Is that how that kind of controversy would be decided in your company? Or would you gather both factions into a conference room and have them argue with each other until they reach consensus? A friend of mine described one such gathering as "a meeting that resulted in a net loss of information." But most of us still make decisions that way.

You're not going to reach consensus over which side of the page should contain the shopping cart. You can't compromise by running it down the center of the page or by having it switch sides on alternate days. There are two opinions, and either one could be "right"—even the one that is "wrong" probably isn't wrong by much. Letting the customers decide is the only way to go.

Lest you think that one percent isn't that big a deal, remember that this was just *one* example. Amazon does tests like these every day, which is why their customer experience is the best in the business. It's amazing how smart you look if you do what your customers tell you.

So how do you do it wrong quickly? Let's break it down.

To do it wrong quickly, you need to know what *it* is. You need to know where to start. How do you know what to try? In Amazon's case, they had an argument to settle, but what if you don't? We'll talk about how you know what to try first.

To do it wrong quickly, you need to be able to measure just how *wrong* it is. How do you know it is wrong? Is it better or worse than what we had—than what we expected it to be? In Amazon's case, they had already decided the metric they cared about—revenue per visit. Amazon calculated the percentage of people that ordered with each design and the average order size and found that the "right" one yielded one percent more money. We'll talk about how you know what it's worth.

To do it wrong quickly, you need to be able to change things, well, *quickly*. You must have the ability to experiment constantly. In Amazon's case, they could show different designs to different sets of customers, but that's not required for most tests. You *do* need to be able to try one design for a week and another design the next week or two different variations of an offer or a different navigation. If you need to justify a change request to the architecture board each time you want to turn a knob, you're not going to make too many changes. We'll talk about how you accelerate your pace of change.

Let's start with the start. (Seems like the right approach, huh?) How do you know what to try first?

Where Do You Start?

What's the "it" in "do *it* wrong quickly?"

Unfortunately, we often choose the wrong place to start. We try to think of the "right" way to do it and then amass all of our resources at that distant target. Let's take a simple example to illustrate this. Suppose your business has no Web site at all. How should you start?

Well, you could try to do it the "right" way:

- **You need to choose your domain name and buy it**—A great deal of discussion revolves around choosing the right name, how the best three names are already owned and will cost a lot to buy, and which of the cheap names (that you really don't love) is the best one.

- **You need to choose a Web hosting company**—Big decision here with all sorts of information that you might not understand about which operating system you want. (What are FrontPage extensions, anyway? And what exactly is FTP?)

- **You need to choose software to make pages**—You see big differences in pricing, and you're not sure you would know how to use any of them.

- **You need to actually build your pages**—Gee, you don't really know how to lay out or design a page or how to do the pictures.

Small wonder that most people drop out along the way and decide, "Maybe we are not ready for a Web site yet." Still others decide to hire someone to do it all for them, but even picking the consultant leads them into gobs of complexity and a hefty bill.

These are the right things to do to build a professional Web site, but that's not where someone with no Web site should start. Instead, do it wrong quickly. Maybe you should start small, by trying to write a blog. You can get a message out there for people to see, you don't need to know very much, and Blogger and Typepad (and others) offer free hosting and easy startup.

Or maybe you just need a page that shows what you sell and where you're located or how to contact you. You can buy a listing in Verizon Superpages or some other Internet Yellow Pages site for a few bucks a month.

If you have no Web site, don't set out to create a professional Web site. An "unprofessional" one might work just fine. It's simple. It's cheap. And you can see how it works before you invest more time and money into it.

You probably already have a Web site, but are you improving it wrong quickly, or are you constantly planning large, costly redesigns as the only way forward?

Think about Web improvement the same way you consider home improvement. How often is it the right thing to knock down the entire house and build a new one in its place? Only if you really hate your house, you have a lot of money, and you can stand a huge disruption in your life. Most improvements should be small, like adding a new piece of furniture or repainting a room, but sometimes it makes sense to rip out a bathroom and put in a new one. Once in a while it makes sense to do something major, such as expand the house so your mom can move in with you. But it's rare that you should tear your house down and start over.

Your Web site is no different from your house. Most Web sites have relatively happy customers, but like most houses, can always be improved. Unfortunately, some people's approach is usually to tear the site down and build a new one where it

"BUT I HAVE NO WEB SITE!"

Nancy Fish was fishing for a way to attract new clients. The Bergen County (New Jersey) psychotherapist had a successful practice but felt unable to market herself to expand further. She did not, at first, think the Web was the way to do that.

> I felt totally out my league when thinking about creating a Web site. I am not very computer savvy, and I also was very skeptical about this form of marketing helping build my practice. I also thought the price would be prohibitive.

A computer-savvy friend came to the rescue, suggesting Nancy use a free Squidoo lens—a simple one-page Web site that is easy to create and update. Her friend told her to "provide a lot of biographical information" and to "write about some of my areas of specialty," which were then used as the content for the Squidoo lens, as shown in Exhibit 6-1. The whole process took just a few hours of work.

Nancy found the update process so easy that she started making her own edits to her lens and said that she feels "relatively confident" doing so. So she had achieved her goal of creating a Web site, and now she waited for results.

Within a few weeks, Nancy's lens was being found in Google and other search engines for "Bergen County psychotherapist," and she had already snagged two new clients, who simply called the phone number posted in her lens. Afterward, Nancy professed shock that people really use the Web to choose a psychotherapist, but she's extremely happy that they do:

> I would definitely recommend this approach and don't think people need to spend an exorbitant amount of money marketing themselves on the Web. At this point, I am very happy with the Web site and don't feel I need to make any changes or additions.

Nancy was not afraid of giving something a try, so she was already attracting clients by the time the people who "do it right" would still be picking a Web hosting company. Remember the old saying that "The smallest deed is better than the greatest intention."

stands—which is called a "site redesign" or a "major re-launch." They don't repaint a few rooms or even put in a new bathroom. They hire a new set of designers and information architects and do something dramatic to justify the cost.

But is that what customers want?

Some companies have learned the hard way that their customers prefer more subtle evolution in their user experience. For example, eBay changed its yellow background in favor of the more typical white and received so many complaints they felt compelled to change it back.

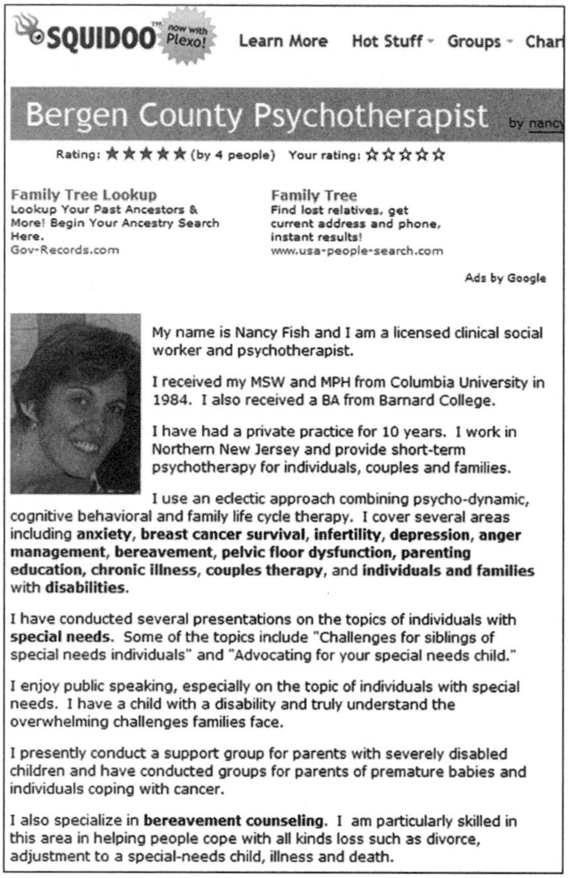

Exhibit 6-1 Web sites can be free and easy.

Now, did those customers really have some intrinsic problem with white backgrounds? Doubtful. White is the most common background of Web pages today. What eBay heard from its customers is that they like the eBay site and don't want anyone mucking around with it. It's an emotional connection with customers any marketer would envy.

So eBay did something very clever—gradually removing the yellow one shade at a time until eventually they had that white background they wanted. This evolutionary approach went unnoticed by customers.

Could eBay apply what it learned to other kinds of changes? Yes. When eBay discovered improvements they could make to the forms on their site based on user testing, they had a dilemma. If customers complained about something as innocuous as a color change, what would they say about modifying the forms that were used millions of times each month?

The personnel at eBay decided to leave it up to their customers. They introduced a new form link on their page that showed each customer the improved version and allowed customers to adopt the new form for themselves. When eBay saw how many people chose the new ones, they developed the confidence to replace the old forms sitewide.

Why does this work? Think of it as the "right turn theory." In countries where traffic stays on the right side of the road, studies show that far more accidents occur when drivers make left turns in front of oncoming traffic than when they make right turns. Big changes in your Web site are left turns. Yes, you get where you are going faster, but left turns are riskier. Instead, make three right turns. You get to the same place, but you've taken in a bit more scenery along the way, and it's much safer. So remember, two wrongs may not make a right, but three rights make a left.

Use a gradual approach when making changes. You can offer new experiences as "beta"—giving your customers the choice of what they want. Usability expert Jared Spool says, "The best teams not only design the changes, but design the process for introducing the change...to overcome the users' natural resistance to change."

Google is one of the biggest practitioners of "beta" experiences—it introduced its Gmail and many other ideas just that way. Google goes even further by testing tiny changes with small groups. If you ever notice that your Google search screen looks different from one shown the person next to you, it's because Google is testing a new feature on a random subset of searchers.

You, too, can tweak your experience a little at a time, rather than gutting it and replacing it every few years. What happens when you don't keep tweaking? One marketing director laments:

> So we're in the situation now where we built our Web site in 2001 and 2002 and it was a great Web site at that point and it provided a really nice jumping off point for individual brands to layer on campaigns and support for their specific business objectives. Well, nobody invested in keeping that foundation solid and current—and online the landscape changes so quickly. We are now in 2007 and we need to spend a ton of money simply to rebuild the foundation. That's a big lesson we are trying to impart to people. We are not going to do a Web design project and walk away from it. We need to turn this project into a program.

Learn from this. Every time you make a change to your Web site, you need to measure its results and make it better. When most people think the project's over, you need to know it's just starting.

If you make small changes, it's far easier to measure their effects. First, you have less data when your change is confined to a small area on your site. Second, if you change only one thing, then any effects can be attributed to that particular change—making multiple changes muddies the waters.

The trick is to make a small change with a large impact. Start with a single page but make sure it is an important page—one that directly leads to conversions. Make it a page with lots of traffic. Later in this chapter, we'll show you the simplest ways to set up an experiment.

Where do you start? That depends on where you are now.

Once, after a speech, a woman approached me and lamented that her small company just couldn't do it wrong quickly. Their Web site was *so* old and so bad that it just had to be redone from the ground up (perhaps even from the basement below ground). Her story of how awful it was reminded me of a description of a sleepy old town: "It was built in 1925 and never repainted." But she despaired of fixing it because they had no budget to upgrade their dowdy old Web site.

So I questioned her: "What is the absolute *worst* thing about your site?" She warmed to the idea and described how the company knows that they get two kinds of visitors, people looking to hire and people looking for work, but that the home page is a mish-mash of links that make it hard for each kind of person to get where they need to go.

I asked her what was stopping her from changing the home page so it highlighted two big buttons—one saying "Looking for a Job" and the other saying "Looking for an Employee." After all, how much can it cost to change one page?

She started to understand. "Yes, and I can check the before and after clicks to the underlying pages and see if I got more people there! And then I can start to rework *those* interior pages to see if we get more employers signed up and more resumes on file!"

That's the idea, and once she starts to show how the Web site is delivering those kinds of business results, she just might get the boss to spring for a designer to do a face-lift.

The idea of "starting small" works at big companies too. Computer manufacturer Sun Microsystems took a big risk by introducing customer ratings and reviews for its products. Curt Sasaki, Vice President of .SUN Web Properties, knew that some people at Sun would be nervous about this idea. "My notion was to start small" with just one product line. "We took that 90-day experience and went to the [next product] group. They were very skeptical but agreed to a 30-day pilot." By building support slowly, the project's success became apparent without the risk of doing something across all product lines that would cost more and be more embarrassing if it failed.

You can do the same thing with *your* Web site. You *can* start with your home page, but you might be better off picking a less-politically charged page that has a single goal, such as a page in your shopping cart experience. Small changes can have big effects, showing people the importance of the whole approach. Whatever you do, make sure to start as small as you can, while still demonstrating some kind of business impact.

Just change *one* thing.

Maybe you should test whether changing the visual design of a page improves your results. Remember, the page's look is the fourth most important part of your Web marketing. If you're now asking yourself, "What are the first three?" STOP! Stop listening to everyone else about what's important! (Yes, stop listening to me, too.) Start trusting your own wisdom about what to try. Start listening to your customers to see if what you tried worked.

Change the design and see what happens. Didn't work? Then change it back. Try something else. Do customers now click through more than before the change? Then see what changing the look of a *group* of pages does.

"HOW CAN I CHECK MY NAVIGATION?"

If you're like most companies, you spend a lot of time obsessing over your home page but maybe not enough time on your destination pages. What's a quick way to check out the information architecture of those pages? Use Keith Instone's Navigation Stress test (www.instone.org/navstress)—Keith is the lead information architect for IBM's Web team.

To start the test, pick any destination page on your site and print it in black and white all by itself (with nothing else on the page, not even the URL). Then pretend that this is your landing page for your first visit to the Web site and answer the following questions:

- What's this page about?
- What does each set of links represent?
- What site is this?
- What are the major sections of this site?
- Which section is this page within?
- What's one level "up" from this page?
- How do I get to the top page for this section of the site?
- How do I get to the site's home page?
- How could I get back here from the home page?

Don't be upset if your pages usually fail this test. Keith reports that he's been doing these tests since 1997, and most pages fail. The questions are designed to test the three major questions customers have when they land on your site: where they are, what is here, and where they can go.

When your pages pass the Navigation Stress test, your customers experience a lot less stress.

You might surprise yourself as to how much you can change over time if you start small and keep at it. For example, if your site does not have a consistent look, you can fix that gradually. Choose one of the designs you have or a new one, if you're ambitious, and start using that one each time you change a page.

Just start *somewhere*. Make a change—maybe you'll get lucky. (But don't call it luck; it sounds better to say "inadvertent competence.") Try a new idea every day—test and adjust—and try again tomorrow. If you're just starting out, perhaps you have a shortage of ideas, so try a few on for size:

- Change your content. Your offers. Your imagery. What happens when you do? Do you show the prices of your products? (Your customers want you to.)
- Are you easy to contact? Do you respond?
- Do you measure how quickly you deliver what you promise? Do you bill people properly? Are your orders being received on time? Can buyers check the status online?
- Can people buy directly from you? Should they be able to? Do you need to put in e-commerce? If people don't buy directly from you, is your downstream experience one that satisfies them?

Start out by making sure your Web site is a store that people want to buy from. When you've turned your Web site into a lean, mean conversion machine, then it's time to start driving traffic there. Focus on search marketing first—it's the most cost-effective way to attract visitors. Once you're drawing your share of searchers, it's time to look at e-mail, blogs, and anything else that seems to work. Try things out and stick with the winners. Treat every page as a landing page. Decide how many different page types you need, what each type should look like, and what content it should contain.

After you do all that, you should have a successful Web site that is drawing lots of visitors. Now it's time to improve your relationships with those visitors.

Get people to *subscribe* to your content so that you can contact them regularly—newsletters, blogs, podcasts. Get them to opt in, and maybe even tell you something about themselves. Cookie them so you know when they come back.

Larger companies should mobilize their employees to do their marketing for them. Set policies for customer e-mail, for employee blogs, and for participation in message boards and other conversations on the Internet. You can encourage employees to get out there with customers while training them in best practices. Monitor the blogosphere and the rest of the Web to see what others are saying about you.

Some marketers can go further.

Use dynamic navigation to make your site more responsive. Let people tell you where they want to go with multifaceted search and start to collect information about people that you can use to show personalized offers.

Start e-mailing them about things they care about. Start personalizing your site in bigger ways. Consider using a portal. Set up a wiki for your best customers to collaborate on strategy—kind of an online customer advisory board.

We've used many examples from the Web because every company needs a Web site, but you must apply this thinking to any Internet marketing work you do. Don't make a six-month commitment to a banner ad network—try it out for a few weeks and see how it works. Don't run the same paid search ad for a month; see if different copy and different keywords bring you a higher return on your investment.

Just start your blog instead of waiting to figure out what you have to say—if it doesn't work, you can always stop. When I started my Biznology newsletter and blog, I had no idea what I was doing. In fact, my first blog entry was about . . . wait for it...blogging. (And when I was a kid, I enjoyed looking into a mirror that faced another mirror.) I'll probably never be an A-list blogger, but I have found an audience, and that's what I wanted.

At all times, remember that Internet marketing is a game of experimentation, just like direct marketing. In fact, Internet marketing is really direct marketing on steroids—you can do more, measure more, and change faster than with offline direct marketing.

Perhaps e-mail marketing illustrates this quality the most. CompUSA, the U.S. technology retailer, uses recontact e-mail marketing techniques, as described in Chapter 5, and does so in a big way. CompUSA sends e-mails to customers that abandon shopping carts, purchasers who might later be interested in a related product, and purchasers who might (years later) be in the market for a replacement product.

But they didn't start out doing it on a large scale. They started out with a very simple experiment, targeting one market segment (purchasers who might be interested in adding another related product) for one product line (personal computers). Only when that worked did they move on to other customer segments and more products.

As we saw in Chapter 5, U.S.-based ScottsMiracle-Gro, maker of fertilizer and other lawn care products, offers personalized lawn care advice, with 125 different geographic regions and multiple grass types (because different grasses require different weed control products). But Scotts worked its way up to this sophisticated service a little at a time, according to Joel Reimer, Director of Interactive Marketing. "We started out by sending a different e-mail to each of our 18 distribution regions—these regions meant nothing to our customers, but at least we knew the product that we were recommending was available in that region."

At its inception in 2001, Scotts' customers liked the service immediately, and Scotts knew they needed to find a way to do more. They automated their e-mail system to more easily send out the personalized messages, allowing them more time to concentrate on improving the content itself.

Scotts shows that personalization doesn't have to be complicated to be effective—they were not afraid to do it wrong quickly. They tried an idea in the easiest way possible, and when they saw it was effective, that's when they invested more heavily and did it right.

Let's recap. We're trying to approach our Web sites and our Web marketing in a brand new way—one that emphasizes incremental improvement over sweeping changes. Evolution over revolution. And we are adopting a new mindset of deciding what is the one thing we should change given where we are now.

Stop embarking on "big bang" site redesigns. Yes, once in a while you need to redesign the appearance of your Web site, but you need to change it a lot more often than that. The problem with site redesigns is that they are *too* big. Because they are done infrequently, you throw in a *lot* of changes, which throws off your customers—they knew how it worked already. (It's well-known that customer satisfaction frequently drops even after a *good* redesign, while customers take stock and adjust.)

You throw in a lot of changes because you do redesigns so infrequently. And because your redesign includes several changes, it always takes longer than you think it will. Your team ends up exhausting themselves from working 80 hours a week to make the deadline. Then everyone falls over the finish line and goes to sleep for a month—during the most critical time for customer feedback.

That first month will tell you how wrong it is. You need to be ready to fix it then—not have everyone on vacation. The project doesn't end when you launch. In many ways, that's when it *begins*. Launch is not the finish line—it's the starting line.

That's why continuous change works better.

Eric Raymond, author of *The Cathedral and the Bazaar*, advises us to "release early and often." You don't need to squeeze a zillion changes into this week's update because you will be doing another one next week. So you don't need to drive your team to get everything in before the deadline because they'll have another chance soon. And whatever is messed up can be fixed the next time. You can see how customers react and fix it next week.

For your situation, what is the very next step?

The answer helps you decide what to do—the "it" in "do *it* wrong quickly." But *why* are you doing it? And *how* do you keep score? You need to know what it's all worth and how far off you are with each attempt.

How Do You Know How Wrong It Is?

"Strategies without metrics are only wishes," says Charles Phillips, President of Oracle. But which metrics are important?

Earlier in this chapter, we saw how Amazon used revenue (in the form of increased orders and order size) to decide which side of the screen should contain the shopping cart. *ACM Queue* magazine quotes Amazon CTO Werner Vogels: "Customers tend to vote with their wallets, so if there is a clear negative result, we know what to do with that."

How does *your* company keep score?

Our friends at Scotts lawn care used a different approach than Amazon. Not being an e-commerce company, they weren't sure how to tie revenue to their personalized lawn care advice, so they surveyed their customers. They found that subscribers to the personalized lawn care advice service make 2.7 applications of Scotts products each year, compared to 1.7 for non-subscribers—a 59 percent increase.

WHAT HAPPENS WHEN IT REALLY IS WRONG?

You know that the "wrong" part in "do it *wrong* quickly" is an exaggeration—we all are doing what we believe is right at the time. But usually what we do doesn't turn out exactly right, and we need to fix it.

Once in a while, you might try something that turns out to be *really* wrong. Dead wrong. What happens then?

Let's hear how the Senior Director of e-commerce for American technology retailer CompUSA handled just such a situation. Al Hurlebaus thought he had a great idea back in 2004.

"Our home page had a large block we called the 'Feature of the Day.' It had become very text-oriented. I thought more graphics would catch the customer's attention and encourage more clickthrough and better conversion."

So like any company with a new idea, they tried it.

Al describes the results: "We found that it reduced clickthroughs, and we had fewer customers moving into the sales environment. I think we let it run for a month and then slowly put the text back in."

This isn't usually the kind of success story people like to tell, but Al was gracious enough to share it. Why is this story important?

It shows what happens when you try something that really is wrong—it's not a disaster. You use your metrics to figure it out, and then you do something else.

The difference between Al's company and most companies is that CompUSA is willing to experiment and to be wrong. Only through this experimentation do they come up with the breakthroughs that really make a difference.

Some other company might have made the same kind of change but suffered with it for months or years because they weren't measuring results or because the boss had such a big ego that he wouldn't admit he came up with a clunker.

Because Al measures everything he does and because he abandons the clunkers quickly, CompUSA continually improves its online marketing results.

Suppose you're marketing cereals for children. You can track enrollments in your Web site's game club as your Web conversion, and you can measure coupon redemption as your sales conversion. After tracking for a while, you might find that club members buy two more boxes of cereal a month than non-members, demonstrating the value of expanding the membership rolls.

Whatever you use, choose a measurement that most people will find persuasive before you make a change on your site. Then check the before and after metrics to see its effect. How do you decide the right metrics for the change *you* want to make?

If you heeded the advice to start small, you can use the metrics from Chapter 4 to analyze each change. Understand your activity metrics—impressions, selections, and conversions—and use the before and after comparison to decide whether the change in question is working.

Sometimes marketers with large Web sites don't feel they can go page-by-page—they need to make many changes at the same time. If you find yourself in this position, you can measure conversions by tracking the mini-conversions with your Web Conversion Cycle. If more people move from Learn to Shop and from Shop to Buy, then you are doing the right thing globally. You can use your metrics system to aggregate all the Learn pages, separating them from Shop and Buy pages, for example, and see the holistic view of what your customers are doing.

Looking at these big numbers across your site can be more useful than a traditional "funnel report" from a Web metrics system. Most funnel reports assume that your customers move around your site in step-by-step fashion—your Web Conversion Cycle assumes they *don't*. You still need to look at individual impressions and clickthroughs to draw conclusions on specific decisions, but this approach lets you change many things simultaneously, while still tracking overall improvement.

Whether you are making big changes or small ones, you need to think in terms of testing and measuring. So far this chapter has talked about how you can decide what to try first, as you tweak your Web marketing. Keep in mind that testing and measuring go on forever and ever, so you can use your metrics system to help you decide what to test next and then measure *that* result (and use it to test again).

You need a metrics system to guide you because you won't catch everything by yourself. Just because you notice when you lose a sock doesn't mean it's the only clothing you ever lose. Similarly, you might be losing lots of conversions without ever noticing. Your metrics can show you what you are missing.

So do your tests. Avinash Kaushik, author of *Web Analytics: An Hour a Day*, says that one test can try out "seven of your ideas and show you which one is wrong very fast." Later in this chapter, you'll see how to design a test, but now let's focus on which metrics to use in your tests.

In Chapter 4, we analyzed metrics such as conversions (for tracking transactions) and subscribers (for measuring relationships), but we didn't look at what it's all worth. We didn't discuss money.

That's what we'll do now. To really measure how wrong your change is, it's best to think in terms of money. Your company might already measure itself using revenue, for example. If so, use that. Perhaps you use profit margin. Fine. Although there are better measurements to use, it's best to use the standard measurements in your company at the start. Sure, it would be great to use the best metrics, but do it wrong quickly by accepting the imperfect measurements and start fixing your marketing and your Web site.

If you have a choice of which metrics to use, it's best to evaluate conversions in terms of profit and to measure customer relationships using Lifetime Value (the next few pages explain how you do that).

Before we dive in, however, a warning: Don't ever believe that your Web site's value can be summed up in a single number. It can't. Even if you use the best metrics, such as profit and Lifetime Value, your Web site is more valuable than what they show. Some conversions, such as a successful customer support experience, have no easily-measured profit value. Branding value is also difficult to quantify.

Baseball player Toby Harrah put statistics in their rightful place when he said, "Statistics are like bikinis. They show a lot, but not everything." (And if you ever saw Toby's batting statistics, you'd know why he wanted to persuade you of that.)

Don't throw up your hands just because no numbers are perfect. Instead, resolve to use the best numbers you can and pay attention to factors that can't be neatly quantified.

We look at how to determine the value of conversions and customer relationships next, which is followed by advice on how to set up and execute tests in simple and inexpensive ways.

How to Value Conversions

In Chapter 4, we learned how to identify and count conversions, but now we need to know what they are worth. When we do, we'll know what our marketing expenditures should be, and we'll know the value of every change we make in our marketing and Web experience.

There's just one catch. Calculating what each conversion is worth ain't easy. That's never stopped us, though.

Let's start by looking at conversions in terms of revenue. Granted, some of your conversions (such as solving a customer support issue) are difficult to express in terms of money, but most marketing is eventually reduced to sales. Our first step is to identify the sales revenue for Web conversions.

If your sales occur online, that's easy. You know exactly how many orders you took, and you know the order size of each one, so you know your revenue. But offline sales are trickier.

Chapter 4 discussed many ways of tracking offline sales back to their origin on your Web site, including special phone numbers, discount coupons, and more. By identifying each offline sale as emanating from your online marketing, you can discretely total the revenue, too. Just as with online sales, you can identify each order, and you know each order's size, so you can add up the offline revenue driven by Internet marketing.

For example, if your company collected 10 orders for aluminum siding where customers presented your "5% Off" coupon printed from your Web site, you know the Web was the catalyst for those 10 orders. If the totals for each of those invoices is $340,000, that shows the value of your Web site.

For some businesses, that's all you'll ever need. If your company has a sales-driven culture, no one might look beyond those orders coming in. If marketing expenditures in your company are merely eyeballed and loosely tracked by sales, then this might be all you need to measure.

But most businesses need to do more. Most of you will want to know much those discounts cost—those discounts reduce the revenue you report on your financial statements. In this case, if each customer presented the "5% Off" coupon, the real revenue collected by your company is reduced to $323,000. For the sake of simplicity, we'll assume that none of your customers will cancel or get their money back, so that $323,000 represents what accountants call *net sales*. (Your company also takes into account—literally—that some customers will not pay their bill, but we'll ignore such complexities to keep the examples simple.)

Real life is messier than this example from the aluminum siding business because most Web sites have multiple conversions that can each lead to a sale of your product or service. Let's look at a more realistic example of a large kitchen cabinet refinisher, called Skin Deep Refinishing.

Skin Deep has a Web site that covers the Learn stage of the customer buying process, closing all sales offline. Skin Deep's Web site offers three different Web conversions:

- Receive an online price quote by entering the number and sizes of the cabinets into a Web form.
- Call a special phone number listed only on the Web site for all customer questions.
- Use a Web form to make an appointment with a salesperson.

Exhibit 6-2 shows what we learn when we look at the metrics. By creating a way to tie the offline sales back to the Web site, you can see that Skin Deep's Web site was the catalyst for $100,000 in July sales.

Once you can measure the conversions of your Web site, you can do a little math to express your goals in purely monetary terms. Exhibit 6-3 shows how to monetize each Web conversion so that you know the value to your business.

July Average Order: $2,000	Web Conversions	Sales Conversion Rate	Offline Orders	Sales Revenue
Online Quote	400	2.0%	8	$16,000
Special Phone Number	500	2.4%	12	$24,000
Sales Appointment	100	30.0%	30	$60,000
Totals	1,000	5.0%	50	$100,000

Exhibit 6-2   Your Web conversion paths have revenue value.

July Average Order: $2,000	Web Conversions	Sales Revenue	Sales Revenue per Conversion
Online Quote	400	$16,000	$40
Special Phone Number	500	$24,000	$48
Sales Appointment	100	$60,000	$600
Totals	1,000	$100,000	$100

Exhibit 6-3   Each individual conversion has revenue value.

Because they needed to get 1,000 Web conversions to get the 50 sales adding up to $100,000 in revenue, you can divide that revenue by 1,000 to find out how much the average Web conversion is worth ($100). Further, although the average Web conversion is worth about $100, each type of conversion (quote, phone, or appointment) can have its own value calculated.

Every time Skin Deep persuades a Web visitor to receive an online quote, it's worth about $40 in revenue. Persuading someone to call is worth about $48, while sales appointments are worth about $600 each. That's because they know how many people must take these actions to get one order, so they can divide up each sale by the number of people needed to take the steps before the order—dividing $60,000 by 100 conversions yields $600, for example. You can see how improving Skin Deep's Web site directly affects sales by prompting more visitors to take these actions.

You can also see how changes that drive more sales appointments are more important than those designed to increase phone calls or online quotes. Perhaps a great first project would be to make the appointment mechanism so compelling that more people would choose that over a phone call. Or perhaps most phone calls are tire-kickers who want to know how much a refinishing job usually costs, so posting the average price on the Web might free up your call center to do more selling.

That's the beauty of monetizing your conversions—it helps you focus on what's really important. But there's more that you can do. If you return to the Web Conversion Cycle modeled in Chapter 4, you can determine how much each visit to the Web site is worth in revenue. Exhibit 6-4 runs the numbers.

July Average Order: $2,000	Total	Conversion Rate	Sales Revenue per Event
Web Visits	50,000	100%	$2
Web Conversions	1,000	2%	$100
Orders from Web	50	5%	$2,000

Exhibit 6-4   Your Web conversion cycle shows each visit's value.

You can divide total sales (in this case $100,000) by the number of orders (50) to determine that the average order size is $2,000. Using the same logic, you can divide sales by the number of Web conversions to learn that each conversion is worth an average of $100. Similarly, if you take the same calculation back one more step, you can divide total sales by the number of Web visitors to see that each visit to your Web site is worth about $2 in revenue.

Why are all these numbers important? Because you can use them to project the value of your marketing efforts. For example, a campaign expected to drive 5,000 more visits to Skin Deep's site projects to earn an extra $10,000 in revenue (because 5,000 visits worth $2 each adds up to $10,000). Or if Skin Deep believes that a change to its Web site would double the number of people who requested online quotes, those additional 400 quotes represent an incremental $16,000 in revenue (400 quotes at $4 a quote). This technique can be used to justify the cost of any Web marketing effort and can be checked against the actual results afterward.

If the flinty-eyed accounting types at your business don't need any more than this, then consider yourself lucky. Go get the money to make your first Web improvement or start your first online campaign. Most businesses, however, need more.

Some businesses use a measurement called *return on advertising spending (ROAS)*. In Skin Deep's case, they are trying for an ROAS of $20, meaning they want to receive $20 in revenue for each $1 of advertising. Because each visit to their site is worth just $2 in revenue, Skin Deep can spend just 10¢ per visit ($2 divided by the ROAS of 20). So, for example, if Skin Deep wants to buy per-click paid search terms, they'd need to average just 10¢ per click to stay within their ROAS guidelines.

When you see that your revenue per visit is as low as Skin Deep's, it usually means that you should focus on improving the conversions you get on your site before going all-out to drive more traffic. That two percent Web conversion rate is too low for the ROAS that Skin Deep requires, so raising the conversion rate is the first step. If Skin

Deep could double its Web conversion rate to four percent, it could double its per-click limit to 20¢ while staying within its ROAS guidelines.

Some companies stop at this point, making their marketing decisions based on revenue, but many go further. They might make decisions based on *profit margin*, the percentage of revenue left over when all costs are paid. If Skin Deep's profit margin is 25 percent, then their $100,000 in revenue yields $25,000 in profit. Exhibit 6-5 shows the same calculations done earlier, except based on profit rather than revenue.

July Average Order: $2,000	Total	Conversion Rate	Profit per Event
Web Visits	50,000	100%	$0.50
Web Conversions	1,000	2%	$25.00
Orders from Web	50	5%	$500.00

Exhibit 6-5   Using profit to determine each visit's value

We see that each visit is worth 50¢ per visit in profit (as opposed to $2 in revenue). What that means is that Skin Deep can decide how much of their profit margin they want to spend in marketing to close more sales. By examining profit margin, Skin Deep might decide that the per-visit spending limit of 10¢ calculated earlier based on ROAS might be too conservative. They could decide to raise that number to be more aggressive about driving more business.

Why would they do that? Because optimizing profit *margin* is not as good as optimizing *profit*. If you cut your profit margin but sold so much more that you made more money in the end, that is the way to go.

Unfortunately, most businesses can't easily measure the profit impact of a marketing campaign or a change to their Web sites. That's why they use stand-ins that are easier to measure, such as ROAS or profit margin.

Some businesses optimize on *return on investment (ROI)*. Often batted around in common usage, ROI is calculated as the percentage of profit returned from your spending, so $200 in profit divided by $20 in advertising spending (paid placement fees) yields an ROI of 1000 percent. Like ROAS, ROI can identify your worst expenditures so that you can eliminate them or reduce them. Conversely, if your budget increases, the highest ROI investments might be the ones you should test to see if higher bids result in higher profits (even if ROI decreases) because the highest ROI does not always lead to the highest profit.

Other businesses use *cost per action (CPA)*. If you can't measure profit, you might settle for minimizing costs. For companies selling a single product, minimizing the costs required to generate each action (Web conversion) might work out just as well as maximizing profit, but there are dangers. Remember that your ultimate goal is to have the highest amount of profit—not the lowest cost for each item sold. You might minimize cost per action with small investments that generate far fewer sales than you could profitably make. CPA is calculated as the advertising costs divided by the number of actions, so 20 conversions that cost $20 in click fees yield a CPA of $1.

If you engage in pay-per-click search campaigns, you'll find that *bid management* software can use any of those formulas to adjust your bidding minute by minute. You can instruct the software to optimize your bids to maximize profit margin, for example. Just be aware that because the highest total profit is your ultimate goal, none of these stand-ins will necessarily provide that. Exhibit 6-6 shows an example.

Metric Optimized	Sales	Profit Per Sale	Ad Fees	CPA	Profit Margin	ROAS	ROI	Overall Profit
CPA	20	$10	$20	**$1**	10%	$100	1000%	$200
Profit Margin	20	$10	$20	$1	**10%**	$100	1000%	$200
ROAS	20	$10	$20	$1	10%	**$100**	1000%	$200
ROI	20	$10	$20	$1	10%	$100	**1000%**	$200
Overall Profit	50	$6	$250	$5	6%	$20	120%	**$300**

Exhibit 6-6 Optimizing for different metrics yields different results

If you have no accounting background, you can see that this can quickly get complicated. In truth, this treatment isn't even as complex as an introductory Accounting 101 course. The table shows all the same values each row, except for the final row, optimizing overall profit. In real life, you're likely to get what you optimize for, so a marketer optimizing for CPA will likely end up with lower costs per action than a marketer aiming for return on investment. If you'd rather have higher profits than any of these other measurements, then you better start thinking about how to optimize for *that*.

You need to work closely with your financial advisors to see how to apply these principles for your company. The idea behind all of this analysis is to spend your marketing budget wisely. By analyzing the Web Conversion Cycle, Web metrics, and financial results for your business, you can run your business by the numbers to increase your success.

How to Value Customers

As complex as it is to value conversions, you ain't seen nothin' yet. Driving more conversions is always a good thing, but you might want to differentiate between driving more purchases from existing customers and acquiring new customers. Both are important to any business, but conversion value is too simple to help us differentiate. Let's look at why.

To decide how much to spend on increasing conversions from existing customers, conversion value metrics work just fine. Suppose the goal of your campaign (or of a change to your Web site) is to raise the number of orders or to increase the order size of existing customers. In that case, optimizing for profit (or profit margin, or ROAS, et al) is exactly what you want to do. You want to spend a bit more on marketing to those customers and take in well more than you spend.

But new customers are worth more than the value of their first order with you.

For most businesses, you can assume that once you've sold something to a customer, you have a better chance of them buying from you again. If they like what they got from you, then they might be back. Certainly there are some businesses where repeat business is unusual, but most industries live off their repeat customers.

Repeat customers are easier to persuade to buy if only because they have fewer questions. In some cases, they require no marketing at all. Because that is true, it stands to reason that the value of acquiring a new customer should take into account more than the initial order.

Suppose you manage a car repair business that specializes in BMWs called Car Groomers. Your Web site attracts many of your new customers, who are looking for the absolute best care for their pricey cars. Your site explores why BMWs need special treatment and how your staff is trained to provide it. You offer a free 150-point inspection as part of the first service for any appointment made on the Web.

Because of that free offer, the first service appointment is quite low in profit. You really start to make money when the customers come back, especially when they eventually need major repairs. So how do you know what you should budget for each new customer?

Get to know *Customer Lifetime Value*—usually called simply *Lifetime Value* (*LTV*). LTV calculates the total profit that a new customer is worth to your business.

Car Groomers can use LTV to think about their new customer acquisition costs. Suppose their profit on an initial appointment is only about $20, but they average $80 on subsequent appointments.

How do you decide what a lifetime is? If it really stretched for a human lifetime, you wouldn't be able to calculate it until your customers were dead. (At that point, you might not be as interested.)

If you've been in business a while, you might be able to estimate the length of a "customer lifetime." Car Groomers' records show that the average customer returns regularly for three years after the initial visit—averaging four times each year—before disappearing.

No one at Car Groomers knows exactly why people stop coming back. Perhaps some have bought a new Mercedes instead of a BMW. A few might have been turned off by a bad experience. Others move away. No matter. Some people are regular customers for many years, while others drop out after one or two visits. The average is three years, so Car Groomers can use three years as the duration of a lifetime. If you don't have this information for your business, take a guess—but be conservative because that keeps your spending lower (and more likely profitable).

So how could Car Groomers calculate LTV? Four visits per year multiplied by three years gives you 12 visits in a lifetime. The profit on the first visit is $20, but the other 11 visits provide $80 of profit each ($880), yielding a total value of $900.

But it's not that simple, unfortunately. Although the numbers total up to $900, the truth is that $900 payable over three years is not worth $900 today—it's worth less. The question is, "How much less?"

Net Present Value (NPV) tells us *that* answer. I won't show you the formula for NPV because it has been known to frighten small children (and math-averse adults). You can find NPV calculators on the Web that ask you for your cash flows and your *discount rate* (which you can think of as inflation or interest rates—it's the cost of money over the three-year customer lifetime). With a three percent discount rate, the NPV of $900 paid over three years is around $850. That means that $850 is the Lifetime Value for a new customer—if Car Groomers spent $850 in acquisition costs for each customer, they'd break even. Every dollar saved becomes more profit.

As with valuing conversions, calculating Lifetime Value is not always easy, especially in a large company where it can be hard just to get everyone to agree to the same formula. Some people believe that you should consider the attrition rate of your customers for each repeat purchase, rather than just using the average number of purchases from a customer over a lifetime. Others argue that new customers referred by that customer have value that should be counted. I chose to present the formula as simply as possible here, ignoring these complicating factors.

Despite the roadblocks, some companies, such as Hewlett-Packard and Bass Pro Shops use LTV to measure their online marketing. Instead of arguing about the complexities, I recommend that you "do it wrong quickly" by using these principles if you can, even if the metrics themselves are not as accurate as you'd like in the beginning.

Remember that the $850 we calculated for LTV is an average. Some of Car Groomer's customers will be worth more than $850 (because they deliver more than $900 in profit over the three-year customer lifetime), and some will be worth less. You'll raise your profits if you can concentrate on acquiring more of the customers that are above the average.

To concentrate on the high end of the market, use the RFM analysis we did in Chapter 5. Some of your marketing tactics will draw customers who show higher recency in the first few months. For example, Car Groomers might notice that more customers acquired through paid search have returned for their second visit, while other customers have not. So they might shift more of their marketing budget to paid search.

This example demonstrates a larger truth about LTV (and most marketing metrics): The more you can segment your customers, the more valuable the measurements become for decision making. In this case, segmenting customers by the way they were acquired helps you to make a better budget allocation decision.

If you use a multichannel marketing approach, you must constantly decide how to allocate the budget among competing marketing tactics. Imran Khan, Chief Marketing Officer for Internet lender E-LOAN, uses a portfolio approach to determine which tactics get "credit" for each new customer.

E-LOAN spreads 70 percent of its marketing budget across TV and search marketing and uses rules to determine which gets the credit for a new customer. When people who have never been to the site before search for the word *e-loan*, they must have heard the name through an awareness channel such as television. Therefore, E-LOAN credits any conversions from that search to its awareness marketing channels, rather than to the search marketing channel. On the other hand, when people search for a generic non-branded term, such as *home equity loan*, the search marketing channel gets the conversion credit because that customer would never have found E-LOAN if it did not come up in the search results.

The tactics that get more credit become larger parts of the marketing mix over time. "To do a good job of budget allocation, we need to do a good job of credit allocation," Imran says.

Some marketers use *matchback systems* to allocate credit across channels. By matching information known about those making purchases (such as names and addresses) with information known about those targeted with promotions, matchback systems can allocate credit to the marketing promotions likely to have influenced the sale. In this way, printed catalogs might get credit for Web sales, while e-mail marketing might be credited for in-store sales. Matchbacks do have drawbacks. Many marketing messages are delivered anonymously on the Web, so matchback systems can't credit those channels accurately for the sales they drive. Even if no one can identify the searcher looking for your product, search may still be driving a lot of sales (both online and offline). Use matchback systems to provide you with more accurate data but understand their limits as you make decisions.

Now you have two different ways of knowing the value of the changes you make. You can calculate your return per *conversion* or per *customer*. Either can show you what worked and what didn't.

Just don't go overboard by using metrics to replace your good judgment. Few situations allow optimizing based on a single metric—you need to control costs and maximize revenue, both short-term and long-term. And even if you have perfect information about what to do, it won't last. Isn't it always that way? Just when you figure out the meaning of life, they change it.

Your only option is to keep testing so that when they change it, you'll figure it out right away.

Test, Test, and Test Again

Yes, I am going to talk about testing again. I know by now I must sound like a broken record (MP3s don't break, thankfully), but testing *is* the best way to get feedback on a new idea. Remember what British Prime Minister Benjamin Disraeli once said: "To be conscious that you are ignorant is a great step to knowledge." The question is: How do you design the right tests to elicit that knowledge?

It all starts with your theory of what your customers want.

At the risk of sounding overly scientific (as opposed to just scientific enough), you need to formulate a theory to test, just like a scientific experiment. For example, your theory might be that customers get confused by too much text on your home page, so you'll create a version of your home page with more pictures and fewer words. Then you can test which variation works better.

To test the theory, you must decide what to measure—just what it means to "work better." You can use business results such as revenue, profit, or Lifetime Value, or you can use customer activity, such as conversions or selections (clicks). Everyone involved in the decision must agree up front on which measurement you'll use to keep score.

How much improvement will be considered a success? Any improvement over the present? Improvement that is worth more than the cost? A certain level of improvement? Decide these questions when you design the test.

For example, everyone might agree that if the less-text version of your home page causes fewer customers to abandon the site, that's a success. Or you might decide that if more conversions come from the less-text home page visitors, then *that's* a success. Or you could do a survey of which version people like better.

Regardless of what you decide, that's what you need to stick with *after* the test. You might personally like the new home page better, but if it doesn't succeed according to the criteria set for the test, you shouldn't leave it up.

In general, it's easier for everyone if you try to use the same kind of success metrics for as many tests as possible. In the previous section, we looked at how to value conversions and customer relationships—if you can pick one of these metrics and stick to it, it will simplify your testing. More importantly, it produces more persuasive results because people will become comfortable with the same measure of success for each decision.

Why is that? Economist John Kenneth Galbraith once said, "When people are least sure, they are often most dogmatic." If people don't understand your metrics or are not moved by them, they'll fall back into their own preconceived notions—exactly the opposite of what you want. So if you consistently measure your marketing campaigns based on profit, you'll prompt fewer questions each time you show test results. People will gradually become comfortable with your methodology.

Sometimes, of course, you'll have to make exceptions. Even if you use profit to measure your conversions, your TV ads designed to increase brand awareness might demand different measures. It's OK to decide that. For this one test, we'll check the increase in search keyword usage for the name of the new product the day after the TV ads run. You can use profit, too, to see how those keywords drove conversions, but if the main goal of the campaign was to raise your public profile, then you should measure whether it did.

The hard part in all of this? Giving up on being right. Although you are formulating a theory of what's going on, you need to let the test show what's *really* happening. You can't design tests to prove yourself right. You need to listen to what customers say regardless of whether they prove you right or wrong. You don't make assumptions. You test them.

For example, you could just assume that it doesn't matter which search engine your customers find you with—that searchers who use the same search keywords convert at the same rate, even if some are coming from Yahoo! and others from Google. The best marketers, however, don't make such assumptions.

Internet lender E-LOAN theorized that different search engines might attract different kinds of searchers, so they tested conversion rates across Yahoo! and Google. They found that Google searchers converted at far higher rates from search ads with the tag line "Perfect Credit Not Required," while Yahoo! searchers responded better to "Bad Credit OK."

The best marketers know the truth of what metrics expert Jim Sterne says: "Ask good questions because we have all the answers." An overstatement? Sure, but that's what makes it quotable. Regardless, it's the right attitude to have.

Your job is to ask those good questions and to develop those intriguing theories—and then devise the tests that show what the answers are. If, as too many do, you start by poring over your metrics reports, trouble lies ahead.

Let's take an example. The first time you look at the "most popular pages" report from your fancy Web metrics system, it will likely show that your home page attracts the most page views. (This is the Web equivalent of learning that "Is this thing on?" is the question most frequently uttered into a microphone.)

Of course your home page gets the most page views. But does that mean that your home page should get most of your attention? No. Your home page, in fact, is frequently a difficult page to improve because the customers arriving there have many different goals. If you perform too narrow a test, you might improve one goal's conversion rate but decrease another's. Which goal is more important? Home pages often require optimization for multiple goals.

On the other hand, your newsletter subscription page is dead simple. Your customers want to subscribe, and you want them to also. It's easy to make a few changes to the page to see if subscriptions go up—you can be sure that you've improved. Typically, the pages closer to the actual conversion events are easier to test and improve than top-level pages such as your home page because those conversion pages have only one goal.

It's still a good idea, though, to improve your home page, but most companies spend too much time thinking about their home pages and not enough time on the other areas of their Web sites. Don't focus solely on your most popular pages. Many companies have found focusing on conversions to be more valuable.

What's the easiest way to start a testing program at your company?

First, don't get hung up on having large numbers of test subjects. Usability expert Jakob Nielsen advises that usability tests with as few as five people can often tell you the major flaws in whatever you are testing. For that same reason, when you change something in your Web marketing or on your Web site, you don't need a mountain of evidence to draw a conclusion.

Even if you're not dealing with big numbers, have someone with a strong statistical background on your test team if possible. Remember, there are three types of statisticians: those who can count and those who can't. When it comes to the big decisions, statisticians can help you know when a one percent improvement is something you can count on.

But you don't need a statistician in most situations. Most of the time, you can simply accept what the raw numbers tell you. Sometimes, the numbers will lead you in the wrong direction, but the great majority of the time, they will tell you what you need to know.

You can have confidence that if you follow the numbers over and over again, you will gradually go in the right direction. Sometimes the numbers will lead you astray, but usually they won't. It's not important to be right for each individual test—you need to trust the methodology of experimentation and correction to work in the end. As mathematician Charles Babbage noted, "Errors using inadequate data are much less than those using no data at all." So trust that you'll make both fewer and smaller errors with metrics than without.

Now then, what do you make of all this? It's simple. Do your testing wrong quickly, too. Don't immediately go out and spend half your budget on a big metrics package and then wallow in data. Instead, pick one thing to change and decide what results you are looking for.

Those results don't have to "wow" a statistician, and they don't require huge investments. Google Analytics is a free metrics package that allows you to track activity simply and easily. Of course, those big metrics packages still have their place. As your testing program matures and your site grows, you'll need those high-end packages to test more and more—but don't start there.

Start with simple *A/B Testing*, so named because it pits two choices ("A" and "B") against each other. You can design almost any test around two choices. Just decide on your criteria at the start—such as "the one that gets more clicks wins." Then run your test.

You can send out one version of your e-mail to a small part of your mailing list and send a different version to another subset of the list. You can provide two different landing pages to catch the clicks and simply count which ones attract more. Once you have a winner, you can mail that version to the rest of your list.

You can do the same thing with a paid search ad. Run one version of the ad this week and run a different version next week. You can see which one gets more clicks (or more conversions, as you wish) and use that ad going forward.

A/B testing works for more than e-mail marketing. Design two versions of a Web page—they could use the same copy but different designs, or vice versa. Use one version for one week and the second for another and see which one puts up better numbers. Or if you have a personalized Web site, you can use one version of the page for a small randomly-selected set of visitors and another for a different group, showing both versions at the same time.

If you can test both versions at the same time, you get more reliable results because you eliminate other variables. For example, you might design a lovely test of two different versions of a Web page, but during the second week of your two-week test, your top competitor announces a new model. Traffic to your site drops by half. Can you be sure of the results of your test?

It could be that visitors you attracted in the second week are different (more loyal?) from those of the first week. Testing both versions at the same time (through personalization techniques) would have made the test more reliable.

So if you can't test choices "A" and "B" at the same time, then just don't bother testing, right? Well, no. Instead, do it wrong quickly. Do the best testing you can—one after the other, if that's the best you can do. Over time, you'll end up in a better place than if you just gave up.

Testing is very important, but it doesn't answer all questions. Too often, tests are designed around a single metric, but perhaps that is not the only purpose of your Web page. For example, your home page might be just as important for answering customer support questions as it is for selling things. If you measure only sales conversions, you might mess up the support end of your business without even knowing it. Make sure your tests are designed with your whole business in mind.

You must also aim to test the true causes, not just whatever you happen to think of. Sometimes that's hard to do, but it's critical.

For example, suppose I tell you that I performed a test that proves that using more text in the name of a link causes more customers to click. Does that mean we should start adding words to all of our links?

No. The reason that longer link text garners more clicks is because the really bad examples of link text ("Click this") tend to be short. *Those* cases get few clicks, thereby skewing the results. A better finding would be to avoid *dumb* link text, not short link text.

Despite our focus on testing, we must recognize that it's merely a tool that tells us which alternative works better—it does not uncover unmet needs. Use customer surveys, focus groups, and other qualitative sources of customer "wants" to find the holes in your experience. Keep in mind the advice of management guru Peter Drucker:

"There is nothing so useless as doing efficiently that which should not be done at all." Make sure you're doing the right thing the wrong way before improving it.

Similarly, testing shows you only the best of what you tested, so you run the risk of what statisticians call "sub-optimizing"—picking the best choice among essentially similar alternatives. To break out of the trap, it's best to try something crazy once in a while. It's only a test, so it won't kill your results. Cultivate a culture of innovative thinking that tests the strangest ideas in addition to what consensus tells you are the "best" ideas.

By now, you should understand how to choose "it" and how to measure how "wrong" it is. But can you do it "quickly"? Can you efficiently experiment and measure and experiment again? If your marketing process is too slow-footed to keep up with the pace of today's business, the next section is for you.

How Do You Speed Up?

Did doing all that testing sound easy? If you keep testing, it's true that you'll eventually lurch into the right answer for whatever question you have. Unfortunately, "eventually" can take quite a while for thorny questions. Sometimes you have to kiss a lot of frogs to find one prince.

So how can you find your prince faster? By finding more frogs and kissing them faster and faster. (Geez, this analogy is really starting to break down.)

Do companies really work this way? More and more, the answer is "yes." Netflix, the DVD rental company, changes its site every two weeks. It might surprise you to know that they consider 90 percent of what they try to be wrong.

But Netflix has such a great site! How can 90 percent of what they do be wrong? The only way to improve is to stick with the 10 percent that works. By ruthlessly dumping every "wrong" change immediately and building on the ones that do work, you'll be amazed how much progress you can make.

When you see how the odds are stacked against even the smartest companies, such as Netflix, you can see how important it is to speed up your pace. If you try 10 changes a year, and 90 percent are wrong, then you find only one good idea each year. If you try 10 changes a day, you'll find 365 good ideas a year, even if you still get only 10 percent of them "right."

So every day you decide to live with your existing marketing is a day you didn't learn anything. Every day you avoid the hard decisions of changing is another day you missed a new idea. Today is the day to start the experimentation. Don't procrastinate. You should, uh, anti-crastinate.

Inventor Thomas Edison once said, "I have not failed. I've just found 10,000 ways that won't work." That's the attitude you must take towards experimentation. You must speed up the pace so that you can find those 10,000 wrong answers as quickly as possible.

Each time you find a "wrong" answer, you try something new. You don't sit around wondering what else to do. You don't leave it broken while you are thinking—you launch Plan B, C, and Z until you figure out something better. Confucius says, "A man who has committed a mistake and doesn't correct it is committing another mistake." (I've always wanted to write, "Confucius says...")

You learned in Chapter 4 how to measure the results of what you do. In Chapter 5, you learned what kinds of things you can change. Now, let's see how to do everything faster. You need to quicken your company's metabolism.

If you don't, you're just a sitting duck for a competitor that does. The faster pace is starting with highly successful Internet companies, such as Netflix, Google, Amazon, and eBay, but it's coming to an industry near you.

Change is the new *status quo.* (OK, I don't know what that means either, but the ISO standard for business books requires at least one slogan like this.)

As you embark on Marketing 2.0 in your company, you must focus on speeding up three things. First, you need to accelerate changes in *targeting*—you must use technology to target new customers and target more relevant messages to your existing customers. Second, you need to quicken changes in *messaging*—you must use technology to tweak messages for maximum effectiveness. Last, you must accelerate how you collect customer feedback so you can act on it even faster.

So pull up a chair (I can't believe you were standing up all this time) and learn how to quickly change your targeting for any campaign.

Speed Up Your Targeting

Direct marketers obsessively fine-tune their address lists so that they send their catalogs and mail pieces to the people who they believe will be most profitable for them. The most sophisticated marketers segment their lists based on which products and messages customers have responded to in the past.

Internet marketing allows even finer-grained segmentation.

You already know that Internet marketing is cheaper than offline direct marketing because printing and mailing costs disappear—it costs next to nothing to send e-mail to even those who don't buy. You already know that personalization and multifaceted search techniques allow customers to segment themselves. But you can apply even more segmentation techniques, and you can use them more efficiently than any offline marketer ever dreamed.

To understand how to speed up targeting, we can return to its basic meaning. *Targeting* is the selection of a marketing message for a particular person or segment. So to speed up your targeting, you can speed up selecting the person or selecting the message. Let's focus on the person first.

The most striking example of people selection is for e-mail marketing. Just as with direct mail and catalogs, e-mail marketers have an explicit list of people to target. What can be done to speed up e-mail targeting?

Most marketers store their mailing lists in databases so that they can perform "pulls" of targeted lists for particular campaigns, based on demographics or other characteristics stored in that database. But targeting takes thinking, and e-mail marketers don't have as much time to do that as they need because they typically have not automated some basic tasks that waste time.

The first time waster is *list suppression*—removing from your list the e-mail addresses of anyone who has opted out. In the United States and in other countries, sending an e-mail to someone who has opted out can be illegal, so you need to perform list suppression—you just want to do it in the least amount of time. The second time waster surrounds bounced e-mails. Every e-mail campaign results in "bounced" (returned) e-mails—it takes time and effort to scrub those invalid e-mail addresses from your list.

Coping with these problems falls under a category known as *list management*. All e-mail marketers must continually update their mailing lists (their targets) to suppress opt-outs, to correct or remove bounces, and for other reasons, but for most marketers, it doesn't come easy. A 2004 Jupiter Research study showed that 69 percent of e-mail marketers struggle with e-mail list churn, which is not surprising.

What is a bit baffling is that only 35 percent of e-mail marketers focus on list management functions when selecting an e-mail vendor. If e-mail marketers make list management features a top priority when choosing their e-mail vendors, they could free up more time to do better and faster targeting.

Marketers that buy e-mail lists or acquire them from affiliates and other partners have even more daunting list management issues—they are counting on the original list creator to inform them when a customer opts out. Luckily, some companies, such as UnsubCentral, are now providing clearinghouses of opt-out lists that you can use to synchronize opt-outs across your sources of lists.

Internet retailer Motorcycle Superstore found that automating its list management improved its delivered e-mail rate from 85 percent to over 99 percent. The retailer used ExactTarget, an e-mail services provider, to do even more. By automating delivery and watching the resulting conversions, they discovered the optimum delivery frequency was weekly, not monthly, which increased sales.

Every minute you spend using duct tape and bailing wire to address these common list management tasks is one less minute you're spending to target your customers more effectively. And you might find that improving your e-mail automation helps you improve the frequency of mailings also, speeding your feedback on what is working and what is not.

Now let's turn to other online marketing tactics. Unlike e-mail, most tactics don't involve people selection—searchers and Web surfers segment themselves, as we discussed in Chapter 1, "They're Doing Wonderful Things with Computers." Even so, you can speed up targeting within these groups also. You can use personalization software, covered in Chapter 5, to efficiently target your Web visitors by segment. For paid search, you can use bid management software to remove most of the drudgery from keyword selection.

SET PAID SEARCH ON AUTOPILOT

If you have any experience using paid placement in Google, Yahoo!, or other search engines, you've experienced the pain of *bid management*. Although the major search engines all use click rate and other factors to help decide which ad is shown first, your pay-per-click bid still carries most of the weight.

Because your competitors are constantly adjusting their bids, you might need to adjust yours to continue to drive your profits. Most paid search marketers use *bid management software* to drastically reduce manual monitoring and adjustments.

If you use only one paid search vendor (just Yahoo! for example), you can use that vendor's free tool to manage your bids. However, if you use more than one search engine or you have a large paid search budget, you'll probably want to use a third-party bid management tool that can monitor bids across search engines and provide enhanced tracking and adjustment of bids. If you are working with a search marketing agency, they might handle the tracking and reporting for you, so you need not choose a tool yourself (25 percent of search marketers go the agency route).

The best bid management tools can adjust your per-click bids moment-to-moment based on the success metrics talked about earlier in this chapter, such as cost per action (CPA), profit margin (PM), return on advertising spending (ROAS), and return on investment (ROI). To date, however, no bid management tools monitor total profit or Lifetime Value.

Bid management software can raise your efficiency while reducing your workload but can't completely eliminate human monitoring. For example, they might lower your bid to the minimum amount if it gets few conversions, but it won't drop the keyword completely, which might be the best thing to do with a real loser. Regardless, the higher your paid placement budget and the more competitive your keywords, the more you'll need a strong bid management tool.

And the less time you spend monitoring your bids, the more time you can devote to deciding which keywords to target and adjusting those targets for maximum benefit.

As I said earlier, you can speed up selecting the person or you can speed up selecting the message—either one will quicken your pace of targeting. We've discussed choosing different landing pages for different search keywords—that helps you select different messages for each segment. But the use of *dynamic content* allows the quickest means of selecting a targeted message.

Dynamic content is nothing more than words and pictures that are generated by a program when the message is needed. A dynamic Web page is one that is pulled together from different content objects at the time the page is displayed—perhaps your personalization software selects the best ad for each customer depending on what market segment they occupy. Or maybe your e-commerce system can show your product's standard description but remind your customers of personal purchase histories on the same page.

Dynamic content offers even more possibilities. It allows e-mails to be generated with personal salutations ("Dear Louie") or personal information ("We noticed that it has been three months since you've had your 2006 Acura serviced..."). Dynamic content allows you to write the copy for a single paid search ad but insert the keywords that the searchers used into that ad to make it appear more relevant, as shown in Exhibit 6-7.

Some searchers look for "bmw 330" and others for "bmw 330i"—but they are served the exact same ad for each one.

Dynamic content capabilities insert the keyword used into the title of each ad, making each look more relevant.

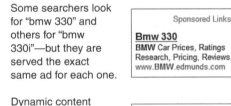

Exhibit 6-7   Dynamic content in paid search ads

Perhaps the most common use of dynamic content is to speed up changes to your messaging—we'll look at that next.

Speed Up Your Messaging

To "do it wrong quickly" you must be able to make fast changes to your marketing messages. In the old days, you had several ideas for your direct mail or catalog copy. You test mailed them and found which one was best, but it was expensive and time-consuming. The testing took a few weeks, and you could only afford to test a few variants before deciding which one you would send out for real.

For each change that you contemplate, you must have backup plans—alternate changes ready to go if the original is unsuccessful. Unlike traditional direct mail, you can't wait weeks to get your feedback. You must accelerate your speed of experimentation.

To understand how to quicken your pace, you need to know how computers assemble content—let's take a Web page as our example. Every message, including a Web page, has three distinct parts: the text itself, the markup of that content, and the formatting style, as shown in Exhibit 6-8.

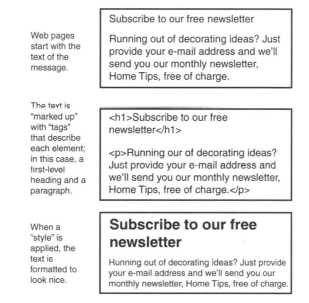

Exhibit 6-8   The anatomy of a marketing message

Your Web pages use what geeks call a *markup language* (called *HyperText Markup Language*, or *HTML*). Markup languages describe the elements of text, such as a heading, a list, or a paragraph. Your Web pages are "marked up" using HTML, using tags, such as "<h1>" for the most important heading on the page.

Most Web sites consist of what's called *static content*—the text and the markup are all brought together in an HTML file. It sounds simple, but because many of your pages share content (mastheads, navigation bars, ads, and other stuff), having those elements copied over and over into files makes them hard to change. Many of those files contain not only the content, but exact formatting instructions on how the content should look, which then makes the appearance hard to change, too.

The better way is to separate the text from the markup from the style. Start with the styles, which work the same way as styles in a word processor. *Cascading Style Sheets (CSS)* define how that heading looks in the browser—what typeface, size, color, and many other factors. Get your Web team to remove the formatting instructions from your HTML files and to use style sheets instead—that way you can change the look of your pages quickly and often, based on customer feedback.

Next, get the techies to create one master copy (called an *include file*) of content items used on many different pages, such as your ads. Once you do, you'll be able to update every page that contains a particular ad simply by editing its master copy. You can accomplish the same ends using dynamic content, as discussed earlier, but including files is a cheaper way to do it for small sites.

If you've got lots of content, you can use a *content management system* to keep all your content items straight and a *portal server* to assemble and display the items in Web pages and other messages. Large companies need high-end systems to manage their huge collections of multi-lingual content assets, but small companies can use inexpensive tools to serve their needs.

SPEEDY IN ANY LANGUAGE

How can you make quick content changes when you have to translate into other languages at the end? Well, the first tip is: don't wait until the end. Get your translators involved early so they don't object later—German needs a lot more space on the screen than English, for example.

To increase speed and control costs, many Business-to-Business marketers use a *tiered globalization* approach—each country site, for example, is assigned to a tier that defines how much content is translated. So the countries that garner your highest sales might be fully translated, the second tier might have only your top products translated, while the lowest tier has only the home page and a few high-level navigation pages in native language (with the rest possibly in English).

When you translate any page, make sure that you re-engage your search marketing experts to use the popular keywords in the new language; otherwise, you risk getting a semantically correct translation, but you aren't using the words that most people will search for.

Most multilingual sites use on-staff or contracted professionals to do their translation, but a few pioneers have asked volunteers to do it—Google is probably the most famous example. Library Thing, an Internet cataloger, offers no money for volunteer translators but displays an honor roll of those who have translated the most phrases. You need a rabid following to work this way, and you probably can't have a great deal of content. If you go the volunteer route, you might need to control what types of people you allow to volunteer. For example, a pharmaceutical site might prefer to be translated by medical professionals rather than by hypochondriacs.

But maybe you don't want to change the content itself—you want to experiment with the design. Some aspects of your content's design are specific to a particular page, such as the choice of what image to show on a product page, but the overall look can be standardized and managed centrally—that's what those style files are for. Style files can be used for Web pages, blogs, wikis, e-mail, and other content.

The power that style files provide allows you to do it wrong quickly—your designers can make changes across your Web site, and they can make them quickly. You can change your style files, see how it affects your conversion metrics, and then decide to keep the change or change it back—or change it to something else. Style files allow you to change your site's design both quickly and frequently.

In fact, the quick change process possible with CSS points out another advantage for dynamic content: *templates*. Templates can be thought of as the structure of your message—the guts that define its layout. With dynamic content, you can change your template to change the structure of every page on your site. With simple HTML files, you'd have to change each file to get the same effect, which slows you down.

And why is a slow pace of change such a problem? Miguel de Cervantes, author of *Don Quixote* (and maybe a closet Web designer), said that "Delay always breeds danger and to protract a great design is often to ruin it." He wasn't tilting at windmills— speed is an important part of listening to your customers. If it takes six months to do what they said, don't bother because they want something else now.

Speed Up Your Feedback

We've examined how you can watch what your customers do and how you can listen to what they say, but how can you do each of them faster? How can you get information sooner than you do now? First, let's think about the way you gather feedback now.

You probably use focus groups. Focus groups are expensive, so you don't do too many of them. And they aren't exactly quick—they take weeks to plan and execute.

What focus groups tell you is inherently limited, like a description of the scenery viewed through a straw. Pretend for a minute that you head marketing for a food company entering a brand new market in a poor country. You have no idea which of your vast product line will be the best first choice for you, so you ask each of your product managers to commission focus groups.

The first results come in: "They loved our meat. They couldn't get enough of it. They raved about the quality. They said no one else has meat like this." The second group's results come in: "They went crazy for our bread. You should have seen them." And on and on it goes, as marketers argue about which food to offer to starving people.

Often we don't know when our customers are starving for something—when they would take what we're selling in any of ten different ways. We try a couple of ways and fixate on what the focus group said, even though we might really have several better ideas that we didn't try.

Focus groups have their place, but you can't learn everything that way. Focus groups can be invaluable for finding out *why* customers do something, but they are a very expensive (and often inaccurate) way to find out *what* customers will do. We've already talked (in Chapter 3, "Marketing Is a Conversation") about monitoring your reputation by listening to what customers say on blogs and elsewhere. But how else can you listen to customers? How can you get customer feedback that's accurate and fast?

- **Interviews and surveys**—Make polls and feedback mechanisms a prominent part of every campaign. Create a customer advisory board you can e-mail or call when you need an opinion.

- **Use paper testing**—To find out what features are most important, use *card sorts* (in which customers rank order ideas or nomenclature from most to least important) and *paper prototypes* (mocked-up drawings of what a campaign or Web site could look like, with none of the expense of actually building it).

- **Use surrogates**—When it's too expensive or time-consuming to test with real customers, use employees or friends. Do it wrong quickly—what you lose in accuracy you might make up in speed. You can always bring in one or two groups of real customers at the end to double-check your conclusions.

And, as we've been saying throughout the book, there's no substitute for testing new ideas in real campaigns and on your real Web site. You can take any two alternatives—A/B tests—and find which one is better. You can do that day after day, but what if you could test alternatives far faster than A/B testing can?

In the 1950s, Japanese engineer Genichi Taguchi improved on A/B testing, describing a process now called *multivariate testing*. His insight was that testing just two possibilities against each other was very slow when you had many different variations to test. Taguchi showed how you can test several variables at the same time by carefully selecting different combinations so that the total test reveals which version of each variable is best. For example, if you want to test five versions of the copy and five versions of the image on your mailing piece, you can use different combinations of each so that you can test all 25 combinations at the same time, getting your answers for both variables at once.

But even Taguchi might be blown away by what computers now do with his original idea. Because computers can combine dozens of variations for dozens of variables, it's multivariate testing to the third power. Computers can assemble every permutation of a page—dozens of copy and image variations for a dozen places on your Web page. The possibilities can be in the billions! Even a site that has heavy traffic can't test even a thousand variations for a page unless you use multivariate testing software.

Multivariate testing software can select which version of each variable should be tested on each page and can boil down those billions of possibilities to a few dozen. After testing those few dozen, you can run a second multivariate test with a dozen versions and then get it down to three or four for the last wave before you decide the right variants for every variable.

But does multivariate testing really work?

Ask Time-Life, the publisher of books and other media that spends a great deal of money on direct response TV ads. Time-Life decided to use multivariate testing to improve the sales of their compilation album called "70s Music Explosion." They found that their ads drew traffic to their Web site, but few people added the album to their cart, and even fewer actually purchased. They designed a multivariate test that could yield a better design of this part of their Web site.

Time-Life identified ten variables they wanted to test, with several different variations of each. They had different copy they wanted to test, different images, and different offers. They wanted to know if showing a seal with their "money back guarantee" caused more sales (it did) and whether the order of the content mattered (it did).

Over a period of a couple of months, Time-Life took literally a billion possibilities and tested in a few waves to identify two different winning designs that improved the number of shoppers that dropped the album into their carts by 75 percent and increased actual sales by five percent.

There are many more examples of the success of this approach. Internet recruiter monster.com tested two alternatives for each of seven different variables in a software download experience using multivariate testing. In less than three weeks, the best design was chosen, which resulted in a 35 percent increase in downloads.

Internet lender Quicken Loans has also seen striking success. Regis Hadiaris, a Team Leader at Quicken Loans, teases the value of multivariate testing by asking, "What if you could walk into your CMO's office and confidently say, 'I can show you how to grow revenue 30 percent—are you interested?'"

Let's look at a detailed multivariate testing case study. ReallyGreatRate.com is an American online financial lead generation company that connects lenders to people looking for student loans, debt consolidation loans, and home mortgages. The company does all of its marketing online, passing loan applicants to up to four lenders (getting compensated for each valid lead passed). You can imagine how valuable it is to increase the number of leads passed, which requires convincing more people to complete the online application form.

But how do you do that? Everyone has an opinion about what should be changed. Multivariate testing boils those opinions down to testable sizes. ReallyGreatRate.com started with the submission form you see in Exhibit 6-9. The president of ReallyGreatRate.com, Matt Schaub, worked with Optimost, a leading multivariate testing vendor, to identify 13 separate areas on the page that could be modified and came up with seven or eight different treatments for each area.

For example, the masthead at the top of the page was one such area. Matt worked with Optimost to come up with several variations, such as changing the location of the image to the left side, changing the words in the tag line, and many others.

ReallyGreatRate.com started with a good page…

…but ended up with a great page, after testing.

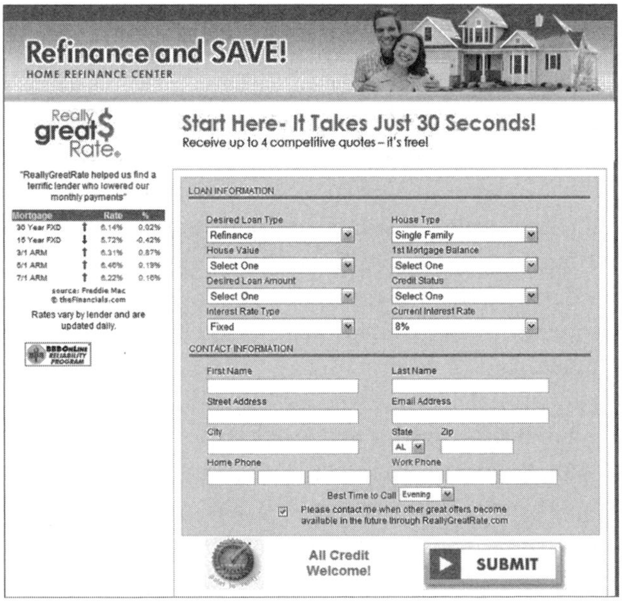

Exhibit 6-9 Multivariate testing in action

Optimost ran several rounds of testing to cycle through each variant, identifying the ones that seemed to outperform the rest—the ones that correlated with more loan applicants pressing that "Submit" button. Within four months, a winning design was chosen.

It doesn't look all that different, does it? It's a bit less cluttered on the left side, removing some things that proved more distracting than helpful, and the most noticed text in the middle of the screen has been reworded to emphasize starting the process. But it looks very similar to what Matt already had.

Here's what wasn't so similar: Form completion went up 116 percent! A new form that didn't look all that much different than the old one had dramatically different results. Without testing, even experts might not know which of those two forms would produce better results. And, remember, thousands of different variants were tested, which no expert could do either.

So now Matt is happy he's got the best one, right? Wrong. "I'm starting a new round of testing this week," he told me. "I'm going to constantly change my form. You have to! What works now might not work next month."

Such is the essence of "Do it wrong quickly." Experiment. Measure. Keep what is working and change all of it, working or not. Matt advised all Web marketers, "Never get complacent."

Don't be left behind in the optimization race. Multivariate testing is your best ticket to higher conversions for your Web site. And if you think you can't afford this technique, think again. Google has begun offering a free multivariate testing tool called Website Optimizer.

Just as when Google began offering the free Google Analytics traffic metrics service, some people have questioned whether marketers should allow Google access to the highly valuable multivariate test results provided by Website Optimizer. When a company you buy advertising from also knows how much you sell—and what it is about your site that sells it—are you letting the fox into the hen house? For most small businesses, "free" is of utmost importance to them, but larger marketers concerned about data privacy can opt for fee-based analytics and multivariate testing tools instead.

No matter how you try to speed up getting feedback, *listening* to that feedback is what's most important. If you aren't acting on the feedback you get, there's no point in getting it faster. There are those who look at things the way they are and ask why. I look at my metrics reports and ask why aren't they clicking?

You might have noticed a pattern in the advice for speeding up your targeting, your content changes, and your feedback mechanisms—automation. Applying new technology is the primary method of increasing the pace of marketing. Unfortunately, technology is something we all do wrong frequently—and not very quickly. You'll have to wait for Chapter 8, "This Won't Work Where I Work," to see how to increase the speed and effectiveness of technology at your company.

Summary

No Web site is ever done until its customers are all dead. The same is true for any marketing campaign. To cope with these facts, the advice is simple: When what you're doing isn't working, try something else. And the corollary is this: If what you're doing *is* working, try something else anyway because you can always improve.

Technology consultant Bob Lewis, author of the *Keep the Joint Running* newsletter, says that "There is no best practice. There are practices that fit best." The only way you discover a best practice for your company is to experiment—to do it wrong quickly.

In this chapter, I broke up our mantra of "do it wrong quickly" into three parts:

- **Where do you start?**—We looked at how you choose the "it" in "do *it* wrong quickly." Where *do* you start? How do you decide what to do next? Well, it depends on where you are today. You need to look at your Web site and your marketing campaigns and start somewhere. Instead of embarking on a massive overhaul, just change one thing.

- **How do you know how wrong it is?**—When you do it *wrong* quickly, just how far off are you, anyway? We looked at several new ways to quantify results in business terms, whether it was cost per action or profit based on conversions, or lifetime customer value based on relationships. We also covered how to design tests that allow you to choose the best alternative to be a little less wrong every day. Inventor Thomas Edison summed it up when he said, "I am not discouraged because every wrong attempt discarded is another step forward."

- **How do you speed up?**—Finally, we addressed our need for speed—how do we do it wrong *quickly?* We reviewed technology for speeding up e-mail and other targeting. We covered tools and techniques for adjusting marketing messages every day. We also saw how to use new testing methods to accelerate the rate of feedback we can collect and act on because customers vote with their mice.

And that wraps up Part 2. You've learned how to watch what your customers do and what you can do about it. And you've learned how to do it wrong quickly. More important than any specific technique is your mindset—can you now go out and start experimenting? In Part 3, we'll take on the roadblocks that stop you from acting on what you know. If you have the knowledge but don't know why you can't get seem to get started, read on.

PART **3**

That Newfangled *You*

Chapter 7 ▪ This Doesn't Work for Me   255

Chapter 8 ▪ This Won't Work Where I Work   275

Chapter 9 ▪ This Stuff Changes Too Fast   315

Y ou've learned, in the first two parts of this book, how Internet marketing has changed the old marketing rules. You've learned how to listen to what your customers say and do. You've learned what you can do in response to make your marketing a little bit better every day.

But somehow, that's not enough for most people.

For some reason, even after you understand everything going on around you, even after you're convinced that these changes are really happening and you know what other companies are doing, you may have some objections. Part 3 helps you work through your objections.

Chapter 7, "This Doesn't Work for Me," helps you work through your personal resistance. If, as you've read ideas and suggestions in this book, a little voice in your head tells you, "Gee, I could never do that," then you need this chapter. You *can* do it if it's important enough to you. We explore where that resistance comes from and what you can do to overcome it.

Chapter 8, "This Won't Work Where I Work," helps you with a different problem. You may be personally ready to change how you work, but you feel powerless to do that without the rest of your colleagues. Maybe your company culture is not terribly innovative.

Maybe your boss will frown on coloring outside the lines. This chapter equips you to assess your environment and decide how you can succeed in it.

Chapter 9, "This Stuff Changes Too Fast," gives voice to another objection you may have. You may already feel exhausted just from all the information that's been thrown at you so far in this book. And you *know* that it will keep changing—probably at a faster pace than it has up until now. This chapter equips you to think about the changes that are coming so that you can assess how each one can be analyzed and adapted to—even ones we can't see today.

At the end of Part 3, you'll be able to identify the obstacles that stand in your way and take action to correct each one. Day by day, you'll make the right decisions to improve your marketing effectiveness. Appoint yourself that captain of your destiny, rather than feeling tossed about on the waves of change.

So let's sail into Chapter 7.

7

This Doesn't Work for Me

"If at first you don't succeed, try, try, again. Then quit. There's no use being a damn fool about it."

—W. C. Fields

Chapter Contents

- The Reasons Why Not   257
- Fear   266
- Change   270
- Summary   273

OK, let's get a show of hands. How many of you enjoy waiting for a bus? I mean, everyone has a hobby—haunting bus stops until you get picked up just happens to be yours.

Hmm. No hands went up. I'm not sure anyone relishes that lonely wait for the bus, and I'm no exception. So on a windy, bitterly cold day in February, when I found myself waiting for a bus, I was just hoping it would come early so I could warm up. But it didn't.

It didn't arrive on time either.

So as I waited for five minutes, ten minutes, and longer, I started to wonder. Did I have the schedule wrong? No, it is posted right here at the bus stop. What could have happened?

Finally, 20 minutes late, the bus arrives. I start to get on, but the bus driver waves me off. "I don't take pickups at this stop—I only drop people off here."

I protested, "But the bus I am supposed to catch is 20 minutes late! I'm cold, and you're going to the same place, and I can see you have plenty of seats—why can't you take me?"

The driver was resolute. "No pickups—if you don't like it, you can speak to my dispatcher. I don't make the rules."

The door closed in my face and the bus sped off.

My bus did finally arrive at the bus stop, 45 minutes late, victimized by an accident that closed a highway with the bus stuck between exits, just sitting there until it was reopened. By that time, I was frozen stiff and just happy to get warm and be on my way. I didn't even bother to protest. I just made a mental note to investigate how easily I could catch a train the next time.

That delay *had* given me plenty of time to ponder an age-old question: What makes some people customer-oriented, while others are content to keep their heads down and follow the rules?

This story is a familiar one. All of us have been in situations where "following the rules" was the worst thing to do for the customer, but no exceptions were made. We've felt that frustration and have vowed to never patronize the business again.

But we've all been in the situation of enforcing those pointless rules, too. We *know* that we're doing the wrong thing, but we also know it isn't worth fighting the system that imposes those rules. There's no percentage in our crusading for the customer in this situation—it has the potential to bring us only trouble.

That's the type of company our bus driver works for—one where helping the customer is not a priority. But that's too easy an explanation. Any of us can decide that we'll be more responsive to our customers, if we really want to be. Even if it means quitting your job to work somewhere else, we each have the power to change the way we work.

That's what this chapter is about—making the decision to change how you work. If you feel like that bus driver, you need to analyze why you feel you *can't* change it. You need to understand what's stopping you before you can do something different.

Now some of you don't need this chapter. Maybe nothing is stopping you. If you're raring to go, chomping at the bit, and (insert your own anticipatory cliché here), then you can skip this chapter. You can start "doing it wrong quickly" a bit more, er, *quickly*.

But if you're more cautious about this new way of operating, perhaps mentally listing your "reasons why not," then you need to read this chapter carefully. You *can* change if you can figure out what obstacles are in your path—and get past them.

So what's stopping you from taking all the advice I've dished out so far? What's holding you back from "doing it wrong quickly"?

The Reasons Why Not

So, what *is* that little voice in our mind telling us? Psychologists know that our self-talk helps define our attitudes and our confidence in facing every situation in our lives. Too often, our self-talk is providing a list of "reasons why not"—a set of excuses that help us to rationalize sticking with what we do now.

What we do now is comfortable. It's safe. It doesn't force us to think. It's defensible to others.

But maybe it's not working. That's the challenge. As Jim Collins, author of *Good to Great*, says, "Good is the enemy of great." What that means is that it is much harder to become great when you are already good because you are comfortable. It's the crisis of being bad that spurs most big changes.

That's your challenge. Your marketing program is probably not in crisis at the moment—but it will be if you ignore the changes that the Internet has caused. So, ask yourself: Am I just making excuses? Am I in denial?

Take a look at the set of "reasons why not" later in this section and ask yourself if you are using them to avoid changing your approach from the traditional way to "do it wrong quickly." When you see one that resonates with you—one that matches your self-talk—it's time to examine whether what you are telling yourself is *true*. It turns out that we tell ourselves things all the time that aren't exactly true.

We're not lying to ourselves—we're telling ourselves a story that doesn't quite mesh with reality. For example, when we tell ourselves, "I must not lose this customer," that's probably a bit extreme. You certainly don't want to lose the customer— you, in fact, *strongly* prefer not to lose the customer—but if you do, you will somehow handle it.

Most of us carry around a set of "musts" that govern our responses. We tell ourselves that we "must" do one thing or another, and we believe that if we don't, life will be intolerable. But it's not true.

We're all resilient creatures, and we can adapt—that's what most of this book is about. Often what we tell ourselves—our beliefs—are holding us back from real change. A whole branch of psychology, called *cognitive therapy*, helps people to identify their beliefs and examine them to see if they are true. If your beliefs are holding you back, you can dispute your beliefs with rationality to help you change your self-talk and allow yourself to change.

WHAT'S COGNITIVE THERAPY?

Cognitive therapy, sometimes called *cognitive behavioral therapy (CBT)*, helps you make big changes in your life. Cognitive therapy starts with the premise that our innermost beliefs are reflected in self-talk, which affect our emotions—and our emotions often handicap our efforts to change our behavior.

A great book, *Three Minute Therapy* by Michael R. Edelstein and David Ramsay Steele, explains the ABCDEF method—the simple steps anyone can take to help them change deep-seated behavior:

A. **Activating Event**—"My boss criticized me for trying to do the new advertising campaign wrong quickly. He said that it doesn't matter how fast we can do things if we do them wrong."

B. **Irrational Belief**—"I must *never* be criticized by my boss. It's intolerable to have my boss believe I messed something up."

C. **Emotional and Behavioral Consequences**—"I fear that if I stick to my guns, my boss will give me a bad review this year and a lower bonus. Maybe he'll lay me off if I keep this up! I should probably go back to the old way."

D. **Disputing Your Belief**—"Why am I fearful about my job? I do a good job, and my boss just doesn't see the value of this new technique yet. From time to time, my boss criticizes everyone—sometimes he's wrong when he does so."

E. **Effective New Thinking**—"Although I *strongly* prefer not to be criticized by my boss, there's no law of the universe that says I *must* not be. I can handle being criticized while still doing things the way I know they should be done. Once I show him that the campaign succeeded and that we did it faster and cheaper, he'll be happy I did it this way."

F. **New Feeling or Behavior**—"I don't like being criticized, but if I can change the way we approach marketing, that will be a big win for me. Maybe I won't try to do every campaign this way, but I will stick with it for this one as a test. If it works, maybe I can really start to change things around here."

Not everyone needs cognitive therapy to "do it wrong quickly," but if your self-talk is holding you back, it can be very helpful.

Take a gander at some of the self-talk that follows and see if you've been hearing any of it inside your brain.

"That's not my job."

One of the scary things about Internet marketing is that it crosses traditional professional boundaries. Yes, marketing requires both technical skills and marketing skills now, but online marketing also erases the clear lines between marketing and sales. No wonder it seems challenging.

Unfortunately, it's not enough to try to redraw those traditional boundaries in fluorescent ink. If, as you've read up to this point, you've told yourself that technology is not your job, and that design is not your job, and that metrics are not your job—think again. You need to understand enough about each of them so that you can be a successful marketer.

And, no, it's *not* your job to change your company's culture from its traditional "plan ahead and get it right" mentality to "do it wrong quickly." But that's what *leaders* do. They go beyond their jobs and do what the company needs, not only what it hired them to do.

Let's be honest. Even if your title is the same, the job you have now probably isn't really the same as the one you had just a few years ago. You've had to change as the demands of your job have changed.

The challenges of online marketing are no exception—they just might be causing a bigger-sized change than the ones you've handled in the past. The people who go beyond their job responsibilities and take on this challenge are the ones who will be running the show, rather than acting in it (or buying a ticket just to watch).

Instead of telling yourself that it's "not your job," why not remind yourself that you are the type of person who does more than expected. Going beyond your job is your way to shine.

"I don't have permission."

Computer pioneer Grace Hopper liked to remark that "it is better to beg forgiveness than to ask permission," and nowhere is that more true than when it comes to new paradigms, such as online marketing.

No one is going to give you permission.

The powers-that-be will ignore the new paradigm until it is a crisis. Then they will conduct a blame hunt for the one who caused the crisis, and they'll order that the problem be addressed. Some leaders will even order exactly *how* the situation should be addressed.

But no one will give you permission. They'll practice neglect until it becomes their top priority and then order it to be dealt with.

Instead of seeking permission (or even worse, waiting for it to be bestowed), think about how the Internet is affecting your company in its industry. How are your customers changing? What core values of your company allow you to address this head on?

Your company's leaders might say that they are customer-centric, but perhaps they don't reward employees that go above and beyond their responsibilities to satisfy a customer. Study what behaviors are punished (and rewarded), and you'll see what your company's beliefs really are.

You can be like my bus driver who needed permission to pick me up from the freezing bus stop, or you can do it wrong quickly by listening to what your customers need and responding. Maybe no one gave you permission, but no one told you not to do it either.

"No one will listen to me."

Perhaps no one *will* listen to you. It is possible. Maybe you are just a terribly unpersuasive person—but I somehow doubt that.

Most marketers communicate rather well—marketing is all about persuading your customers to do something. If you're telling yourself that other people at your company won't listen to you, why should your customers listen to you?

A basic role of any leader is to get people to address problems. You don't have to be "in charge" to be a leader. You just need to be persuasive.

It is possible to be in a difficult situation where your company has hired lots of people who themselves aren't very adaptable. If that is truly your problem, then you'll want to read Chapter 8, "This Won't Work Where I Work," closely, which discusses how to deal with that situation.

But maybe the people you work with are highly adaptable (or at least average), and your problem is lack of confidence. Ask yourself to think about situations in your past where you knew the right thing to do. Were you able to persuade others of your point of view? Would you do things the same way today?

Reframe the way you talk to yourself. Instead of saying, "No one will listen to me," say "Not everyone will listen to me," or "In the past, many people did not listen to me." Just saying things differently changes how you think. If "not everyone" will listen to you, or "in the past" people did not always listen, those statements prompt you to ask yourself what you could do differently this time so that more people do.

If, in contrast, you tell yourself that no one will listen to you, you're likely to look for evidence that your prediction is correct—and you will always be able to find such evidence if you look hard enough.

Change the way you talk to yourself, and you'll see your actions change, too.

"I don't have time."

Feeling as though you have more to do than you have hours in the day is perfectly natural in our busy modern world. How on earth can you move any faster than you do now? After all, you already work too many hours, and you already do too much. Maybe this experimentation stuff works, but who has time for it?

The truth is that you have the same amount of time as anyone else—it's a question of what you do with it.

When people say they have no time for something, what they are really saying is that it is not a high enough priority. Think about it. Some things are critically important for you get done, no matter what. If you make changing your marketing practices a priority, you'll get that done, too.

A variation on "I have no time" is "If you don't have the time to do it right, how will you have time to do it over?" It's a great sound bite, but it isn't true. The truth is that it's only by doing it wrong that you find out *how* to do it over because it isn't about the *time* it takes. It's about not knowing what to do until you've done it wrong and your customers tell you so.

Instead of telling yourself you have no time, ask yourself to be honest about what's important to you. If you're not working on the things you say are important, then you need to change your words or your actions.

"I'm no numbers person."

You don't have to be. Some marketers have been doing analytics for years, but many marketers have not spent their lives with spreadsheets. Not to worry.

Maybe you aren't a technology person, either, but you can still work with technology people. If you are in the minority of marketers that are truly spooked at the thought of calculations, then find someone to help you with them. You don't have to personally do them anymore than you have to design your own Web site.

Don't worry about the numbers themselves—focus on what they mean. If your brain just isn't wired for numerical data, insist that your metrics folks explain the numbers in words. Don't let them out of the room until you understand what they are telling you. Even if you lack *any* ability to do numeric analysis, you should be able to pose questions about what your customers are doing and get answers from people who *can* crank the numbers. When you really get down, remember Albert Einstein's words: "Do not worry about your difficulties in mathematics. I can assure you mine are still greater."

Instead of lamenting that you are "no numbers person," why not remember that your perspective has advantages, too? Sometimes "numbers people" can get so fixated on their calculations that they miss the bigger picture. While the numbers person is torturing the data to reveal the statistical significance of two different calls to action, you might notice that the color of the text is too hard to read—a potentially bigger problem than the wording.

"I've never been fast at decisions—it's too much pressure."

You don't need to be. Think of the *final* decision—the one you've always done deliberately and slowly—as continuing to take a long time. You're just going to make a lot of other decisions along the way, and each one that you make is low-stakes. You're going to see how it works, and that helps you deliberate on where you need to go toward your final decision.

Some people—maybe even you—are more comfortable with deliberation. But it's important in the world of the Internet that you make choices as quickly as you can. Will Rogers could have been talking about online marketing when he said, "Even if you're on the right track, you'll get run over if you just sit there."

STATISTICAL SIGNIFICANCE IS OVERRATED

One of the most intimidating parts of the numbers game is *statistical significance*. Many marketers struggle with this concept, even those normally comfortable with numerical analysis.

To the uninitiated, when a statistician says that a number is not statistically significant, they interpret that as meaning that no conclusions can be drawn from that number—but that's wrong. Let's take an example.

If you tested three different e-mail messages to see which one has the highest click rate, the statistician (or your computer statistics program) might tell you that the third version was significantly worse than the first two but that the difference between the first two was insignificant. What do you do?

You could run another test. You could eliminate the third version and retest the first two. Your numbers person will tell you that you need many more e-mail recipients to achieve statistical significance because the two e-mails are quite close to each other in effectiveness.

If you want to "do it wrong quickly," then just send out the one that tested better, regardless of whether it is a statistically significant difference. Why? Because the two e-mails are close enough to each other that sending either one is probably OK, and chances are that the one that tested slightly better really is better, even if you don't know for sure.

To understand why this is true, you need to understand what "statistical significance" means—it is generally used to mean that you are 95 percent sure that

Besides, you probably have better skills in this area than you give yourself credit for. Think about the last time you conducted a negotiation. It might have been for that big contract with your new dealer or with the contractor who is renovating your kitchen. It doesn't matter what example you think of.

Just go over in your mind exactly how that negotiation went. Could you have possibly planned the final agreement yourself? No matter how long you sat and pondered, could you have anticipated every objection raised? Could you have predicted how each disagreement was resolved?

You probably went into the negotiation thinking you understood what you wanted, but you learned more from the negotiation process itself. ("Oh, I guess we really don't want the refrigerator next to the stove after all.") And the other side probably made some compromises, too.

your conclusion is correct. That means that even when you achieve statistical significance, you have a one in 20 chance of being wrong.

A different statistical methodology is gaining traction, called *Bayesian probability*, which takes a different approach, based on the persuasiveness of the data. Bayesian aficionados argue that when you know where you are starting from, such as the conversion rate for your shopping cart page, you can persuade yourself that a new page design is "working" with a very small number of successes. That small sample size is *not* statistically significant, but it is probably the right conclusion to influence your decision.

If you can't stop yourself from aiming for statistical significance, remember that the bigger the change, the smaller the sample size you need. So try to go after things that raise your conversion rate ten percent rather than one percent. That might sound obvious, but often we need to make a concerted effort to "think big" rather than shooting only for small improvement.

Better yet, don't get hung up on statistical significance at all. It's better to make ten decisions in a row with 70 percent confidence than just one that you are 95 percent sure of. By making frequent changes, the ones that turned out to be wrong will be found out soon enough. So ask your statistician to find statistical significance with 70 percent confidence instead of 95 percent.

If you're still thinking that you need statistics to prove that your results aren't random, just remember the words of comedian Dick Cavett: "Just think of all the billions of coincidences that *don't* happen."

Only in the most one-sided negotiation can either party anticipate the final outcome. Every other negotiation is done step by step. You ask for something, and then the other party counters with something else. Eventually you come to agreement.

Your Internet marketing can work the same way. Think about every decision you make as a negotiation between you and your customer. Every time you try something on your Web site, think of it as an offer in a negotiation. If you are suddenly converting a lot of customers, then you can consider your offer accepted. If, instead, your customers run screaming into the night, then you can take that as a rejection, and you might want to make a counteroffer.

So think about every change you make in your marketing campaigns and your Web site as a negotiation in that each offer can be accepted or rejected by your customer. Eventually, you'll arrive at a something that seems like an agreement, but you can take all the time you want to deliberate along the way. Web analytics expert Jim Sterne goes so far as to call each customer click a "micro-negotiation." Regardless of how you look at it, it's better to tell yourself that your new approach to marketing is just another negotiation instead of thinking you can't handle the pressure of quick decisions.

"We tried that already."

Well, you probably didn't try *exactly* the same thing, right? And even if you did attempt precisely the same idea, conditions have changed. The Internet makes it far easier to measure everything and to move quickly to make changes. If you tried these techniques before these conditions existed, you might find they work better now.

Often we tell ourselves that we tried something already when we only experimented with something similar. People have a tendency to draw broad conclusions that aren't always true. Things fail due to very small problems. Curt Sasaki, Vice President of .SUN Properties at Sun Microsystems, says that "Rather than dumping stuff, we rework things." Now sometimes dumping a dumb idea is the right thing to do but only after you've given it several tries.

You might need to try a good idea many times before it suddenly "works." Dre Madden, Channel Manager of Internet ticket seller StubHub, talks about a "chain of pain" for the customer. Each time one problem in the ticket-buying process was addressed, it opened up another that became glaringly obvious. Only by addressing each problem in turn was the experience eventually optimized.

Perhaps you succeeded because you finally lurched into the formula where everything is clicking. Other times, things start to work because the time is right.

You might have been slightly ahead of your time. That great idea for an ad that has been disappointing for three months might suddenly resonate with your audience. Maybe they need it now, or their perception of your brand suddenly makes that promise credible. Your customers might have needed to be exposed to similar messages a few times before they were attracted by yours.

I'll go further than that. A great way to "do it wrong quickly" is to resurrect ideas from the past that never panned out. Your team thought they were good, but they failed when they were first tried. Try them again and see if times have changed. Tweak them a few times to see if they work now.

Instead of saying "we tried that already," it might be the case that you haven't tried it enough different ways. But sometimes when people say, "We tried that already," they don't want that idea tried again because if it worked, it might prove them wrong. Economist John Maynard Keynes once said, "When the facts change, I change my mind. What do you do, sir?" Let's talk about what *you* do next.

"I can't stand being wrong."

You're not alone. No one relishes admitting they screwed up, but some people do seem to have an easier time with it than others. What makes those people different from the rest of us?

It might be merely a question of attitude. Some people approach life as a series of experiments—each one designed to help them learn a little more so that the next decision is better. Develop your playful side and think about what you're doing the same way you'd approach a guessing game.

If you break out a crossword puzzle, do you expect yourself to read the clues and fill in every last letter? Of course not. You know that you'll figure out some of them right away, but many of them require you to take a guess. You try filling in a word for "1 across" and see if the words for "1 down" and "2 down" and "3 down" seem to fit with the word you guessed. Doing the puzzle in pencil lets you erase guesses that did not pan out and try again.

The difference between crossword puzzles and Internet marketing is that crossword puzzles are far easier. A few people *can* whip out a pen and methodically fill in a crossword puzzle in just a few minutes. In contrast, *nobody* can solve the Internet marketing puzzle in one try—it is truly a case of trial and error.

If you expect to conduct thousands of trials with no error, that's crazy. Instead, you need to play the game. You need to take guesses and see what customers do. They'll tell you what is working and what should change. If it bothers you to think of yourself as being wrong, then just treat every decision as a guess. By the time you draw a conclusion (many experiments later), you'll most definitely have it right.

But maybe some of you are still resisting "doing it wrong quickly"—preferring the old, slow consensus way sometimes cynically described as "often in error, but never in doubt." In contrast, "do it wrong quickly" says that you are *always* in error and *always* in doubt—you know you're wrong. There's no doubt about that.

Rocket pioneer Werner von Braun once remarked that "Research is what I'm doing when I don't know what I'm doing." Maybe we can take the same approach to what we marketers do every day. After all, Internet marketing ain't rocket science.

Even when you understand the "do it wrong quickly" concept in your rational mind, you still might feel more comfortable searching for a best practice. The problem is that when things are changing as fast as they are in interactive marketing, no one knows what the best practices are yet. That unheralded Internet marketing expert Will Rogers summed it up when he said, "It isn't what we don't know that gives us trouble, it's what we know that ain't so."

If Werner von Braun can admit he doesn't always know what he's doing, so can you. Just call it research.

"It feels too overwhelming."

It *can* be overwhelming, but you can still do it. It might seem overwhelming because you are trying to do it perfectly. Doing it wrong perfectly is as dumb as it sounds, but you might still *feel* that way. You need to recognize this feeling and overcome it. You don't always have to make decisions based on how you feel. Sometimes you can notice that your feeling is not rooted in reality and you can decide to do something else, even if it's a bit uncomfortable.

Besides, it's natural for you not to know what to do all the time. That's why we have to experiment, right? American journalist Edward R. Murrow knew what he was talking about when he said, "Anyone who isn't confused doesn't really understand the situation."

If you're truly feeling overwhelmed, then you might be taking on too much. Break down the problem into a series of small tasks and take them one by one. The idea of proposing an optimal Web experience for your customers *is* overwhelming. Instead, start small and take each question individually. Start with one page, such as your shopping cart checkout page. In fact, start with just one decision on that one page, such as whether customers should type in their credit card expiration date or pick it from pull-down menus. Add up a million decisions like that, and suddenly you have a strong Web experience.

When you find yourself saying you feel overwhelmed, remind yourself to think granularly so that you cut your problem down to size. But maybe when you're feeling overwhelmed, it's actually a symptom of something else. Fear. Fear of change, fear of doing it wrong, or fear of getting fired—there are lots of fears to go around. What are *you* afraid of?

Fear

Maybe you have a "reason why not" that I didn't list. I left out a lot of things people say to themselves because many of them are caused by one thing: fear.

Fear is an easy emotion for me to help you with because writers deal with fear all the time. Some writers (including me) have to battle fear over every word they put on a page. They fear being criticized. What if I am wrong? What if I make a mistake?

What if someone doesn't think my joke is funny? In the solitude of writing, it's easy for your mind to spend a lot of time imagining all sorts of scary possibilities. I actually took the time to read Ralph Keyes' excellent book, *The Courage to Write: How Authors Transcend Fear*.

Some writers are so fearful of putting words on paper that they suffer from writer's block. ("If I don't write anything, it can't be criticized.") More commonly, writers retreat into lack of clarity. ("If I abandoned the jargon, they would understand me and might think I am dumb. Or they'd be able to argue with me better.")

One of my favorite book titles is *Everyone's Normal Until You Get to Know Them*. One of the things you find about everyone is that we all have fears. You might not see them until you get to know us, but they are there. And they drive a lot of what we do. Marketers are in no way immune from fear.

Even when we know that we should do something—rationally—fear can hold us back. Some of you are afraid of trying these ideas. I know this because every time I speak to an audience on this subject, people ask questions driven by fear.

Once, in fact, I ran into someone so fearful that she was visibly agitated.

I had completed my speech and I was packing up my stuff when she approached. Some people have jokingly said that to "do it wrong quickly" I must have the attention span of a gnat, but this woman asked me a question I had never heard before: "Do you have ADD?"

As it happens, I don't have attention deficit disorder, but that is how some people react to the idea that you should try many things instead of having one set plan. Fast change is so threatening that they need to tell themselves that those who move quickly have some kind of psychological condition. (Now if you do happen to have ADD, maybe you've found your dream career, but, trust me, you can do just fine either way.)

Maybe we all ought to act a bit more like we have ADD. We love to convince ourselves that we know the agenda and that we have things under control, but we don't. If that scares you, then you need to think about how to overcome your fear of experimentation.

Comedian George Carlin knows fear. "I'm not concerned about all hell breaking loose, but that a *part* of hell will break loose...it'll be much harder to detect." That kind of irrational fear can be paralyzing in the face of change.

Too many people are simply afraid to try something new. Jazz great Miles Davis liked to say, "Do not fear mistakes. There are none." That does sound like a jazz musician, doesn't it? But Internet marketing is like jazz because it depends on improvisation. And, like jazz, the risks are low. Playing one wrong note is not the end of the world—neither is making one wrong decision in your interactive marketing.

Marketing guru Seth Godin might have said it best: "There's never been a marketing problem that turned out just the way the book said it will. That's what makes it interesting." And that's the point. Like jazz, there's no sheet music. There are no best practices—there are merely the best decisions we can make in each situation.

Baseball player Yogi Berra summed it up when he said, "In theory, there is no difference between theory and practice. In practice there is." All right, all right, I don't really know what he meant either, but I am completely out of inspiring quotes for this section of the book. At some point, if you are afraid, you just need to get over it.

Or maybe you need to use your fear to motivate yourself. Here's a quote that isn't meant to inspire you but instead to scare you—*really* scare you. Mark Twain once said that "The man with a new idea is a crank, until the idea succeeds."

What does that mean to you? At some point, *not* changing will be more dangerous than changing ever would have been.

You see, if you've become convinced over the course of this book that online marketing really *is* different, if you've been persuaded that experimenting and changing at a fast pace is the new way to succeed, *and* if you can see that other companies are jumping on the bandwagon, then what happens when everyone has changed but you?

So far, we've looked at how fear can hold you back and how you might use it to motivate you to change. But is fear ever healthy? Isn't it sometimes valuable to be fearful?

Actually, it is.

A study by the Cranfield School of Management (U.K.) revealed how useful it can be to accurately assess the danger in a situation. Fifty entrepreneurs were character-

"I WANT ANALYST MARKETERS"

When Imran Khan started his business career, he didn't fit anyone's idea of a marketer—he had a background in public accounting and no marketing degree. "When I came to America, I sent out 500 résumés and didn't get a single internship offer," he recalled. "People told me that I had no idea about American culture and what makes Americans tick." But Imran is not the kind of person who is easily dissuaded.

He kept at it and finally met the director of global business development at Hewlett-Packard, whom he recognized as a former entertainer from his native Pakistan. The director finagled him a part-time contract position, which Imran worked at night and day, eventually landing a full-time permanent marketing position.

Imran decided to pursue Internet marketing because it was an "unexplored territory where there were no experts." Imran worked in Internet marketing for several companies before joining E-LOAN, the Internet lender, in 2003 as Director of Search Marketing.

He brought a keen insight in Web metrics to his new position, building an $18 million search marketing program. In 2004, E-LOAN expanded his position to

ized by their appetite for risk and their feelings of self-confidence. Guess which entrepreneurs had the strongest sales and profit growth? The ones that tested highest in risk-taking *and* lowest in confidence.

These are not people lacking fear—they *know* how hard it is to succeed. That's why they are never confident that their decisions are correct. But they also know something else—that their fear can't prevent them from taking risks, from trying things, from experimenting. They play the game, but they never assume they are going to win.

And then they *do* win—most of the time.

As the study showed, these winning entrepreneurs are different from the rest. Some people are overconfident—perhaps they think of themselves as "born leaders" and use that as an excuse to do whatever they want. Others lack the risk-taking gene—maybe they think they are not leaders, so they shrink from the big decisions.

Successful entrepreneurs, in contrast, "do it wrong quickly"—they take constant risks, with no confidence that they are right.

Are they afraid? Probably. But it doesn't stop them. Instead, they take action. Fear is paralyzing. If you take action, you'll overcome your fear, at least temporarily.

Perhaps you don't think you're "wired" for that. Maybe you are not a risk taker. You have two options. One is to get a lot more confident in this process so that you realize

---

oversee their affiliate program and their banner advertising spending. 2005 saw Imran, now Director of Marketing, take over all media spending, both online and offline, including a large TV and radio budget. In 2006, he was named Chief Marketing Officer of E-LOAN, which has written $27 billion worth of loans in its history.

To what does he attribute this rapid success? "Every day I come to work to see if yesterday's test improved the numbers," he enthused. "If I unearth one more nugget, it makes my week!"

Imran no longer worries about getting a marketing job. Now *he's* the one hiring. And what kind of people is he looking for? "I want analyst marketers—they use Excel and do their own number crunching." He once hired a Ph.D. in Statistics and readily admits that not everyone on his team has marketing degrees. Imran ticked off the qualities he is looking for: "how intelligent and hard working they are and how analytical—some have degrees in Investment Banking or Computer Science."

If you're fearful of what will happen if you change the way you've always worked, maybe you should balance that against the fear of *not* changing. Ask yourself: If you sent Imran Khan your résumé, could *you* get hired?

that you are *not* taking a big risk to try things. In fact, you are taking a huge risk *not* to try things. So even if you aren't a risk taker by nature, you can talk yourself into taking risks here.

Note that developing confidence in the process is *not* the same as developing confidence in the decisions (which the study shows does not work). You can simultaneously have high confidence in the process, which helps you take the risk, and low confidence in each decision—that low confidence is actually a critical key to success. The process calls upon you to do it *wrong* quickly, which shows how much confidence you should have in each individual decision.

If you don't like that option, your other option is to change. We look at about how to do that next.

Change

Change can be difficult. There's no getting around it. Every person, no matter how flexible they might appear, struggles with some kinds of changes. Why?

There's no one reason, and you've undoubtedly read lots of studies that give all sorts of explanations. There's one very powerful reason that too few people know about, however.

All changes aren't the same.

Some changes just seem harder than others, don't they? Let's look at an example. Suppose you've decided that you want to get up an hour earlier each day. Perhaps you want to pray in the morning, do some exercise, or start writing that book. Logically, if you go to bed an hour earlier each day and add this activity first thing in the morning, you should be able to pull it off, right?

But no matter what you do, you just can't seem to get to bed an hour earlier, and you just can't get up an hour earlier. It feels like a *big* change.

It *is* a big change. It requires you to alter longstanding habits. You might have to forgo watching your favorite show to go to bed earlier. You might have to give up the time you spend talking to your spouse each night. You might not see these implications as the root of your problem, however. Instead, you might tell yourself, "I just can't get up an hour earlier" or "My body clock just won't adjust to this schedule."

For you, getting up an hour earlier might be an *adaptive* change—one that requires you to change your beliefs about yourself or change other habits that you consider to be part of who you are.

Let's consider another example. Come spring in many countries, the clocks are adjusted to Daylight Savings Time. The entire country sets their clocks an hour ahead—that means that everyone is essentially going to bed an hour earlier and getting up an hour earlier. No one has any trouble with it despite the fact that it requires exactly the same behavior change. What's going on here?

TECHNICAL AND ADAPTIVE CHANGES

We make *technical* changes every day. We call upon our expertise to solve routine problems, such as unhappy customers or lower-than-expected sales. We can survey customers and set up an action plan to address the problems. We can run a sale. These are technical changes—they change the externals only.

Adaptive changes are transformative—they require us to change ourselves on the inside. We want to reign in our temper because it is affecting our relationships with customers and colleagues, but no matter how hard we try, we can't "control" it. Our frustration spills over, and now we have to fix the damage.

Only by addressing our inner feelings of frustration can we make an adaptive change. We could decide to use cognitive therapy ("What am I telling myself when I feel frustrated?" and "Where is it written that I would be free of frustration or that no customers would make mistakes or misunderstand me?"), or we could choose other methods of internal change.

To make such changes, you need to recognize when you're facing an adaptive change—one that requires this level of thought and effort. For more background on adaptive changes, read *Leadership on the Line* by Martin Linsky and Ronald Heifetz.

Adjusting to Daylight Savings Time is a *technical* change, rather than an adaptive one—a technical change alters something external only and requires no personal adaptation. Because everyone is changing their schedule at the same time that you are, no huge adjustment of your life priorities is triggered.

This example demonstrates that a good deal of the pain involved in change goes on inside your own mind. Clearly, your body clock is adjustable enough to change your bedtime by an hour—you do it every year—but if you *tell* yourself that you can't adjust, you'll undoubtedly prove yourself correct.

For me personally, changing my mental model from the old "plan ahead and get it right" approach to "do it wrong quickly" wasn't hard—for me it was a technical change rather than an adaptive one. But I've had my share of adaptive changes, and I know their challenges.

I woke up one day several years ago weighing more than 230 pounds, and I knew I had to do something about it. I decided to go on a low-carbohydrate diet and began losing weight, but my wife pointed out to me that I'd made only a technical change and that I was unlikely to keep the weight off.

Most diets fail because they are technical solutions to problems that require adaptation. Diets restrict what foods you eat or restrict how much you eat, which is trying to make the food behave instead of yourself. I lost 70 pounds, but, more importantly, five years later I have gained back only 10 of them because I made adaptive changes to the way I eat.

I now eat carbohydrates in normal amounts (unlike when on my low-carb diet), but I have learned to be very careful to eat only when I am hungry and to stop eating when I am no longer hungry. I had to change the way I think about eating, and I needed to pay attention to what my body was telling me—those were adaptive changes. (My wife, Linda Moran, wrote a book about this kind of thinking, called *How to Survive Your Diet*.)

Changing my thinking (the adaptive change) was much harder than changing what and how much I ate (the technical changes of most diets), but if I had not done so, I am certain I would have regained the weight I lost.

So what does all this have to do with marketing?

For some of you, changing your thinking to "do it wrong quickly" is a technical change. You've always been an off-the-cuff kind of person, more likely to try something than to research it.

But for others, this mindset seems foreign. Some of you might feel as though every fiber in your being resists this change. It's very uncomfortable.

You've always been a planner, a researcher, a consensus builder, a person who checks out everything thoroughly before proceeding. Maybe that's why you're reading a book about Internet marketing before you try it. You can soothe yourself by checking out this methodology thoroughly before adopting it, but you might still be wracked with doubts (maybe even fears) each time you experiment with something untested and unproven.

If this sounds like you, you are wrestling with an adaptive change. You'll need to address your thoughts, your beliefs, and your feelings to weather this transition. You'll need to ask yourself what feelings this change conjures up. What beliefs are being spoken by that voice inside your head?

One common feeling when confronting an adaptive change is disloyalty. All of us want to look good in front of other people, and the beliefs we hold are often reflections of those other people. Perhaps we want our boss or our co-workers to like us, and we fear that bringing up this new way of doing business will imperil those relationships—even make us seem disloyal to the reigning culture of the group. You can use the cognitive therapy techniques discussed earlier to identify your beliefs, dispute them, and then begin the adaptive change your rational mind wants to try.

Adaptive changes are also riskier than technical changes because often the results take longer to appear. When you first begin "doing it wrong quickly," your projects might actually appear worse than before—at the start. Over time, the feedback loop will work and will make your project a bigger success than it ever could have been the old way, but it doesn't feel very safe. You might need to overcome your fears of being criticized to attempt this change.

Evangelist Norman Vincent Peale, who wrote *The Power of Positive Thinking*, liked to say, "Change your thoughts and you change your world." When you realize that you *do* have the power to change—even big scary adaptive change—you really experience the *power* of positive thinking.

Summary

"Dad," asked my eight-year old son, "Why do we put scarves on snowmen? They *like* the cold." I had no good answer for that one. It was just something that I never questioned.

The deeply-held beliefs that drive your self-talk might be something *you* have never questioned. If you're wrestling with the changes that online marketing seem to be imposing on you, or if you're feeling afraid or overwhelmed by what's happening, then you might need to tune into those feelings and find out what's causing them. It's probably a lot easier than pretending nothing is changing or sticking with what used to work but no longer does.

Gee, this chapter was a change of pace, wasn't it? There you were innocently reading a marketing book, when suddenly it turned into something from the self-help section. It sounds like that old Rodney Dangerfield joke: "I went to a fight and a hockey game broke out."

You might not have needed this chapter, but I run into people every day who do—good people, hardworking people. They're people who feel as though they just can't do it, even though they know they should. If this describes you, I hope you feel a little more in control of your growth. I'm hoping you can start to "do it wrong quickly," even though it doesn't come naturally.

So now that you have plumbed the depths of your inner psyche, fumigated your beliefs, and started down the path of real change, it's time to turn your attention to everyone else. No matter who you are, you can't change the way marketing is done at your company by yourself—not even if you own the company and not even if you are the only employee.

You work with other people every day to do your marketing, and you need to persuade *them* to change their marketing philosophy, too. It's no use for you to be ready to "do it wrong quickly" when the rest of your company is entrenched in the old ways. Even if you are a one-person show, you still depend on other people to help you with your marketing, whether it is the support person at the Web hosting firm, the salesperson who sold you that e-mail delivery service, or the freelance copy writer who does your product descriptions.

That's why you need Chapter 8, which examines what techniques you can use to successfully lead people to change. We examine why you need to treat different people differently and how understanding what motivates them is the key to real persuasion.

8

This Won't Work Where I Work

"The brain is a wonderful organ. It starts working the moment you get up in the morning and does not stop until you get into the office."

—Robert Frost

Chapter Contents

- Leading People to Change   279
- Specialist Disease   287
- Personality Parade   307
- Summary   313

275

How many times have you sat in a conference room, sifting every last detail of the proposal? How many times have you spent hours (or weeks) building consensus? Oh, and how many times must an executive approve before they call it a plan?

The answer, my friend, is not blowing in the wind, but I bet it is blowing your budget and draining your profits—and frustrating everyone no end.

What causes seemingly sane people to work this hard to get every last thing right before trying something new? Often, it's driven by an unseen force called *organizational culture*.

Organizational culture (sometimes called corporate culture or company culture) is found in the behavior of people at work. And while the name *corporate* culture brings to mind large companies (or at least medium-sized ones), *every* business has a culture, even if it merely reflects the personality of the owner. For a small business, culture is reflected in the behavior of both employees and its *extended* employees—the lawyer, accountant, the advertising agency, and other specialist consultants that provide advice and services for that business.

IMD professor Andrew Denison has created a model that identifies adaptability as one of just four major traits of an organizational culture. Big business or small, the adaptability of your culture helps determine whether your company can make the changes required by the advent of Internet marketing.

Unfortunately, companies vary widely in their adaptability. It's sad but true that most good companies have just one breakthrough idea, one innovative product. Even great companies often catch only a couple of "waves."

Sears caught the catalog wave in the 19th century. They were also among the pioneers in self-serve retail department stores. But Sears failed to adapt to the rise of the discount store (dominated by K-Mart and Wal-Mart) and to "category killers" (specialty stores and catalogs) while they mistakenly diversified into financial services (focusing on insurance, real estate, and revolving credit). Neither has Sears become a force in online retailing.

Another great company, IBM, caught the mainframe computer wave but missed minicomputers. IBM helped pioneer personal computers but realized that it needed to diversify into software and services and leave commoditized businesses behind.

Sears tried to diversify and failed. IBM succeeded. So deciding to change is not the moral of the story. All businesses face changes in their industries, but some companies just seem to be more adaptable than others. 3M, for example, is well-known for its ability to churn out innovative new products, but most companies come up with just one big idea and survive by perfecting it.

When a change as big as the Internet comes along, most companies struggle to adapt. It's true that *some* businesses won't be affected much—Coca Cola might not have a whole lot to change, for example. Some other businesses are being shaken to the core—think Barnes and Noble bookstores, Blockbuster video rentals, and Merrill Lynch investments. Most companies will need to change their marketing, at least. Can yours?

If not, you might need to switch to a company that does. If it *really* won't work where you work, maybe you should change where you work because it is *going* to work somewhere, and you want to work there. (I'm not sure that sentence worked...)

Comedian Fred Allen once remarked that "A committee is a group of men who individually can do nothing but as a group decide that nothing can be done." So what leads to decision by committee? What is it that locks the group in that conference room to reach the dreaded consensus?

Organizational cultures can become dysfunctional in some ways. Some dysfunctional cultures reward the "herd mentality." "Don't attract undue attention," you are advised. "Be a team player." Yes, the competition picks off another member of your herd every day, but the herd itself survives by sticking together. This defensive behavior does nothing to make a company adaptable, however.

In other organizational cultures, whenever a project fails, the "blame hunt" begins. Someone must be the scapegoat. If you work at a place where people get fired for making mistakes, but no one gets fired for bumbling along with the status quo, it's no wonder people spend hour after hour in that conference room. It had better be right, whatever they do. And, the more people in the conference room, the less likely any one person will be the one blamed if it all goes wrong. So people can hide in the herd at the same time that they tirelessly go over the plan one more time for any "showstoppers."

Your company's culture might even suffer from both of these problems. Often the bigger the herd, the safer people feel, which is why some big companies can be so conformist. Any company can break out of this mold—yours can, too. But it has to start with you.

In Chapter 7, "This Doesn't Work for Me," we saw how you can fight the fears that stop you from trying something or from just being different. In this chapter, I help you to persuade the others around you to do the same. You'll need to convincingly lead people to a new way of working before you'll be able to do it wrong quickly.

From reading this book, you undoubtedly understand intellectually what doing it wrong quickly is all about. Perhaps you've even wondered how the idea would be received in your own organizational culture.

Think about what it's like where you work. It's really embarrassing to have to tell your boss that this project that you planned for six months—that everyone agreed to—might be wrong, that it could miss the mark. Despite how much we spent, all the smart people who worked on it, and how hard everyone worked, we might lay an egg.

You can't get people to work that hard for that long and defend the plan that many times unless they've talked themselves into it. Your team must have convinced itself that *this will work*. That's how the herd mentality works to stave off being targeted by the blame game.

But suppose you were trying to do it wrong quickly? If you know that you're doing the project wrong—you just *know* it—then you will undoubtedly do the project a bit differently than if everyone sat around that conference room arguing until they reached consensus. If you haven't spent all your time convincing each other how smart you are, if you are in fact sure that this project will miss the mark in some ways—perhaps major ways—then you will take a different approach.

Instead of indulging in the groupthink that everything will be OK, you will instead spend your time thinking about what might go wrong and asking yourself, "If that goes wrong, what will we do about it?" You start to spend your time answering those questions. You have a Plan B and a Plan C for each thing that could go wrong.

Obviously, this philosophy applies to marketing but not to everything your company does. Sometime risk mitigation is important, even critical. You can't do every project wrong quickly. Who would want to take an airplane's first flight where they did it wrong quickly? But redesigning your home page does not have the same danger as a plane crash, and we should not run that project as though it does.

We talked about adaptive change in Chapter 7—and how it's not easy for most people. In fact, the first instinct of most managers is to resist the idea that an adaptive change is even required—it's that distasteful. To avoid confronting the adaptation involved, big companies might try to reorganize or to install a Vice President of New Media. Small companies might ask "their agency" to handle it, or they hire a crack consultant. Unfortunately, those approaches won't work.

You can't centralize these new marketing techniques. There won't be any blogging department, for example. Hiring a search marketing consultant is not all you need to do. The problem with each of these Internet marketing tactics is that they pervade your entire company. Many of your employees (and *extended* employees) must know what to do to make online marketing successful.

Think about it. To make organic search marketing work, your Webmaster must ensure that the spiders can crawl your pages. Your product manager must research what words your customers search for. Your copywriter must use the right words on the pages. Each person must add tasks to their already busy day. And it doesn't matter whether these people work for your company or not—nor whether yours is a big company or a small one. Someone is doing these tasks and must do them in a certain way for search marketing to work.

Take another example. You can't develop content written in a personal voice using the same process that creates your company's Web product catalog. *One* person writes a blog. And it sure is hard to *translate* blogs, podcasts, and wikis into other languages—bloggers are almost always read in just their own language. (If you do translate them, what do you do when the first comment comes in on your Bulgarian translation?)

No, you can't centralize these new marketing techniques. But you must *control* them. To be effective, you must be sure that your employees (and extended employees) are doing what you need them to do. In this chapter, I show you how to persuade them to care about this stuff and how to help them change the way they work.

So how do you convince the people at your company to experiment, to start listening to what customers say, and to start watching what they do? How do you persuade them to change a longstanding organizational culture?

First, you must understand how to lead people to change. In this case, you want to create a feedback-based culture, one where what the customer says and does is what drives decision-making. For some companies, it's a big change, so you need to understand how to approach it.

Along the way, you'll run into marketers, salespeople, Webmasters, copywriters—specialists of every stripe. And each of these nice people might suffer from "Specialist Disease"—that professional malady that prevents people from seeing past their specialty. To create a feedback-based culture, you'll need to challenge people to transcend their professional training to really put the customer first.

Before closing this chapter, we also look at the "personality parade." People are more than their professional roles—they have behaviors and beliefs that you'll need to identify and address to win them over to this new way of thinking.

It's hard to make these changes, but this chapter helps you get started. First up, let's look at how to lead people to change.

Leading People to Change

In my defense, I was very tired.

It was late at night, but before I went to bed, I needed to take my vitamins. My wife had persuaded me that I should start taking vitamins each night, and this was my first night doing it. So I took the pill bottle off the shelf and stared at the small print on the back to determine how many vitamins to take. It was at this moment that I realized I was trying to figure out the dosage for One-A-Day® vitamins. (If you're like me, I need to tell you it turned out to be one pill a day.)

Most of us have moments like that—moments where we just aren't thinking. (Some of us, like me, have more of those moments than other people do.)

One of the tough parts of making an adaptive change, such as the change to a feedback-based culture, is that you have to do a lot of thinking. You can't go on autopilot. You need to pay attention to each situation, to learn, and to make thoughtful decisions.

You need to *adapt*.

Whether you are a big company or a one-man show, you can't do it all yourself. You need to get other people to adapt, too, or you won't be able to make the change. You must consider the critical people who must implement the new way, and you must take into account the working environment itself. After all, you can't make changes in a vacuum (unless you work for Electrolux).

Now, you might not be very happy at the prospect of leading all these other people to change. Your self-talk might be, "I am a specialist, not a politician." And you're right. Of course you are a specialist—most of us possess specialized knowledge that makes us valuable to our companies. But to get your organization to change, you need to be a leader of people also.

Some people mistakenly believe that the boss is *the* leader—that people follow the boss because, well, he's the boss. But the power that derives from the boss's position is not the only kind of power. Many people who are not in positions of power are nonetheless leaders. They have the social power to influence people, or they possess expert power because they simply know more than others about a subject.

In my experience, people don't always follow the person who is the boss, but often the person they do follow becomes the new boss. If you happen to be a boss, all the better, but anyone can be a person who leads. You need to be willing to be different, to go out on a limb, and to persuade others to join you. Anyone can be the person who rallies the troops to change the way you are fighting this marketing war. Let's look at what you're up against when you try to recruit allies to your cause.

Rally Your Allies

Studies show that 37.4 percent of all people are not adaptable. (OK, there's no study that really shows that, but you bought it for just a split second, didn't you?) Regardless of numbers, *many* people are just not capable of adaptive change. Now understand, they're nice people. On Thursdays, they volunteer at the youth hostel. Their kids trick or treat for UNICEF. But they are, well...*limited*.

Luckily, you don't need to persuade everyone. Some people are born followers. When doing it your way seems safe to them, they'll happily follow you. You need to persuade the *right people*—your fellow leaders—those who *are* adaptable.

Your first job is to identify who you need to convince. You probably know who they are. One or two of them might be bosses, but most of them are not—they are individuals with key positions in your organization. They are the ones who must be convinced to do anything really big in your company.

Your first step is not necessarily to call them up and start pitching your big idea. In most companies, it's far easier to do something small than to make a huge change in how people work. In the next section of this chapter, we decide what the right first project should be, but for now, just make a mental note of who the powerful people are that must eventually be persuaded to "do it wrong quickly"—to start listening to what customers say and do and change what your company does in response.

Sometimes it's very clear who to work with, and you can go to them directly. When CompUSA introduced product ratings and reviews, Senior Director of e-commerce Al Hurlebaus recalled, "All I needed to do was sell it to two individuals." But it might not come that easily for you. In fact, you might not feel that the people you've identified are even approachable. In that case, you need to work your way up. Who do you know that can influence the unapproachable ones? Who *can* you approach? Where can you start?

Regardless of the place you start, use the same philosophy for this task that you use for everything else. That is, accept the fact that you won't convince *everyone* on your list, so have contingency plans. (If you can't convince Mabel, then would persuading Sergio be almost as good?) You'll find that you don't need to convince every last person—once you get a strong core, others who turned you down at first will be attracted to what you are doing. Others will convince them.

So if your company is large enough that you have choices about who to convince, don't spend too much time on any one person. After all, perseverance is great, but don't take it to extremes. Bono from U2 has been singing, "I Still Haven't Found What I'm Looking For" for 20 years. At some point, I think he should really consider giving up.

Likewise, you must recognize that some people will not be able to adapt to the new approach. At first, when I was struggling to obtain funding to start a paid search program in IBM, I approached a manager responsible for a sizable advertising budget. Despite everything I showed him, he would not agree to divert any money from his precious banner ads to paid search. At one point, I showed him how much more effective paid search was than other programs (a chart very similar to Exhibit 3-2 from back in Chapter 3, "Marketing Is a Conversation") and told him, "Look, either you can show this chart to your boss, or I will, but either way, your boss will give me the money."

That wasn't an easy thing for me to do, but I felt so strongly that his decision was hurting IBM that I had to speak bluntly with him. He still refused, so I did show it to his boss, who *did* approve the money for search. It's an important part of leadership to realize that some people won't be able to change, and you must leave them behind, go around them, or tunnel under them.

Sometimes you lose people once you begin to "do it wrong quickly." Usability expert Jared Spool tells the story of a Web designer at Netflix who just could not accept that the beautiful feature he designed did not test well with customers. Rather than adapt to a feedback-based culture, the designer left his job.

When you've identified the right people to convince, you need to do it with the *right attitude*.

We spent all of Chapter 7 examining our own self-talk to see why we might be resisting this change in how we work. Don't expect the change to a feedback culture to come more easily to everyone else. Just because you've converted doesn't mean that others will now see the light any faster than you did.

Consultant Andrew Draheim advises leaders to "acknowledge loss." The people you are asking to adapt are giving up behaviors that have served them well. So instead of saying, "Take one for the team," instead be real ("I know this is hard, but it's important"). If you show people that you understand that adaptive change is difficult and uncomfortable, they'll at least know you understand what it's like for them, even if they still don't like it. Help them work through their own set of "reasons why not" the way you did for yourself in Chapter 7.

You'll also find that different people experience different kinds of loss. Some people really like working the old careful, deliberate way—it fits their personalities. Others prefer doing something they consider "safe." Some people experience feelings of disloyalty. ("My old boss—the one I liked—never thought we needed to do this.")

Still others can't handle "wasted time." They hate having to throw away completed work because the customer didn't take to the idea. When you do it wrong quickly, however, everything you do is disposable either because it didn't work or because something better came along. Tossing out losing approaches is the price of gaining

ADOPTING A FEEDBACK CULTURE

The basic idea behind "do it wrong quickly" is that if customers are not responding to your marketing, you should do something different. (Deep, huh?) That kind of flexibility requires a special kind of organizational culture, however.

There's no universal name for the kind of culture that adjusts its marketing based on what customers say and do. Some call it a "feedback" culture, others a "responsive" or "open" culture. Several marketers referred to a "metrics-driven" culture. Whatever the name, successful marketers know it when they see it.

Some of these marketers were starting from scratch. Listen to Curt Sasaki, Vice President of Sun Microsystems' Web team: "Sun was not at all a metrics-driven culture when I arrived. When I took over, the Web was an information resource. I began to ask folks, 'What are our customers doing?' And they didn't have the answers. I noticed that the first thing people did at our Web site was to leave. [Now] every single week, we measure everything. We look at the funnels of promotions to clickthroughs to sales." Sun's culture of "openness" is a clear contributor to the marketing transformation they've made—people must listen to be persuaded.

Some companies have always had a "numbers" culture but needed to learn to apply it to online marketing. Joel Reimer, Director of Interactive Marketing at ScottsMiracle-Gro, explained, "Scotts is very data-driven. Consumer research drives everything we do. But we've always struggled with justifying this internally because we have had a hard time isolating the impact [on offline sales]. With online, we're trying to foster a relationship approach."

Michael Petillo, e-business Leader at manufacturer W.L. Gore describes their transition. "Gore is very much a metrics-driven company—it's an engineering company. We're educating marketing in the power of Web metrics. We've seen an amazing revolution—there's so much passion."

better understanding. Later in this chapter, we look at more of the personalities you'll encounter and provide advice for working with them.

Once you are approaching the right people with the right attitude, you need to provide the *right motivation*.

People respond to both positive and negative motivation—you might be more comfortable using one or the other, but you'll probably have more success using both. Positive motivation is often more palatable—the opportunity to improve business results or get promoted—but some people respond better to negative motivation.

Devashish Saxena, Texas Instruments' Manager of Worldwide Internet Marketing, tells a similar story. "We have a culture where numbers talk. I've always found that if I can back up my story with the right data, people who were dead set against it are willing to change. It's not just the culture of the company, but the openness of the leadership team. We've been able to educate them on Web metrics. One approach is to tie back to customers: 'Hey look, here is what customers are telling us.' Anytime you can bring that customer perspective and customer insight, that's very helpful."

CompUSA's Al Hurlebaus noted that "Numbers play an important part of convincing anyone around here. We look at bottom-line gross margin and profit." Still, when talking about when he proposed adding customer reviews to the Web site to raise conversion rates, he says, "I don't think one executive thought there'd be any change." So they experimented—trying it on one product segment to see if conversion rates increased. (They did, markedly.) In a company without a feedback culture, Al's bosses might have said "no" instead of "give it a try."

Successful online marketers almost universally agree that the way to persuade companies to experiment is to emphasize listening to customer feedback. Web analytics expert Avinash Kaushik summed it up: "Most people don't care what I think—my opinion, my analysis—they think I don't understand their business problem, which may be true. They will be doubtful of my analysis as long as they think it is mine. But when I manage to clearly articulate the customer voice shining through, that is when they seem to accept the data."

The thread that runs through each of these stories is the need for a change and the need for someone to persuade people to make that change. In your company, will that someone be you?

Later in this chapter, we'll look at the kinds of motivations people bring to work each day, some shaped by their roles (Web designer or financial analyst, for example) and others shaped by their individual personalities.

Sometimes negative motivation ("we're falling behind the competition") is just what's needed to get people to change. As a leader, it's critical to apply the right level of pressure—not too much or too little. Ronald Heifetz and Marty Linsky, co-authors of *Leadership on the Line*, call this the "Productive Range of Distress." Without pressure to change, most people lapse into their former ways, but too much pressure causes people to panic—they either become overwhelmed and immobilized, or they spin out of control. To relieve the pressure, people choose scapegoats for their problems, they propose fake solutions, convene a task force (there's that herd mentality again), or even ostracize people socially.

Some find the changes so difficult that they go into denial. Early in my career, I found that I was unable to persuade some of my colleagues that mainframe computers were losing importance to personal computers. Many denied what I thought were obvious facts, but I vividly recall one man coming up to me after another "the sky is falling" presentation and saying admiringly, "Wow, you're a visionary." I know it was meant as a compliment, but I quickly realized what he really meant is, "There's nothing that you said that I have to do anything about right now." Realize that a form of denial is to greet your message as an interesting treatise on the future, when your goal is to bring about change today.

Approaching the right people, adopting the right attitude, and offering the right motivation gives you the best chance of persuasion. Now let's look at what you want to go after first—your first target.

Pick Your Target

How do you persuade people to do it wrong quickly? How do you convince people to measure how customers respond—to be accountable? You do it by treating a mistake as a less-than-fatal disease. The *real* fatal disease is to be unaccountable and defensive, pretending to always be right. Instead, you want to take the ideas we've looked at in the first six chapters of this book and put them to work.

At most companies, the place to start is the "wrong" part in "do it *wrong* quickly." In the "blame hunt" culture, doing anything wrong is fraught with danger. (Why is nothing ever fraught with safety?) This fear of being blamed is the first thing you must attack. Usually, a good way to start is with an intractable problem.

What marketing problem do you have that no one has been able to solve? Perhaps your Web leads have been flat for two years, or maybe fewer people open your marketing e-mails each month. Have your online sales for a key product mysteriously dropped?

Those kinds of problems are perfect to take on because they are painful to your company and because no one expects anyone to have the right answer. If there were an easy answer, you'd have found it already. But if your company has taken multiple swipes at a certain problem with little success, that's a great one to propose an experiment for. It's even better if that problem has many possible solutions but no consensus on what's best.

Try them all!

Pick every simple, easy-to-try possibility and show how you'll test each one. To do that, you need to ensure that everyone agrees on how you measure success. Resist the temptation to explain the concept of Lifetime Value at this moment. Instead, simply validate the metric that they are complaining about.

If they say the problem is that leads are flat, then any solution that causes the number of identified leads to go up is a success. Yes, I know that is a flawed metric, but this is not the time to fight that battle. Now is the time to show how experimentation works. (Remember to do adaptive change wrong quickly—you can perfect the metric later.)

If fewer people are opening your e-mails, then whatever gets customers to open more is good. Yes, it could be a delivery problem, or it could be a problem with the subject lines or with the offers themselves, but that's what you'll test. If you can get more opened, that is a success. Later, after people see the value of testing, you can ask whether any of these customers actually bought anything from those e-mails—but not now. And don't argue about whether they are measuring the open rate properly. Just assume that whatever errors are in the old measurements will be in the new ones, too, and move on.

Similarly, accept the fact that dropping online sales really *is* the problem. Don't question whether people are buying offline or whether profits are unaffected. That's later. For now, be happy to get approval to try a number of ideas in rapid-fire sequence.

By choosing an intractable problem that your company really cares about, you're more likely to be allowed to experiment. The right target will be seen as a problem big enough that unusual measures are needed. You'll be allowed to put a "full court press" on it, to "swing for the fences," or to [insert another tortured sports analogy for risk-taking here].

Some of you might be cringing at this point—it's a lot less scary to choose a small problem to do wrong quickly, one that no one will notice if it goes wrong. I don't advise that approach.

Only by picking an important problem will you get the backing of the leaders to do something different. Choosing a small problem leads you right into the legion of naysayers. Small changes arouse the corporate immune system (the one that rejects foreign ideas), but big problems are often given latitude for unusual solutions.

Moreover, choosing a big problem gets you more attention when the method works. When you show an early success on a difficult problem, you'll find it far easier to attract support to go further—to institutionalize the new marketing approach in a larger way that goes beyond the first problem you targeted.

Declare Success

After your first few experiments, declare success.

What? What do you mean? Oh, did we skip the part of it actually *being* a success? Well, what's important is the way you describe what you're doing.

When you pick your target, explain why fast experimentation is so important. Remind everyone that we don't know what the right answer is for this difficult problem, so we'll be successful even if all we do is to rule out more wrong answers much more quickly than we did before because eventually we'll lurch into an improvement if we keep trying. Thomas Edison once said, "Just because something doesn't do what you planned it to do doesn't mean it's useless."

You can declare success no matter how it turned out. We'd all be thrilled if you actually came up with an improvement that got more of those pesky e-mails opened, but merely showing how you can test several different titles each week is a success because you'll eventually find one that works.

And when you do find one, trumpet it.

Don't just tell the bosses. Don't just tell the team. Don't just tell the people who care about the problem you've solved. Tell everyone you can. "A little success is a good example to use with others," says Curt Sasaki of Sun Microsystems. Curt and other adaptive marketers build internal case studies of successful experiments, which help them persuade folks to go along with the *next* idea.

Some marketers spread the word even more widely. Joel Reimer, of ScottsMiracle-Gro, advises, "Get external publicity for everything you do—it always adds credibility when our programs get discussed. We won a Web award in 2003 and made it a big deal." He laughed and added, "Whether it really *was* a big deal is irrelevant."

Modesty aside, that Web award *was* a big deal—they're not easy to win. Most companies pay far more attention to outside voices than they do to you the employee, so every shred of external recognition you can attract makes a difference. The truth is that Joel and these other first-rate marketers deserve to be heard inside their companies.

To gradually win over your company to a feedback culture, you need to continually bring forward ideas for new experiments, and you must regularly celebrate success. Sam Decker, Vice President of Marketing and Products for software maker BazaarVoice, tells marketers, "You need to be both a woodpecker and a peacock. A woodpecker is persistent—if they don't see you, they will hear you. A peacock puts on frequent events that the organization can't miss."

Joel described a couple of "peacock" events at Scotts:

We're about to kick off a site redesign project. We're bringing in an external speaker to talk about trends online, what consumers are doing online, rather than getting right to the project. Let's do twice as much communication and get a project team that is involved, aware, and supportive.

We {also} do brown bag lunches—we brought in Yahoo! to speak. External resources are always trusted more than internal ones.

If this kind of persuasion sounds slow, well, it can be, especially in larger companies where many more people can say "no." But even in small companies, you can think about what kinds of celebrations you can stage to get attention, even something as simple as asking the owner to take the successful team out to lunch. While the boss is having lunch with you, the conversation will inevitably turn to how we are now doing this Internet stuff better. It will make an impression.

So start small, but on a big problem. Your campaign for a new approach to marketing will take time for people to get accustomed to. After all, nothing happens overnight (except sleeping).

Remember, you can orchestrate culture change by doing it wrong quickly, too. Just start with one thing and then celebrate when it works.

Specialist Disease

A consultant, an engineer, and a statistician were in a car traversing a steep mountain road. Suddenly the brakes failed, and the car careened out of control. The engineer, who was driving, somehow was able to stop the car by brushing it against the side of the mountain until it finally came to rest. Thankfully, no one was hurt. As the three emerged from the car after their harrowing experience, each one began to think about their situation.

The consultant said, "We need to convene a committee to assess the brake failure, draft a report, and utilize a continuous improvement process to develop a solution."

"Give me a break," said the engineer. "That never works, and it takes too long. I will take apart the brake system with my Swiss Army knife, use a problem determination process to isolate the root cause, and then correct it."

The statistician exclaimed, "You're both wrong! We must push the car back up the hill and see if it happens again. You can't rely on a sample size of just one."

If these attitudes are common where you work, your organization might have "Specialist Disease." That's the mind-numbing condition where people retreat into their professional disciplines and can't look at what your customers need. All they see is their specialty, whether it is marketing, technology, design, or something else.

Specialist Disease often strikes without warning, such as the day I was a conference panelist at the "Fix My Site" session. People could walk into the session and project their company's Web site up on the big screen, asking the panel to provide advice. The moment one Web site was projected, I knew we were dealing with Specialist Disease.

The site was an over-designed mess. Someone had apparently decided that no information should fall "below the fold" (in the lower area of the page that would require the customer to scroll down). That design rule is useful enough for a home page, but the entire site was designed that way. Deep information pages explaining complex financial products to sophisticated audiences had a small tabbed area on the screen that forced you to click five or six times to get a total of ten paragraphs of information.

They had replaced the typical detailed product specs page with a design more befitting a Rolodex.

Misguided designers had run roughshod over the writers and anyone else in their path as this site was conceived—a clear case of Specialist Disease.

You probably don't call it by that name, but I bet you've seen Specialist Disease where you work. You are looking at Specialist Disease when people make recommendations to you that are entirely in concert with their training and background but display no critical thinking and no understanding that there are other specialties that affect the final decision.

Each of us exhibits knee-jerk reactions once in a while—we each must actively work to avoid contracting Specialist Disease. Most specialists are able to rise above their specialty when needed, but some find comfort in retreating to their discipline, especially when under pressure.

And it happens in companies large and small. The only difference is that the specialists in small companies usually aren't quite so specialized. In very small companies, these specialists aren't always employees—they might work for a Web agency or an accounting agency or be hired on as a consultant when they are needed. Small companies often find the sales manager at odds with the "tech guy." Big companies find the designers at odds with the information architects. But the disease is the same—people don't think holistically about what the company or the customers need, but rather view the world through their narrow professional prism.

Sometimes, these problems feel structural in nature. Traditional roles, such as public relations and marketing communications, are no longer separated with neat lines. Some jobs, such as reputation monitoring and search marketing, may seem to be no one's job. Rob Key, CEO of Converseon, notes, "In the digital realm, the lines of delineation between public relations, direct marketing, advertising, customer service, and sales have inalterably blurred."

How can you get people to look beyond their safe professional roles to work together so they really listen to the customer and think about what should be done?

First, you must attack the culture that allows Specialist Disease by explicitly replacing it with one that puts your business and your customers first. Almost everyone gives lip service to valuing customer feedback, but you must address specific situations where professions collide, lest the customer get lost in the shuffle.

Next, you need to understand where your specialists are coming from so you can speak their language. Professional knowledge exists for good reason—it is crucial to getting the job done. If professionals feel under attack, they'll be even more likely to retreat into their professional shells. Marketers must understand how to work with each type of specialist to persuade them to put the customer above their professional best practices.

But that's not enough. Once you understand what is important to each kind of specialist and you are committed to addressing the values of placing the customer first, you must create an environment that makes it easy. You must bring the specialists together into a single team that crosses traditional organizational lines to work together. It's not easy, but it is the most likely path to long-term success.

Before we can solve the professional specialty problem, we must understand it better. Let's start by understanding how to get professionals to abandon their specialist religions and put the customer first.

Put the Business First

When your Webmasters tell you that you can't start up a blog just because there are no corporate standards yet, that's Specialist Disease. When your authors tell you that your company name needs to be the first word in the title of every page (even though your search marketing suffers because of it), that's Specialist Disease. When your designers tell you that landing pages must all look the same (even though you know that they each ought to look like the collateral that drives customers to the page), that's Specialist Disease.

The shame of it is that all of these specialists fervently believe that they are doing the right thing. And they are, if you only think within their own specialist channel. When you apply critical thinking to these situations, however, you quickly realize that the best practice called for by each specialty in question must yield to the greater good—specialists must compromise their specialties at times, and the best specialists know this. The best specialists know that customers come before professional allegiance.

It's very easy to dogmatically follow a set of beliefs that are promulgated by your specialist religion and to castigate naysayers as pagans who don't understand the one true way. What's more, many professionals see specialization as the easy way to job security because piling up the certifications and working with a community of similar specialists is easier than developing the broad skills that let you make proper trade-offs.

The problem is that we're in danger of losing the generalists. We talk about the beauty of cross-functional teams, but where are the cross-functional people? Where are the people who have strong backgrounds in several different specialties who can choose the perspective they use for each problem? Cross-functional teams are great, but they require a lot of communication and often result in a contention system where specialists veto and bargain their way to consensus—maybe that results in a good decision, but maybe it doesn't. It certainly can slow things down, regardless.

Now don't get me wrong. Specialists are critically important to everything we do in online marketing (and just about everything in life) but only when they add their ingredients into a stew, rather than pretending their spices are the whole meal.

There's a better way. Persuade your specialists to drop their preconceived professional notions and give a customer feedback culture a try.

One way to approach your specialists is to capitalize on their good intentions. As we discussed earlier, all specialists are convinced they are doing the right thing, and that is one of the keys to curing Specialist Disease. Recognize that your specialists want the best for your site. When they go overboard with their specialties, it is out of a good heart, not malice or laziness. So that is the first place to start, by helping specialists to see that there is a wider world out there. Allow your specialists to mingle with each other. (OK, force them to mingle.) Arguments will erupt, but they will be forced to confront the trade-offs that warring specialties demand, and that will help them put their specialties into perspective.

When your copywriters demand that your company name be the first part of every title, the search marketing consultants will scream bloody murder, demanding that your critical search keywords be first. But instead of having to referee this dispute, let them work it out together. Make sure that both sides understand that they are all professionals and that they have reasons for what they do, but sometimes those reasons come into conflict with each other and everyone needs to make compromises.

Your copywriters need to defend their practice, so the search marketers need to hear them out. Perhaps they say that it is important to have a common style for each title, for usability reasons. If so, bring in the usability specialists to see what they say. Or maybe the copywriters believe that having the name of the company first will help visitors to find sites they bookmark, and that will increase return visits. So bring in the metrics experts to see if that is true. If you don't have a team so large as to have these usability and metrics specialists, then challenge the copywriters to back up what they say with whatever studies or expert opinion they can find. Whatever you do, have a conversation where the issues get aired.

Sometimes warring factions won't come together just by having a calm discussion. Two specialties collide, and neither is particularly adept at listening or at compromise. Make sure all specialists know that the path to success involves more than just their specialties. Successful specialists must be able to think and speak in business terms. They all work in a business, and a business approach provides a common language and a common goal (making a profit) that every specialist needs to agree on. Satisfying the customer is the best way to make a profit.

If the copywriters and the search marketers can't agree on how to standardize titles after their discussion, encourage them to think in business terms. Can the copywriters describe the business value of their existing company name standard? Can the search marketers explain how removing the standard would improve sales? Once the search marketers explain how important it is to have critical search keywords in the first few words of each page's title, the copywriters might relent because they understand the business value of higher search rankings to the sales of their Web site.

But even when people talk in terms of business value, they can't settle all disputes. Perhaps the metrics people really have data that shows increased bookmark visits when the company name begins the title, and maybe the search marketing people can't prove that the increased search referrals would make up for the lost bookmark visitors. What do you do then?

You make sure you have an agreed-to process for ending the standoff. One person (or a committee, perhaps) should have the final word. Don't let these decisions fester and cause lack of harmony on the team. Make them and move on.

But how you make the decision and how you follow up on the decision is just as important as the decision itself. First, listen to both sides and make your reasoning public. If you decide to change the title standard so that company names are no longer *first* but are still included as the *last* part of the title, explain why. Tell people you believe the search marketing arguments but that you also believe that your company name ought to continue to appear somewhere. By doing so, you teach each side the rationale you use in applying business value to the question, which will develop their abilities to handle such questions without resorting to tie breakers in the future. The better the specialists understand the business approach for your Web site, the fewer impasses you will have.

You also should follow up on the decision. Challenge the search marketers to show the results of the change. Ask them to project what the improvement will be and make sure they report back to the team to show what happened. If the results were disappointing, you might reconsider the decision in the future by trying a new experiment.

This is how you put business first. If your specialists can be shown that every decision should be motivated by what the customer says and does, you can make the trade-offs between the purism of each professional discipline. Gradually, you might help each specialist to think more holistically.

Sometimes, the problem is more insidious. Rather than competing specialists with conflicting opinions, instead, each professional has different advice, and they all want their advice heeded before the project is ready to go. Everyone has an ornament they want to hang on the tree. Everyone knows the *one* thing more that you need to do to before it's "ready"—reminiscent of the quote from 19th century writer Samuel Johnson that "Nothing will ever be attempted if all possible objections must first be overcome." Besides the extra time that all this extra work imposes, changing many small things can give you a "Frankenstein design" (complete with the bolts on the neck).

Another way to combat Specialist Disease is to put the customers in each professional's face. Amazon rotates many of its employees into customer service periodically so that they interact with real customers. They return to their regular roles a little wiser about what their customers are like.

To treat Specialist Disease, you must focus on a shared sense of mission—the customer and the business comes first—but you must also understand each specialist's perspective to influence behavior change. That's what we tackle next.

Speak Their Language

Every profession has its own jargon, but that's not what we'll be talking about. To really speak the language of specialists, you must appreciate their unique viewpoints. If you know what motivates each one, you can be more persuasive.

Let's start the "role" call with the wide variety of business people.

It's dangerous to lump everyone from the business side into one big pile, but marketers should have the least trouble talking to these groups because marketers *are* business people. Most business types will readily understand the need to quantify the results of what is done, but some will be uncomfortable with the faster pace and the need for experimentation. Devashish Saxena of Texas Instruments noted that "It's difficult for marketers to change the way they look at things because it's easier to do it the same way [we always have]."

Often, the best way to persuade this group to try things in a new way is to share case studies of other successful companies. I've tried to include stories and quotes throughout this book to make the advice real, but there's only so much room. I've provided expanded versions of all the case studies in this book on my Web site (www.mikemoran.com/resources). I'm always looking for a good story, so if you have a case study to share, I'd love to add yours too.

One secret to persuading business people is to start small. Several small successes lead to greater freedom to do more. David Seifert of Bass Pro Shops describes how "I built up the trust that I am paying attention to the fiscal realities and measuring everywhere, so there is very little resistance now."

The best way to work with business people is to get into the trenches and do their work with them side-by-side. You probably have the skills to help them more than you can help other specialists. So sit with your public relations person and show her why using the right keywords in the press release will help the company's search rankings—help her craft the press release she is working on for your product. Likewise, your lawyer might be filled with dread about blogging—show him some examples about how shrewd companies defused charged situations so that they did not become lawsuits, all by being a little more honest than lawyers like to be. Similarly, your procurement person does not know that she should ask for a supplier testimonial and a link to your Web site when negotiating a new contract—once she knows, then she can consider it.

TALKING TO THE BIG BOSS

My son once asked me, "Why do you itch only on the outside of your body and not the inside?" If you enjoy tackling questions like these, then you'll relish proving the business value of online marketing to the big boss. No matter how much you think you've prepared, you'll always get asked something you don't know—which is the point, really. You want to get them thinking about your business in a new way. They might have insights that no analyst can uncover. If you can get them to think about what they are seeing, you might learn something.

So who is the big boss?

In a small company, it might be the owner, while a large company has an executive. No matter what the job title, it can be intimidating to be face to face with the real decision maker—the person who can decide whether what you want happens or not.

Joel Reimer of Scotts remembers the day he was in the middle of his executive pitch for funding to improve their Web site, when the company president stopped him cold. "I'm skeptical whether we can use the Web to drive our business and find new customers," the boss said. But Joel was prepared with metrics that proved his point—by the end of the meeting, the project was approved.

That's what the boss is looking for—bottom-line results. Bosses don't want to hear about branding or Web traffic or how many comments are on the blog. They want to know what was sold and how you know your marketing efforts had something to do with it. They want to know whether the customers are coming back because of what you did. They want to talk business.

You can also score points if you tie your proposal to whatever your competitors do. If your competitors are already doing what you propose, show that ("Let's not fall farther behind"). If your competitors are *not* doing it, then trumpet your opportunity to lead the industry and beat them to the punch. Big bosses are usually very competitive, and this argument will get their juices flowing.

But the biggest advice for working with big bosses is to understand their priorities. What are the broad goals for your company or for your division, and what problems stand in the way? How can you propose a quick, low-risk, low-cost solution to a problem that is part of your company's biggest initiatives? Why will this benefit our customers?

If you can answer those questions persuasively, few big bosses will stand in your way.

Gore's Michael Petillo believes that business people are yearning to change the way they work, but they don't know how. "The key is painting the picture—connecting the dots. A marketer sees he's running a campaign but doesn't see all the way to a conversion. When they get feedback, they feel ownership." When Curt Sasaki introduced customer product reviews on Sun's Web site, he knew (as discussed in Chapter 7) that "You have to address the fear of a product manager who doesn't want to be the one with a one-star rating. Will my personal review be bad if my product gets one star?"

Some business people, such as the company accountant (in a small company) or the Finance Department (in a large company) are most swayed by numbers. If you don't have a metrics system or feel you can't afford one, get a free one, such as Google Analytics. Then explain to the numbers-oriented groups what you expect to happen from your project (using specific numbers) and then show them what really happened. Tell them that your experiment with testing the subject lines for marketing e-mails should raise the open rate ten percent. Better yet, if you can express the outcomes in terms of cash, do it. You can be conservative, but you can't be vague.

To have the numbers at your fingertips, you'll need to have a good relationship with your Web analyst. In a small company, the person responsible for analyzing Web traffic or e-mail responses is doing it part-time—it might be your "Web person" (who's also responsible for updating your Web site) or someone also doing marketing or sales. In some very large companies, whole departments of Web analysts pore over the numbers all day, every day.

Regardless of who tracks the numbers, you, the marketer, need to be in control. Marketers ought not to be on the receiving end of analyst reports—the analysts should be answering the marketers' questions. If you don't know what questions to ask, here are a few to start with:

- From which Web pages do the most people leave our site? Why?
- What's the difference between the subject lines of the most-opened and least-opened e-mails?
- What issues about our company do we see most repeatedly discussed in the blogosphere?
- Which conversions are we most successful in driving? Why?
- Why do some product lines attract more search traffic?
- What kind of posts on our company blog attract the most positive comments? The most negative? No comments at all?
- What time of day or what days of the week do we get the highest conversions from our paid search traffic?
- For our most popular products, what Web pages do customers tend to view the most before purchasing?

WHY MARKETERS IGNORE METRICS REPORTS

Avinash Kaushik, author of *Web Analytics: An Hour a Day*, explained to me why marketers ignore reports. "The problem with most analytics reports is they are pushed." I immediately made a connection that marketers should understand.

You don't want to receive metrics reports for the same reason that customers don't want to receive your marketing message—irrelevancy.

Avinash advises marketers to stop asking for reports and start asking for answers. Pose the questions to your analyst and let them do the research and give you the answer. Marketers don't want to know the site's conversion rate. They want to know whether showing pictures of people using the company's products will convert more people than showing the products alone. They want to know which page in the conversion process has the highest abandonment rate. They want to know why some products have a higher conversion rate than others.

Avinash correctly draws the distinction between "measuring things" and "understanding customer behavior." You need to measure to understand customer behavior, but too many analysts treat the reports as an end in themselves.

Don't let them get away with it. Instead, get them to answer your questions, and you'll know what to try next.

Your analyst probably won't know any of these answers without doing some research. That's OK—you can wait a few days for each one. Unlike receiving a report, when you get the answers to these questions, you'll be equipped to try some new experiments to improve your results. To get more examples of real-life questions that companies needed answered, check out my Web site (www.mikemoran.com/resources).

One thing for you to be aware of, however, is that the more questions you ask, the more answers you'll get—and the more questions you'll then have. Once you get started answering questions, you'll never stop. There will always be something more to learn, something else to check, and more questions—and it's your analyst's job to answer them with data.

Some analysts will be uncomfortable with the shift from reports to questions. Reports are easy. Once they are set up, the computer does all the work. Answering questions, in contrast, is difficult. The analyst must render an opinion to answer all those "why" questions, but that's exactly what you want. Marketers need analysts to distill their expertise into answers they can act on, not long dry rows of figures.

Analysts might struggle with this new role, however, because they are not always the strongest communicators. Some went into this number-focused profession as a refuge from having to speak or write. And if forced to speak, they'd rather explain multivariate testing than analyze why the latest ad on the home page got only 17 clicks all week.

Use the primer in Chapter 4, "Going Over to the Dark Side," to understand just enough about metrics that you can ask the right questions. Some analysts won't like the simple metrics approach outlined there ("You've oversimplified things to the point of idiocy—you've dumbed down my numbers."), but it's important that *you* understand what the numbers mean because the only purpose of those numbers is to assess success and generate a new experiment. If you don't understand what they mean, you'll be capable of neither.

So let's get to those pesky experiments. To carry them out, you'll need to work with the friendly people we met in Chapter 5, "The New Customer Relations," your creative people—the copywriters, the designers, the art directors, and perhaps others. That's what they call them in big companies, but even small companies have people who write the words, design the look of an e-mail or a Web page, and choose the pictures.

In a small company, you might have one person who writes the copy and chooses the images, or maybe you have an agency that does your Web site design. These folks might not even work for your company, and they are in no mood to hear about your philosophy. The clock is ticking, and they just want to know what you want done so they can do it. Once.

It might take a couple of attempts for you to get them to understand that you'll need to try several different approaches each time you come with a request. You'll need to accept the fact that this will cost you more—you are not coming back to them to redo something because they screwed up. (They'll be suspicious that you want them to fix it for free.) Instead, you want them to understand that you need to budget for several versions so that you'll pick the best one.

In larger companies, where you have your own creative folks on staff, you'll run into different fears: "You mean that you're not going to use the design *we* recommend? You're seriously going to let some metrics program tell you what the right brand image should be?"

If your Web designer fancies himself as the czar of color, he might not understand what you want. Web analytics expert Jim Sterne advises you to say, "Instead of knowing the right shade of teal, tell us which 27 colors to test." In the end, you'll need to persuade creative team members that they'll achieve greater job security and bigger success not by being experts, but by being part of successful campaigns and projects. If the customers buy, then the design and the writing really worked.

Unfortunately, the mindset of many designers is to win design awards rather than sales. If you can't show your designer that keeping a job depends on what customers think, rather than what the awards committee thinks, it might be time to get a new designer. In my experience, designers usually care about the customer once they see they can get valid feedback about what works.

Some designers and writers chafe at the restrictions that metrics impose on their creativity. They feel that their artistic freedom is being constrained. Well, it *is*. But that's nothing new.

Writers have never written whatever they wanted—they needed to stay on message. That marketing message was non-negotiable. Now they need to do even more. They need to use the right terms for search engines. They need to write persuasively enough for customers to convert, and your job is to ensure that writers understand why they need to do it.

Designers are in the same boat. They don't have total freedom either. The designer's colors can't clash with the company logo. Brand image limits choices also—designers can't use cartoon characters for a law firm, and that e-mail describing a retirement community probably shouldn't use an eight-point font.

As you can see, none of the creative folks behind our marketing materials have ever had total creative freedom, so adding metrics as one more constraint shouldn't be the end of the world for anyone. If it is, it's time to get someone else.

Sometimes your problem is not with the designer. Sometimes the problem is that the big boss—let's call him Matt Finish—fancies himself as a designer. Rather then gathering feedback from customers or even letting the color czar decide, Matt steps in and chooses the shade of teal. Often a designer will be too intimidated to go against Matt's wishes.

You'll need to step in to change the dynamics. Matt is not a bad guy, but he's out of his depth. He's probably frustrated that the designs haven't worked that well in the past or that he never understood the basis on which they were chosen, so he took control. You need to show him a new way to control things.

Gently point out that in the end, what Matt really wants is a better customer experience that will improve sales and profits. So Matt's frustration can be put to use by experimenting to improve these metrics. Allow Matt to give you four or five ideas to test and then re-test them. That way, neither he nor the designer needs to "get it right"—your customers will tell you what works and what doesn't. That is how Matt can get the control he craves—and the higher sales and profits he needs to have.

But even the all-powerful Matt has trouble controlling the technologists. It's not always easy to know what they do, but we know we need them. Small companies need the "tech guy" to keep the Web site up—and up to date—while large companies have departments full of Webmasters, programmers, information architects, and other technology personnel.

You can spot technologists because they don't think the glass is half empty or half full—they think it has unused capacity. With the rise of the Internet, marketers now need to work more than ever with technical specialists because the tactics we've focused on throughout this book require technical people to make them work.

Technologists are usually very analytical, so they'll warm to the idea that customer feedback should drive what we do, but they might not be keen on the experimentation part—or on the "quickly" part.

Technologists usually prefer to carefully plan everything up front. In our next section, we explore how to bring the specialists together with a process that allows even technology to change to a "do it wrong quickly" approach.

Bring the Specialists Together

We've already talked about how Specialist Disease can divide your team into separate camps that aren't focused on your customer and your business, and we've looked at how marketers can be more persuasive by speaking each specialist's language. Now let's take positive actions to forge one team united in its mission.

As a leader, you have many options in shaping organizational behavior, but three approaches are best employed to "do it wrong quickly:" *evangelism*, *training*, and *process*.

We've spent most of this book arming you with all the reasons to adopt a more feedback-driven marketing approach. Doubtless you've already begun preaching to your congregation.

In any area of fast-moving technology, training also plays an important role. Fortunately, the Web itself is a great training ground, where informational Web sites, e-mail newsletters, blogs, and all the other tactics we've discussed in this book can be used to keep up-to-date as the pace of marketing change marches on. Chapter 9, "This Stuff Changes Too Fast," will help you keep your knowledge and skills sharp.

For most companies, *evangelism* and *training* seem to come naturally. The bugaboo is *process*. Most small companies don't have enough policies and processes to really simplify their jobs. At big companies, they frequently have too many—or at least too many of the wrong ones.

For some people, *process* is a loaded word, bringing to mind endless red tape and bureaucracy, but it needn't be so. Policies, procedures, or processes should be designed to make the job more standardized and error-free, not to impose sameness where none makes sense. Done well, processes free you to think about the real problems.

Perhaps your company culture downplays the importance of process. If even the word *process* itself seems stifling, then picture a really *simple* process—a checklist. If you are a one-person show, you might only need to post a list on the bulletin board of everything you need to do when you send a marketing e-mail or when you change a Web page. To make it easy for you, I've posted several of these checklists on my Web site (www.mikemoran.com/resources)—simply print them and post them.

Larger companies need more than checklists. They need full-blown policies and procedures—processes with a capital "P." The Internet is changing every part of your marketing, so take the time to think about all the marketing tasks your company performs. Where do you need new or updated policies and procedures?

Let's take one example: product naming. At first, you might not think about how the Internet makes a bit of difference in christening your newest creation. But do you name your products with search in mind? Or are you still calling your new widget a "Series I" and expecting Google to find it? The words "series" and the Roman numeral "I" occur all over the Web already. You should search for your proposed names and see what you get.

But your product name must be more than unique—it must be memorable. Is your new software called "Enterprise Management Content Server"? (...or was that Enterprise Content Management Server...or Content Management Enterprise Server?) If customers can't remember (or spell) your product name, they can't search for it. It might have been a clever name in the old days, but this ain't the old days. Your product-naming policy and process must consider how customers find your product and must cater to this new behavior.

As your Internet marketing approach evolves to support customer feedback, you'll likely find dozens of tasks (such as product naming) that need to be adjusted and tweaked to provide better results. In most companies, however, the biggest process problem surrounds technology.

In big companies and small, anything that requires technology can often be an impediment to experimentation because the technologists insist on a slow, deliberate process of understanding everything up front and "doing it right" (slowly). To combat this, the most important process of all is your process for experimenting with technology.

Most of us are frustrated with the "tech guy" (small company) or the "IT department" (large company) because nothing ever happens quickly, and often we don't get what we expected. The best companies, however, don't have as many problems with technology because of the way they approach it. Web 2.0 expert Dion Hinchcliffe says that photo-sharing site "Flickr can update its software every 30 minutes and uses feedback loops to see what's working." "How is that possible?" you might be asking yourself. Technology projects are notorious for their slow pace.

The secret is a shared process—one that brings all the specialists together.

For those of you unfamiliar with how technology projects are traditionally planned and managed, here is a quick introduction to the *waterfall method*. You might never have heard that term, but you'll recognize the pattern.

The project begins when marketers explain what they want ("the requirements"), the technical team designs a "solution," documenting exactly what they intend to do in a book full of prose and diagrams ("the specs") that can be hundreds of pages long—to ensure that all details are plainly explained. The marketers read the book and suggest modifications, eventually agreeing to what's in the revised book (the "sign off").

After sign off, the technology group "estimates" when the solution will be complete by breaking down the project into low-level tasks and judging when each can be done by the team assigned. (They usually create a GANTT chart that shows all the dependencies of each task on another.) The team then builds the solution according to the specs. And they all live happily ever after.

Some of you are snickering. "Technology projects are the riskiest and slowest things we do around here," you might be thinking. "I never understand why this technical stuff takes so long, and I don't know why they so often turn out badly, but they do." If this has been your experience, you're not alone. But let's play out the rest of the waterfall story.

Once the waterfall project is underway, the marketers (inevitably) think of something new that is required, so they must get a "change request" approved. As the project drags on, it's clear that the system will be delivered later than promised, and often it fails to meet some of the important requirements requested.

THE EMPLOYEE BLOGGER

Blogging is great for companies but carries real risks. Your lawyer and your marketing folks should collaborate on a blogging policy. Here are the basics for a corporate blogging policy:

- **Set out an approval process**—Maybe you'll let anyone start blogging, but most companies want the blogger to get approval of immediate management. During that process, you can ensure the blogger knows what is expected before starting. Make the training about more than your policy. Share the tips offered in Part 1 of this book and encourage them to learn more.

- **Clarify who's responsible**—Is it a company blog, one that speaks for the company? Is it a personal blog? If so, the company usually wants a disclaimer as to whose opinion the blog represents. Does the employee blog on company time or personal time? Regardless, ensure that the blogger is clearly identified as the author and as a company employee and that he can be contacted by readers.

- **Confidential information is off-limits**—Trade secrets of your company and any other company are not for public consumption. Public companies must be especially careful about financial information staying under wraps until officially released. Privacy laws must be upheld. Don't write about something that could later be patented.

- **Define proper behavior**—Ensure that copyright and trademark laws are upheld for company property and the intellectual property of others.

All too often, waterfall projects end up getting cancelled, or they deliver less than expected later than expected. Because the tech team is under great pressure at the end to "get it done," waterfall projects also tend to have more than their share of bugs. (Testing and repairing the software is the last step of a waterfall project, so it frequently is performed in a rushed and slipshod manner.)

Waterfall methods can work well when you know exactly what you want and the technologists are so familiar with the tasks that they know how to do them and how long they will take. If you want a cake, you have to tell the bakers at the start what you want and exactly how much of it you want. The bakers measure the ingredients up front, they mix them up, and they put them into the oven. If you asked for the right thing, then you'll be happy when the cake is done. On the other hand, if you change your mind about what you want, or you'd rather get half a cake in half the time, you're out of luck. Once it's in the oven, you really can't change it. In fact, you

---

Obviously, racist remarks, sexual innuendo, and other bad behavior are not tolerated, but is it OK to use obscenity? Can bloggers speak ill of a competitor? How nicely do you expect readers and commenters to be treated? Do you expect bloggers to quote people only when they know they are speaking on the record? Are unnamed sources OK? How many sources do they need?

- **Be clear about what's at stake**—If the blogger violates the policy, what happens? Loss of blogging privileges? Demotion? Job loss? Whatever punishments you might mete out should be explained up front so that people take your policy seriously. Explain the legal problems that could ensnare your company and the blogger.

If your company's culture is not very open, blogging is not going to come naturally. Instead of expecting a restrictive policy to make it work, it might be better to admit that your company is not ready for a blog yet. If you try to force it, expect it to show.

But policies are not enough. Bloggers need training and support. Sun Microsystems, the poster child for widespread employee blogging, believes in team blogging. Sun's Curt Sasaki notes, "Getting someone to write their first blog is easy, but getting them to write weekly is hard. Rather than giving up on it, we instituted group blogging so others could collaborate on a blog."

The employee blogger is a powerful force, so be sure you have the policy and the process in place for the force to be *with* you.

shouldn't even open the oven too often to check on it. You just wait until the whole thing is done.

Baking is precise. On the other hand, making soup is not.

Agile development is more like making soup, while waterfall methods are closer to baking a cake. With agile methods, you don't necessarily need to know exactly what you are making at the beginning, although it helps if you do. Not only can you watch soup simmer, you can taste it early in the process and add more ingredients, unlike the cake, which you can't eat until it is done. If you're really hungry, you can eat the soup early in the process, although it tastes much better if you can wait.

You can even start out making vegetable soup and then at the end decide you'd like to add some cooked chicken. Now you've got *chicken* vegetable soup. Try that when you bake a cake. With a cake, one small mistake in your ingredients can ruin everything—because you can't taste it until it's finished. Once, my wife inadvertently left the sugar out of a cake—it tasted about as good as you imagine it did.

Agile development tolerates mistakes—that's the essence of "do it wrong quickly," after all. Agile teams always set out to do the best they can—they believe they are doing it right. The process allows them to take a quick stab at it and see how well they did and then adjust it with another try based on an improved understanding of what's needed. The waterfall process requires that you get it nearly exactly right up front.

Most things that we make are like cake—anything we manufacture or build out of physical materials needs a baking-like waterfall process, but software is soup. Yes, we can approach it the same way as making cake, and you'll still get your software at the end. But why be that rigid if you don't have to be? We could approach making soup in the same way we bake, but no one does because soup is easier to make (and comes out better) if you don't.

Waterfall development is akin to calling all the plays in a football game before the game starts. Now you can have a set of plays that you think will work, that you practiced, and that you believe the other team is susceptible to. That's fine—that's just having a plan. But you wait until the right situation for each play. Some of the plays you practiced are never used because it turned out you didn't need them. That's how agile development works.

In football, you might run three plays that don't work and have to give the ball to the other team, but you haven't lost the game—you just wasted a small opportunity. Agile development breaks up a project into a series of small opportunities, delivering a working system every week, every two weeks, or every month, depending on which particular agile methodology you use. So the worst that can happen is that you blow a small opportunity—you've wasted a couple of weeks. When something goes wrong in a waterfall project, in contrast, you just might lose the game right there.

THE BENEFITS OF AGILE DEVELOPMENT

"Everyone had a sense that we needed to do something different," says Devashish Saxena of Texas Instruments. "Back in 2003, we moved from a traditional approach to a consistent development model—we have a release every month."

It's a common story with the fastest-moving companies these days—they've moved to agile development to speed their pace. Scott Ambler, an agile development expert from IBM and the author of 19 books, including *Agile Modeling*, explains the key benefits these companies are seeking: "greater quality, greater accountability, and greater value."

Agile development relies on constant testing so that at the end of each phase (often a month or less), you get working software that does *something* useful, even if it doesn't solve world hunger—that leads to higher quality and higher accountability. Moreover, because as Scott says, "We work in priority order," the marketers' most important needs are handled first—providing greater value.

Agile development is not "quick and dirty." It *is* quick, but the technical team works hard to ensure that a correctly working version of the software is always available for marketers to examine, both to assess progress and to provide feedback. People are more likely to try things when there's less danger of breaking the whole shebang. (There are never any partial shebangs, for some reason.) Because the technology under development is always working, it provides the stability that frees people to experiment more. Stability is the new flexibility. (I think that because I said it, that quote qualifies as an "oxyMoran.")

Floyd Marinescu explained how the infoq.com site was built using agile methods. "We launched with no SEO [(search engine optimization)]. Every month afterward we launched new features. I would always have a chance to change the next [version]. Our SEO launched later because it was not the most important [feature], instead of delaying the go-to-market for a few months." Floyd's site was producing value when a waterfall project would still be waiting to launch.

Without a speedy technology process, it's hard to do Internet marketing quickly. Agile development is the easiest way to do technology wrong quickly.

In football, the quarterback is the person who calls the plays, while each of the other players decides how to do his own job on that play. Sometimes the plan for a play "breaks down," and each player has to improvise. In agile development, one person acts as the quarterback, deciding exactly what the development team should be working on. You, the marketer, *are* the quarterback. You set the priorities.

Just as in football, the hallmark of agile development is teamwork. Each player on the team has an assigned role. Each player decides the right way to "run your play"— that's when each specialist's knowledge is required. The quarterback decides the "what" (which play we are running), but each player decides the "how" (how to execute that play). The quarterback may call a running play, but it is up to the running back as to how to evade the other team's tacklers to make the biggest gain possible.

Let your development team decide "how" to implement agile development by picking which particular methodology they want to use—there are many to choose from. Some of the most popular ones are Scrum, Extreme Programming, and OpenUP. (Can you tell that programmers chose these names and not marketers?) Marketers probably don't care exactly which agile method is used, but they should insist that all technology that supports marketing be implemented using some kind of agile method.

Your technology team members might resist. Some of them like to do all the design work up front, but you're better off teaching them to make soup. The major advantage of agile development for marketers is that you don't need to know everything at the beginning of the project. You need to know only the most important two or three things for the technologists to do right now.

For example, if you want to add product reviews to your Web site, the old way would be for you to demand support for ratings, reviews, and a sign-on procedure— and demand to do it for every product in every country. The IT people would want those requirements so that they could select a service provider, pick a software package, or develop the long-term architecture to build it themselves.

What's the new way? Do it wrong quickly.

If you are developing the system in-house, implement only the barest of functions at first. Perhaps start with ratings alone—anonymous ratings, with no sign-in function. And do it for just one set of products, not your whole catalog. Then month after month, you can add reviews and other capabilities. You can test to see whether customers participate and whether the pilot products convert better than before.

In contrast, if you are licensing software or using a service provider, you won't need to compromise on function, but you should still start with a pilot set of products. Negotiate a trial period with the vendor or a money-back guarantee if the results are not positive.

As empowering as it might be for marketers to be in charge of what the technologists deliver, you'll find that it is a lot more work than the old waterfall way. You'll need to be constantly available to the team to set priorities, to answer questions, and to provide feedback on work-in-progress. This is how an agile process brings all your specialists together.

Setting priorities gives you more responsibility than with a waterfall process, too. If what the technologists built is not what your customer wants, that's your fault, not theirs. (If the customer wanted vegetable soup, shame on you for deciding to add the chicken.) But the "do it wrong quickly" approach means that you'll have a plan for how to fix what's wrong, and an agile development process means that your technologists can deliver small fixes at breakneck speed.

Agile development focuses on doing the most important things first in the simplest possible way but with the highest quality—no bugs. So instead of dropping every last function into a requirements document ("We need to ask for *everything* because the tech people always deliver less."), ask for only the most minimally necessary things—and have the technologists make dead sure those functions work. With a small list of requirements, you get it much faster.

Agile development depends on delivering business value on a regular basis—say, once a month. Each month a new function or feature appears, quality tested and ready to use within real marketing campaigns with real customers. You don't delay the deadline to complete the whole job—you ship whatever is working when the deadline comes around. The train leaves the station on time no matter how many passengers are on board. If a particular function misses one train, it catches the next one.

You can do the same thing with design—have the designer do several versions and keep updating them. You can even use multivariate testing to see which one is better.

Duane Schultz, Vice President of Internet Marketing at Xerox, sums up why marketers care about this technology process:

> *We use agile methods—Extreme Programming. We think that if you need to write it down, you blew it. We still do projects, but we have reasons to do them now. The old model was* build *then* measure, *but the new model is* measure *then* improve. *We must shift from "What?" to "Why?" to "What are we going to do?"*

But how do you convince your technologists to go along? The history of failed waterfall projects, complete with the hunt for the guilty afterwards, has caused mistrust between marketers and technical types. You might have some fence-mending to do before you win the trust of the techies. But agile methodologies have great benefits for technologists:

- **Agile projects are smaller**—That makes them easier to estimate and easier to complete. Most waterfall projects fail because too many things change or go wrong over the many months they span. Agile projects allow you to shift the plan every month, so it's harder to get off track.

- **Agile projects are shared**—Marketers work side-by-side with the technologists, constantly answering questions and providing feedback so that communication is improved and mistakes are caught early, making them easier to correct.

- **Agile projects require less debugging and little documentation**—Many technologists would rather build things than shake out the bugs or write a manual, so agile development helps them do more of what they love.

- **Agile projects are less stressful**—The end of a waterfall project requires untold overtime hours and endless stress, as techies fix remaining problems after the original deadline has passed. Agile projects usually deliver on time by removing a function and moving it to next month's release—a technique that lowers blood pressure considerably.

DO SMALL BUSINESSES NEED TO BE AGILE?

Most small businesses don't do much software development, but they can still use agile methods. The basic idea is for the marketer to continually guide and check in with the specialist so that gradually you get what you want. It's a lot easier than having to painstakingly write a document that perfectly describes your idea.

Matt Schaub, President of ReallyGreatRate.com, now uses agile methods for Web design, although he might never use the name "agile." Matt creates a detailed outline and a *wireframe* (shown in Exhibit 8-1) of the page to be designed, spelling out the exact words he wants used, if he knows them. Matt is no designer—he uses Powerpoint to demonstrate what he has in mind—but these instructions get the designer off to the right start.

In the past, Matt expected that just describing what he wanted to the designer over the phone would be sufficient, but that hardly ever worked. "I took a lot of shortcuts in the past because I thought he'd know what I was thinking. I thought everyone would be a good interpreter of what I say, but they're not."

Even today, the key to his success is what he does *after* the first version of the design comes back. He insists on going over the design on the phone, explaining what he likes and what misses the mark. "I fired designers who only wanted to do e-mail. I need to talk to them on the phone."

This intense communication after the work is "done" is the most critical part of agile development. The marketer and the designer collaborate until they both feel it is ready to test. Matt works with his designer to develop multiple versions of each page, which he then uses with multivariate testing so that customers pick the real winner.

Marketers can sketch simple wireframe drawings to communicate with a designer, as this PowerPoint diagram from Matt Schaub of ReallyGreatRate.com shows.

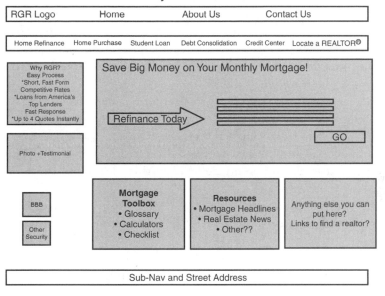

Exhibit 8-1   A sketch of a Web page layout

Once the technologists realize that you want to work in the trenches with them and that this methodology will result in more successful projects, they're usually willing to give it a try. But a few will continue to be pained. It's just their personalities.

Personality Parade

Early in my career at IBM, I was part of the heady rush of the newest thing—the personal computer. (I know, I know—I am *really* old.)

Inside my department, IBM was replacing "dumb terminals" with PCs, but they hadn't figured out an easy way to get people all the software they needed to run those PCs. IBM had been distributing hardware to employees for years but had no system for doing the same with software because terminals didn't use any software (that's where the "dumb" part comes in).

I knew we needed a way to let employees get whatever software they needed and soon came across the concept of an internal "PC Store"—an office stocked with useful software that employees could charge to their department's budget. It seemed like a great idea, but I knew I had a big problem.

The big boss would never go for it.

The boss—we'll call him Stan Patt—never liked *any* new idea. Stan was actually a nice guy, a good person to work for, hard-working, and intelligent—but he was incredibly risk-averse. Anything new was automatically suspicious.

It took us a while to come up with the right approach for Stan's personality, but we found it. We began clipping articles in trade magazines about how companies were getting sued when their employees made illegal copies of software they needed to use their PCs. Anytime we saw an article, we'd cut it out and secretly leave it on Stan's desk. This went on for a couple of months.

At the same time, we worked on the proposal for our department PC store. We analyzed the software people needed and estimated what it would cost and how we would pay for it. Then we were ready to pitch the idea to Stan.

In the middle of the presentation, he fixed his gaze on us and said "You! You're the ones leaving these scary stories on my desk! Does this idea fix all those problems?"

"Yes, it does," we assured him.

"What does it cost?" Stan wanted to know. After we told him, he said, "Fine, just do it and stop leaving stuff on my desk—I don't want to hear about this stuff anymore. Just make the problems *go away*."

Stan hated risk, so the winning approach to persuade Stan to do something new was to make the status quo riskier than the new idea. By understanding Stan's personality, we got a "yes" rather than a "no."

Businesses grow and improve by making "yes" decisions. "No" decisions are made all the time, but they just maintain the status quo (possibly after it has lost all of its status). Getting "yes" decisions depends on understanding the personalities of the people you must persuade.

With Stan Patt, change was scary, so getting him to change required scaring him about the current situation. Contrast that approach with Willie Nilly, who is always looking for a good change. It's much easier to get Willie to try something new—your challenge is getting him to stick with his decision when the next shiny object catches his eye. You might want to continually present your experiments as great new ideas for Willie so that the thrill of something new continues unabated.

Regardless, thrill-seeking and risk-aversion are just two of many personality characteristics that your colleagues and bosses possess. You need to accept the fact that understanding what makes people tick can help you to gain support to do it wrong quickly.

Perhaps you're thinking, "I don't have time for that folderol" (no one ever seems to have time for folderol) or "I hate politics." I'd like you to reconsider that stance. No matter how powerful a position you might have or how small your company might be, to adapt to the changes in marketing requires persuasion. You have to persuade other people, whether it's your boss, your "tech guy," or your customers. You need to understand where other people are coming from and how to deal with them.

If this feels manipulative, you're not doing it right. Your goal is not to get them to do something by fooling them. It's to open up their thinking so they can really improve themselves. Some people won't respond well, but if you treat everyone with respect, then enough people will. To be honest, I personally don't always do this right, so I am letting myself off the hook, too—I can do this wrong quickly. If I don't treat someone with respect, then I can do it the next time or with the next person—or I can go back and say I'm sorry.

It's also OK to prioritize. Doing it wrong quickly means that you can choose who to work on the most—the ones requiring low effort who can make a high impact. And you might find that you do better working on some kinds of people while others tire you out. That's OK, too.

Just do your best and keep improving.

All the people you work with have certain traits that make them more or less receptive to what you're proposing. If you'd really like to change the way you do marketing, but you cringe each time you think of proposing experimentation to your boss, if the other two departments heads just won't seem to cooperate, or the assistant to the big boss always cancels your appointments, then you need to spend some time thinking about what is stopping them from going along.

Comedian Whoopi Goldberg says that "'Normal' is nothing more than a cycle on a washing machine." That's a good attitude to have when working with people. In wrapping up this chapter, we'll take a quick look at different personality types that you might run into along the way and what you might do and say to enlist them in your cause. Let's start with the ones who just aren't paying attention.

The Inattentive

I'm a Marxist—of the Groucho variety. And one of Groucho's characters was Professor Wagstaff in the movie *Horsefeathers*, whose contribution to management decision making was this little ditty:

I don't know what they have to say.
It makes no difference anyway.
Whatever it is, I'm against it.
No matter what it is or who commenced it,
I'm against it!

Your proposition may be good,
But let's have one thing understood:
Whatever it is, I'm against it.
And even when you've changed it or condensed it,
I'm against it!

If your proposals get the same level of attention, you'll need to find a new approach, depending on exactly who you're dealing with:

- Neil Befourmey doesn't accept suggestions from below—only from his boss and his peers. Rather than wringing your hands about working for him, go convince his boss and his peers. (*Related species*: Mary O'Nette, who won't do anything without her boss' approval.)

- Myles Away never seems to pay attention when you are talking. He's usually fingering his Blackberry or answering a cell phone call. Maybe *you* need to call him on his cell phone.

- Oscar Nominee is never really paying attention to anything substantive because he just wants to look good. This one is simple. Explain to him how doing what you want will make him look good (or how not doing it will make him look awful). (*Related species:* Scott Free, who cares only about avoiding blame for mistakes.)

- Emmanuel Follower won't do anything that is not written down. Your best approach is to change the procedures—as soon as you do, he'll follow them. (*Related species:* Marc Time, who is just waiting to retire.)

- Frank Assessment thinks he is being candid, but he just rejects everyone else's ideas. When dealing with this breed—a "negasaurus"—sometimes the easiest way forward is to work closely with Frank and slowly make it all his idea. American president Harry Truman once said, "It is amazing what you can accomplish if you do not care who gets the credit." (*Related species:* Ike Cue, who always needs to be the smartest boy in class—the one with the best ideas.)

- Roman Thoughts can't seem to stick with the subject—he's always interjecting unrelated questions and ideas. Perhaps you're providing more information than he can handle. Simplify, simplify, and repeat what you are saying in many different ways. You might need to have frequent short interactions to build up to a bigger decision.

Sometimes when you're ignored, you need to get attention in a dramatic way, as one person confided to me. "One business unit just would not engage with us no matter what I did—it was a 'person' problem," he recalled. So at the next review meeting with the CEO, he put up a blank chart where that business unit's measurements would have been. That prompted the CEO to speak with the head of that unit, and they were very cooperative after that.

Sometimes the problem isn't lack of attention—it's lack of spine. Next up, the wishy-washy decision maker.

The Indecisive

As painful as it can be to be ignored, it can be tougher to have someone listen to everything—14 times—but still not be quite ready to get off the fence.

You might have to deal with people who just can't make up their minds. No matter what you suggest, they can think of a reason to delay, even if it's as flimsy as, "Don't be reckless." (Make sure you have at least one "reck.")

Some people are naturally more detail-oriented than others. What they consider to be "thorough" you consider "obsessive compulsive." (If you just asked yourself whether the words *obsessive compulsive* should have been hyphenated, you might be a "thorough" person yourself.)

Although it can be frustrating, chronic fence-sitters *can* be coaxed to make a decision, but different people need different approaches:

- Lotta DeBait checks with everyone before deciding. She desires consensus above all else and loves to say, "That's a good point." (Are there ever any bad points?) To persuade her, find a way to persuade those she trusts. If she wants a consensus, give her one—an agreement that we should try several ideas to attack this problem.

- Juan Moore continually requests more data. No matter how much information you have, it's never quite enough. To convince Juan, you might provide data that shows how much it's costing you to delay the decision. (*Related species:* Ken Fused doesn't understand the significance of the data and needs far simpler evidence to weigh.)

- Isaiah Lott talks a blue streak but never does anything. Luckily, you might also find that he never *stops* anything, either. Just go around him. (*Related species:* Noah Pruvall forces every decision to "go through channels" but lifts not one finger to grease the skids.)

- Hugo Ferst will never be the first one to do anything, thinking "We'll let someone else prove it works…it won't take long to catch up." It might be frustrating, but you need to get another group on board before he'll bite. Once you do, he will follow along.

The indecisive believe in the aphorism from cartoonist Charles Schultz: "No problem is so big and complicated that it can't be run away from." But you can use this avoidance behavior to your advantage. When Sun's Curt Sasaki introduced customer ratings and reviews, he recalls that at times, "We didn't get an enthusiastic *yes* as much as 'We won't object.'"

As hard as it can be to get that "yes," sometimes it's not as difficult as what happens afterward. Some people just can't execute the project after it is approved.

The Inept

It sounds harsh, but some people really *are* inept. (The rest of us are "ept.") Even if you persuade them to experiment, they might not be the right people to carry it through. How you handle the situation depends on who you get from central casting:

- Rick O'Shea bounces from one trend to another. He'll approve your experiment and agree to a conflicting project a week later. To overcome this, stay in his face—have daily status meetings if you need to. Make sure you are always the last project he's heard about. (*Related species:* Peter Rout starts strongly behind it but always fades over time.)

- Helen Bakk drives the team relentlessly to make changes and just can't rest, even when you really get it working well. She just can't help but ask for change after change after change. You need to show her that burning out the team actually makes things worse and to use the metrics to identify what the biggest problems are. In a crisis—your company is going out of business—driving the team is understandable, but you can't declare any situation a crisis for more than a couple of months.

- Rex Plans agrees to all ideas but botches their execution. He doesn't do it on purpose, but it doesn't matter. Usually people like Rex know they cause train wrecks, so you can usually persuade them to assign the project to someone who won't kill it. (*Related species:* Rocky Relationships drives everyone nuts, so he alienates anyone working on his project.)

- Les Metrix flies by the seat of his pants, rather than relying on measurements. He likes to say he has "a golden gut." You might alert Les that you're going to keep track of how well your decisions work. Once Les sees that he might be called on mistakes, he'll be less prone to shoot from the hip. (*Related species:* Max Effort ignores measurable results but rewards how hard people work.)

- Rosie Glasses always sees something positive in the numbers no matter how bad they look. ("I'm an optimist, which I think is a good thing.") It's imperative that you get her to agree on what numbers you should expect ahead of time so she can't "go relativist" when numbers hardly improve. (*Related species:* Ray F. Sunshine and Sonny Outlook, who can find a reason why things will turn around without us doing anything. Nineteenth-century author Andrew Lang described someone who "uses statistics as a drunken man uses lampposts, for support rather than illumination.")

- Nick F. Time always waits until the last minute to decide things, making it harder to turn problems around. Show him how many more experiments you could run—maybe he'll like more frequent adrenaline rushes. (*Related species:* Will Power can always tough it out without changing anything.)

- Chuck Everything believes that, no matter what the problem, we need to start from scratch with something big, sweeping, and new. "Don't embroider around the edges," he likes to say, "We need a new quilt!" If you can show Chuck that you can succeed with smaller changes, he'll go along. (*Related species*: Hugh Fired always thinks that mistakes need to be handled by dumping the staff.)

Each of us suffers from some personality challenges. (Personally, I resemble Ike Cue and Rick O'Shea in my weaker moments.) Why does this happen to us? In the immortal words of Roger Daltrey, "Can't Explain."

The truth is that working with people means dealing with idiosyncrasies. These personalities on parade are listed to get you thinking—you need to think about the people you work with and help them overcome their blind spots.

Summary

Comedian W.C. Fields once said, "I am free of all prejudices; I hate everyone equally." Sometimes working with people can be frustrating, but getting changes made in marketing requires you to persuade others.

In this chapter, we've looked at three major points:

- **We must lead our colleagues to change**—The adaptations required to do it wrong quickly don't come easily to everyone. If you rally your allies, choose your initial experiments carefully, and declare success, you'll make progress toward a feedback culture.

- **Some people retreat to their specialties**—Challenge your experts to put the business first and connect with them by understanding their perspectives. Institute a process that brings your specialists together so they can collaborate with maximum impact.

- **Adjust your approach to persuade each personality type**—Each of us exhibits different traits—not all of them lend themselves to experimentation and customer feedback. If we can challenge and support our colleagues to transcend our comfort zones, we'll help our companies adapt to the new marketing realities.

One more chapter to go. In Chapter 9, we look at how to cope with the dizzying pace of change. It's moving fast and will move faster in the future, but you can keep up if you know how.

9

This Stuff Changes Too Fast

"The future ain't what it used to be."

—Yogi Berra

Chapter Contents

- How Do You Cope with Change?   317
- What's Changing?   321
- How Do You Keep Up?   331
- Summary   333

Yes, I really did this.

When I was in college, a couple of weeks before Easter, a friend and I walked around New York City for a few hours wearing bunny suits—complete head-to-toe bunny suits. We walked down Broadway. We shopped. We took the subway. We got thrown out of a diner when we sat down and ordered "salads—hold the salad dressing." Whenever bystanders were in earshot, we argued with each other in animated fashion about which of us was getting stuck with more of the Easter preparation work.

This might not sound like a fun way to pass a day, but it was. The people gawking at us thought we were the show, but to us, *they* were the show. Some of them laughed. Some of them recoiled. Others, like those diner employees, got angry. Most of them just stared. All of the kids thought it was hysterical.

I hadn't thought of that day in years, but recently it struck me as a good metaphor for the changes in marketing. (Thank God, or this chapter would have had no opening.)

The marketer of Energizer batteries literally dresses in a bunny suit, but all marketers have routinely donned the equivalent of rabbit outfits to get customers' attention. And until now, those marketers in the bunny suits *were* the show.

But today's savvy marketers know that the customer is the show. We still dress in bunny suits to get the customer's attention, but now we have to watch what customers *do* in response. That's what this book has been all about—shifting our focus from merely *getting* attention to also *paying* attention.

Early in this book, we called it "Millennium Marketing." Maybe we'll all end up calling it "Marketing 2.0," or "Adaptive Marketing," or even "Open Source Marketing." Eric Raymond, in his seminal book *The Cathedral and the Bazaar*, noted a tenet of open source software development: "Treating your users as co-developers is your least-hassle route to rapid code improvement and effective debugging." Likewise, treating your customers as collaborators for your marketing is your least-hassle route to rapid improvement. That's what "do it wrong quickly" is all about.

But it's not easy.

In Chapter 7, "This Doesn't Work for Me," we looked inside ourselves to see what's stopping us from making the change to the new marketing. In Chapter 8, "This Won't Work Where I Work," we looked at the other members of our teams to help them do the same. In this chapter, we look at the world around us—that fast-paced, changing world around us.

Some of us find change invigorating. Others find it a little scary.

If you feel like those spooked diner employees when you see something new, you don't have to make the bunnies go away. Instead you can notice each new bunny that comes along and decide to take it all in stride and just strike up a conversation.

But it takes time.

Some of you don't know where you'll find that time. You're already working too many hours in the day now. (If the same disc jockey is on the radio when you go to work in the morning as when you drove home last night, that's a sign you're overworked.)

The good news is that reading this book is probably the biggest investment of time you need to make. It's harder to learn something new than it is to stay on top of a subject as it changes. Just remind yourself of why you picked up this book in the first place. That motivation will help you stay with it every day.

After all, it really *does* change too fast, but does that mean you can just ignore it? Nope. Hockey superstar Wayne Gretzky described how all marketers must think about their craft: "I skate to where the puck is going to be, not where it has been." Where are *you* skating?

This chapter helps you anticipate where the puck is going to be. We start by looking at how you can cope with change—how to think about what's changing and what's staying the same. Next, we examine the specific areas in marketing that are still changing so that you'll be prepared for what's to come. Lastly, we learn how to keep up with the changes in marketing, with specific resources to make it manageable.

So let's dive in. Just how *do* you cope with change?

How Do You Cope with Change?

It's undeniable. Technology changes around us every minute. The changes of the forces described in this book aren't slowing down—they're accelerating. And if we're being honest, many of us don't cope all that well. Change seems stressful, risky, and fear-inducing. In this chapter, we look through a very cloudy crystal ball at some of the trends you will need to know about, but before we do, let's examine something more basic—coping with change.

One way to cope with change is to reassure ourselves that most of what we know is still true. In the first couple of chapters of this book, we saw that the old offline tactics still work to a great degree and that many of the new interactive techniques can be understood as variations of what we already know.

For example, organic search marketing has similarities to public relations. Banner ads remind us of print advertising. Viral marketing feels a whole lot like good old word-of-mouth.

We should also remember that our biggest challenges are not technical at all, so they are *not* changing. Look at Exhibit 9-1, which shows the major issues that large companies face in improving their customer experience. Changing technology didn't cause any of those issues, and neither will it solve any of them by itself. (Geez, "implementing technology" is Problem #2, anyway.)

This book addresses each of these obstacles. You just finished reading about the top three problems in Chapter 8. We've spent most of the book looking at how to measure the customer experience and how to listen to customers to better understand their needs—and design better interfaces for them.

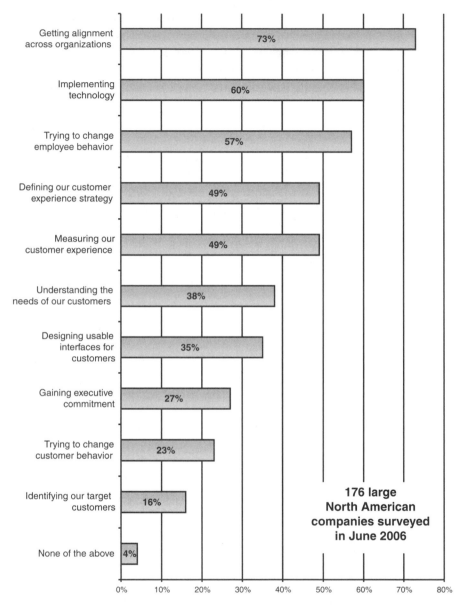

Source: Forrester Research, June 2006

Exhibit 9-1   What are the obstacles to improving your customer experience?

Although this study surveyed large companies, small companies have many of the same issues. These "big picture" problems never really change—we change to better handle them. We adapt.

Some things really do change, however. Technology moves quickly, dragging marketers with it (kicking and screaming, at times). A few years ago, there were no blogs or wikis or podcasts. (Oh my!) A mere 15 years ago, there was no Web. Surely we'll look back a few years from now and laugh at how little we understood what was coming.

To cope with that kind of change, your best hope is to look at the big picture—the goals that you have for marketing to your customers. When you do, it helps to answer the same set of questions for each new marketing tactic that comes along—the following answers them for viral videos:

- **What's in it for me?**—You need to understand how the tactic advances your marketing agenda to improve sales, brand awareness, or customer relationships. Are competitors doing it already? For example, you might have assessed viral video as a way to send a rich marketing message to the youth market that is paying less attention to TV—and that you can do it before your competitors do.

- **What's in it for my customer?**—You must clearly understand why the customer cares. What benefit does the customer receive? The benefit does not have to be tangible—customers share videos with their friends simply because it is fun. That can be enough.

- **Are there sensitivities to be aware of?**—List the reservations that customers might have. Does it raise privacy concerns? Is it too much work? See if it fits with being real, relevant, and responsive. If you sell a consumer product, customers might be reluctant to pass along viral video while at work in case the boss is watching, but that might be the only downside.

- **How can its success be measured?**—New marketing tactics often are hard to measure, but is there at least a crude measurement you can use? For viral videos, you can count the number of viewings on YouTube, so set an expected number for the first week and see how you do.

- **How easily can it be undone?**—If it doesn't work, how damaging is it? Will you have spent a lot of money on it? Would it be publicly embarrassing? Can it be stopped quickly? Viral videos don't cost much to produce or distribute and can be taken down immediately, but if you do something embarrassing, it will be copied and archived on the Internet—you can't undo it.

If you learn how to think about each new tactic that comes along, you'll be one step ahead of your competitors. If you pursue tactics that your customers care about, that will differentiate your marketing from that of your competitors.

As with anything you try, you'll assess its results against the metrics you chose, and you'll keep tweaking it so that you continuously improve—or you'll drop it in favor of a new experiment. Remember that different market segments might respond to different tactics, so a tactic that might seem like a loser overall could be a big winner for a particular group of customers.

As each new technique pops up, you'll need to assess what it does for you and for your customer—that way you'll figure out which ones matter for you and which don't. You needn't be afraid to wait to see if something takes off before trying it yourself, but neither should you feel pressured to jump on every new thing that comes along. As an example, while doing my research for this book, I interviewed a top marketing executive for a very forward-looking company. I was incredibly impressed with the ways they've adapted their company culture and how responsive they are to customers.

But as the interview progressed, I sensed a growing discomfort. He seemed to be weighing his every word. Finally, I asked him what was wrong. He admitted that the culture in his company was so team-oriented that he was becoming concerned that the interview might glorify him personally and alienate him from his colleagues. Now that I understood the sensitivity, I promised him that I would keep that in mind as I used the quotes. He relaxed immediately, and the interview continued.

Why am I telling you this story? It's because that company is *not* ready for blogging. Blogs, like interviews, require a personal opinion. A company culture that de-emphasizes individuality so much that interviews are uncomfortable would render blogging absolutely painful. That company's culture is more compatible with the homogenized "voice of the company" found in a press release—and they are better off recognizing that fact rather than writing a blog that might feel forced.

It's entirely valid to see a new marketing tactic arise, even one that is successful for other companies, but decide to wait because you can't easily see how it will work for your firm and your customers. Just because all the kids are doing it doesn't mean you should, too. (Thanks for that advice, mom.) Don't feel pressure to keep up with the Dow Joneses.

Conversely, if you see something that you immediately feel would be useful, don't wait to see if other people try it first. Experiment and see what your customers think. That same company that has avoided blogging was measuring its conversions way back in 1999! Why? Because they immediately saw its power—they treated those measurements the same way they approached any sales analysis. For their company, it just made sense.

Don't stereotype your company as being either forward-looking or hidebound. Joel Reimer, Director of Interactive Marketing for ScottsMiracle-Gro, believes that more companies are beginning to treat online marketing expenses as an enterprise-level investment, just as they do manufacturing. If he's right, more and more companies will be making decisions on each new marketing tactic on a case-by-case basis, instead of thinking of themselves as being "too conservative for that kind of risk."

As online marketing tactics become more commonplace, companies will increasingly apply critical thinking to each opportunity that comes along. They'll judge whether the work involved for this tactic seems to be worth the opportunity—and whether it is a good fit for their business and for their customers. The best advice is to identify the promising candidates and give them a try.

But don't be too picky about which candidates you find promising. Remember that "the new thing" is often easier for you to succeed with than the tactics that everyone is already using. The first banner ads got heavy clickthrough until customers decided they weren't terribly relevant—if you were one of the first ones, banner ads worked for you. The first paid search marketers made oodles of cash at just pennies per click—before other marketers got in the game and drove up the price.

The point is that new marketing tactics are often under-priced. If a new marketing tactic comes along that really doesn't seem right for your company or your customers, fine. But take a close look before you let it go. It might give you a strong opportunity to make a mark—at least for a while.

So let's look at what *is* coming along. What exactly is changing?

What's Changing?

You can't avoid the changes that are coming—the handwriting is on the wall. (You really *should* keep those indelible markers away from the kids.) The tricky part is knowing exactly what those changes will be. As physicist Neils Bohr noted, "Prediction is very difficult, especially about the future."

But that won't stop me. Whether spurred by bravery or foolhardiness, let's plunge into the big trends in interactive marketing. You'll see lots of small changes and probably a few big ones that get missed here, but let's focus on the three broad categories of change to help organize our thinking:

- **More participation**—As important as the Internet has become to our marketing efforts, we ain't seen nothin' yet! More customers will participate in online life. They will participate in more activities online, and they will participate for a higher percentage of their time than they do now.

- **More context**—Customers tend to interact with marketers anonymously today. Increasingly, you'll be able to identify customers, sometimes by name, but frequently by context—geographic location, behavioral characteristics, and demographics, for example.

- **More integration**—Today, interactive marketing materials are generally sought by the customer, rather than being sent. In the future, marketing and sales will become more integrated with other online activities and with your customers' daily lives.

First up, let's see how the growth of Internet usage affects marketing.

More Participation

Time was that marketing to people on the move involved newspapers, radio, and billboards, and marketing to people in their homes and offices was based on catalogs, yellow page ads, phone calls, salespeople, and TV.

The Internet is changing the way marketers reach customers. It's already transformed marketing to people at home: In some countries, time spent online outstrips time spent watching TV. Marketing to people on the move is next.

Cell phones are already Net-capable—in the U.S., more than 60 percent of American cell phones can access the Web, with that number increasing every year. Browsing the Web on a cell phone has always required that marketers have a version of their Web site tuned for a phone's small screen size. Soon, mobile Web browsers will handle Web sites designed for display on computer monitors, opening up a world of content for mobile devices.

Beyond cell phones, wide-area wireless networking is becoming a reality for computers. Soon you'll see the Internet-connected car. Each of these technological advances will increase participation in online life. More people are getting connected to the Web, more of the time, at higher speeds, to do more things.

What does this mean to marketing? It means that more marketing moments will happen online. Marketers have traditionally thought of these moments as raising *brand awareness*. Of course, you need customers to be aware of your brand so that they will seek you out when they need you. But instead of thinking in terms of brand awareness, it helps to use a more customer-focused term. Customers want to "Discover" new and useful products and services. Discovery is how customers first notice what you sell. Exhibit 9-2 shows Discover inside the Web Conversion Cycle because it is a necessary condition to take any of the other steps.

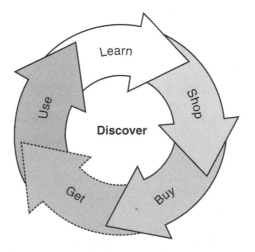

Exhibit 9-2   The Discover step begins the Web Conversion Cycle

In the future, customers will increasingly Discover your product online.

Orbitcast blogger Ryan Saghir notes that "Social networking will become a way for people to find information"—that also means more and more discovery happens online. Pontiac, for example, is offering free "land" in the Second Life virtual world on "Motorati Island." Why? To have their cars discovered by customers. We might someday look back on this as a quaint attempt to get attention for a real-world brand in the middle of a far-more-exciting fantasy world, but give Pontiac points for trying something rather than sitting on the sidelines. If we all keep experimenting, someone will figure out how to market through virtual worlds.

There's a generational shift underway also. Internet users over the age of 40 are more likely to use the Web to satisfy needs, rather than for entertainment. Younger adults typically do far more online—watching videos, downloading music, and playing games. Younger customers are spending their free time online—that's more and more where they will Discover your company and your product.

So many experiences that once were offline are moving online. It wasn't long ago that the only way to get a feel for student life at a university was to visit the campus. No more. Prospective students now use MySpace to Discover colleges based on the opinions of current students, eliminating some from consideration without ever visiting. The MySpace profiles for students at some schools feature students out having fun, while others show students drinking in their rooms. The Admissions department can't control this venue where customers talk to other customers. The generation now checking out colleges online will Discover many other brands that way, too.

There's also a generational shift in attitudes toward contributing content, such as writing a product review or commenting on a blog. One-third of all American Web users over 30 have contributed content to the Web, but one-*half* of all those under 30 have done so. Younger people are just plain doing more things online so that is where marketers must be to get discovered.

Discovery will increasingly occur online—the seeds of this trend are visible today. Just look at what's happening to some traditional venues for offline discovery. The advertising-supported newspaper and magazine industries are losing revenue to Web upstarts. Newspaper classified advertising is under fire from craigslist.com and monster.com. Display advertising in both newspapers and magazines are losing ground to the cheaper and more measurable pay-per-click search ads. Magazines as disparate as *Life*, *Child*, and *InfoWorld* have retreated to an online-only business model, ceasing a print version altogether. Bloggers and other Web sites deliver news and analysis faster than a periodical. FlickR displays many more photos than *Life* magazine ever could.

Whether because its editorial content is being cannibalized by blogs and other free Web alternatives or because its advertising lifeblood is under fire from Web alternatives, periodicals dominate less time for our customers than they have for decades. If people were not reading *Life* magazine, then they didn't Discover the products advertised there.

Increasingly, they'll Discover what their favorite blogs and search engines tell them instead.

As technology improves, everyone does more online, forcing marketers to focus their brand awareness efforts on interactive marketing. Moreover, as the younger generation ages, their purchasing power will demand that marketers accommodate younger customers' desire to live online—marketers will need to be online, too.

So customers of the future will Discover online. They already Learn online today. What about the Shop and Buy steps?

In most industries today, customers use the Web for research (the Learn step), but they clearly Buy offline. The average American searcher spends $2.56 offline for every $1 dollar spent online and 87 percent of shoppers research products online but head to the store to buy them. Apparently, something about online shopping and purchasing is lacking or else all those people completing the Learn step online would follow through the Shop and Buy steps online also. Some of this preference for offline purchase might be explained by impatience with shipping or the cost of shipping—customers want it now with no shipping fees—but we need to face the fact that the online shopping experience still leaves much to be desired.

In the future, the Shop and Buy steps will increasingly be completed online, as technological advances remake the online shopping experience to be more social and more interactive—transforming today's analytical online shopping into a more emotional experience that offline shoppers will enjoy.

Clearly today's online shopping experience lacks the intensely social possibilities of its offline counterpart. Marketers of the future will provide more opportunities for customers to interact with each other when shopping online. Someday, customers looking at your site will have the option of online chat with other shoppers examining that same merchandise—or maybe just with their friends on a virtual shopping trip. They could answer each others' questions and swap opinions. If that starts to sound like more of a MySpace-style social network than today's e-commerce experience, you're not the only one who has thought of that.

Marc Andreesen, the one-time wunderkind of Netscape browser fame, is now running Ning, a company that sets up private social networks. Will they catch on? No one knows, but many companies might like a branded social networking experience tailored to their particular target markets. Today's public social networks are relegated to the Discover step, but a branded social network could be geared to customer relationships across the Web Conversion Cycle.

Some pioneers are showing the way, even today, to our private social networking future. Webkinz is a branded social network for children who own one of their $10 plush toys. Each toy comes with a code the child can use to create an avatar representation of that toy in the Webkinz virtual world. Webkinz has provided the ability to interact with other avatars but has provided safeguards that protect children from revealing too much information to others. Do you think that children who interact in the Webkinz social network might want more plush toys?

Your customers, too, might want to interact with a community of people outside the commerce experience, perhaps to share their thoughts on message boards while they research a purchase. They might want to see what their friends are buying or what their business colleagues are reading. The future of online shopping and purchasing will clearly include more social elements.

Beyond social features, faster networking speeds and Web 2.0 techniques (such as Ajax) will fuel more interactivity in the shopping experience itself. Two-thirds of shoppers today say they want their shopping experiences to be more interactive, with the ability to get more information about products and add them to their carts without leaving the page they're on. It won't be long before people, especially younger people, require much more.

Anyone who grew up playing the Sims game will expect a furniture retailer to offer that same kind of simulation of whatever furnishings they buy. They'll want to simulate the appearance of that couch they are considering—right there inside that image of their living room. Today, Second Life simulates an imaginary world, so why can't those same techniques simulate the real world?

Marketers will face challenges with these new Ajax interfaces. Today's Web sites can be measured by counting impressions, selections, and conversions, as discussed in Chapter 4, "Going Over to the Dark Side." In this new Ajax world, every slight move of the mouse tells a story. Today, you can collect your data and analyze it later, but Ajax interfaces generate too much data to collect it all. Web analytics expert Avinash Kaushik says the new interfaces demand that you "decide up front what you want to collect," which means you'll need to know in advance which metrics you want to analyze. Because you already know how to think about metrics, you'll be more prepared than most to handle this shift when it happens.

Advances in technology will provide a more sensory and more intense online experience that packs a bigger emotional punch—perhaps more similar to a gaming experience than anything we associate with interactive marketing today. In turn, that will prompt more people to spend even more time doing even more things online. And marketers will be there every step of the way.

As more and more people participate, they'll also have higher expectations for the experience—they'll require that it be personalized.

More Context

As customers spend more time online, they'll come to expect smarter experiences based on their personal preferences, rather than the anonymous interactions taken for granted today. Customers will want marketers to understand the context in which they approach you.

Customers will demand much more from their interactive marketing experiences than they get today. They'll expect that you'll recognize them when they come, that you'll know what they've bought from you before, and that you'll use that information to interact with them. Amazon and other excellent Web experiences do that today. As discussed in Chapter 5, "The New Customer Relations," there's no question customers will demand that from many more marketers in the future.

The tougher question is, "What *more* will customers expect?"

They might want their past interactions with multiple Internet marketers to form a *context* for future interactions—a context formed from more than just their interactions with you. No matter what any individual marketer knows about a customer, combining the information from several different marketers—a banner ad network, a search engine, and a retailer, for example—would provide a much more complete picture of customers that can be used to improve relevance.

So customers might expect you to know that they have been searching for a new car for three weeks when they arrive at your site. They might want you to know that they started out not knowing which car they wanted, but now know they want a hybrid sedan. Customers might desire that you know these things so that you can provide a more relevant experience that saves them time and money.

Clearly, understanding that kind of context requires sharing among multiple marketers—a search engine, perhaps some car research sites, and finally the auto manufacturer. That kind of context sharing will require customer approval—sharing that information would otherwise violate customer privacy. But customers might want to share their information to obtain a better, more relevant experience.

If marketers prove trustworthy in the ways they use information—creating more relevant offers rather than interrupting people with spam—customers might decide to share more information with them. Certainly, some customers will want privacy, and nearly all customers will prefer to make some of their purchases anonymously, but many customers might allow the sharing of information when it benefits them. Customers will likely choose to share information with only certain marketers that they trust—the ones that save them money or, more likely, time. Think about how valuable it will be for you to possess that kind of relationship with your customers. Let's look at how such information can make your marketing more relevant.

Even today, search engines are toying with *personalized search*, providing different results for the same search words to different people. They've long known where searchers are located, allowing them to show different results to people in different places, but they are now extending beyond simple geography into demographics and more.

How do search engines know which searchers are women over 65? They need searchers to tell them. That's why Google, Microsoft, Yahoo!, and other search engines are racing to provide services that entice searchers to identify themselves. When people register with one of these companies, they might provide demographic information that the search engines can use to personalize searches.

If your customer has a Google account, for example, Google knows the customer's Web history, maybe even the contents of e-mails (through Gmail), and increasingly knows which Web pages have been visited (through the Google toolbar and Google Analytics). Google might also know what your customer has bought (through Google Analytics and Google Checkout). This information can form a powerful context for marketing, if customers permit Google to share it with marketers.

To take another search example, Microsoft today sells paid search clicks for higher prices when the customers fit desirable demographics. With demographic targeting, marketers can raise their bids for searchers based on gender, age, or other characteristics. So you can raise your normal per-click bid three percent for women over 65, if that's your highest-converting market segment.

But when those customers click through to your site, you don't know anything else about them, even though Microsoft might. Microsoft might know where they live or what other searches they've performed recently, but it can't tell you without the customers' permission.

How much more could Microsoft charge per click if they had permission from the customer to pass more information to you? Microsoft would make more money, you could prepare more targeted (higher converting) messages, and customers would see more relevant offers. Everyone wins. Securing that kind of permission requires that customers trust Microsoft and trust the other marketers to use the information to the customer's benefit. Increased use of mobile devices will add even more context. Customers might be willing to reveal their geographic location to marketers in return for relevance. Would loyal Starbucks customers want to be able to press a button on their cell phones or on their car dashboard displays to indicate they were ready for another cup of coffee?

By revealing their location, customers could then be directed to the closest Starbucks. Perhaps if Starbucks discounted each cup for these loyal customers, they'd give up that aspect of their privacy. If customers permitted it, perhaps Dunkin' Donuts would send an offer for a free cup of coffee when their store is closer than the nearest Starbucks. We will all be experimenting to find out what customers want in return for permission—and we'll test how much more relevant we can make the offers as a result.

Some of these ideas, broadly called *behavioral targeting*, are being experimented with today. As an example, Snoop Dog Care might buy banner ads from an advertising network. Whenever a customer clicks one of Snoop's ads, but does not make a purchase, a cookie is left on the customer's computer noting that fact.

Snoop can then target that particular customer with a new banner ad, perhaps one that offers a discount on the price of that same product. The ad network can then show that targeted banner ad whenever the customer visits a site within the ad network. (And the ad network can charge a lot more for that targeted ad than for the original banner ad.)

Yahoo! has introduced SmartAds, which use customer behavior to personalize banner ads. For example, if a registered Yahoo! user is known to live in Detroit, but frequently checks the New York Yankees page on Yahoo! Sports or the Yankees message board on Yahoo! Groups, he might be shown ads for Yankee merchandise, because he is assumed to be a fan of that baseball team. If one day he searches for tickets to a particular Yankees game, he might then be shown ads for flights and hotel accommodations to New York around that date. Think about how much more behavioral targeting could be possible if customers someday permit marketers to share customer context with each other. Because the offers would be far more relevant, customers might provide such permission for marketers to snoop at what they are doing.

Customers could benefit from shared context in other ways, beyond relevant offers, as they begin to connect to the Internet more and more—at work and at home through computers, through their cell phones, their MP3 players, in their car, and through methods we've not even thought of yet. Customers might want an experience that recognizes them as the same person no matter what device they are using. An anonymous Internet won't pull that off.

All this added context leads to more relationship-building with your customers. Marketers dealing with younger, more connected customers are already noticing. Snack maker Frito-Lay, in targeting 16- to 24-year-olds, is building relationships by emphasizing authenticity and relevance. They're employing social media marketing campaigns which challenge customers to create their own marketing messages for Doritos tortilla chips. As this new generation of customers flexes its purchasing muscles, all marketers will be forced to address these issues.

As more people participate and expect the experience to be tailored to them, the relationship with your company can become embedded into many aspects of the customer's life. You would no longer be merely a Web site to them or just a product they use once a day. A successful product or service will become a part of your customer's life—it becomes *integrated*. How will your product fit into your customer's daily life?

More Integration

Web feeds, such as RSS (and e-mail before that), are part of a new wave of information integration—content that is part of your customer's daily experience. Just as marketers have always depended on television and radio to slip their messages into a customer's day, now Web feeds can do the same. More than ever, interactive content will come to your customer just as offline messages do today.

But because the customer subscribes to the feed and could cancel if unhappy, the marketing message must be far more subdued—the softest of soft sells. To reach busy, hard-to-reach people, you must make it easy for them to consume the content they want, when and where they want it. Sun's Curt Sasaki notes, "We may have zero people coming to sun.com [someday] because they subscribe. We want to make sure all of our content is subscribable."

Because those customers use feed readers to closely control both *what* they see and *when* they see it, it's challenging (as we saw in Chapter 4) to know exactly which content they actually looked at. Depending on how technology advances, it might become harder yet. You might have heard of the concept called the *Semantic Web*, in which software can understand the meaning of content. Such software would allow customers to take in thousands of feeds and have the most relevant information extracted for viewing. It's possible that you might not know whether your message was seen. You might even have to pay customers to read them.

Semantic software might put pressure on marketers in other ways. If your customers prefer messages that are "real"—rather than bombastic—a semantic filter might serve as a "hype meter," eliminating anything a bit too "sales-y." Google's Eric Schmidt has spoken about developing a "truth detector" that discerns the honesty of politicians, so marketers might not be far behind.

At some point, as John Batelle points out in *The Search*, the information (or even the products) that searchers are looking for can start to find *them*, rather than the other way around, just as if your customer's wish list was one big Google Alert. Customers could register their interests and let the right information and products come to them. Similarly, Peter Morville's seminal book, *Ambient Findability*, describes how every object in the world (and every piece of information) must be designed with findability in mind. In such a world, marketing messages find the people that are interested in them—so you'd better create an interesting message.

This concept of integration goes far beyond the idea that content finds your customer, however. The more you can integrate your marketing to the customer's task at hand, the more relevant and the less intrusive it will seem.

Let's look at an example from offline marketing to see where online marketing can go. A friend of mine is a wholesale distribution consultant. Guess where he works? For a commercial real estate company. Yeah, I scratched my head when he told me that, too.

His company advertises consulting services to optimize distribution costs for manufacturers and their suppliers. As my buddy works his way through each consulting engagement, he pays careful attention to the warehouses. Inevitably, any company that has paid little attention to their distribution costs is using an antiquated warehouse facility that wastes both space and energy costs. Almost always, the old warehouse is not designed to be easily adaptable to changes in the distribution processes—the very types of changes such a consultant recommends to solve their problems.

Before you know it, the friendly distribution consultant is pitching the idea of relocating the customer's warehouses to more modern facilities: "We have a few right here that I can show you. Let me run the numbers for you to prove how much you'll save."

How many of these customers do you think will say to my friend, "Gee, that's a great idea, but we'll go buy a new warehouse with a different real estate firm?" That's right, none. Not every client gets a new warehouse, but every one that does uses the consultant's real estate firm to do it.

More and more, this is the way business is headed. When you integrate your marketing with real problems that your customer need solved, even when they seem outside your traditional industry, that's when you develop a powerful value proposition that differentiates you from your competitors.

Increasingly, technology will make these new integrations possible. Close your eyes and imagine the possibilities in *your* industry. Oh, uh, I guess you had to open your eyes again to keep reading. Anyway, here are some things to get your brain in gear:

- Refrigerators that order groceries to be delivered
- Printers that order their own supplies
- Cars that make their own service appointments
- Electronic calendars and organizers that make travel plans

None of these ideas are original, but in the next few years, they might just become possible, as sensor technology and Internet connections become universal. I'm not sure that I believe my fridge will replenish itself, but the business model is powerful. Just as with the realtor who sells supply chain consulting, the grocery store whose service is sold with that refrigerator gets a locked-in customer because it is so convenient. That grocery store has suddenly gotten on that customer's payroll—it's become a regular monthly bill, just like a utility.

How do you get permission to be on the payroll? How do you become a company that can make transactions without explicit permission for each one? Integration.

You can see how B2B marketers will work their way through a similar progression from "Buy from us on our Web site" to "Buy from us on an extranet site set up just for your company" to "Order through your company's procurement system" to "Replenish as needed." You want your company on the receiving end of a single mindless "standing replenishment order," rather than getting stuck fighting for a positive decision on *every* tiny order. By integrating what you sell into the solution of a larger problem, you allow your customer to make you a trusted supplier. Be on the lookout for technology that offers new integration opportunities for your business.

MARKETERS GONE HIGH TECH

We've spent this whole book looking at how technology is changing marketing, but how will technology change the way marketers work every day?

Just as content will come to our customers, content will come to marketers, too. Your marketing dashboard will track all of your conversions, highlighting in-progress tests that you want to watch closely—and the conversions whose results have diverged from their norms.

Your dashboard will also show you the most important content that mentioned your company in the blogosphere or anywhere on the Web. *Sentiment analysis* filters the content so that the most positive and the most negative mentions can be clipped for you to read.

Excerpts of customer comments from your online market research will be shown to you, noting two very promising new product ideas from customers.

Your marketing dashboard will be available to you whenever you want, wherever you are, alerting you to urgent conditions as they occur, such as a significantly lower replenishment order from your best customer. Your dashboard will automatically take actions in certain situations using responses you've already approved, such as increasing today's paid search budget because conversion rates are higher than normal.

The technology to perform each of these feats exists today, but few marketers have access to such time-saving automation. Stay tuned and watch that change.

You'll see many other kinds of changes, for sure, but more *participation*, more *context*, and more *integration* are three trends that you can get a head start on now. Think ahead about how these kinds of changes might affect your marketing so that you are more prepared as they happen.

Next, we see how you'll know when they occur.

How Do You Keep Up?

If this book was about accounting, it could have been researched and written within a year without becoming out of date. Not so a book on marketing.

During the year that I wrote the manuscript, I had to constantly go back to each chapter, updating it based on new events with new tactics emerging. Once I was finished, it took another five months to publish and distribute it.

So I could have been depressed about the fact that this book was out of date the first day it was on sale—but that's not my style.

Instead, I'd rather create resources that will help you stay up to date, resources that I can update every day because they are on the Web. So you can use this book for the basics and use the Web to stay in touch with the latest trends.

Or you can take the attitude of Albert Einstein, who once said, "I never think of the future. It comes soon enough." Well, if we were as smart as Einstein, we might be able to get away with that. Most of us, however, need some help to stay abreast of the fast pace of change in online marketing.

I've created a section on my Web site designed to provide you the resources you need to keep up with the changes in interactive marketing (at www.mikemoran.com/resources). Here's what you'll find there:

- **My Biznology newsletter and blog**—Subscribe to a once-per-month newsletter or to a more-frequent blog message to get my take on what's going on in Internet marketing. If you liked this book, you'll probably like Biznology because a good chunk of this book actually started as Biznology content.

- **Case studies**—You've come across many case study anecdotes in this book. At my Web site, you'll find expanded versions of many of these cases. I'd love for you to contribute your own case studies so that we can all learn from each other.

- **Checklists**—Many simple interactive marketing tasks can be improved by following a routine that frees you to concentrate on the creative side of marketing.

- **Skinflint guides**—If you really have no money to spend on marketing, don't fret. The Internet is the best place for free marketing ever invented. Find out how much you can do for nothing.

- **Reference materials**—First off, you'll find a list of all the reference materials used to research this book. So if I said that 42 percent of customers want something, I've included that citation on my Web site, so you can read about it more. You'll also see a list of every other book mentioned in these pages, along with my capsule review. Be sure to check out the blogroll of the best Internet marketing blogs as well as the list of other Web resources.

You'll find that this book has given you some information to get started—I hope my Web site will point you at the resources you need to keep you going in the right direction.

Summary

So you've reached the end—well, the end of this book anyway. It's just the beginning of your new role as a Millennium Marketer. Now it's time to put the words into action.

More than anything you learned in this book, the most important lesson is to use your own judgment, to test everything you do with customers, and to respond to their feedback. Your wisdom in your particular situation will be better than any prescription you found in this book—I'd love to hear from you when you find something wrong here so that I can fix it. After all, I didn't invent these ideas—they were invented by marketers unafraid to experiment with something new. As you do that, you'll invent the future of marketing, too.

We spent this whole chapter talking about the future. For some of us who are still trying to cope with the changes we've seen already, the thought of an even faster pace of change is a bit scary. But take heart in the words of American Vice President Dan Quayle, who assures us that "The future will be better tomorrow." (Or maybe it will be *here* tomorrow. Uh, never mind.)

In this chapter, we looked at how marketers can think about the future:

- **How do you cope with change?**—Remind yourself that many things you know are not changing—the laws of marketing have not been repealed. And remember that by thinking about what your business needs and about what your customers need, you can put into perspective any change that comes along.

- **What's changing?**—More customers will participate in the Internet world, performing more tasks online than ever before—exposing them to more online marketing messages. You will also have more contextual understanding about these customers than ever before. Marketing is becoming more integrated into real life, rather than remaining an interruption in your customer's day.

- **How do you keep up?**—While the Internet has posed a challenge to marketers by forcing change in the way marketing is conducted, it also provides the information for us to adapt. Start with the resources on my Web site (www.mikemoran.com/resources) and go from there. And remember that it will be easier to keep up than it was to learn the basics in this book in the first place.

So what's the modern marketer to do?

Spend as much time paying attention as getting attention. That means that you still need to dress in your bunny suit to attract attention, but you'll need to do more than that. You must embrace your inner bunny.

Use your big bunny ears and sharp rabbit eyesight to pay attention to what your customers are saying and doing. Become both a good listener and an impartial observer so that your actions reflect customer feedback.

And, like bunnies, we must do the math. Rabbits multiply, don't they? Oh, that's a different kind of multiplying. Regardless, we must do *that* type of multiplying too—it's up to us to produce more and more marketers who think this way. Let's lead our colleagues to do it wrong quickly even if they believe it's a hare-brained scheme.

Maybe this new trend in marketing won't be called "Millennium Marketing," or "Adaptive Marketing," or "Marketing 2.0" at all. Maybe it will be just our luck for it to be christened "Bunny Marketing."

Glossary

A

A/B testing   A simple form of user testing, so named because it pits two choices ("A" and "B") against each other to see which one performs better.

accessible Web site   A Web site designed so that customers with disabilities can use all the major features. Some countries require certain specific accessibility features by law.

action   Customer behavior that ultimately results in a Web conversion, sometimes the purchase of your product. Typically used in "call to action" to describe copy written to induce a conversion and in "cost per action" to describe the fee for each successful conversion.

adaptive change   A behavior modification that requires internal, transformative changes, in contrast to the easier *technical* changes that require external behavior changes only.

advertising agency   A company that helps clients plan and purchase promotional announcements. *Interactive* agencies handle e-mail, banner ads, search, and other electronic promotions. *Traditional* ad agencies cover TV, radio, and print media but might cover interactive media, too.

adware   A more benign form of *spyware*, where the customer (often unwittingly) downloads a program that shows advertising while the computer is being used.

affiliate   A Web marketer that is compensated for sending Web visitors to an e-commerce site (the *merchant*) that pays a commission for every lead that results in a sale. In the Amazon Associates affiliate marketing program, the associate is the affiliate, and Amazon is the merchant.

affiliate marketing   A technique of marketing and selling products in which a Web site (the *affiliate*) directs Web visitors to another site (the *merchant*) and is compensated with a commission for the visitors' purchases.

agile development method   A process for developing software characterized by intensive teamwork between business and technical personnel, fast turnaround of requirements, and constant testing so that the software is almost always working. Agile development methods are a key part of doing things wrong quickly—it facilitates quick experimentation.

Ajax   Like Flash, Ajax is a form of rich media that can respond to mouse-over actions as well as to clicks, so an Ajax user experience within a Web browser can seem just as interactive as one within a desktop computer application.

astroturfing   An unethical marketing technique used to plant negative stories and comments without revealing their origin, in the hopes of fooling customers into believing the information comes from an unbiased source. "Astroturfing" is so named because it is a "fake grass roots" uprising. The situation resembles a public outcry against a company when it is actually carefully staged by an interested party, usually a competitor.

Atom   A form of *Web feed*, similar to *RSS*, which delivers subscribed information from an information provider (such as a marketer) to a feed reader.

audience   A Web term analogous to *market segment* in offline marketing that describes a particular group that a Web site's message is targeted to. Audiences are broader than market segments because they reach beyond customers. Typical Web site audiences include stock analysts, the media, and distribution channels, as well as each of their customer market segments.

authenticating e-mail   A technique that protects Internet users from some kinds of spam. E-mail marketers should become familiar with authentication so that they are identified as trusted senders.

authority   The perceived expertise level of a Web site, as measured by its network of inbound hypertext links. Search engines typically place great importance on sites that have many inbound links from other well-linked sites and place those sites at the top of search results for queries on subjects that match the site's subjects.

authority page   A Web page that has many links to it on a certain subject.

B

B2B   Business-to-Business, one business (the marketer) that sells to another business, in contrast to *Business-to-Consumer (B2C)* businesses.

B2C   Business-to-Consumer, a business (the marketer) that sells to consumers, in contrast to *Business-to-Business (B2B)* sellers.

back links   Also known as *inbound links*, the hypertext links from a page *to* your page. Inbound links to your page from outside your site are highly valued by search engines performing link analysis when they rank search results by relevance.

banner ad   Also known as a *display ad*, a promotional message, typically presented as a large colorful rectangle in a prominent part of the page, analogous to an advertisement in a newspaper or a magazine. Clicking a banner ad takes the visitor to the Web site of the sponsor of the ad.

behavior model   An abstract embodiment of the activities of a group of people performing a task that is used to measure and analyze what they are doing. This analysis can suggest improvements to the process being followed for the task.

behavioral characteristic   A quality of a market segment based on how its members act. For example, customers who rarely use a product might be placed in a different segment than those who use the product every day. That way, marketers can provide different information to each segment based on the behavioral characteristic of usage.

behavioral targeting   A marketing technique that selects particular customers based on previous actions to receive special marketing messages. For example, a banner ad network might target customers who have not made recent purchases to be shown a different offer than those that are regular customers.

bid   The price paid to a paid search engine for each referral to secure a ranking in paid search results. In its simplest form, paid search results show a link to the highest bidder's page at the top of the list, and that bidder pays the bid price to the paid search engine each time a visitor clicks the bidder's link.

bid management   The technique used by search marketers to track and control the prices they pay to paid search engines to have their pages listed. Bid management is crucial for large paid search campaigns comprising multiple search keywords over several paid search engines, usually performed with software tools that automate bids based on constraints chosen by the search marketers.

bid management software   A program that automatically adjusts the prices paid for each click in paid search campaigns based on constraints provided by search marketers.

blog   Short for "Web log," an online personal journal, a kind of a periodic column on the Web. Some blogs are reminiscent of a private diary, but others resemble magazine columns focused on a particular subject of interest.

blogosphere   The collective opinion of the totality of all blog posts and all comments in response.

bookmark   Also known as a *favorite*, the browser function that enables surfers to store the URLs of a Web pages so they can return at a later time.

bounced e-mail   E-mail that is returned to the sender because it cannot be delivered, due to an invalid e-mail address or some other reason.

brand awareness   A measurement of the degree to which potential customers think of a certain company, product, or service when they have a need for it. Marketing campaigns are often focused on increasing brand awareness, which is typically measured with surveys assessing brand recognition or unprompted naming of brands.

brick-and-mortar retailer   The Web-savvy name for a traditional physical store, to contrast it from a Web retailer.

browser   The program that a Web site visitor uses to view and navigate the Web site, such as Microsoft's Internet Explorer.

bulletin   A private message posted for a MySpace user from another.

business rule   A constraint placed on the way software behaves in an attempt to automate the decisions that emulate what a smart person would do under the circumstances. For example, a marketer can create a business rule that causes the system to suggest the purchase of an extended warranty whenever a high-priced technology product is placed in the shopping cart.

C

call to action   The sales term for the message that causes the prospective customer to do something that closes a sale or gets them closer to a sale. Web pages that ask you to "add to cart" or "sign up for an e-mail newsletter" contain calls to action.

campaign   A marketing term for a marketing effort of relatively short duration with specific goals for success. A search marketing campaign might last a few months, during which specific keywords might be targeted for paid search, with success measured by the number of sales made from visitors referred by the paid search engines.

card sort   A method of soliciting feedback by asking customers to rank ideas or nomenclature from most to least important.

Cascading Style Sheet (CSS)   A set of formatting instructions for each tag in an HTML file that can be customized so that the same tagged file can be formatted in different ways with different style sheets.

click   The action that Web users take with their mouse to navigate to a new page. Web metrics programs capture all visitor clicks for measurement and analysis.

clickthrough   The Web metrics term for visitors clicking a link and navigating to a new page. In Web marketing, clickthrough rates of links can show marketers the effectiveness of copy, design, and navigation of Web sites and of other marketing tactics.

clickthrough rate   The Web metrics term for the ratio of visitors seeing a link versus clicking that link and navigating to a new page. In Web marketing, clickthrough rates can show marketers the effectiveness of copy, design, and navigation of Web sites and of other marketing tactics.

cloaking   Also known as *IP delivery*, a technique by which a spammer, for the same URL, designs a program to return one page for human visitors and a different version of the page for a search engine's spider—one full of keywords designed to attain a high search ranking. The term *cloaking* originated from the way site owners blocked visitors from viewing their HTML code to reveal their search optimization secrets.

cognitive therapy   A branch of psychology that helps people to identify their beliefs and examine them to see if they are true. When their beliefs are holding people back, they can dispute their beliefs with rationality to help bring about behavior change.

color blindness   Also known as *color deficiency*, it causes people to perceive some colors differently, especially those containing shades of red and green.

color deficiency   Also known as *color blindness*, it causes people to perceive some colors differently, especially those containing shades of red and green.

color vibration   A fatigue-producing condition where adjacent objects with clashing colors seem to vibrate.

community   A group of people sharing information about a particular subject. Marketers can take advantage of communities to answer their customers' questions and provide them with more reasons to remain loyal to the product.

company culture   Also known as *corporate culture* or *organizational culture*, a sociological term describing the environmental climate and behavior of people at work.

consumer-generated content   Also known as *user-generated content*, any information created by the customers themselves, rather than by the marketer. Amazon reviews, blog comments, and many other customer contributions comprise consumer-generated content.

content   A Web term for the words and pictures shown on a Web page, e-mail, or another Internet marketing tactic. Web marketing frequently depends on content for attracting attention and persuading customers to follow through on a Web site.

content management system   The system software that manages the process of creation, update, approval, and publishing of Web pages to a Web site.

contextual advertising   A paid merchandising spot displayed on the same page as an article about a related subject. Yahoo! Content Match and Google AdSense are the two leading programs.

conversion   The sales term for closing a sale—*"converting* a prospect to a customer."* The traditional definition can be expanded to include *Web conversions*—any measurable, successful outcome of a Web visit—such as registering an account or donating to a cause.

conversion rate   The ratio of Web site visitors to Web orders—how many people came to the site versus how many actually purchased.

cookie   A method Web browsers use to store information that Web pages need to remember. For example, a page can store your visitors' names in cookies so that their names can be displayed on your home page each time they return.

copy   The words that appear on a Web page. Web marketing frequently depends on content for attracting attention and persuading customers to follow through on a Web site.

copywriter   The Web specialist responsible for crafting the words that appear on a Web page designed to sell products.

corporate culture   Also known as *company culture* or *organizational culture*, a sociological term describing the environmental climate and behavior of people at work.

cost per action (CPA)   A method of calculating fees whereby money is owed only when the Web visitor converts—typically by purchasing your product. CPA pricing has long been used in fixed placement or shopping searches and now is beginning to be used for paid placement search ads. CPA costs typically range from $5 to $50.

cost per click (CPC)   A method of calculating fees whereby money is owed only when the Web visitor clicks the paid placement advertisement. CPC prices range from about 10¢ (usually the lowest bid allowed) to $30 or sometimes more, with the average around $1.

cost per thousand (CPM)   A method of calculating fees whereby money is owed for each impression of an advertisement—each time it's displayed. Usually referred to as CPM (cost per thousand—M is the Roman numeral for one thousand), it is usually used for fixed-placement advertising, not bid-based advertising, and it varies from $10 to $30 per thousand impressions (or about 1¢ to 3¢ per single impression).

CPA Cost per action, a method of calculating fees whereby money is owed only when the Web visitor converts—typically by purchasing your product. CPA pricing has long been used in fixed placement or shopping searches and now is beginning to be used for paid placement search ads. CPA costs typically range from $5 to $50.

CPC Cost per click, a method of calculating fees whereby money is owed only when the Web visitor clicks through on the paid placement advertisement. CPC prices range from about 10¢ (usually the lowest bid allowed) to $30 or sometimes more, with the average around $1.

CPM Cost per thousand—M is the Roman numeral for one thousand—a method of calculating fees whereby money is owed for each impression of an advertisement— each time it's displayed. CPM is usually used for fixed-placement advertising, not bid-based advertising, and it varies from $10 to $30 per thousand impressions (or about 1¢ to 3¢ per single impression).

creative The copy written for an advertisement or other marketing message.

CSS Cascading Style Sheet, a set of formatting instructions for each tag in an HTML file that can be customized so that the same tagged file can be formatted in different ways with different style sheets.

customer lifetime value Also known as *lifetime value*, a method quantifying what each new customer is worth, not just for the first purchase but for the lifetime of purchases from that customer.

customer rating A technique for soliciting quantitative feedback for products and services in which Web visitors provide a numerical assessment of the offering's quality. Amazon's five-star rating system for books may be the most famous example of a rating system. Amazon's system solicits customer ratings and customer reviews in combination, but each can be used in isolation.

customer reviews A technique for soliciting qualitative feedback for products and services in which Web visitors provide a written assessment of the offering's quality. The textual book reviews provided by Amazon's customers may be the most famous example of a customer review system. Amazon's system solicits customer ratings and customer reviews in combination, but each can be used in isolation.

D

demographics Characteristics of the members of a target market, such as age, gender, or marital status.

destination page   A page on a Web site where it is likely that a visitor may complete a task, such as your newsletter sign-up page. Destination pages are contrasted with navigation pages, whose primary purpose is to lead visitors to other pages on your Web site where they might complete their tasks.

developer   A specialist who develops software. *Web* developers develop programs or HTML to display Web pages in your visitor's Web browser.

direct marketing   A form of marketing characterized by measurable response from the customer to a specific marketing tactic. Direct mail, catalogs, and television infomercials can all tie specific customer responses to the marketing that caused them, while brand marketing campaigns in television and other media typically cannot.

directory   A list of hundreds or thousands of subjects (such as fly fishing or needlepoint) along with links to Web sites about those subjects. Yahoo! Directory is the most famous example, but most directories are lightly used in comparison to text search technology.

directory listing   One of many hypertext links about a particular subject. Site owners submit a page to request that it be listed in the directory and say that they have a "directory listing" when their submission is accepted. Yahoo! Directory and Open Directory are the most famous examples of Web directories.

discount rate   A factor in the calculation of net present value that you can think of as the cost of money over time—such as interest rates or inflation rates.

display ad   Also known as a *banner ad*, a promotional message, typically presented as a large colorful rectangle in a prominent part of the page, analogous to an advertisement in a newspaper or a magazine. Clicking a banner ad takes the visitor to the Web site of the sponsor of the ad.

domain name   The spoken language label for an Internet Web site that can be used for Web surfing or e-mail. The domain name (dell.com) follows the "at" sign (@) in an e-mail address (michael@dell.com) and the www. in a Web URL (www.dell.com).

dynamic content   In contrast to *static pages*, a Web page or other interactive marketing message that is generated by a software program at the moment it is displayed. Dynamic content allows change based on the visitor, such as an order status screen, which contains information about that specific order. A software program must retrieve the order status for the visitor from a database and build the HTML that shows the correct information on the screen.

dynamic navigation   Links and other selectable choices on a Web page that are generated by a software program at the moment it is displayed so that it can be different for each customer interaction.

E

e-mail   Electronic mail, a method of sending and receiving messages between computer users. Marketers use e-mail as one more way to send marketing messages and accept feedback from their customers.

e-mail marketing   The use of electronic mail by marketers to send a marketing message to a customer.

e-mails opened   A measurement used to determine the number of people who actually viewed the contents of an e-mail message sent by a marketer. Some sent messages are never delivered, while others are delivered but not opened by the recipient.

eXtensible Markup Language (XML)   A standard for a markup language, similar to HTML, that allows tags to be defined to describe any kind of data you have, making it very popular as a format for data feeds.

F

facet   A characteristic of a product or service that can be selected to narrow down the remaining choices. When shown a list of camcorders, for example, customers can choose facets—their preferred price range, brand preference, media format, and optical zoom capabilities—to narrow down the list of camcorders to choose from.

feed reader   A program that customers can use to subscribe to *Web feeds*, such as RSS and Atom. Web feeds deliver subscribed information from an information provider, such as a marketer.

field   A term in database design for a certain kind of information. A payroll database would typically contain fields for employee names, addresses, and salaries, for example.

firmographics   Characteristics of companies within target markets, such as industry and number of employees. Firmographics are the B2B marketing analogue to *demographics*.

focus group   A market research technique that determines the attitudes of several members of a targeted market segment toward a marketing message or offering.

fixed placement   A technique by which a search marketer negotiates the appearance of an advertisement in a particular place on a page for a given search query, usually paying for impressions (the number of times the ad is shown), rather than for clicks.

Flash   A technology invented by Macromedia that brings a far richer user experience to the Web than drab old HTML, allowing animation and other interactive features that spice up visual tours and demonstrations.

flog   A "fake blog" in which the author of the blog hides or misrepresents his identity to mask the source of the blog's opinion. Flogs typically criticize a competitor or boost a company's own offerings without revealing the company as the obviously biased source of the point of view.

folksonomy   Also known as *social bookmarking* or *social tagging*, readers can categorize and vote for your content to alert other prospective readers of its quality, newsworthiness, or importance.

forum   Also known as a *message board* or a *news group*, a technique for multiple Web visitors to ask questions and share opinions on a particular subject. Typically, broad subjects are broken up into smaller conversations, known as *threads*, for each specific question or comment.

frequency   A measurement used by direct marketers to segment their best customers based on how often an action occurs. The more frequently an action (such as a purchase) occurs, the more likely it is to be repeated, so your most frequent purchasers are most likely to repurchase soon.

G

grid layout   A technique of aligning content for a Web page, e-mail, or other marketing message in which multiple messages of the same type have the same content in the same place. For example, Web sites that use a grid layout will have the name of the Web site, the site navigation, and the promotions in the same places on each page that shares that grid.

H

hate site   Also known as a *negative site*, a Web site whose primary purpose is to discredit another organization or Web site. These sites frequently use the name of another site with the word *sucks* appended to the domain name, such as yourdomainsucks.com.

heading   The HTML element that contains an emphasized section name that breaks up the body text.

home page   The page on a Web site that is displayed when the domain name (such as www.sony.com) is entered into the browser.

HTML   Hypertext Markup Language, the markup tagging system used to denote the precise document element of every piece of text on a Web page. For example, all paragraphs are marked with a paragraph tag, and all headings are identified with heading tags. Web browsers interpret each tag to determine how to format the text on the screen when displaying that page.

hyperlink   Also known as a *link*, a set of words, a picture, or other "hotspot" on a web page that, when clicked, takes the visitor to another Web page.

Hypertext Markup Language (HTML)   The markup tagging system used to denote the precise document element of every piece of text on a Web page. For example, all paragraphs are marked with a paragraph tag, and all headings are identified with heading tags. Web browsers interpret each tag to determine how to format the text on the screen when displaying that page.

I

image blocker   A program, often employed by e-mail providers, that prevents pictures from being displayed within e-mails. Many e-mail providers routinely block all images from being shown in e-mail to thwart those sending pornographic offers.

impression   A term derived from banner advertising that denotes each time your content is shown to someone. The number of clicks for your ad is divided by the number of impressions to derive the *clickthrough rate*.

inbound links   Also known as *back links*, the hypertext links from a page *to* your page. Inbound links to your page from outside your site are highly valued by search engines performing link analysis when they rank search results by relevance.

include file   A piece of content that can be reused on many separate pages so that you can change just one place to update the content on multiple pages.

information architect   The Web specialist who decides the navigational structure of a Web site—how information is divided into separate pages, which pages link where, what nomenclature is used on a link to ensure people know what it is, and many other tasks.

instant message   A real-time communication from one computer to another that allows people to have interactive conversations. AOL Instant Messenger is probably the most famous program that allows people to send and receive instant messages.

integrated design system   A consistent and systematic appearance for all your customer communications that provides a unified brand image.

interactive advertising agency   A company that helps clients plan and purchase online promotional announcements, such as e-mail ads, banner ads, search, and other electronic promotions.

interactive media   Electronic promotions such as e-mail, banner ads, and search, that drive visitors to your Web site. Advertising agencies often handle client purchases of interactive media.

Internet   The computer network that connects different computers enabling the Web and e-mail, among other uses.

Internet Yellow Pages   Online listings of company names, phone numbers, and addresses reminiscent of printed phone directories.

J

JavaScript   A programming language that can provide special effects inside a browser that cannot be performed in HTML.

K

keyword   A particular word or phrase that search marketers expect searchers to enter frequently as a query.

keyword research   The step in the search marketing planning process during which search marketers discover all the possible words and phrases they should target.

keyword stuffing   A spam technique by which words or phrases are overused in content merely to attract the search engines.

keyword volume   The number of times within a specific period that searchers enter a particular word or phrase.

L

landing page   The first page that a marketer expects a customer to see after responding to a marketing tactic. For example, an e-mail landing page is the one the recipient would see after clicking on the link in the e-mail message.

lead   A prospective customer passed from one business to another (or passed from one part of a company to another) who might eventually complete a transaction to become a customer. The number of leads passed is a critical measurement for businesses that cannot close a sale on the Web—they must attract interest in their products on the Web but "pass the lead" to an offline channel to continue the sales process that might culminate in a sale.

lifetime value (LTV)   Also known as *customer lifetime value*, a method quantifying what each new customer is worth, not just for the first purchase but for the lifetime of purchases from that customer.

link   Also known as a *hyperlink*, a set of words, a picture, or other "hotspot" on a web page that, when clicked, takes the visitor to another Web page.

link farm   A spam technique in which search marketers set up dozens or hundreds of sites that can be crawled by search engines, just so they can put in thousands of links to sites they want to boost in search rankings.

liquid design   A design technique that allows Web pages to dynamically change their layouts when the browser window is resized.

list management   A blanket term for a host of actions marketers take to continually update their mailing lists (their targets) to suppress opt-outs, to correct or remove bounces, and for other reasons.

list suppression   A task that falls under the general category of *list management*, in which marketers remove from their mailing lists the e-mail addresses of anyone who has opted out from being contacted again.

look and feel   A layman's term that describes how the experience looks to the customer and how it feels to use it. For the Web, it includes everything from the visual design (colors, typefaces, layout, and white space) to the way customers interact with the information (how the site responds to a mouse, how the site is navigated, and what customers are expected to know).

LTV   Lifetime value, also known as *customer lifetime value*, a method quantifying what each new customer is worth, not just for the first purchase but for the lifetime of purchases from that customer.

M

market segment   A group of customers with similar needs that receive the same marketing messages for your products. For your Web site, market segments are usually defined as *audiences* that include groups beyond your customers (stock analysts, press, and others). Your Web site messages are usually targeted to several market segments (audiences).

market segmentation   The marketing term for the activity of dividing up the pool of potential customers based on shared characteristics. So a consumer marketer might segment markets based on demographics (such as age or gender) while a business-to-business (B2B) marketer might use firmographics (such as company size or industry).

marketing communication   Any activity by which a marketer sends a marketing message to a target market. Advertising, catalogs, Web sites, and e-mail are all forms of marketing communication.

marketing impression   A measurement that counts whenever a customer saw a marketing message that drove that customer to come to your Web site. If a customer opened an e-mail and clicked on a link within the e-mail to visit your site, that action would be counted as a marketing impression.

marketing mix   The combination of ways in which you spend your marketing budget (TV, radio, print, and so on). Making a commitment to Web marketing usually implies that some other expenditure must be reduced in your marketing mix.

Marketing Performance Measurement (MPM)   A philosophy of marketing that emphasizes the use of metrics to determine the value of every marketing tactic, allowing marketing tactics to be measured as a portfolio designed to maximize return on investment.

markup   A publishing technique where text is *tagged* according to its meaning within the document so that computers can format and find the text more easily. Markup languages such as HTML allow content authors to "mark up" parts of their documents with tags denoting each document element. For example, a title tag (<title>About Our Company</title>) identifies the title of a Web page.

match   A Web page found by a search engine in response to a searcher's query. Search engines use various techniques to determine which pages match each query and then rank the pages by relevance so the best matches are presented first.

matchback system   Automated program designed to allocate credit for sales across marketing channels. By matching information known about those making purchases (such as names and addresses) with information known about those targeted with promotions, matchback systems can credit the marketing promotions likely to have influenced the sale. In this way, printed catalogs might get credit for Web sales, while e-mail marketing might be credited for in-store sales.

meme   An idea that is spread from person to person. Memes are often discussed by those engaged in viral marketing, as a way to analyze just what properties an idea should have to spread rapidly.

merchant   The party in an affiliate marketing program that actually completes the sale. For the Amazon Associates affiliate marketing program, the associate is the affiliate, and Amazon is the merchant.

message board   Also known as a *forum* or a *news group*, a technique for multiple Web visitors to ask questions and share opinions on a particular subject. Typically, broad subjects are broken up into smaller conversations, known as *threads*, for each specific question or comment.

metadata   Information that applies to an entire piece of content, such as the subject or the author of an HTML page. Information that applies to a single data element is in contrast called a *field* or a *tag*.

metrics analyst   The Web specialist responsible for compiling and reporting statistics—how many visitors come to the site, customer satisfaction survey results, the number of sales, and many more.

monetary   A measurement used by direct marketers to segment their best customers based on how large the value of their actions. The higher the value of the action, the more likely it is to be repeated, so customers with the largest orders are more likely to repurchase.

MPM   Marketing Performance Measurement, a philosophy of marketing that emphasizes the use of metrics to determine the value of every marketing tactic, allowing marketing tactics to be measured as a portfolio designed to maximize return on investment.

multifaceted search   A search technique that allows searchers to restrict the search results by responding to choices offered by the search engine. Multifaceted search allows searchers to continually narrow down their results by choosing another constraint on their search.

multivariate testing   A form of user testing, so named because it can analyze multiple combinations of content to determine the one that results in the most conversions.

N

natural search   Also known as *organic search*, the technique by which a search engine finds the most relevant matches for a searcher's query from all of the pages indexed from the Web. Natural search contrasts with *paid search*, in which bidders vie for the highest rankings by topping each others' bids.

navigation page   A page on a Web site whose primary purpose is to lead visitors to other pages on your Web site. Your home page is a navigation page, as is the main page for your best-selling product. Your navigation pages are the most-used pages on your site, but customers don't complete tasks there. Navigation pages are contrasted with *destination pages*, where they might complete their tasks.

negative site   Also known as a *hate site*, a Web site whose primary purpose is to discredit another organization or Web site. These sites frequently use the name of another site with the word *sucks* appended to the domain name, such as yourdomainsucks.com.

net present value (NPV)   A financial metric that determines the current worth of an amount of money to be received in the future. NPV allows marketers to calculate the return on investment possible for future sales caused by today's marketing expenditures.

net sales   A financial term for the money that flows to your company as revenue after deducting pricing discounts, returns, and other reductions.

news group   Also known as a *forum* or a *message board*, a technique for multiple Web visitors to ask questions and share opinions on a particular subject. Typically, broad subjects are broken up into smaller conversations, known as *threads*, for each specific question or comment.

newsletter   A free periodic communication from a company to its customers containing items of interest. Most newsletters nowadays are sent by e-mail.

NPV   Net Present Value, a financial metric that determines the current worth of an amount of money to be received in the future. NPV allows marketers to calculate the return on investment possible for future sales caused by today's marketing expenditures.

O

offline sales   Revenue from product purchases in which customers began the sales process on the Web but transacted the purchase on the phone, in person, or through some other off-Web channel.

online commerce site   A Web site that transacts sales of products, even though it might use offline distribution channels to ship the product to the customer. (*Pure online sites*, in contrast, need no physical shipment.) Examples include retailer amazon.com and competitor buy.com.

online panel   A community representative of a target market that provides feedback on marketing, products, and services using Web sites and other electronic means. Marketers can perform market research by inviting participants matching demographic or other target market characteristics to register for a Web site in which they share ideas with the company and each other to combine the best aspects of both surveys and focus groups.

open rate   The Web metrics term used to show the percentage of e-mails recipients have looked at compared to the number that were sent.

opened e-mail   The Web metrics term used to count how many e-mails have been looked at by the recipients.

opens   The Web metrics term used to count how many e-mail messages have been looked at by the recipients.

optimizing content   A search marketing term for modifying the words and pictures shown on a Web page so that search engines can more easily find that page for a relevant query.

organic search   Also known as *natural search*, the technique by which a search engine finds the most relevant matches for a searcher's query from all of the pages indexed from the Web. Organic search contrasts with *paid search*, in which bidders vie for the highest rankings by topping each others' bids.

organizational culture   Also known as *company culture* or *corporate culture*, a sociological term describing the environmental climate and behavior of people at work.

organizational psychographics   A specific form of firmographics that B2B companies use to target their market segments. Whether a firm is fast or slow at making a purchase decision is an example of organizational psychographics.

outbound link   A hypertext link *from* your page to a different page on the Web, perhaps within your site or maybe to another site.

P

page view   The Web metrics term used to count how many Web pages on a site have been viewed by individual visitors. If three people view a page once, and two people view that same page twice, that page is said to have seven page views.

paid link   A hypertext connection to a target site that has been purchased from the source site.

paid placement   The technique by which a search engine devotes space on its search results page to display links to a Web site's page based on the highest bid for that space. Most search engines distinguish paid placement results from *organic* results on its results page, but some do not.

paid search   Any service offered by a search engine in return for a fee, including paid inclusion, paid placement, and directory services.

paper test   A method of soliciting customer feedback by showing mocked-up drawings of what a campaign or Web site could look like, with none of the expense of actually building it.

per-click fee   An amount charged by search engines or other advertising sellers for each mouse click made by customers for a particular ad. Search's paid placement programs, such as Google AdWords, is the most famous example of a program based on per-click fees, known as pay-per-click advertising.

personalization   A technique that presents information to a customer based on that customer's past behavior, characteristics, or his company's characteristics. Marketers can use personalization to present the most targeted offers to each customer, raising the likelihood that an offer will be accepted. Amazon's suggestion of books you would enjoy based on those you've already purchased is probably the most well-known example of personalization.

personalized search   A technique through which a search engine provides different results for the same search words to different people based on what it knows about each searcher.

personas   A method of Web site design that uses shorthand caricatures of your real customers to help designers tailor the experience to their real needs.

phishing   An illegal impersonation of a legitimate company in an attempt to fool that company's customers with a counterfeit message. Phishers steal company names, e-mail addresses, logos, visual design, and anything else they can think of, fabricating a message asking the recipient to log into their account after clicking a link in the message. This allows the phisher to capture access to the account to enable monetary or identity theft.

podcast   An audio file downloaded from the Web and played on demand using an Apple iPod or any MP3 media player.

pop-up ad   An interactive marketing message that creates a new Web browser window, covering the window that was previously displayed. Pop-up ads are considered so annoying that most people use some kind of software to block them from appearing on their computer screens.

portal server   The system software that manages the display of Web pages for some Web sites, frequently including the use of personalization rules that dynamically choose what content to display based on what is known about the customer.

press release   A news story written by a company in the hope of getting newspapers to print it or at least to write about it.

privacy policy   A written public statement that discloses what a company will and won't do with personal information divulged by a customer.

product placement   A marketing technique that displays a product as part of a movie scene or a video game, with no overt marketing message. Product placement can help raise the "cool" factor for your product by associating it with movie and game characters loved by audiences.

profile   A computer file that stores information a company has gathered about each customer so that the customer's experience can be personalized. Personalized sites often require registration with a user identifier and password before allowing profile information to be viewed or changed.

profit   A financial term denoting the money left over from sales for use by a company after all expenses have been paid.

profit margin   A financial term, the measurement of return on the sale per item. Profit margin is calculated as (Revenue–Cost)÷Price.

programmer   The Web specialist responsible for developing the software that runs the Web site.

psychographics   A specific form of demographics that B2C companies use to target their market segments. Whether consumers are laggards or trendsetters is an example of psychographics.

pure online site   A Web site that not only transacts sales of products but also delivers products to customers without any physical shipment. Examples include stock purchases at schwab.com and music downloads at itunes.com.

Q

qualified visitor   A person coming to your Web site who is within the targeted market segments for your product—a person you are trying to attract because he is able to buy.

query   The words that a searcher types into a search engine to identify what information should be searched for. Some queries are a single word, but others can consist of multiple words and might contain search operators.

R

ranking   The technique by which a search engine sorts the matches to produce a set of search results.

ranking algorithm   The software instructions that control precisely how search matches are sorted into the order in which they are displayed on the search results page.

real   One of the "Three Rs" of Web marketing, a tone of authenticity that ought to pervade all online messages.

Really Simple Syndication (RSS)   A type of *Web feed*, a method of delivering subscribed information from an information provider (such as a marketer) to a feed reader. RSS and Atom are two popular types of Web feeds.

recency   A measurement used by direct marketers to segment their best customers based on how recently actions have been taken. The more recently an action has been taken, the sooner it is likely to recur, so those who have purchased most recently are more likely to repurchase soon.

recontact   A marketing action designed to follow up with a specific customer on an offer not accepted the first time. For example, if a customer responded to a previous offer but did not buy, a marketer could send a recontact e-mail with a sale offer for the same product a few days later.

redirect   An instruction to Web browsers to display a different URL from the one the browser requested. Redirects are used when the URL of a page has changed, but they are also used by phishers trying steal identity information.

referral   The Web metrics term for the event of a page being viewed after viewing a previous page. Web metrics systems capture the referrer URL for each page view so that referrals from particular places, such as search engines, can be counted and analyzed.

referrer   The URL of the page that a visitor came from before coming to the current page. Web metrics systems capture the referrer for each page view so that *referrals* from particular places, such as search engines, can be counted and analyzed.

relevance   1. The degree to which an organic search match is closely related to the query. A match with extremely high relevance is a candidate to be the #1 result for that query. 2. The applicability of a marketing message to a customer's situation, problem, or interest.

relevance ranking   The technique by which a search engine sorts the matches to produce a set of organic search results whose top matches most closely relate to the query. The software code that decides exactly how the relevance ranking is performed is called the *ranking algorithm* and is a trade secret for each search engine. Relevance ranking algorithms use a myriad of factors, including the location on the page that matches the query, the authority of the page (based on link analysis), the proximity of different words in the query to each other on the page, and many more.

relevant   One of the "Three Rs" of Web marketing, the degree of applicability of a marketing message to a customer's situation, problem, or interest.

response   The action that a customer takes based on a direct marketing message. For example, when a customer calls a phone number to order from a catalog mailed by a direct marketer, that phone call is a response.

responsive   One of the "Three Rs" of Web marketing, a quality of quick reaction to customer actions and communication.

return on advertising spend (ROAS) A financial term measuring the revenue impact of media expense using a formula such as Revenue ÷ Expense. Calculating the ROAS of several advertisements can help increase spending on the best ones.

return on investment (ROI) A financial term measuring the monetary impact of an investment using a formula such as Profit ÷ Cost. Projecting the ROI of several possible investments can help you choose the best one.

RFM rating A measurement used by direct marketers to segment their best customers based on Recency, Frequency, and Monetary factors. The more recently and frequently a particular customer has taken action, and the higher the monetary value of that action the more likely that action is to recur. So your best customers are those who have purchased in the recent past, multiple times, and with high order sizes.

ROAS Return on advertising spend, a financial term that measures the revenue impact of media expense using a formula such as Revenue ÷ Expense. Calculating the ROAS of several advertisements can help increase spending on the best ones.

ROI Return on investment, a financial term that measures the monetary impact of an investment using a formula such as Profit ÷ Cost. Projecting the ROI of several possible investments can help you choose the best one.

RSS Really Simple Syndication, a type of *Web feed*, similar to *Atom*, which delivers subscribed information from an information provider (such as a marketer) to a feed reader.

S

search engine marketing (SEM) All the activities designed to improve search referrals to a Web site using either organic or paid search. Search engine marketing is also known as *search marketing*.

search engine optimization (SEO) The set of techniques and methodologies devoted to improving organic search rankings (not paid search) for a Web site.

search marketing All of the activities designed to improve search referrals to a Web site using wither organic or paid search. Search marketing is also known as *search engine marketing* (SEM).

search query The words that a searcher types into a search engine to identify what information should be searched for. Some queries are a single word, but others can consist of multiple words and might contain search operators.

search result A link to a matching Web page returned by a search engine in response to a searcher's query.

search spam   Also known as *spamdexing*, unethical (but legal) techniques undertaken by a Web site designed to fool organic search engines to display its pages, even though they are not truly the best matches for a searcher's query.

search term   One word or phrase from the search query. Words enclosed in double quotation marks (the phrase operator) are treated as a single search term, but other words are treated as individual single-word terms.

search toolbar   A program used to enter search queries on your browser screen without first going to a search engine's Web site.

searcher   The Web user who enters a query into the input box of a search engine and requests that a search be performed.

selection   A measurement that counts how often an item was chosen, usually by a mouse click but sometimes by a mouseover or other method.

self segmentation   The way the interactive selection capabilities of the Web allow customers to divide themselves into target market segments. Marketers can provide product choices or message choices that customers select so that they see the right information for them.

SEM   Search engine marketing, the activities designed to improve search referrals to a Web site using either organic or paid search. Search engine marketing is also known as *search marketing*.

Semantic Web   A concept of the future of the Web that allows some of the meaning of the information encoded in Web content to be understood and processed by software programs. The semantic Web will allow programs to take actions on behalf of people according to rules that those people set. For example, using the semantic Web, a customer could instruct software to purchase a plane ticket for a vacation when its price drops to the right level.

sentiment analysis   An automated method of characterizing customer feedback as positive or negative in tone.

SEO   Search engine optimization, the set of techniques and methodologies devoted to improving organic search rankings (not paid search) for a Web site.

server   A computer (or a program running on a computer) that responds to a client program's request. For example, a Web server responds to its client, a Web browser.

session   Synonymous with a *visit*, a Web metrics term for a single series of pages viewed from a single Web site. If a visitor comes to a Web site and views five pages before leaving to go to a new site, the metrics system logs five page views but just one session.

site map   A page consisting of links to the rest of your Web domain. For a small site, your site map can have direct links to every page on your site. Medium-to-large sites use site maps with links to major hubs within the domain (which in turn allow eventual navigation to every page on the site).

sneezers   People with huge social networks who are constantly spreading ideas. Sneezers are ideal targets for viral marketers for ideas for their campaigns.

snippet   The short paragraph that a search engine generates under the title (on the results page) to display the relevant passages on the page for the query.

social bookmarking   Also known as *folksonomy* or *social tagging*, readers can categorize and vote for your content to alert other prospective readers of its quality, newsworthiness, or importance.

social computing   Sometimes known as *social media*, a way of using technology to enable connections between people. Blogs, wikis, social networks, and social bookmarking are all examples of social computing.

social media   Sometimes known as *social computing*, a way of using technology to enable connections between people. Blogs, wikis, social networks, and social bookmarking are all examples of social computing.

social network   1. A group of people that an individual knows and passes ideas to, which viral marketers rely on. 2. A Web site such as MySpace, FaceBook, or LinkedIn, where people post profiles of themselves and connect with (offline or online) friends and colleagues. Depending on the site, profiles can be private (seen only by those invited by the owner) or public (viewable by any member of the networking site).

social tagging   Also known as *folksonomy* or *social bookmarking*, readers can categorize and vote for your content to alert other prospective readers of its quality, newsworthiness, or importance.

spam   1. Unsolicited illegal e-mail, usually containing a sales pitch or a fraudulent scheme offered to the recipient without permission. 2. Also known as *spamdexing*, unethical (but legal) techniques undertaken by a Web site designed to fool organic search engines to display its pages, even though they are not truly the best matches for a searcher's query.

spam filter   A software program designed to stop unwanted e-mails from reaching inboxes. E-mail marketers must test their outbound messages to assure that they are delivered properly.

spamdexing   Also known as *search spam*, unethical (but legal) techniques undertaken by a Web site designed to fool organic search engines to display its pages, even though they are not truly the best matches for a searcher's query.

spider   Also known as a *crawler*, the part of a search engine that locates and indexes every page on the Web that is a possible answer to a searcher's query. Successful search engine marketing depends on spiders finding almost all the pages on a Web site.

splog   A "spam blog" that is created for the sole purpose of fabricating links to other Web sites the spammer wishes to improve in search rankings.

spyware   Software that takes control of some or all functions of a computer without the knowledge of the computer's user. Some unethical marketers use spyware to collect information about customers without their consent.

static content   Information, such as a Web page, whose data is stored in a file for display. Static content typically does not change based on the visitor—it looks the same to each person who views it—in contrast to *dynamic* content.

statistical significance   A concept from the field of statistics indicating that a result is unlikely to have occurred at random—there is some assumed correlation between the test and its result.

style sheet   A set of formatting instructions for each tag in an HTML or XML file that can be customized so that the same tagged file can be formatted in different ways with different style sheets.

subscriber   A person who has requested to regularly receive a content delivery, such as an e-mail newsletter or a blog's Web feed.

subscription   The relationship between a content provider and a regular content recipient in which the recipient requests periodic delivery of a type of content, such as an e-mail newsletter, which continues until the recipient cancels.

syndication   A method of delivering content using a Web feed, such as RSS or Atom.

T

tag   1. A method of marking text in a document with its meaning so that computers can format and find the text more easily. Markup languages such as HTML allow content authors to "mark up" parts of their documents with tags denoting each document element. For example, the title tag (<title>About Our Company</title>) identifies the title of a Web page. 2. A social bookmarking label that identifies the subject of a piece of content. For example, readers of a Web page about Cadillac automobiles might use del.icio.us to set and share bookmarks (links) named "Cadillac," "autos," or "cars."

technical change   A routine behavior modification that requires merely external changes, in contrast to the more challenging *adaptive* changes that require internal, transformative changes.

template   A computer file that provides a framework or structure to multiple Web pages, e-mails, or other pieces of content. Dynamic Web pages, for example, allow changes to a single template to effect the structure of many pages on a Web site.

term   One word or phrase from the search query. Words enclosed in double quotation marks (the phrase operator) are treated as a single search term, but other words are treated as individual single-word terms.

thread   A specific question or conversation within a forum, message board, or news group.

tiered globalization   An approach for managing content for multiple countries that assigns each country to a level that defines how much content is translated. Countries that produce high sales might be fully translated, while the lowest tier countries might have just the home page and a few high-level navigation pages in native language (with the rest possibly in English).

title   The headline that entices customers to read the full piece of content.

title tag   An element of an HTML document that stores the main heading of the entire page, which will be used on the title bar or bookmarks for its page.

toolbar   A program that adds a function on your browser screen you can execute without having to first navigate to a Web site. A search toolbar, for example, allows Web users to enter search queries without first going to a search engine's Web site.

traditional advertising agency   A company that helps clients plan and purchase promotional announcements for TV, radio, and print media but might cover interactive media, too.

trackback   A comment a blogger makes about someone else's blog, except the comment is actually stored in the blogger's own blog, with a link to it from the blog commented on.

traffic   The Web metrics term to describe the number of visits to a Web site. Web metrics reports will frequently analyze increases or decreases in traffic.

U

UCD   User Centered Design, the practice of creating online customer experiences around the needs of the customers. UCD begins at the earliest conception of the project, extending all the way to user testing and deployment.

Uniform Resource Locator (URL)   The address of a Web page that a visitor can enter into a browser to display that page. For example, www.bn.com is the URL of the Barnes & Noble home page.

unique visitor   Synonymous with *visitor*, a Web metrics term for a person who visits a Web site at least once in a period of time. If the same person came to a Web site three times in one month, the metrics system would log three visits for that month, but just one unique visitor.

URL   Uniform Resource Locator, the address of a Web page that a visitor can enter into a browser to display that page. For example, www.bn.com is the URL of the Barnes & Noble home page.

usability engineer   An expert in human learning and behavior responsible for the process that creates online experiences around the needs of customers.

use case   A detailed depiction of each step that your customers take to complete a task—a task such as buying your product.

User-Centered Design (UCD)   The practice of creating online customer experiences around the needs of the customers. UCD begins at the earliest conception of the project, extending all the way to user testing and deployment.

user experience   The total environment a Web visitor is exposed to that shapes satisfaction with each visit to a site, including content, visual design, navigation, and technology.

user-generated content   Also known as *consumer-generated content*, any information created by the customers themselves, rather than by the marketer. Amazon reviews, blog comments, and many other customer contributions comprise consumer-generated content.

user testing   A method for soliciting feedback in which real customers sit down in front of your Web site and try to complete their tasks, with varying degrees of success.

V

vidcast   Also known as a *video podcast* or a *vodcast*, a video file downloaded from the Web and played on demand using an Apple video iPod or any video MP3 media player.

video podcast   Also known as a *vidcast* or a *vodcast*, a video file downloaded from the Web and played on demand using an Apple video iPod or any video MP3 media player.

visit   Synonymous with *session*, a Web metrics term for a single series of pages viewed from a single Web site. If a visitor comes to a Web site and views five pages before leaving to go to a new site, the metrics system logs five page views, but just one visit.

visitor Synonymous with *unique visitor*, a Web metrics term for a person who visits a Web site at least once in a period of time. If the same person came to a Web site three times in one month, the metrics system would log three visits for that month, but just one visitor.

visual design The appearance, often called the look and feel, of a Web page, including page layouts, colors, fonts, images, icons, and buttons.

vodcast Also known as a *vidcast* or a *video podcast*, a video file downloaded from the Web and played on demand using an Apple video iPod or any video MP3 media player.

W

waterfall development method A software development process that consists of a set of steps in which the end product is documented in more and more detailed fashion until it is finally built and tested.

Web Known formally as the World Wide Web, an interlinked network of pages that display content or allow interaction between the Web *visitor* and the organization that owns the *Web site*.

Web analytics Also called *Web metrics*, the measurement, research, and reporting of Web activity by customers and other Web site visitors.

Web 2.0 A name made popular by Internet expert Tim O'Reilly to connote the next generation of Web usage that provides more interaction and participation rather than passive consumption of information and products. *Social media*, *consumer-generated content*, and other trends are all considered part of the larger Web 2.0 trend.

Web application server The system software that executes the programs that run a Web site. Web application servers, also know as application servers, are typically used to display dynamic pages.

Web conversion Any measurable, successful outcome of a Web visit—such as registering an account or donating to a cause—based on the behavior model developed for the Web site's specific goals.

Web Conversion Cycle A behavior model that describes what visitors do when they come to your Web site and that helps you count your successes as Web conversions.

Web conversion rate The ratio of Web site visitors to Web conversions—how many people came to the site versus how many successfully achieved the goal (buy the product, sign up for a newsletter, fill out contact information, and so forth).

Web designer   The Web specialist responsible for the visual appearance of the page, frequently handling the HTML templates and style sheets used.

Web developer   A Web specialist who develops programs or HTML to display Web pages in your visitor's Web browser.

Web feed   A technique that delivers subscribed information from an information provider (such as a marketer) to a feed reader. Really Simple Syndication (RSS) and Atom are two popular types of Web feeds.

Web log   1. A file on your Web server that serves as a record of every action the server has taken. Log files can be analyzed in complex ways to determine the number of visits to your site (by people and by search engine spiders) and the number of pages that they view. 2. Also known as a *blog*, an online personal journal, a kind of a periodic column on the Web. Some blogs are reminiscent of a private diary, but others resemble magazine columns focused on a particular subject of interest.

Webinars   Online Web seminars usually delivered as a set of slides with a voiceover by phone to a remote audience interested in a certain topic. Marketers often use free Webinars directed at interest areas for members of their target markets in order to identify leads.

Webmaster   The Web specialist responsible for planning and operating the servers that display Web pages when visitors arrive.

Web metrics   Also called *Web analytics*, the measurement, research, and reporting of Web activity by customers and other Web site visitors.

Web page   A combination of text and pictures, often augmented by software, that allows visitors to interact with the organizational owners of the *Web site*.

Web sales   Revenue from product purchases in which customers conclude the sales process on the Web, usually using a form of shopping cart to directly transact with a seller.

Web server   The system software that displays *static* Web pages from HTML files and can execute some programs to create *dynamic* pages.

Web site   A set of interlinked Web pages managed by a domain team that allows interaction between visitors and the site's owner. For example, visitors speak of "going to Amtrak's Web site," which is at www.amtrak.com. All pages whose URL starts with www.amtrak.com are considered part of the Amtrak Web site.

Web site impression   A measurement of the number of times customers see a marketing message or other piece of content when they came to your Web site. Most metrics systems call this a *page view*, but rich media (such Flash and Ajax) are creating customer experiences outside of traditional Web pages (which metrics systems don't count as page views).

wiki Derived from the Hawaiian word wiki-wiki, meaning "quick," a group word processor whose documents are always available for viewing and updating. The most famous wiki is Wikipedia, an encyclopedia created and maintained by the public.

wireframe A visual representation of the design for a Web page or other piece of content.

word of e-mail An interactive form of *word of mouth* marketing in which customers pass along interesting information about products or services to other customers using electronic mail, thus spreading a marketing message.

word of IM An interactive form of *word of mouth* marketing in which customers pass along interesting information about products or services to other customers using instant messages, thus spreading a marketing message.

word of mouth Also known as *buzz marketing* or *viral marketing*, word-of-mouth has traditionally referred to the way that customers talk to other customers about an interesting product or service, thus spreading a marketing message. Interactive marketing has expanded the pass-along possibilities beyond personal conversations to include *word of e-mail*, *word of Web*, and other formulations.

word of Web An interactive form of *word of mouth* marketing in which customers pass along interesting information about products or services to other customers using electronic means (message boards, news groups, and others), thus spreading a marketing message.

World Wide Web Usually abbreviated as WWW, or simply "the Web," an interlinked network of pages that display content or allow interaction between the Web visitor and the organization that owns the Web site.

X

XML eXtensible Markup Language, a standard for a markup language, similar to HTML, that allows tags to be defined to describe any kind of data you have, making it very popular as a format for data feeds.

Y

Yellow Pages A printed phone directory listing businesses by categories that has traditionally been the way small businesses are found in the offline world. Internet Yellow Pages are beginning to make inroads on their print counterparts.

Index

A

A/B Testing, 238
ABC blogs, 77
ABC, Cyrus, 77
accessibility of Web sites, 160
Adams, Douglas, 149
adaptability, 276
adaptive changes, 270-273
adopting a feedback culture, 282-283
advertising, 4
  advertising-supported media, 7
  online advertising
    adware, 36
    banner ads/display ads, 35-37
    community building, 39
    contextual ads, 38-40
    paid search ads, 37-38
    pop-up ads, 36
    product placement, 40
    social network marketing, 40-41
    sponsorship, 40
    Yellow Pages, 40
adware, 36
affiliate links, 94
affiliate marketing, 98-101
agile development, 302-307
  benefits of, 303-306
  small businesses, 306
  teamwork, 304
  tolerance of mistakes, 302
Agile Modeling, 303

Ajax, 172, 325
Allen, Fred, 277
Amazon.com, 197, 214, 224
Ambient Findability, 329
Ambler, Scott, 303
America Online, 81
analyst marketers, 268-269
analytics. *See* metrics
Anderson, Chris, 198
Andreesen, Marc, 324
Anheuser-Busch, 41
Antin, Randy, 101
Apple, 34, 79
Apple iTunes, 111
Arbor Networks, 184
astroturfing, 82
AT&T, 78
Atom, 42
attitude, importance of, 281
authenticating e-mail, 161
avoiding misrepresentation, 70-73

B

B2B (Business to Business) marketers, 195
B2C (Business to Consumer) companies, 195
Babbage, Charles, 238
banner ads, 35-37
banner blindness, 7
barriers to change. *See* change, overcoming
    barriers to

Bass Pro Shops, 78, 207
Batelle, John, 195, 329
Bayesian probability, 263
BazaarVoice, 286
Become, 156
behavioral models
    for customer relationships, 114-116
    extended behavioral model, 123
    for influencer sites, 120-121
    for lead-oriented businesses, 118-120
    for offline sales businesses, 117-118
    for Web sales businesses, 116-117
behavioral targeting, 327
Berra, Yogi, 211, 268, 315
Best Buy, 164
betas, 219
bid management software, 232, 243
Biznology, 332
blogosphere, 48
blogs, 48-51
    BuzzMachine, 78
    company blogs, 66-67
    corporate blogging policies, 300-301
    Engadget, 84
    flogs, 82-83
    Hacking Netflix, 49
    hate blogs, 85-89
    listening to customers via, 77-79
    Orbitcast, 33, 80
    splogs, 73
    trackbacks, 67
BMW, 73
Bohr, Neils, 321
Book Yourself Solid, 187
bookmarks (browser), 58
bosses, convincing of need for change, 293
bounced e-mail, 138, 161
brand awareness, 106, 322
brand loyalty, 27
brands, 4
Braun, Werner von, 265
brick-and-mortar retailers, 111
Brilliant, Ashleigh, 188
bringing specialists together, 298-307
Burger King, 40
business partners, recommendations from,
    98-100
business rules, 202-203
Business to Business (B2B) marketers, 195
Business to Consumer (B2C) companies, 195
BuzzMachine blog, 78

C

call to action, 112
Calvin Klein, 181
card sorts, 248
Carlin, George, 70, 267
Carphone Warehouse Plc, 198
Cascading Style Sheets (CSS), 245
case studies
    DreamHost, 28-29
    Netflix, 49
    Wal-Mart flog, 83
catalog marketing, 16
The Cathedral and the Bazaar, 224, 316
Cavett, Dick, 76, 263
CBS Sportsline, 50
change, overcoming barriers to
    adopting a feedback culture, 282-283
    agile development, 302-307
        benefits of, 303-306
        priorities, 305
        small businesses, 306
        teamwork, 304
        tolerance of mistakes, 302
    betas, 219
    cognitive therapy, 257-258
    common objections, 257-258
        "I can't stand being wrong," 265-266
        "I don't have permission," 259-260
        "I don't have time," 261
        "I'm no numbers person," 261-262
        "I've never been fast at decisions," 262-264
        "It feels too overwhelming," 266
        "No one will listen to me," 260
        "That's not my job," 259
        "We tried that already," 264-265
    coping with change, 316-321
    fear of change, 266-270
    gradual approach, 219
    identifying changes, 321
        context, 325-328
        integration, 328-331
        participation, 322-325
    keeping current with changes, 331-332
    leading people to change, 279-280
        attitude, 281
        declaring success, 286-287
        motivation, 283-284
        rallying allies, 280-284
        targeting problems, 284-286

measuring success, 224-227
  bid management software, 232, 243
  conversions, 227-232
  CPA (cost per action), 231
  Customer Lifetime Value (LTV), 232-235
  ROAS (return on advertising spending), 230-231
  ROI (return on investment), 231
  testing, 235-240
metrics reports, 295
overview, 256-257, 277-279
personality types, 307-309
  inattentive, 309-310
  indecisive, 311
  inept, 312-313
Specialist Disease, 287-289
  bringing specialists together, 298-307
  putting business first, 289-292
  speaking their language, 292-298
speeding up change, 240-241
  feedback, 247-251
  messaging, 245-247
  targeting, 241-244
starting small, 219-224
talking to executives, 293
targeting items for change, 215-224
technical and adaptive changes, 270-273
value of experimentation, 212-224
Charles Schwab, 110
Chrysler, 18
clickthrough rate, 65, 134
clickthroughs, 132
cloaking, 73
The Cluetrain Manifesto, 10
Coca-Cola, 34, 88, 92, 213
cognitive therapy, 257-258
Collins, Jim, 257
color blindness, 160
color deficiency, 160
Color Schemer, 160
color vibration, 160
colors in Web sites, 159-160
commercial-free media, 7
committees, 277
communication
  Internet communities, 10
  interruption model versus permission model, 9
  markets as conversations, 10
  overview, 6-11
  public relations, 10
  with specialists, 292-298
communities (Internet), 10

community building, 39
company blogs, 66-67
complaints. *See* negative feedback, responding to
CompUSA, 7, 44, 78, 223, 225, 280, 283
consumer-generated content. *See* Web 2.0
consumers
  compared to participants, 23
  control over marketing, 8-9
content-based social media, 24
content management systems, 203, 246
context, 325-328
contextual ads, 38-40
conversations (marketing), starting. *See also*
    listening to customers
  avoiding misrepresentation, 70-73
  customer-initiated conversations, 58-63
    hyperlinks/inbound links, 60-61
    offline marketing, 59-60
    searches, 62-64
  marketer-initiated conversations, 63, 67-70
    company blogs, 66-67
    mailing lists, 63-64
    recontacts, 70
    subscriptions/opt-in rates, 68-69
    trackbacks, 67
    wikis, 64
  overview, 56-58
conversations, markets as, 10
Converseon, 24, 88, 288
conversions, 227-232
  conversion process, 131-135
  counting, 127-131
cookies, 143-144, 202
CooperKatz, 67
coping with change, 316-321. *See also* change,
    overcoming barriers to; objections to change
  betas, 219
  gradual approach, 219
  identifying changes, 321
    context, 325-328
    integration, 328-331
    participation, 322-325
  keeping current with changes, 331-332
  measuring success, 224-227
    bid management software, 232, 243
    conversions, 227-232
    CPA (cost per action), 231
    Customer Lifetime Value (LTV), 232-235
    ROAS (return on advertising spending), 230-231
    ROI (return on investment), 231
    testing, 235-240

speeding up change, 240-241
  feedback, 247-251
  messaging, 245-247
  targeting, 241-244
starting small, 219-224
targeting items for change, 215-224
value of experimentation, 212-224
copywriting (Web sites), 175-182
  for search rankings, 179
  text ads, 177
  titles, 176
  for viral marketing, 180-181
CoreMetrics, 134
corporate blogging policies, 300-301
corporate culture. *See* organizational culture
Cosby, Bill, 21
The Courage to Write: How Authors Transcend Fear, 267
CPA (cost per action), 231
crisis listening, 84-85
cross-functional teams, 289
CSS (Cascading Style Sheets), 245
culture. *See* organizational culture
Customer Lifetime Value (LTV), 232-235
customers
  behavioral model, 114-116
  customer-initiated conversations, 58-63
    hyperlinks/inbound links, 60-61
    offline marketing, 59-60
    searches, 62-64
  cynicism, 30
  Lifetime Value (LTV), 232-235
  listening to
    blogs, 77-79
    crisis listening, 84-85
    fake feedback from competitors, 82-84
    focus groups, 74-75
    hate sites/hate blogs, 85-89
    importance of, 75-76
    listening in a crisis, 85
    online panels, 75
    ratings and reviews, 78-79
    responding to negative feedback, 79-82
  market segmentation, 190-196
  measuring customer activity, 125-127
    conversion process, 131-135
    conversions, 127-131
    impressions, 132-142
    selections, 132-142
  meeting customer needs, 121-125
  opt-in rates, 68-69

participation, increase in, 322-325
paths to purchase, 125
purpose, 113-114
recommendations from, 90-93, 96
recontacts, 70
relationships, 107
  measuring, 142-147
responses, 106
self-segmentation, 12-13
targeting, 188-190
  RFM ratings, 188-190
  speeding up messaging, 245-247
  speeding up targeting, 241-244
userIDs, 143

D

Davis, Miles, 267
day trading, 111
decision-making, 262-264
Decker, Sam, 286
declaring success, 286-287
Del Monte, 75
Dell, 13-14, 78
demographic targeting, 327
Denison, Andrew, 276
designing e-mails, 161
designing Web sites
  accessibility, 160
  colors, 159-160
  copywriting, 175-182
    for search rankings, 179
    text ads, 177
    titles, 176
    for viral marketing, 180-181
  destination pages, 167-169
  grid layouts, 162
  images, 184-186
  information architecture, 164-169
  integrated design systems, 162-163
  interactivity, 169-175
  landing pages, 156, 159
  liquid design, 162
  look and feel, 153-156
  market segmentation, 190-196
  navigation, 164-169
  navigation pages, 167-169
  overview, 150-153
  personalization, 186-187, 197-204
    business rules, 202-203
    content management system, 203

cookies, 202
dynamic pages, 203
metrics-based personalization, 202
multifaceted searches, 198-200
profiles, 202
podcasts, 182-184
privacy policy, 192-193
progressive disclosure, 169
targeting customers, 188-190
UCD (User-Centered Design), 154
use cases, 155-156
user experience, 151
user testing, 154
video podcasts, 185-186
visual design, 159
destination pages, 167-169
Digg, 93
digital video cameras, 186
Digitas, 123
direct mail marketing, 16
direct marketing, 41-44
  e-mail, 41-42
  overview, 15-19, 103-104
  testing, 18
  Web feeds, 42-44
disclosure, 72
display ads, 35-37
Do Not Call Register, 8
Don't Make Me Think, 151
DontDateHimGirl.com, 10
Dove, 59
Doyle, Sir Arthur Conan, 124
DreamHost case study, 28-29
Drucker, Peter, 239
Ducati, 49
DuPont, Teflon® product, 33
dynamic content, 244
dynamic navigation, 198
dynamic pages, 23, 203
dysfunctional organizational cultures, 277

E

E-LOAN, 15, 176, 235, 268
e-mail
  authenticating, 161
  bounced e-mail, 138, 161
  design, 161
  direct marketing, 41-42
  image blockers, 161
  list management, 242
  list suppression, 242
  mailing lists, 63-64
  newsletters, 45-46
  open rates, 139
  opened e-mail, 107
  personalization, 204-207
  phishing, 204-205
  spam, 41, 71
  spam filters, 161
  welcome e-mails, 69
  word of e-mail, 90
eBay, 218
Edelstein, Michael R., 258
Edison, Thomas, 240
Einstein, Albert, 261, 332
Eisenberg, Bryan, 162, 197
eMarketer, 15
employee blogs, 300-301
employees
  as marketers, 30-31
  recommendations from, 96-98
Engadget blog, 84
entrepreneurs, 4
evangelism, 298
Everyone's Normal Until You Get to Know Them, 267
ExactTarget, 242
Executive Travel magazine, 64
executives, convincing of need for change, 293
experimentation, value of, 212-224
extended behavioral model, 123

F

facets, 198
fake feedback from competitors, 82-84
fantasy-based social media, 24
fear of change, 266-270
feature-oriented marketing, 32
feedback
  fake feedback from competitors, 82-84
  negative feedback, responding to, 79-82
  speeding up, 247-251
feedback culture, adopting, 282-283
FeedBlitz, 44
feeviews, 82
Ferrari, Vincent, 81
Feynman, Richard, 214
Fields, W. C., 255, 313
findability, 166
Fish, Nancy, 217

flogs, 82-83
focus groups, 74-75
folksonomies, 92
frequency, 188
Frito-Lay, 328
Frost, Robert, 275

G

Galbraith, John Kenneth, 236
game logs (glogs), 50
Gap, Inc., 172
General Motors, 49, 59, 66, 95
GlaxoSmithKline, 185
globalizatiom, tiered, 246
glogs (game logs), 50
Gmail, 93
Godin, Seth, 9, 94, 192, 267
Goldberg, Whoopi, 309
Good Experience, 121
Good to Great, 257
Google, 26-27, 93, 219, 327
GORE-TEX®, 112
gradual approach to change, 219
Gretzky, Wayne, 317
grid layouts, 162

H

Hacking Netflix blog, 49
Hadiaris, Regis, 249
hate sites, 85-89
Heifetz, Ronald, 271, 284
herd mentality, 277
Hewlett-Packard, 195, 268
history of marketing, 4-6
honesty in marketing, 29-32
  customer cynicism, 30
  DreamHost case study, 28-29
  feature-oriented marketing, 32
  role of employees, 30-31
Hopper, Grace, 259
Horsefeathers, 309
How to Survive Your Diet, 272
HTML (HyperText Markup Language), 245
Hunt, Bill, 114
Hurlebaus, Al, 7, 44, 78, 225, 280, 283
Hurst, Mark, 121

hype, 30
hyperbole, 30
hyperlinks
  affiliate links, 94
  link farms, 73
  as marketing tool, 60-61
HyperText Markup Language (HTML), 245

I

IBM, 99, 196, 276, 281
image blockers, 161
images, selecting for Web sites, 184-186
impression fees, 35
impressions, 107, 132
  counting, 135-142
impulse purchases, 110-111
inattentive personality type, 309-310
inbound links, 60-61
include files, 246
indecisive personality type, 311
inept personality type, 312-313
influencer sites, behavioral model, 120-121
infoq.com, 32
information architects, 164
information architecture (Web sites), 164-169
*Information Architecture for the World Wide
    Web*, 164
Instone, Keith, 221
integrated design systems, 162-163
integration, 328-331
interactivity (Web sites), 169-175
interest-based social media, 24
Internet communities, 10
  community building, 39
Internet marketing
  advertising, 35
    adware, 36
    banner ads/display ads, 35-37
    community building, 39
    contextual ads, 38-40
    paid search ads, 37-38
    pop-up ads, 36
    product placement, 40
    social network marketing, 40-41
    sponsorship, 40
    Yellow Pages, 40

affiliate marketing, 98-101
behavioral model
for customer relationships, 114-116
extended behavioral model, 123
for influencer sites, 120-121
for lead-oriented businesses, 118-120
for offline sales businesses, 117-118
for Web sales businesses, 116-117
behavioral targeting, 327
communication
interruption model versus permission model, 9
markets as conversations, 10
overview, 6-11
public relations, 10
compared to old-style marketing, 25-26
consumer control, 8-9
conversations, starting
avoiding misrepresentation, 70-73
customer-initiated conversations, 58-63
marketer-initiated conversations, 63-70
overview, 56-58
customer relationships, 107
customer responses, 106
demographic targeting, 327
direct marketing, 41-44
e-mail, 41-42
overview, 15-19
testing, 18
Web feeds, 42-44
dynamic Web pages, 23
history of marketing, 4-6
Internet communities, 10
introductions
outreach by employees, 96-98
outreach by partners, 98-100
overview, 90
recommendations by customers, 90-96
listening to customers
blogs, 77-79
crisis listening, 84-85
customer ratings and reviews, 78-79
fake feedback from competitors, 82-84
focus groups, 74-75
hate sites/hate blogs, 85-89
importance of, 75-76
listening in a crisis, 85
online panels, 75
responding to negative feedback, 79-82
market segmentation
overview, 11-12
self-segmentation, 12

measuring customer activity, 125-127
conversion process, 131-135
conversions, 127-131
impressions, 132-142
selections, 132-142
measuring customer relationships, 142-147
metrics, 107-109
negative publicity, responding to, 33-34
offline marketing, 59-60
overview, 1-2
publicity, 45-53
blogs, 48-51
message boards, 51-52
newsletters, 45-46
podcasts, 46-47
press releases, 45
vidcasts/video podcasts, 47-48
wikis, 51
questions to ask, 319
reality/honesty, 29-32
customer cynicism, 30
DreamHost case study, 28-29
feature-oriented marketing, 32
role of employees, 30-31
relevance, 26-28
reputation, monitoring, 88
responsiveness, 32-34
search marketing, behavioral models and, 122-124
social media marketing, 24-25
viral marketing, 90-96
copywriting for, 180-181
Web 2.0, 22-25
Web sites
call to action, 112
impulse purchases, 110-111
leads, 112
meeting customer needs, 121-125
offline sales, 112
online commerce sites, 110
page views, 107
pure online sites, 110
purpose, 109-113
interruption marketing, 9, 36
introductions
outreach by employees, 96-98
outreach by partners, 98-100
overview, 90
recommendations by customers, 90-96
Israel, Shel, 67
iTunes, 111

J–K

Jarvis, Jeff, 78
Jo-Ann Fabrics, 12
Johnson, Samuel, 291

Kahn, Alice, 55
Kaltschnee, Mike, 49
Kaushik, Avinash, 19, 226, 283, 295, 325
Keep the Joint Running, 252
Key, Rob, 24, 88, 288
Keyes, Ralph, 267
Keynes, John Maynard, 265
keyword stuffing, 72
keywords, 64
Khan, Imran, 15, 235, 268
Killer Web Content, 181
Kraft Foods, 59
Krug, Steve, 151
Kryptonite lock company, 84-85
Kuler, 160

L

L. L. Bean, 153
lack of time, 261
landing pages, 64, 156, 159
Leadership on the Line, 271, 284
leading people to change, 279-280
  attitude, 281
  declaring success, 286-287
  motivation, 283-284
  rallying allies, 280-281, 284
  targeting problems, 284-286
leads, 112
  behavioral model, 118-120
Lewis, Bob, 252
Lincoln, Abraham, 30
link farms, 73
links. *See* hyperlinks
Linsky, Martin, 271, 284
liquid design, 162
LISA (Localization Industry Standards
    Association) conference, 99
list management, 242
list suppression, 242
listening to customers
  blogs, 77-79
  crisis listening, 84-85
  customer ratings and reviews, 78-79
  fake feedback from competitors, 82-84
  focus groups, 74-75
  hate sites/hate blogs, 85-89
  importance of, 75-76
  listening in a crisis, 85
  online panels, 75
  responding to negative feedback, 79-82
Live Nation, 68
Localization Industry Standards Association
    (LISA) conference, 99
Locke, Chris, 10
The Long Tail, 198
look and feel of Web sites, 153-156
LTV (Lifetime Value), 232-235
Lutz, Bob, 49, 66

M

Madden, Dre, 264
Magun, Harrison, 106
mailing lists, 63-64
Marinescu, Floyd, 32, 303
market personalization, 13
market segmentation, 190-196
  overview, 11-12
  self-segmentation, 12-13
marketers, 4
  analyst marketers, 268-269
  marketer-initiated conversations, 63-70
    company blogs, 66-67
    mailing lists, 63-64
    recontacts, 70
    subscriptions/opt-in rates, 68-69
    trackbacks, 67
    wikis, 64
  misrepresentation, avoiding, 70-73
Marketing Performance Measurement
    (MPM), 107
markets, as conversations, 10
Marx, Groucho, 3
matchback systems, 235
McDonald's, 33
McGovern, Gerry, 181
measuring success, 224-227
  bid management software, 232, 243
  conversions, 227-232
  CPA (cost per action), 231
  Customer Lifetime Value (LTV), 232-235
  ROAS (return on advertising spending), 230-231
  ROI (return on investment), 231
  testing, 235-240

media, 6. *See also* Internet marketing
  advertising-supported media, 7
  commercial-free media, 7
meeting customer needs, 121-125
memes, 95
Mentos, 92
merchants (affiliate marketing), 100
message boards, 51-52
messages, 4
  speeding up messaging, 245-247
metrics, 107-109
  conversions, 227-232
  CPA (cost per action), 231
  Customer Lifetime Value (LTV), 232-235
  measuring customer activity, 125-127
    conversion process, 131-135
    conversions, 127-131
    impressions, 132-142
    selections, 132-142
  measuring customer relationships, 142-147
  metrics-based personalization, 202
  multiple metrics facilities, 145
  response metrics, 16
  ROAS (return on advertising spending), 230-231
  ROI (return on investment), 231
  testing, 235-240
metrics reports, 295
Microsoft, 7, 82, 106
mikemoran.com, 332
Milgram, Stanley, 186
MingleNow, 41
Minoli, Federico, 49
misrepresentation, avoiding, 70-73
monetary metrics, 188
monitoring reputation, 88
monster.com, 249
Moran, Linda, 272
Morville, Peter, 164, 329
motivation for change, 283-284
Motorcycle Superstore, 242
MPM (Marketing Performance
    Measurement), 107
multifaceted searches, 198-200
multiple metrics facilities, 145
multitasking, 7
multivariate testing, 248-251
Murrow, Edward R., 266
MySpace, 40, 323

N

Naked Conversations, 67
navigation (Web sites), 164-169
navigation pages, 167-169
Navigation Stress test, 221
needs-based segmentation, 191
negative feedback, responding to, 79-82
negative publicity, responding to, 33-34
Neistat, Casey, 79
Net Present Value (NPV), 234
net sales, 228
Netflix, 49, 240
newsletters, 45-46
Nielsen, Jakob, 153, 169, 177, 208
Ning, 324
NPV (Net Present Value), 234

O

O magazine, 64
objections to change, 257-258. *See also* coping
    with change
  "I can't stand being wrong," 265-266
  "I don't have permission," 259-260
  "I don't have time," 261
  "I'm no numbers person," 261-262
  "I've never been fast at decisions," 262-264
  "It feels too overwhelming," 266
  "No one will listen to me," 260
  "That's not my job," 259
  "We tried that already," 264-265
offline marketing, 59-60
offline sales, 112
  behavioral model, 117-118
Omniture, 134
online commerce sites, 110
online marketing. *See* Internet marketing
online panels, 75
online trading, 111
open rates (e-mail), 139
opened e-mail, 107
opt-in rates, 68-69
Oracle, 224
Orbitcast blog, 33, 80
organizational culture, 276
  adaptability, 276
  adopting a feedback culture, 282-283
  committees, 277
  dysfunctional cultures, 277

P

page views, 107, 132

paid search ads, 37-38

panels, 75

paper prototypes, 248

participants, compared to consumers, 23

participation, increase in, 322-325

partners, recommendations from, 98-100

paths to purchase, 125

Peale, Norman Vincent, 273

per-click fees, 37

Permission Marketing, 192

permission model, 9

permission, need for, 259-260

personal logs (plogs), 50

personality-based social media, 24

personality types, 307-309

  inattentive, 309-310

  indecisive, 311

  inept, 312-313

personalization, 13

  e-mail, 204-207

  software, 12

personalized searches, 326

personalizing Web sites, 186-187, 197-204

  business rules, 202-203

  content management system, 203

  cookies, 202

  dynamic pages, 203

  metrics-based personalization, 202

  multifaceted searches, 198-200

  profiles, 202

personas, 197

Petillo, Michael, 16, 282, 294

Phillips, Charles, 224

phishing, 204-205

plogs (personal logs), 50

podcasts, 46-47, 182-184

  measuring, 139

  video podcasts, 185-186

pop-up ads, 36

Porsche, Ferdinand, 153

Port, Michael, 187

portal servers, 246

Post (Kraft Foods), 59

The Power of Positive Thinking, 273

press releases, 45

privacy policy, 192-193

probability, Bayesian, 263

problems, targeting for change, 284-286

process, 298

product placement, 40

profiles, 202

progressive disclosure, 169

proximity, 26

public relations, 10

publicity, 45-53

  blogs, 48-51

  message boards, 51-52

  negative publicity, responding to, 33-34

  newsletters, 45-46

  podcasts, 46-47

  press releases, 45

  vidcasts/video podcasts, 47-48

  wikis, 51

purchases, paths to, 125

pure online sites, 110

purpose

  of customers, 113-114

  of Web sites, 109-113

Q–R

rallying allies, 280-284

Ramsay, David, 258

Ramsey, Geoff, 15

ratings (customer), 78-79

Raymond, Eric, 224, 316

reality in marketing, 29-32

  customer cynicism, 30

  DreamHost case study, 28-29

  feature-oriented marketing, 32

  role of employees, 30-31

Really Simple Syndication (RSS), 42

ReallyGreatRate.com, 249, 306

recency, 188

recommendations

  by customers, 90-96

  by employees, 96-98

  by partners, 98-100

recontacts, 70

referrals, 136

referrers, 135

Reimer, Joel, 7, 282, 286, 293, 320

relationships, 34, 107

  behavioral model, 114-116

  measuring, 142-147

relevance in marketing, 26-28

reputations, monitoring, 88

Request for Proposal (RFP), 119

response metrics, 16
responses, 106
responsiveness in marketing, 32-34
return on advertising spending (ROAS), 230-231
return on investment (ROI), 231
reviews (customer), 78-79
RFM ratings, 188-190
RFP (Request for Proposal), 119
ROAS (return on advertising spending), 230-231
Rogers, Will, 266
ROI (return on investment), 231
Rollins, Henry, 85
Rosenfeld, Lou, 164
RSS (Really Simple Syndication), 42
Rubel, Steve, 67
rules, business, 202-203

S

Saghir, Ryan, 33, 80, 323
sales
   net sales, 228
   offline sales, 112
      behavioral model, 117-118
   paths to purchase, 125
salesmen, 4
Sasaki, Curt, 79, 220, 264, 282, 286, 294, 301, 329
Saxena, Devashish, 15, 283, 292, 303
scapegoats, 277
Schaub, Matt, 249, 306
Schmidt, Eric, 329
Schultz, Duane, 16
Schwartz, Jonathan, 66
Scoble, Robert, 67
ScottsMiracle-Gro, 7, 197, 223, 282, 286, 320
Seagate, 181
The Search, 195, 329
Search Engine Marketing, Inc., 114
search engines, 26-27
search marketing, 62-64
   behavioral models and, 122-124
search spam, 72-73
searches, 12
   copywriting for search rankings, 179
   multifaceted searches, 198-200
   paid search ads, 37-38
   personalized search, 326
   search spam, 72-73
Sears, 276
segmentation. *See* market segmentation
Seifert, David, 78

selections, 132
   counting, 135-142
self-segmentation, 12-13
Semantic Web, 329
sentiment analysis, 331
Sephora, 64
servers, portal, 246
single-pixel tracking, 136
Sirius Radio, 80
Skin Deep Refinishing case study, 228-230
small changes, starting with, 219-224
SmartAds, 328
social bookmarking, 92
social computing. *See* Web 2.0
social media marketing, 24-25
social network marketing, 40-41
social tagging, 92
sound, podcasts, 182-184
spam, 41, 71
spam filters, 161
spamdexing, 72-73
Specialist Disease, overcoming, 287-289
   bringing specialists together, 298-307
   metrics reports, 295
   putting business first, 289-292
   speaking their language, 292-298
speeding up change, 240-241
   feedback, 247-251
   messaging, 245-247
   targeting, 241-244
splogs, 73
sponsorship, 40
Sportsline, 50
spyware, 36
Squidoo lens, 217-218
St. Claire, Laurie, 83
Staples, 167
starting conversations
   avoiding misrepresentation, 70-73
   customer-initiated conversations, 58-63
      hyperlinks/inbound links, 60-61
      offline marketing, 59-60
      searches, 62-64
   marketer-initiated conversations, 63, 67-70
      company blogs, 66-67
      mailing lists, 63-64
      recontacts, 70
      subscriptions/opt-in rates, 68-69
      trackbacks, 67
      wikis, 64
   overview, 56-58

statistical significance, 262-263
Sterne, Jim, 237
stocks, online trading, 111
Stonyfield Farm, 67
StubHub, 264
subscribers, 136
subscriptions, 12, 68-69
success, declaring, 286-287
success, measuring, 224-227
  bid management software, 232, 243
  conversions, 227-232
  CPA (cost per action), 231
  Customer Lifetime Value (LTV), 232-235
  ROAS (return on advertising spending), 230-231
  ROI (return on investment), 231
  testing, 235-240
Sun Microsystems, 66, 79, 172, 220, 282, 286
.SUN Properties, 264
.SUN Web Properties, 220
Super Size Me!, 33
Swasey, Steve, 49

T

Taguchi, Genichi, 248
Target, 160
target markets, 4
targeting
  behavioral targeting, 327
  demographic targeting, 327
targeting customers, 188-190
  RFM ratings, 188-190
  speeding up targeting, 241-244
targeting items for change, 215-224
technical changes, 270-273
technology, future of, 331
Teflon® product, 33
telephone solicitation, 8
templates, 247
testing, 18, 235-240
  A/B Testing, 238
  multivariate testing, 248-251
  user testing, 154
  Web site navigation, 221
Tew, Alex, 45
Texas Instruments, 15, 93, 283, 292, 303
text ads, 177
theserverside.com, 32

"Three R's"
  reality, 29-32
    customer cynicism, 30
    DreamHost case study, 28-29
    feature-oriented marketing, 32
    role of employees, 30-31
  relevance, 26-28
  responsiveness, 32-34
Thresher, Jim, 83
tiered globalization, 246
Time magazine, 18
time, lack of, 261
Time-Life, 249
titles of Web sites, 176
trackbacks, 67
trade associations, 100
traffic, 145
training, 298
Travelocity, 101
TurboTax, 122
Twain, Mark, 268
Tylenol, 33

U–V

UCD (User-Centered Design), 154
Uniform Resource Locators (URLs), 58
unique visitors, 145
Unleashing the IdeaVirus, 94
URLs (Uniform Resource Locators), 58-59
use cases, 155-156
user experience, 151
user testing, 154
User-Centered Design (UCD), 154
userIDs, 143
UserLand, 67

Veloso, Maria, 176
vidcasts/video podcasts, 47-48, 185-186
viral marketing, 90-93, 96
  copywriting for, 180-181
Vision Critical, 75
visual design, 159-160
vlogs, 50
Vogels, Werner, 224

W

W. L. Gore & Associates, 16, 112, 282
Waiting for Your Cat to Bark, 162
Wal-Mart, 83, 206

WatchThatPage.com, 87
waterfall method, 299-302
Web 2.0, 22-25
Web Analytics: An Hour a Day, 19, 226, 295
Web beacons, 136
Web Conversion Cycle, 322
Web Copy That Sells, 176
Web developers, 169
Web feeds, 12
  direct marketing, 42-44
Web metrics. *See* metrics
Web sales businesses, behavioral model, 116-117
Web sites
  call to action, 112
  cookies, 143-144
  design
    accessibility, 160
    business rules, 202-203
    colors, 159-160
    copywriting, 175-182
    destination pages, 167-169
    grid layouts, 162
    images, 184-186
    information architecture, 164-169
    integrated design systems, 162-163
    interactivity, 169-175
    landing pages, 156, 159
    liquid design, 162
    look and feel, 153-156
    market segmentation, 190-196
    metrics-based personalization, 202
    multifaceted searches, 198-200
    navigation, 164-169
    navigation pages, 167-169
    overview, 150-153
    personalization, 186-187, 197-204
    podcasts, 182-184
    privacy policy, 192-193
    progressive disclosure, 169
    targeting customers, 188-190
    UCD (User-Centered Design), 154
    use cases, 155-156
    user experience, 151
    user testing, 154
    video podcasts, 185-186
    visual design, 159
  impressions, 132
  impulse purchases, 110-111
  leads, 112
  measuring customer activity, 125-127
    conversion process, 131-135
    conversions, 127-131
    impressions, 132, 135-142
    selections, 132, 135-142
  measuring customer relationships, 142-147
  meeting customer needs, 121-125
  Navigation Stress test, 221
  offline sales, 112
  online commerce sites, 110
  page views, 107, 132
  pure online sites, 110
  purpose, 109-113
  referrals, 136
  referrers, 135
Webinars, 40
Webkinz, 324
Weblogs, 48-51
Website Watcher, 87
Weigend, Andreas, 197, 214
welcome e-mails, 69
WFWM (Working Families for Wal-Mart), 83
Wikipedia, 51
wikis, 51, 64
Wilde, Oscar, 77
Winer, Dave, 67
wireframes, 306
word of e-mail, 90
word of IM, 90
word of mouth, 90
word of Web, 90
Working Families for Wal-Mart (WFWM), 83
Worldwide Web Consortium, 160
Wright, Steve, 203

X–Z

Xerox, 16
XM Radio, 80

Yahoo! SmartAds, 328
Yellow Pages, 40
YELLOWPAGES.COM, 78
yourdomainsucks.com, 86

ISBN: 0131852922

Search Engine Marketing, Inc. **is a step-by-step guide to setting up and managing a search marketing program, with best practices and tips from two of the world's premier experts.**

"A very comprehensive, yet light-hearted guide for internet managers that demystifies search engine marketing and provides practical advice for success."

—*Piers Dickinson, Global Internet Marketing Manager, BP*

"Outlines every one of the major strategic steps to develop your search marketing initiatives. This book teaches Web marketers what to do from the beginning so they can implement a successful search marketing program—the strategic steps to define the scope and cost of your search marketing program, develop a team, create a proposal, get executive approval, manage, and measure your search marketing program. You have to read it to appreciate it!"

—*Cynthia Donlevy, Web Marketing & Strategy, Cisco Systems, Inc.*

"Getting your site indexed is the most fundamental, yet one of the most challenging, aspects to search engine marketing. *Search Engine Marketing Inc.: Driving Search Traffic to Your Company's Web Site* is a detailed and comprehensive guide through the pitfalls and opportunities of this complicated subject. I started reading Chapter 10, "Get Your Site Indexed," and haven't really put it down since. It is a wonderfully well-written and detailed reference that you will come back to again and again to get more out of your SEO efforts. From price engines to paid placement, Chapter 14, "Optimize Your Paid Search Program," covers everything you need to know about paid search. I have yet to come across a more useful book for SEM pros. From budgeting to bid strategy and optimization, Mike and Bill take you through the steps to create successful paid search campaigns. Whether you are just starting out in paid search or are already a power player, you will learn something new from this book."

—*David Cook, Search Marketing Manager, Buy.com*

"This book has no silver bullets or snake-oil potions that will magically propel your site to the top of every search engine. What it offers instead, is the most comprehensive, well-thought-out, and well-motivated treatment to date of all aspects of search engine marketing, from planning to execution to measuring. If you are involved in any way in the economic aspects of Web search technology, you need this book on your shelf."

—*Dr. Andrei Broder, IBM Distinguished Engineer & CTO, IBM Research Institute for Search and Text Analysis*

Visit *www.ibmpressbooks.com/title/0131852922* to learn more and read Chapter 1: "Why Search Marketing Is Important...and Difficult"

THIS BOOK IS SAFARI ENABLED

INCLUDES FREE 45-DAY ACCESS TO THE ONLINE EDITION

The Safari® Enabled icon on the cover of your favorite technology book means the book is available through Safari Bookshelf. When you buy this book, you get free access to the online edition for 45 days.

Safari Bookshelf is an electronic reference library that lets you easily search thousands of technical books, find code samples, download chapters, and access technical information whenever and wherever you need it.

TO GAIN 45-DAY SAFARI ENABLED ACCESS TO THIS BOOK:

- Go to **informit.com/safarienabled**

- Complete the brief registration form

- Enter the coupon code found in the front of this book on the "Copyright" page

If you have difficulty registering on Safari Bookshelf or accessing the online edition, please e-mail customer-service@safaribooksonline.com.